UNDERSTANDING AND CREATING DIGITAL TEXTS

UNDERSTANDING AND CREATING DIGITAL TEXTS

An Activity-Based Approach

**Richard Beach, Chris M. Anson,
Lee-Ann Kastman Breuch, and
Thomas Reynolds**

ROWMAN & LITTLEFIELD
Lanham • Boulder • New York • London

KH

Published by Rowman & Littlefield
A wholly owned subsidiary of The Rowman & Littlefield Publishing Group, Inc.
4501 Forbes Boulevard, Suite 200, Lanham, Maryland 20706
www.rowman.com

16 Carlisle Street, London W1D 3BT, United Kingdom

British Library Cataloguing in Publication Information Available

Library of Congress Cataloging-in-Publication Data

Library of Congress Cataloging-in-Publication Data Available

ISBN 978-1-4422-2873-3 (pbk. : alk. paper)—ISBN 978-1-4422-2874-0 (electronic)

∞™ The paper used in this publication meets the minimum requirements of American National Standard for Information Sciences Permanence of Paper for Printed Library Materials, ANSI/NISO Z39.48-1992.

Printed in the United States of America

11/18/15

CONTENTS

PREFACE

At Michigan State University, first-year writing students participate in the online game *Ink* http://writing.msu.edu:16080/ink. In this game, students assume the roles of members of a fictional neighborhood and city council. The game involves extensive reading and writing of texts to address problems facing the neighborhood. As they enter the game, students receive the following writing prompt:

> "Welcome to Ink," the stranger says. "This is a great place. But we have a problem right now, and I'm hoping you can help. Our neighborhood isn't doing well. We need to get a group of people together to address this problem. Can you help us? We need to design a flier that will motivate people to come to a meeting where we can talk about this problem. We need to draft a resolution that we can circulate to those who show up. We also need a brochure that explains why other citizens should vote for our proposal. And we're going to need a white paper to explain to City Council the principles that inform our proposal. We've got a lot of work to do. Can you help us?"

To advance in the game, students share journal entries to veteran players who judge whether the entries serve to convince audiences, particularly voters, of the validity of their positions. Students also have to create an appealing brochure that requires the use of multimodal design techniques. As part of the game, students reflect on what and how they are learning through their writing in the game. Their teachers then receive copies of the writing produced in the game and report on students' participation in it.

Students in Elizabeth Erdmann's 12th-grade writing class at Jefferson High School, Bloomington, Minnesota, were upset about their school's Internet policies, which allowed the school to block or filter websites that they perceived as providing them with relevant information they needed to complete their assignments. For example, in writing about the issue of gun control, they found that the National Rifle Association's site was blocked.

To address this issue of whether or not access to these sites should be blocked, Elizabeth engaged her students in a role-play via an online discussion forum (Beach & Doerr-Stevens, 2011; Doerr-Stevens, Beach, & Boeser, 2011). Students adopted the roles of administrators (principals, superintendent, technology people), teachers, students, librarians, lawyers, counselors, coaches, parents, businesspeople, computer hackers, and so on, with half the students assigned roles positing the need to unblock sites and the other half, to not unblock sites.

To do so, students created fictional biographical profiles with avatar images describing their roles in terms of their expertise, experience, traits, and attitudes, in a manner similar to creating Facebook profiles—profiles that they drew on to create a convincing ethos for their arguments. They then had to respond to one another's arguments with counterarguments, both during and after class. During class, students caucused with similar pro and con roles to engage in collaborative writing. They also consulted a digital map projected onto a screen in their classroom portraying the allegiances between the pro and con roles.

After the completion of the role-play, students stepped out of their roles and wrote argumentative essays for or against unblocking the websites by drawing on material from the online role-play. In a meeting with the school administration, they used their writing to argue for the need to unblock the sites, which the administration agreed to do, leading the students to perceive themselves as successful given the quality of their arguments derived from the online role-play experience.

These two snapshot examples of the use of digital writing to teach writing represent a marked shift away from traditional print-based writing instruction. Rather than writing essays solely for the teacher, students were writing

- for their peers, who were actively engaged in reading texts to evaluate them in the *Ink* game or to formulate counterarguments in the online role-play;
- within a defined rhetorical context based on particular tangible purposes—to address neighborhood problems in *Ink* or to consider changing their school's Internet policies in the online role-play;
- through use of multimodal communication and design in creating a brochure in *Ink* or through use of avatars and a digital map in the online role-play;
- collaboratively by reviewing and responding to one another's writing;
- over an extended period within and outside the classroom.

They were also learning through participating in activity. A meta-analysis of 225 studies of learning in the sciences, engineering, and mathematics found that engaging in active learning results in higher levels of performance when compared to learning through lectures (Freeman et al., 2014).

These writing activities are possible given the use of digital reading and writing tools—online discussion forums, digital design tools, and digital maps. However, this instruction involves more than simply learning to use these tools. In these cases, students were actively learning to use these tools to achieve certain social purposes inherent in the effective design of these activities by instructors. All of this suggests that the use of digital reading and writing tools is insufficient to foster student engagement in learning. Student learning occurs through development of engaging *activities* that exploit the uses of digital reading and writing tools. As Jeff Wilhelm (2014) notes,

> Even with the latest and most powerful technologies, the teaching/learning situation requires a teacher 1) to make learning matter, 2) to provide a meaningful situation that requires and rewards learning, and 3) to offer focused assistance in that context in order to develop the strategies necessary to complete the project at hand. (p. 60)

Knowing how and why to create these activities exploiting the use of digital reading and writing tools is the focus of this book. Teachers do perceive the benefits of using digital tools for literacy instruction. The Pew Research Center (Purcell, Buchanan, & Friedrich, 2013) conducted a national online survey of 2,462 middle and high school teachers of Advanced Placement classes and those involved with the National Writing Project in March and April 2012, in which teachers indicated increased use of digital tools in their teaching:

> Ninety-six percent agree (including 52% who strongly agree) that digital technologies "allow students to share their work with a wider and more varied audience"; 79% agree (23% strongly agree) that these tools "encourage greater collaboration among students"; 78% agree (26% strongly agree) that digital technologies "encourage student creativity and personal expression." (p. 3)

Teachers are using these tools. In another survey, 61% of middle school students and 74% of high school students now access their assignments, teacher notes, and grades online; and 47% of high school students create multimedia productions (Speak Up, 2013). Teachers find that these tools are particularly useful for fostering student collaboration as well as for writing for audiences beyond the classroom. One teacher noted,

> Digital technologies have allowed my students to be more collaborative in their writing experiences and to experience writing for a larger audience. My expository writing class is now a high school version of a blended course. Students are able to respond to one another through an online academic social network. Through this site they brainstorm together, share responses to writing in forums, and share resources through shared links and wiki creation. They also share their writing through sites like Google Docs or Wiggio. We even collaborate on how we pace our writing assignments through

an online calendar. Students research together by sharing links through Diigo. In my freshman class, students are able to use elireview.com for online peer review, which is especially nice for them so they can easily share their writing and focus their responses on each other. We also collaborate with other classes. We have six American Literature classes at my high school, and we're all connected through our online academic social network. We post on forums and create wikis together and share resources across classes. Students now have around 180 peers as their audience for a lot of their writing, instead of just a teacher or one class. (p. 30)

Furthermore, teachers recognize the value of drawing on students' use of mobile devices outside of school, with 65% of middle school students and 80% of high school students using smartphones, and 39% of middle school students having access to their own digital reader (Speak Up, 2013)—tools that support digital reading and writing. In the previously cited Pew survey, 73% of teachers indicate that they and/or their students employ mobile phones for classroom work; 45% employ e-readers; and 43% employ tablet computers (Purcell, Heaps, Buchanan, & Friedrich, 2013). In a study of students' use of iPads in a British school, 71% of students used their iPads outside school for completing homework, 47% for online research, and 39% for design and creative activities; in addition, 69% of students and 67% of teachers indicated that students were more motivated to learn given the use of iPads (Heinrich, 2012).

GOALS FOR THIS BOOK

These research findings indicate a marked increase in the use of digital tools to support reading and writing instruction. The challenge remains how to effectively use these tools in new and different ways to enhance students' digital reading and writing.

It is often the case that the digital tools described in this book are perceived primarily as technological add-ons designed to support a largely print-based literacy curriculum. In a national survey of 1,441 U.S. literacy teachers, most perceived technology integration primarily in terms of a technological rather than curricular framework—that technology serves more as supplementing rather than redefining their curriculum and instruction (Hutchison & Reinking, 2011). For example, teachers may assign students to use a blog to write a five-paragraph essay, as opposed to using a class blog to foster students' collaborative sharing of ideas. Students could simply write their essays with a word processor; in using a class blog, they can then readily add hyperlinks to blog posts/websites, embed images/videos, and add comments to one another's posts—features that invite them to employ the practices of making intertextual connections, use multimodal communication, and interact with peer audiences.

While teachers are employing the use of digital tools in the classroom, there remains a disconnect between students' active use of digital tools outside the classroom and within the classroom. Sixty-one percent of 9th graders and 59% of 12th graders make regular use of the Internet to support their learning, as opposed to only 21% of teachers assigning Internet-based homework or projects on a weekly basis (Speak Up, 2013). In the British study of iPad use, students indicated that they wanted teachers to make more use of iPads for creating wikis, for writing and reading, and for communicating with teachers (Heinrich, 2012).

We believe that this disconnect stems from how teachers frame the use of digital tools simply as technological add-ons, versus the use of these tools to transform their curriculum. As was the case with the printing press and the typewriter, the uses of digital tools are transforming literacy learning and instruction in ways that redefine what has largely been a print-based literacy curriculum and instruction. Rather than simply substituting a digital tool for a print-based tool, such transformation involves augmentation, modification, and redefinition of curriculum and instruction employing digital tools (Puentedura, 2011). However, instead of totally transforming instruction in one fell swoop through use of digital tools, we are suggesting moving gradually from augmenting instruction to modifying and redefining it.

Using Digital Tools Within an Activity-Based Curriculum

Integrating uses of digital tools entails much more than simply learning how to use a particular tool—for example, how to set up a blog. Students need to know how to use digital tools to accomplish certain purposes within particular contexts, such as those represented in the *Ink* and online role-play activities.

To consider how the use of digital tools can ultimately redefine or transform literacy learning, in this book we provide an activity-based curriculum framework for teaching secondary and college English language arts using digital tools. By an *activity-based curriculum*, we mean a curriculum that focuses on goal-driven reading and writing activities supported or mediated by uses of digital tools. By *goal-driven activity*, we mean activity in which students have a clear sense of purpose for using digital reading and writing tools to accomplish a certain goal.

Goal-driven activity is mediated by use of digital tools designed to achieve certain social or rhetorical purposes (Engstrom, 2009; Russell, 2009). Students are familiar with use of digital tools to achieve certain social and rhetorical purposes outside the class-room, through texting, Facebook, e-mail, or social networking (Dredger, Woods, Beach, & Sagstetter, 2010). In one study, college students indicated that text messages, e-mails, and lecture notes were, in addition to writing academic papers, three of the most frequent types of writing that they employed; they also employed these tools largely for social purposes to interact with and coordinate social relationships with others (Pigg et al., 2013).

Transferring this social, goal-driven activity outside the classroom into the classroom to achieve academic goals requires providing students with the same sense of purpose and audience that motivates them to achieve certain social and rhetorical goals outside the classroom. In creating a collaborative writing activity involving use of wikis, your activity needs to provide students with some reason for engaging in collaboration so that they are not just learning how to use a wiki per se—that is, they are learning how wikis can be used to engage in collaborative construction of knowledge.

How then can you foster digital writing for social purposes within the classroom? Having students go beyond simply replicating or transmitting knowledge to collabora-tively constructing it for audiences provides them with a sense of purpose and audience (Mateos et al., 2010; Pennycook, 2010). For example, if students are collaboratively creating a script with Google Docs to produce a public service video on examples of pollution in their town's local rivers, they are exploiting the use of an online tool for the social construction of knowledge within a goal-driven activity to convince local residents to address pollution in the town's rivers.

Integrating Understanding and Creation of Digital Texts

Students are not only learning to transfer uses of digital reading and writing from outside to inside the classroom. They are also learning to transfer ways of understanding digital texts to ways of creating them. In reading digital texts, students are acquiring knowledge of the features and conventions that constitute certain types of digital texts. For example, in reading blog posts, students are acquiring an understanding of the use of hyperlinks to other blogs and the content of reader comments, leading to their writing of their own blog posts. Through reading digital texts, students are also acquir-ing ideas for use in their own writing.

Reading and writing are therefore highly integrated. Students' reading ability influ-ences their ability to self-assess their writing, leading to revisions of their drafts essential to improving their writing (Beach & Friedrich, 2006; de Milliano, van Gelderen, & Sleegers, 2012; Moore & MacArthur, 2012). Unfortunately, many students lack the ability to "determine central ideas or themes of a text and analyze their development; summarize the key supporting details and ideas"—one of the English language arts Common Core standards (Council of Chief State School Officers & National Governors Association, 2010, p. 31). The 2013 reading assessment from the National Assessment of Educational Progress found that only 38% of 12th graders were categorized as *profi-cient*—meaning that students should be able to provide relevant information and sum-marize main ideas and themes (National Center for Education Statistics, 2014).

Students' difficulty in reading then transfers to difficulty in writing (Graham & Harris, 2013). Analysis of students' writing on the 2011 computer-based writing assessment of the National Assessment of Educational Progress indicated that 54% of 8th graders and 52% of 12th graders performed at the *basic* level, while only 24% of both performed at the *proficient* level and only 3% at the *advanced* level (National Center for Education Statistics (2012). Students who write more frequently (four to five pages a week) versus less frequently and those who use a computer for editing their writing had higher scores. Conversely, engagement in digital writing enhances students' reading of digital texts, whereas extensive use of writing enhances students' knowledge of organizational cues and structure contributing to interpreting texts (Hsu & Wang, 2011; Kuteeva, 2010; Mendenhall & Johnson, 2010).

One of the goals of this book is to suggest ways to not only integrate digital reading and writing instruction but also help students acquire new ways of responding to digital texts to enhance their reading ability in ways that enhance their writing ability.

Professional Development for Teachers in the Uses of Digital Tools

Finally, we recognize that you as our reader bring to your teaching different background knowledge and experiences in the uses of digital tools. As a busy teacher, you may simply lack time or opportunities to learn about these tools for their use in teaching. While 62% of teachers in one survey indicated that their school does a "good job" in providing technology support and 68% indicated that it provides formal training, 85% of teachers said that they seek out ways on their own to employ technology in their instruction, and 84% reported themselves finding instructional content for use in their teaching (Purcell, Heaps, et al., 2013).

Our book concludes with a chapter providing a range of resources for acquiring additional information and resources, with links included in the book itself. We also provide you with links throughout the book to the book's website http://digitalwriting. pbworks.com for additional information, resources, and further reading.

ACKNOWLEDGMENTS

We thank our Rowman & Littlefield editor, Sue Canavan, for her encouragement to write this book and her editorial guidance; Andrea O. Kendrick, for her editorial assistance; and Stephanie Scuiletti, for her production assistance. We also thank our reviewers, as well as our own copyediting reviewers, Barbara Horvath and Sumitra Madhuri Ramachandran, and our indexer Ian Anson. And we thank all the teachers who were willing to contribute examples of their teaching activities and student work to this book.

I

INTRODUCTION

In one of his classes, one of the authors—Tom Reynolds—planned and implemented the creation of a class e-zine. Over the course of a semester, students designed and produced individual texts that were grouped into magazine sections, or departments, and then joined into a single digital text. The focus for the e-zine was the experience of the first year of college.

Tom artfully divided this project into several stages:

a *planning stage*, to help the students gain a sense of the magazine's historical shift from print to digital text, to immerse them in the magazine as a multimodal genre, to teach them to make use of digital resources, to have them explore the topic, and to facilitate practice of the written and visual forms of magazines as genres;

a *writing stage*, when students wrote three texts for the class magazine in a variety of genres;

a *curating and reframing* stage, when students took the role of editors, choosing a limited number of individual pieces, gathering them into sections of the magazine, and copying them into iBooks Author, an e-book authoring program—this allowed the students to adjust fonts, draw images, and collect individually authored texts into a single larger text with the current focus of their magazine sections; and

an *editing and finalizing* stage, in which the students joined the various sections into one e-book file, gave the text its final shape as their e-zine, and chose an image for each section.

One student, Kendall, wrote a practical piece that addressed the need to manage one's time carefully. She directed the piece at women and provided a series of annotated websites with live links to magazine articles that provided advice to college women. To make the piece more visually appealing, she designed each section with bold headings that stood out from her annotations, and she used clip art that illustrated each piece of advice. For example, a section titled "Breakfast" included an image with a plate of eggs and toast—a visual sign for a healthy breakfast. Other student projects included video interviews of advanced students on campus offering advice to first-year students, digital sound interviews of campus authority figures, concert reviews with digital photographs, and websites authored on the news and entertainment value of magazines.

Tom's students used a range of digital tools to create their class magazine as multimodal digital productions. Rather than perceiving these multimodal texts as outliers in secondary and college classrooms, Tom's students—through producing these kinds of digital texts—are acquiring skills for 21st-century learning, creativity, and employment in ways that enhance their engagement with the topics of their interest and the materials of their curricula.

We believe that students' uses of digital tools, such as those involved in Tom's students creating multimodal texts, reflect what students need to acquire for success in the 21st century—uses of tools that represent a shift from solely print-based English language arts instruction.

As noted in the preface, we discuss ways to use a range of digital tools for understanding and creating digital texts. To plan instruction in the use of these tools—the focus of chapter 2—it is important to consider how using the tools strengthens students' learning (for more on students' uses of digital tools: http://tinyurl.com/lesxq6d).

AFFORDANCES MEDIATING SOCIAL PRACTICES THROUGH USES OF DIGITAL TOOLS

As shown in Figure 1.1, the affordances associated with the use of digital tools are closely related to social practices that are central to students' learning and educational interaction based on use of Web 2.0 digital tools (Beach & O'Brien, 2014; Castek, Zawilinski et al., 2010; for Web 2.0 digital tools: http://tinyurl.com/mdlt7gx; for research on students' use of digital tools: http://tinyurl.com/k7yh2p4).

If you think about any tool, such as a hammer, it is not difficult to imagine ways that it might be used to do more than one thing. A hammer can drive in nails but also knock something apart, smash in a window, serve as a doorstop, or hold a book open. By *affordances*, we mean the actions associated with the use of digital tools designed to achieve certain goals (Beach & O'Brien, 2014; J. J. Gibson, 1986). Affordances associated with the use of a particular tool depend on how that tool is being used in an activity. For example, one affordance of Google Docs is how it supports collaboration through shared revisions and comments. However, the degree to which that affordance is fully realized depends on your effective design of a collaborative writing activity.

Relationship Between Activities, Affordances, and Social Practices

Activities Involving Use of Digital Tools

|

Affordances

|

Social practices

Figure 1.1.   Relationships Among Activities, Affordances, and Tools

Tools therefore do not have set, predetermined affordances "in" the tool. Rather, they are manifested in the way that you design activities involved in understanding and creating digital texts for different purposes. As such, we describe the use of digital tools in terms of an activity-based approach given the centrality of the activities that you design involving the use of these tools.

Exploiting the affordances of digital tools used in the classroom requires designing activities that are most likely to help students achieve the learning goals that you set for them. As noted in the preface, learning the use of digital tools involves learning to employ them for social purposes. To achieve these purposes, students learn to employ certain social practices as ways of achieving social purposes.

In this book, we focus on six social practices involved in use of digital tools:

1. Contextualizing digital texts
2. Making connections between digital texts and people
3. Collaborative understanding and creation of digital texts
4. Adopting alternative modes of communication
5. Adopting alternative perspectives
6. Constructing and enacting identities

Students employ these social practices in understanding and creating digital texts within a rhetorical context (D. Barton & Lee, 2013). Theresa Lillis (2013) notes,

> An emphasis on practices signals that specific instances of language use—spoken and written texts—do not exist in isolation but are bound up with what people do— practices—in the material social world. . . . Ways of doing things with texts become

part of everyday, implicit life routines both of the individual, habitus in Bourdieu's (1991) terms, and of social institutions. (p. 158)

People use different means to achieve certain social *uptakes*—defined as intended rhetorical effects (Freadman, 2002). For example, when students use a blog post to convince their peers to vote for a candidate for student council president, the intended uptake is that their peers will then vote for that candidate. In Tom's class, when students created magazine texts to inform next year's students on how to survive their first semester of college, the intended uptake was that next year's students would have a better-informed view as they launched into their own first year, avoiding some of the pitfalls along the way.

When we think about the affordances of many digital tools associated with use of these social practices, it is helpful to remember that what might appear to be a "noneducational" tool—maybe even one to "ban" from the classroom—has tremendous potential for enhancing the classroom's social context. For example, as noted in the preface, Pigg et al. (2013) found that texting, e-mail, and lecture notes were the most frequent use of digital writing tools by college students. Their use was not limited to simple academic pursuits; instead, these tools served to maintain social connections and coordinate relationships with friends and family members across time and space. Such coordination

> provides college students an active means for organizing "things" that matter to them within the contexts of the goals, identities, and domains that are meaningful to them: projects, internships, information, personal memory—even their own learning trajectories. . . . By bringing people and things (like events or projects) into alignment, coordination becomes a way for students to actively participate and meaningfully direct their relationship to many of the roles and identities that characterize their lives in college. (p. 19)

In this book, we advocate for a social practices model of literacy education. This model differs from a skills, process, or text-genre model of literacy instruction. While a skills model involves explicit instruction in specific isolated skills, such as being able to infer a main idea when reading in isolation, a social practices model emphasizes understanding digital texts so that students do not experience reading and writing without any purposeful rhetorical context (Ivanic, 2004).

Likewise, in a process model, students can focus on "prewriting," "drafting," and "editing" as ends in themselves simply to meet a regimented requirement in a lockstep set of activities. This can limit their dialogic exploration of alternative constructions of meaning (Aukerman, 2013). In contrast, in a social practices model, students are focusing on how they can achieve certain rhetorical goals or uptakes within a purposeful social context.

In a traditional text-genre model, students focus on writing according to formalist structures and templates that may not consider differences in rhetorical contexts. In contrast, in a social practices model, students focus on how they can best employ different social practices mediated by use of digital writing to engage their audiences to achieve a positive uptake.

Addressing the Common Core State Standards

Our six social practices are related to implementing the English language arts Common Core State Standards (Council of Chief State School Officers & National Governors Association, 2010). They are also related to standards formulated by the National Council of Teachers of English / International Reading Association, Partnership for 21st Century Skills, and the International Society for Technology in Education (for specific standards: http://tinyurl.com/lmyca73).

It is important to recognize that the Common Core State Standards do not dictate what and how to teach; it is up to you to devise activities for implementing the standards. For further resources on implementation, see the resource website for Beach, Haertling-Thein, and Webb (2012): http://englishccss.pbworks.com.

Digital technology strongly informs the Common Core State Standards and their implications for instruction. For example, the eighth-grade writing standard refers to the following outcomes:

- Use technology, including the Internet, to present and cite information effectively in a digital format, including when publishing and responding to writing.
- Demonstrate command of technology, including the Internet, to produce, publish, and update work in response to ongoing feedback, including fresh arguments or new information.
- Incorporate digital media and visual displays of data when helpful and in a manner that strengthens the presentation.

Note that beginning in 2015, the Partnership for Assessment of Readiness for College and Careers and the Smarter Balanced Assessment Consortium will be conducting assessments of students' digital reading and writing skills. In contrast to paper assessments, these assessments will be completed on computers, requiring the use of keyboarding, online searches, spreadsheets, and digitally produced argumentative writing. For example, one sample task in the Smarter Balanced Assessment asks students to assume the role of chief of staff for a congresswoman in their state who needs advice on how to vote on a proposed nuclear plant to be built by a power company (Pierce, 2013). This requires that the student find online information related to identifying three arguments for and three against building the power plant, assess the validity of those arguments, and formulate a statement with supporting evidence for the congresswoman favoring or opposing building the plant.

The results of polls taken in fall 2013 found that only 11% of schools felt well prepared to implement these online assessments, 40% believed that students still need to learn technology skills to successfully participate in the tests, and 38% thought that students need to learn these skills through subject-based instruction (Haber, 2014). A study of 36 states' Common Core State Standards implementation found that while 30 states felt that the new assessments will serve as more valid measures of higher-order thinking and performance than their current state tests, 34 indicated that they face technological challenges involved in the testing, such as having enough computers or adequate bandwidth to administer the tests (Rentner, 2013). All of this points to the increasing importance of digital reading and writing as being central to successful performance on these assessments.

The Common Core gives you an opportunity to develop criteria for assessing students' use of a particular social practice and to monitor students' development of competence in this practice over time. As we describe each of the six social practices, we indicate some of the relevant Common Core standards associated with them.

CONTEXTUALIZING DIGITAL TEXTS

Related Common Core State Standards

- Synthesize and apply information presented in diverse ways (e.g., through words, images, graphs, and video) in print and digital sources to answer questions, solve problems, or compare modes of presentation.
- Produce writing in which the organization, development, substance, and style are appropriate to task, purpose, and audience.
- Present information, evidence, and reasoning in a clear and well-structured way appropriate to purpose and audience.

Students understand and create digital texts in more highly interactive ways than they do print texts. While readers of print texts generally read in a linear, left-to-right manner, readers of digital texts locate and attend to those links or icons that address their purposes for reading—that is, they "read for relevancy" (Kress, 2003). For example, in navigating an admissions website to acquire information about a certain college, students attend to those links or icons that provide information relevant to their questions.

Reading in this purposeful way requires that students engage in the social practice of *contextualizing* a digital text. When students conduct online searches, they need to have a clear sense of purpose for collecting information. In creating a digital video, identifying their purpose and audience helps them to select and edit video content in appropriate ways. Saskia Stille (2011a), for example, describes the way that she, her students, and their parents contextualized a digital video about creating a garden for their school:

> Attempting to deal with these concerns, I involved the students, teacher, and parents in every stage of the project: Selecting events and activities to film, holding the camera, creating interview questions, and editing raw footage. To make the film meaningful, the students chose which footage of themselves to include, and added voice-over narration to help the audience understand the significance of the experiences portrayed. Having students, parents, and the teacher speak for themselves in the film provided context and ensured that they explained and represented the experience in their own words. The choices they made about what to include/exclude and how to narrate their story reveals some of editing that individuals do when they become aware that their experiences will be made public. Creating context also meant providing background information about the school and community so that the audience could understand the significance of the project within this setting. (pp. 105–106)

Identifying Components of a Rhetorical Space

In Stille's project, the students, teacher, and parents contextualized their video production in a *rhetorical space*. Troy Hicks (2013) offers a useful heuristic for understanding and acting on the concept of rhetorical space. His MAPS scheme is based on five components: *mode*, "the genre of the text"; *media*, "the form(s) in which a text is created"; and *audience*, *purpose*, and *situation*. For examples of applying MAPS to digital writing, see his *Crafting Digital Writing* companion wiki at http://tinyurl.com/pcr25xh and links to tools described in the book, http://tinyurl.com/okm8edj.

As illustrated in Figure 1.2, when contextualizing digital spaces, students identify the components of purpose, audience, situation, genre, and form.

> *Purpose*—what students perceive the writer of a text to be saying or doing or what they want their own text to say or do, to achieve a certain effect or uptake—for example, to convince an audience to accept their position on an issue. Students' senses of purpose drive their decisions to use the affordances of digital tools, such as media (genre) and mode (form).

Contextualizing Digital Texts

purpose   audience   situation

digital texts

genre   form

Figure 1.2.   Contextualizing Digital Texts

Audience—how students define a text's intended or potential audience and how they conceptualize that audience's beliefs, knowledge, and expectations, as well as their relationship with that audience—whether familiar or unfamiliar. This requires that they engage in "rhetorical reading"—framing their own text as a reader by adopting their potential audience's perspective and considering the text's effects (Warren, 2013). Determining their audience's characteristics helps students select the media or mode most likely to achieve positive uptake by gaining audience identification with their positions or personae.

Situation—students frame their understanding and creation of a digital text in terms of their familiarity with the digital tools that they are using, as well as the social, political, and cultural contexts within which they are using them. The classroom community becomes what Gee (2013a) defines as an "affinity space" for collaborative construction of knowledge. For example, students might use the affordances of a wiki as a space for collaboratively organizing and sharing knowledge about a certain topic or issue.

Genre—students frame their understanding and creation of a digital text as a socially meaningful genre (argumentative essay, digital storytelling, and hypertext poetry). Perceiving texts as social genres goes beyond thinking of them as textual structures to thinking of them as social actions (C. R. Miller, 1984). For example, rather than think of the genre of the school newspaper editorial in terms of a predetermined structure or template, students can think of the editorial as a set of social actions used purposefully within a context or situation. In doing so, students are using their knowledge of social genres as typified "forms of life, ways of being, and frames for social action" (Bazerman, 1994, p. 79). A student creating a parody remix of a video draws on the genre of video remix to entertain the audience by connecting with his or her prior knowledge and experience.

Form—to achieve their purposes, students select certain forms, such as print text, video, audio production, image presentation, or a combination of visuals/images, video, sound/music, or textual media. Tom's students were asked to build an understanding of writing that made use of compositional skills in the new context of journalism, which involves use of certain forms associated with journalistic writing. In writing their individual texts with the larger context of the magazine in mind, they were challenged to reframe writing concerns, such as clarity, audience, editing, and multimodal rhetorical strategies, in ways that extended their knowledge and practice of writing. The "hurry-up" time frame that often accompanies journalistic writing was also a new challenge.

MAKING CONNECTIONS BETWEEN DIGITAL TEXTS AND PEOPLE

Related Common Core State Standards

- Analyze how two or more texts address similar themes or topics in order to build knowledge or to compare the approaches the authors take.
- Use technology, including the Internet, to produce, publish, and interact with others about writing.
- Integrate and evaluate information from multiple oral, visual, or multimodal sources in order to answer questions, solve problems, or build knowledge.

Another social practice mediated through the affordances of digital tools involves making intertextual connections between texts and people. For example, when students share text messages to organize a social event, those messages reference previous messages and invite further messages. In this intertextual sharing, each text is both the absorption and the transformation of another text (van Meter & Firetto, 2008). Or, when posting to a blog, students can include links that interconnect other posts in ways that extend or elaborate on ideas, but in doing so, they must anticipate whether a reader will select those links. When reading these posts, other students may add comments and include links that continue to extend the initial post.

Making these connections is a social practice related to sharing knowledge or building relationships. When they create hyperlinked connections between their blog posts and a peer's post, students are sharing their knowledge with others, building or maintaining social relationships with peers, and creating intercontextual connections to another writer's activity or context (Bloome, Carter, Christian, Otto, & Shuart-Faris, 2005).

In responding to digital texts to connect to other texts, students need to know how to navigate hyperlinks to access other texts related to their purposes. Students may simply click on links without any clear sense of purpose. As a result, they often become lost in a sea of links without knowing what they are trying to find. As we discuss in more detail in chapter 3 on search strategies, students need to have a clear sense of purpose for navigating links so that they know which links to select or pursue to achieve certain information.

To help students learn to select and navigate links purposefully, you can have them clarify their purposes for reading texts. Similarly, in creating their own hyperlinks between texts, students need to provide cues so that readers will know what to expect if they click on a link. A cue might be a note that, for example, another blog post addresses their topic from a somewhat different perspective or that a website contains information that will further illuminate their topic.

The fact that students can now readily access and create these online connections has led to the formulation of a connectivist model of learning. In this model, knowledge is constructed and located in and through online networked connections (Rainie & Wellman, 2012; Siemens, 2009). If knowledge resides in the network and is constructed through networking, then students need to acquire the social practice of creating and using their own "personal learning networks" (Richardson & Mancabelli, 2011). Raine and Wellman (2012) argue that instead of relying on traditional organizations or institutions to acquire or share knowledge, people now rely more on these loosely defined, fluid networks:

> Many meet their social, emotional, and economic needs by tapping into sparsely knit networks of diverse associates rather than relying on tight connections to a relatively small number of core associates. . . . Networked individuals have partial membership in multiple networks and rely less on permanent memberships in settled groups. They must calculate where they can turn for different kinds of help—and what kind of help to offer others as they occupy nodes in others' extended networks. (p. 14)

A "connected learning" approach (http://connectedlearning.tv) advocates for the need to connect students' social, interest-driven uses of digital tools with academic uses of these tools in ways that enhance their engagement with learning. These processes are helpful in advancing social and civic equity, particularly for students from nondominant populations who are alienated from school (Ito et al., 2013). Designing "peer-supported," "interest-powered," and "academically oriented" online networking builds social relationships with peers and adults around academic content (Ito et al., 2013).

COLLABORATIVE UNDERSTANDING AND CREATION OF DIGITAL TEXTS

Related Common Core State Standards

- Synthesize and apply information presented in diverse ways (e.g., through words, images, graphs, and video) in print and digital sources in order to answer questions, solve problems, or compare modes of presentation.
- Use technology, including the Internet, to produce, publish, and interact with others about writing.
- Participate effectively in a range of interactions (one-on-one and in groups), exchanging information to advance a discussion and to build on the input of others.

Another social practice involves the collaborative understanding and creation of digital texts. Reading digital texts through shared online discussion responses or annotations engages students in creating meaning collectively—what Shirky defines as "social reading" (Findings, 2012), what Reich (2013b) defines as "connected" versus "focused" reading, and what Marshall (2009) refers to as the "sociality of reading," by which students are active participants who collaboratively contribute their own texts in response to the texts that they are reading. However, students often have difficulty engaging in productive collaboration, sometimes because they have had little opportunity to practice it in their classrooms. A 2013 Gallup survey found that only one third of students engaged in collaborative work in the classroom and only 3% reported using videoconferencing, discussion boards, or Skype for collaboration.

Collaboration also involves sharing common interests and knowledge valued by a group. When students come together to explore topics and issues of mutual interest, they are equally compelled to work together without establishing hierarchies or delegating more power or expertise to some members (Gee, 2013a). Working collaboratively requires building social relationships, defining social roles, and providing support for and between peers. Students are also more engaged with reading and writing when they are sharing responses to and writing texts within an affinity space that provides them with a sense of purpose and audience.

Within these local spaces, students adopt socially determined roles and adhere to social or genre-related norms. When students use Google Docs, these norms help them to become cowriters and revisers. When they create Wikipedia articles, students assume the roles of researchers, interviewers, and writers, knowing that a key norm influencing the ratings of Wikipedia articles is the Wikipedia editors' crowdsource-based determination of the article's degree of accuracy, use of references, and number of citations.

Use of class blogs can also enhance collaborative interaction among students and between teachers and students, particularly in terms of providing immediate feedback through comments (Felix, 2008). Cathy Davidson (2012) notes that by writing blog posts on a class blog, her students are writing more and are more engaged than they are in writing essays or term papers because

> the context is so urgent, compelling, and interactive that they enjoy it and it doesn't seem like drudgery. They work so hard to articulate and defend ideas about which they have strong convictions that it does not feel like the exercise of "writing a term paper."

In her American literature class, Elizabeth Barniskis had students work in groups of two or three to assume the identities of characters or authors from different literary movements and create a cartoon using PowToon, Toondoo, or a similar platform to portray how those characters or writers would react differently to a common conflict. For example, to represent three literary authors—Ralph Waldo Emerson, Henry David Thoreau, and Edgar Allan Poe—Connor Tressel created the cartoon in Figure 1.3 for his group using Toondoo, in which the authors are arguing with one another in the woods.

In terms of the larger classroom context, to enhance collaboration, you can encourage students to assume more active roles in shaping the class by providing them with choices in focus and activity. In describing the creation of her class at Duke University—21st Century Literacies: Digital Knowledge, Digital Humanities course site http://bit.ly/WxbGXk, in this course, Cathy Davidson (2013) begins her class by having them reflect on their collaborative peer production. Her students then collaboratively craft statements on Google Docs constituting the importance of collaborative digital commu-

Figure 1.3.   Emerson, Thoreau, and Poe Argument. *Source: Screenshot used with permission of Connor Tressel.*

nication for their university community, resulting in the "Duke 21C Community Manifesto" http://bit.ly/duke21c-manifesto.

Davidson also fosters collaborative construction of the course content by putting her syllabus online two months before the beginning of the class to invite potential student comments about the course content. Her students are given responsibility for shaping learning in that space, leading the class to create a collaborative e-book as its final project (Damasceno et al., 2013). For contributing collaborative writing to Wikipedia, she encourages what she defines as "collaboration by difference," requiring a recognition of "different forms and levels of expertise, perspective, culture, age, ability, and insight, treating difference not as a deficit but as a point of distinction" (Davidson, 2011, p. 1).

For each class meeting, different students select a topic and organize discussion around it using the hashtag #Duke21C on Twitter for participation inside and outside the classroom. Students then assume an active role in constructing their classroom community—for example, by preparing presentations about ways to design and learn in the class (Peddycord & Pitts, 2013). Two students in the class made the following comments:

> We believe that just like their teachers, 21st century students have a vested interest in becoming facilitators and collaborators. Open source style classrooms offer them the opportunity to practice these "soft" skills that become critically important later in life. (p. 2)

In Tom's class, students worked in small groups to form subsections of the larger magazine. This was a process of curating texts from the entire class set and grouping them into areas by common themes. Before the small groups took ownership over their set of texts, the entire class brainstormed and negotiated which belonged in areas. The class then created titles for those sections, and groups took over the editing of their sections. By working together, the students were learning how to negotiate adoption of roles and responsibilities associated with accomplishing their goals.

ADOPTING ALTERNATIVE MODES OF COMMUNICATION

Related Common Core State Standards

- Synthesize and apply information presented in diverse ways (e.g., through words, images, graphs, and video) in print and digital sources in order to answer questions, solve problems, or compare modes of presentation.
- Use technology, including the Internet, to produce, publish, and interact with others about writing.
- Integrate and evaluate information from multiple oral, visual, or multimodal sources in order to answer questions, solve problems, or build knowledge.
- Make strategic use of digital media and visual displays of data to express information and enhance understanding.

Understanding and creating multimodal digital texts requires an awareness of semiotic aspects of design—for example, the placement of objects or persons at the top of a space, as opposed to the bottom, to associate power or status with that object or person (Bezemer & Kress, 2008). Reading digital texts also requires the ability to understand multimodal combinations of images/video, sound/music, and language. As noted by Kress (2003, quoted in McCallum, 2012, p. 39),

> the current landscape of communication can be characterized by the metaphor of the move from telling the world to showing the world. . . . New forms of reading, when texts show the world rather than tell the world have consequences for the relations between makers and remakers of meaning (writers and readers, image-makers and viewers. (p. 140)

Students can employ digital tools to create multimodal texts that mesh the modes of images, audio, video, and print language to engage in digital storytelling or poetry. Students are actively engaged in viewing and producing video, thereby requiring a pedagogical focus on understanding and creating cinematic production techniques. This includes attention to aspects of time associated with editing, sequencing, duration, and rhythm, as well as the tailoring of digital texts for certain audiences (Bazalgette & Buckingham, 2013). In doing so, students use digital tools to create multimodal texts for social purposes. They use digital video or animation tools to parody, satire, or remix texts—for example, remixes of Shakespeare plays as found on the steampunk site http://thesteampunkhome.blogspot.com.

In the design of their e-zine, Tom's students were asked to think in terms of communicating to an audience of next year's first-year university students, using multimodal elements. Students were asked to think rhetorically in making choices about their use of visual, written, and video elements. Students considered whether the use of video, for example, in an interview situation would be persuasive for the e-zine and, if so, in what combination with alphabetic text. They were therefore considering how best to portray their ideas through multimodal communication given their purpose and audience.

Adopting alternative modes involves experimenting with alternative uses of genre conventions through recontextualizing the uses of those conventions. For example, in creating online fan fiction, students may experiment with different ways of creating it based on the genre's current conventions (R. W. Black, 2009b). In devising their own magazine, Tom's students were experimenting with alternative genres and forms, recontextualizing these uses of magazines within their original context for use in their classroom context, in some cases to create parody critiques of representations of race, class, gender, or age difference.

To foster such recontextualizing, you can encourage students to experiment with adopting alternative uses of texts given novel perceptions of the media, purpose, audience, and situation. For example, in his Digital Humanities course http://tinyurl.com/ogecbrg, Jesse Stommel (2013) asked his students to take the Emily Dickinson poem "There's a Certain Slant of Light" and rearrange it into another text using the words in the poem. One student created a mind map of the poem, which "asks the reader to consider the linearity of poetry, responding directly to Dickinson's call to read the poem (all poems) at 'a certain slant.'" Another student created a haiku:

> Winter Oppresses
> Shadows the landscape like death
> Tis heavenly when it goes

Another student used TypeDrawing for the iPad to paint with words, turning Emily Dickinson's poem into the raw material for her own work, "A Certain Slant of Light, Typographically Speaking." In doing so, she moved "from annotations through rough notes, several sketches, coloring, and the final step in which she signed her work in gold across the sky."

These uses of digital remixing of texts build on a long tradition of writers appropriating material from previous texts to create their own in ways that convey shared cultural ideas. Students engage in remixing activities through writing and online sharing of fan fiction that draws on and reappropriates popular culture material in ways that express their own versions of narrative events or character development (R. W. Black, 2009a). For example, Elizabeth Barniskis has her students take a vocabulary word and then use bighugelabs.com (http://bighughlabs.com) to create posters based on that word that parody the motivational posters that hang on the walls in office buildings and schools.

Integrating reading and writing instruction of digital texts also involves having students focus on elements of craft associated with the multimodal aesthetic design of digital texts (T. Hicks, 2013). For example, in creating their own e-books using iBooks Author or ePub, students and teachers are attending to aspects of visual layout and design in terms of integrating images into a page or using white space and font (for more on multimodal theory and text production: http://tinyurl.com/ldaq3jg).

ADOPTING ALTERNATIVE PERSPECTIVES

Related Common Core State Standards

- Assess how point of view or purpose shapes the content and style of a text.
- Write arguments to support a substantive claim with clear reasons and relevant and sufficient evidence.
- Evaluate the speaker's point of view, reasoning, and use of evidence and rhetoric.

Another social practice involves adopting alternative perspectives in understanding and producing digital texts. By applying alternative perspectives, students engage in dialogic thinking about a text that leads them to interrogate assumptions or biases operating in their own or others' texts. In participating in face-to-face or online discussions, students identify others' perspectives and beliefs about an issue or topic to voice their own perspectives, whether distinct or similar, thereby avoiding the "myself bias" (Wolfe, Britt, & Butler, 2009) associated with failing to consider alternative positions on an issue. Students gain an awareness of alternative cultural perspectives through engaging in cross-cultural communication with students in different parts of the country or the world using Skype, Google Hangouts, or PenPals, tools that we discuss in chapter 6.

Students can also use digital tools to adopt a critical perspective. Glogowski (2006) argues that students need opportunities in school to use digital writing to be exposed to alternative perspectives and ideas that challenge their status quo thinking. He cites an activity in which his students began writing about issues of genocide and human rights on their blogs. In doing so, they were writing about these topics from their individual perspectives. However, when they started reading and responding to their peers' posts, they began to perceive the value of links to others' posts to further foster their own thinking. Glogowski recounts this shift in their perspectives:

> Then, one day at the end of April, it all changed. They started linking to each other's work because they found other entries meaningful and relevant. No, I do not mean that they linked to entries that explored the same topics. No. They started linking to entries that helped them expand their own understanding of issues that they were struggling with. I began to see semantic relations.

Glogowski notes that as the students developed a shared interest in the topic of human rights, they "realized that the topics they had chosen brought them all closer together, through debate, through common research ideas, through links and correspondences that they created based on meaning, based on commonly shared research interests."

CONSTRUCTING AND ENACTING IDENTITIES

Related Common Core State Standards

- Analyze in detail where, when, why, and how events, ideas, and characters develop and interact over the course of a text.
- Write narratives to convey real or imagined experiences, individuals, or events and how they develop over time.

Our sixth social practice involves the use of digital tools to construct and enact identities. For example, in creating Facebook profiles, assuming avatars in an online game, or adopting certain personae or ethos in an online discussion or role-play, students are constructing and enacting "projected identities," thereby constituting their identities. Gee (2010) notes,

> Video games are all about identity. The player "plays" some character; the player takes on, carries out, and identifies with some special identity in a virtual world. When I have married my personal goals and values to the virtual character's "in game" goals, I see the game as both a project that the game designers have given to me and, simultaneously, I project my own goals, desires, values, and identity into the game world, melded with the "in game" identity and goals of the virtual character. The "project" now becomes "mine" and not just something imposed on me, because I have "projected" myself into it. (p. 18)

In creating digital texts associated with online argumentative writing, as described in the preface, students are adopting personae or roles associated with establishing ethos designed to engage their audiences. This requires them to project ethos as someone who is knowledgeable and believable about their topic so that they gain their audience's identification (Burke, 1969). Students therefore bring autobiographical identities to their writing to construct projected personae in their writing; as such, they are then perceived as adopting certain identities by their audiences (Burgess & Ivanič, 2010).

How audiences perceive the projected ethos can influence students' self-perceptions as writers, which in turn influences their sense of confidence in their writing abilities. Students are better able to project ethos when they are familiar with their potential audience's knowledge, beliefs, and stances. One advantage of writing in a digital context (e.g., a class blog) is that students readily receive comments from their peers in ways that help them experience actual audience feedback so that they get to know their audience's knowledge, beliefs, and stances.

Students also create digital texts as a way to reflect on their identities. According to interviews with hundreds of adolescents about their uses of digital writing, Susannah Stern (2008) found that adolescents use blogs or social networking sites to share their feelings about their daily experiences. For example, one interviewee noted,

> My blog has helped me to center my feelings and realize that I need to take things one step at a time. It forces me to think about who I am, what I like, and who I want to be. I can think about one of the problems I am going to face, but writing about it allows me to work through the problem and start to look at solutions. (p. 102)

In this study, adolescents also used blogs to chronicle key events in their identity development. As one adolescent noted, "my blog keeps tabs on me" (p. 102). The students were also eager to share their critiques of current schooling or political status quo practices, leading to the need to engage in collective action to address and change these practices.

USES OF DIFFERENT DIGITAL DEVICES

In this book, we describe a range of software and apps designed for use with different devices associated with understanding and creating digital texts. In addition to desktop/laptop tools, this includes iOS, Android, and Chrome OS apps for use on tablets and smartphones (for more on iOS apps: http://tinyurl.com/kz27vwu; Android apps: http://tinyurl.com/lm49mbj; or Chrome apps: http://tinyurl.com/l3pkkor).

Affordances Associated With the Use of Devices

Students' use of tablets and smartphones is increasing in schools; 51% of high school students indicated that they used their tablets at least once a week in English language arts classrooms (C. Harris, 2013). This includes iOS iPads and iPhones; Android OS tablets by Amplify, Samsung, Dell, Google, and others; as well as Chromebooks (for more on uses of smartphones in the classroom: http://tinyurl.com/lheelje).

Results of the 2013 Speak Up Survey conducted by Project Tomorrow found that 89% of high school students have personal access to Internet-connected smartphones; 60%, access to laptops; and 50%, access to tablets (Riedel, 2014). Within their schools, one third of students have access to a school device—laptop or tablet. Sixty percent use mobile devices for research; 43%, educational games; 40%, collaboration with their peers; 33%, assignment reminders; 24%, taking photos of their assignments; and 18%, in-class polling. One third access videos on their own for assistance in completing homework, and 23% access teacher-created videos.

For planning activities, you can therefore consider students' use of certain affordances with the use of certain devices: the use of touch commands, the ubiquity of use, their mobility/portability, their reachability/access to people for contact and communication, and their photo/video production (Beach & O'Brien, 2014). Students can use their smartphones as highly mobile devices to take photos on a field trip to an art museum and achieve the goal of documenting the kinds of art they viewed there. Or, students can use their tablets to store texts or add highlights and annotations/notes to texts.

One reason for the popularity of some of these devices is the increased use of cloud-based sharing through iCloud, Google Drive, SkyDrive, DropBox, Evernote, Box.com, WebDAV, and so on, so that students can store their files/digital texts in the cloud rather than take up space on their tablets, smartphones, or Chromebooks. For example, Jennifer Carey (2013) uses Google Drive to share documents—files, presentations, spreadsheets, and so on—with her class. To do so, particularly when giving them assignments, she employs Share options in terms of providing her students access to these documents. She selects "Can view" if she wants students to only view a document, "Can comment" to allow them to add comments, or "Can edit" to edit a document. To have her students submit assigned writing to her, she creates a shared folder for each class, as well as specific assignment subfolders to which students add their files. She also requires that when they submit their files, that they name them according to the specific assignment and provide their names so that she can keep track of who is submitting what files.

Given the increasing popularity of apps for iOS and Android devices, we provide links to iOS apps (iTunes Store: http://tinyurl.com/bssljs6) and Android apps (Google

Play Store: http://tinyurl.com/cn9oc2t) in addition to links to desktop software, both in the book itself and on the website.

SUMMARY

In this introductory chapter, we posit the need to go beyond perceiving digital tools as technological add-ons to recognizing how they are transforming curriculum and instruction in ways that can engage students in learning. We also describe the need to help students learn to employ the affordances of digital tools to foster the use of our six social practices—affordances inherent in the activities by using these tools. In our next chapter, we provide you with some specific processes for planning instruction based on the use of our six social practices.

PLANNING FOR AN ACTIVITY-BASED APPROACH TO UNDERSTANDING AND CREATING DIGITAL TEXTS

As writing continues to shape and be shaped by digital tools and networked spaces and as standards for teaching and learning how to write broaden to encompass new genres and media, writers are presented with more and more options. The question is no longer whether we should use technology to teach writing; instead we must focus on the many ways we must use technology to teach writing.

—Troy Hicks (2013, p. 2)

PLANNING INSTRUCTION FOR UNDERSTANDING AND CREATING DIGITAL TEXTS

Your students' ability to understand and create digital texts depends on their level of engagement in your classroom activities. That level of engagement depends on how carefully you have planned these activities which foster learning to use tools for understanding and creating digital texts. Given this focus on fostering learning, in this chapter we describe ways to plan instruction designed to cultivate students' acquiring our six social practices through uses of digital tools. Tom describes his processes for planning instruction for his first-year college course, a fall 2013 University of Minnesota freshman seminar with a focus on studying magazines, as well as a unit in which his students created a public service video about an on-campus issue at the university.

In response to concerns about the university administration's decisions about its student union, a group of Tom's students created manifestos in the form of videos designed for the university community as their audience. They planned a video that included images from the union itself, which were significant because they were essential to an understanding by the main stakeholders—namely, other students and admin-

istrators. The fact that the students recognized the importance of including these images reflected their audience awareness.

Tom based his planning on working with students with advanced reading ability,
extensive prior reading and writing experiences, and active use of digital/online tools,
which would require modifications for planning for a sixth-grade class of students with
limited reading abilities and history, few previous writing experiences, and little online
access in their homes. However, we believe that the different aspects of instruction that
he describes apply to teaching at any level, while recognizing the need to vary that
instruction based on differences in students in a particular class.

WHAT FRAMEWORKS EXIST FOR INTEGRATING DIGITAL AND PRINT LITERACIES IN MY CURRICULUM?

Whereas instruction for English language arts revolved largely around print texts in the
past, it now involves a greater focus on integrating print and digital texts. One useful
framework for planning instruction is the "technological pedagogical content knowledge
model" (TPACK) (Mishra & Koehler, 2006), based on integration of technology, pedagogy, and content. This framework posits the importance of focusing not only on using
technology but also on considering how technology changes curriculum and instruction.
Tom had his students create digital magazines as an activity that involved multimodal
ways of communicating that integrated the pedagogy of collaborative knowledge construction with understanding the content of contemporary online communication
through uses of digital tools.

As noted in our preface, another useful framework is the substitution, augmentation,
modification, and redefinition model (Puentedura, 2011) for thinking about integration
of digital tools in terms of four different phases, depending on the degree to which uses
of certain tools reify versus transform traditional ways of learning. (For a "Padagogy
Wheel" aligning these four phases to specific tools, see http://tinyurl.com/oc3uztk (Carrington, 2013); for more on this model, see http://tinyurl.com/l4cbmx6.) In the substitution phase, teachers may simply substitute a digital tool for a print-based tool—for
example, using a screencasting tool such as ShowMe or Explain Everything to have
students present information as a substitute for a written report (Holland, 2013b). In
the augmentation phase, students may use a screencasting tool to augment their learning by using it to demonstrate their knowledge about their interpretation of a poem, for
example. In the modification or redefinition phase, students may use screencasting for
modifying or redefining learning—for instance, creating screencasts for their peers
about ways to employ digital tools so that the students become the teachers in a classroom.

You may also experience variations in your colleagues' or administrators' stances on redefining or revising a print-based curriculum to integrate both print and digital literacies/modes. In a framework that recognizes the need to not simply jettison the print curriculum but mesh the print and digital curricula, Kevin Leander (2009) identified four stances that teachers adopt in addressing this challenge: *resistance* to using digital literacies, *replacement* of old literacies with new, using new literacies to validate or *return* to older print literacies, and *remediation* in which students use digital literacies to "remediate" or transform uses of print literacies. Adopting a remediation stance involves what Leander describes as a "parallel pedagogy" approach that integrates print *and* digital/media literacies. For example, in creating a video to convey one's ideas, students are writing scripts and storyboards while considering ways to integrate images, sound effects, and music along with transition effects as they edit their video.

All of this suggests the need to remediate uses of both print and digital text around activities that serve to foster the use of certain social practices, for example, use of reading and writing wikis for collaboration.

HOW CAN I PLAN ACTIVITIES FOR FOSTERING STUDENTS' USE OF SOCIAL PRACTICES?

As noted in chapter 1, our framework for instruction revolves around fostering students' use of social practices. In planning his instruction, Tom considered how students' uses of the affordances of digital tools involved uses of social practices.

Contextualizing Digital Texts

Contextualizing digital texts involves "rhetorical reading" (Warren, 2013) to assist students in contextualizing their senses of purpose and situation to achieve a certain effect or uptake—for example, to convince an audience to accept their position on an issue. In response to the decision made by the University of Minnesota administration to remove student-painted murals in the student union's cultural centers, a group of Tom's students contextualized their task in terms of their purpose, audience, situation, genre, and form as described in chapter 1. They determined that the manifesto genre using a video form would be the most effective tool given their purpose, audience, and situation.

With this sense of purpose, they were selecting a tool whose affordances would achieve that purpose. Given their concerns about the university administration's decisions about their audience, Tom's students' manifesto video for the university community as their audience represented an attempt to inform that community of the problem with removing the student murals to replace them with what the students perceived to be public relations images about the university.

In employing the social genre of a manifesto, Tom's students were drawing on their genre knowledge of and experience with crafting manifestos related to the need for a call for action in history (Russell, 2010). They selected familiar images from the union itself to gain their audience's identification with that setting. They also planned for music as a soundtrack, a good idea that may or may not have worked in the execution (discussed later in the book).

Students also developed and applied their knowledge of different genres and forms of magazine-based writing and reading, visuals, production, audience reception, and current forms of e-zines. In doing so, they were inferring how these texts positioned their identities in terms of race, class, gender, sexuality, and age differences, as well as audiences with particular interests or needs. For example, several students wrote reviews of rap concerts with the knowledge that doing so would position them as convincing authors with a college-age audience. Adding to this positioning, accompanying photos of performers and crowd shots located the authors as writing in the vein of local urban weeklies aimed at peer audiences.

Making Connections Between Texts and People

In planning activities, it is important to foster students' production of intertextual connections between texts and people. You can provide them with those texts or with access to certain people or have students make their connections. In creating their articles for inclusion in the e-zine, Tom's students built a mini-portfolio of work of different forms, such as the profile, the interview, and the review. In online discussion forums and classroom discussions, students were asked to consider notions of audience, ethos, and approaches to the development of writing within a multimodal space as notions that carried over within each form. Students were asked to comment on one another's work and on professionals' work, developing a network of associations that brought their own, less practiced work in relation to those with a great deal of practice and expertise.

Collaborating

You can devise activities that involve collaboration with peers in ways that require students to define their roles and responsibilities in working with one another. In Tom's magazine class, the e-zine project was planned so that those with more experience in creating multimodal texts could share their knowledge with those that lacked experience. After an initial survey of student skills with writing in digital contexts, Tom distributed expertise in a number of directions. In one group, for example, a student who had created digital videos worked with students who had no experience. She was able to share knowledge of how to edit a collection of video shots in iMovie, a skill that became important for others as well. Similarly, students who had experience working in web-authoring environments were able to tackle the e-book-authoring software that they used. In both cases, other students assumed roles of editors, curators, and readers for the project.

The magazine class was also planned as an introduction to the ways that journalists collaborate. As students wrote their pieces and worked on editing them, activity was happening in organizing sections; that is, groups were choosing and grouping texts into sections designed for overall impact as one magazine text. Students were assigned to work both in a small group and with the entire class to carry out these tasks. Leaders for tasks emerged as the students met deadlines for drafts and edits. This dimension of group work gave students the sense of working with the tools under time and task constraints more like what they will likely encounter as they move forward with their studies and work lives.

In planning activities for working collaboratively, it is important to have students learn to pose questions to one another, as well as provide positive support for one another for making valuable contributions. This collaborative support is particularly important for students enrolled in massive online open courses (MOOCs). Students often do not complete these courses because they lack support associated with collaborative sharing of ideas within an online community.

This suggests the need for focusing instruction more on how the MOOC community becomes the curriculum as collaboratively constructed and negotiated by participants engaged in activities. For example, in one MOOC, small groups brainstormed the creation of their own MOOCs (Morris & Stommel, 2013). Groups of 50 coauthored and revised the same 1,000-word essay, and participants engaged in daily chats using a Twitter hashtag that resulted in 7,000 tweets during the first week of the course.

Adopting Alternative Modes of Communication

In planning activities to foster students' use of alternative modes, you help students mesh the modes of images, audio, video, and print language to create texts. As noted above, Tom planned for students to gradually build awareness of modes in published magazines in preparation for producing the class e-zine. As students wrote their individual articles, they were also assigned to add a multimodal element, whether visual or aural. In class, students were asked to reflect on how images and other nonprint elements communicated along with alphabetic communication. Students were also asked to adjust their usual understanding of print magazines for an electronic medium in terms of using color and design as they composed their pieces. To do so, students were asked to study established webpages and online magazine sites to learn about available resources.

Adopting Alternative Perspectives

In planning activities to encourage students to adopt alternative perspectives, you can create activities in which they are exposed to alternative perspectives that challenge their status quo perspectives. Awareness of alternative perspectives leads students to perceive the limitations of their own perspectives, or their "myself bias" (Wolfe et al., 2009), associated with failing to consider alternative positions on an issue. Tom planned for an exchange of perspectives via the student-authored drafts of their e-zine articles in an online forum in Moodle. In many cases, this involved students considering perspectives that differed from their own in terms of background identities based on a rural/urban split, regional differences, gender, and religious differences.

Constructing and Enacting Identities

In planning activities to foster students' construction and enactment of identities, you are having students think about the personae or ethos that writers adopt in their texts as well as the personae or ethos that they are creating that might differ from their autobiographical selves. In Tom's class, students were asked to study published authors' personae created in their texts and develop their own as budding magazine writers. Students studied stories and articles by famous magazine authors such as F. Scott Fitzgerald as well as writers for contemporary magazines and discussed the persona that each built through his or her writing. Students composed their own "writer" identities through profiles created in Moodle and eventually in the e-zines that they created. Students then created a "Notes From the Author" section to announce and establish ethos for their e-zines. One student, Jenna, announced that she was studying to be a public relations specialist and that she was proud to be "weird, spunky, and insecure" because it made her "interesting" and "inspired her to grow."

HOW DO I SELECT AND EVALUATE THOSE TOOLS OR APPS THAT WILL BEST MEET MY LEARNING OBJECTIVES?

Given the thousands of tools or apps available, it can be a challenge to select and evaluate tools or apps whose affordances serve to achieve your learning objectives. You can turn to the many app recommendation sites http://tinyurl.com/mjmulpy to identify certain apps based on their potential affordances for engaging students in certain activities, as well as to acquire evaluations or ratings of these apps. Again, these affordances are not simply inherent in a tool or app—they are constituted by how you are using a tool or app with your particular activity. To evaluate tools or apps, you are determining their relevancy, customization, usability, engagement, potential for sharing, and degree of fostering our social practices (Vincent, 2012). (See Kathy Schrock's description of the use of apps for remembering, understanding, applying, analyzing, evaluating, and creating http://tinyurl.com/95x4p2x.)

You are then using your learning objectives driving these activities to select those digital tools that may best help students achieve these goals. Rather than organizing the activity around a particular tool, you are designing the activity around what you want your students to learn *through* using the tool.

Given the fact that students may not know how to use these tools to achieve certain goals, in planning instruction, you can identify their knowledge, experience, and dispositions related to use of certain tools. To ascertain your students' prior experiences with digital reading and writing, you could have them complete a questionnaire asking them to describe their previous experiences and level of proficiency in using certain digital tools (databases, digital mapping/note-taking/annotations, blogs, wikis, websites, social networking, online discussion, presentation tools, e-book production, video production, podcasting, e-portfolios, etc.), as well as their reading, viewing, or media preferences. For example, as illustrated below, you can have them indicate their level of previous experience and proficiency—some students may have limited experiences but believe that they are relatively proficient:

Use of Blogs
Previous experience: Little / Some / Extensive
Level of proficiency: Low / Medium / High

For the freshman seminar course, Tom hands out a survey on the first day that asks students about their confidence levels in working with typical digital tools and writing forms that are likely to be used in the course. He also asks about confidence levels in carrying out certain writing tasks, such as "writing a persuasive argument" and "imagining challenges to my written arguments." Joining the digital tools and forms with concerns about writing can give students the idea that these are all parts of the same set of tasks for the course and that the technology is not merely an "add-on" task.

It is also useful to consider your students' dispositions or habits of mind related to uses of digital reading and writing. Representatives from the Council of Writing Program Administrators, the National Council of Teachers of English, and the National Writing Project developed the framework for success in postsecondary writing http://

wpacouncil.org/framework, which identified eight dispositions or habits of mind associated with being "college ready":

> Curiosity—the desire to know more about the world.
>
> Openness—the willingness to consider new ways of being and thinking in the
> world.
>
> Engagement—a sense of investment and involvement in learning.
>
> Creativity—the ability to use novel approaches for generating, investigating, and
> representing ideas.
>
> Persistence—the ability to sustain interest in and attention to short- and long-term
> projects.
>
> Responsibility—the ability to take ownership of one's actions and understand the
> consequences of those actions for oneself and others.
>
> Flexibility—the ability to adapt to situations, expectations, or demands.
>
> Metacognition—the ability to reflect on one's own thinking as well as on the indi-
> vidual and cultural processes used to structure knowledge. (p. 3)

Gaining an understanding of your students' dispositions is most likely to occur during
your class as you get to know more about your students. During the first week of Tom's
class, one student felt comfortable enough to share with the class that she had experience editing her high school newspaper and working with some of the digital forms that
the class would be reading and writing. It was an important moment for her, as reinforc-
ing an identity that she had begun in high school, and for the class, since it was brought
into the world of someone who had been successful in carrying out work with digital
texts. Practically, that student and a couple of others with similar experiences began to
take leadership roles with moving the class e-zine project forward.

WHAT ARE SOME DIGITAL TOOLS I CAN USE TO
ORGANIZE MY INSTRUCTION?

You can employ tools such as social networking sites, websites, blogs, and wikis to create
a class site for organizing your course content to provide students with your syllabus,
assignments, resources/readings, and ways of interacting with you or other students in a
class. One advantage of using social networking sites, websites, blogs, and wikis to
organize your instruction is that your students are familiar with these tools and you can
tailor them to meet their needs.

Another set of tools for organizing your courses involves using the Google Apps for
Education http://tinyurl.com/mn7oygr tools, which includes Google Drive, Docs,
Gmail, Calendar, Forms, Sheets, Slides, Sites, Vault, Chrome, Blogger, Maps, Google+,
Translate, Custom Search, Kaizena, Translate, Scholar, Books, YouTube for Educators,

Moderator, and Picasa Web Albums. Because these tools are free and cloud based, are accessed with one e-mail account, and can be readily loaded simultaneously into Chromebook computers, they represent an ideal option for organizing your class. To organize students' work, you can employ Google Classroom http://www.google.com/edu/classroom to communicate with students, share documents, organize assignments, and provide feedback about students' writing. Google Classroom uses Google Drive to create folders for each assignment so that students have deadlines; you can then determine who has completed those assignments and when.

You can also use the free Wiggio site http://wiggio.com to set up a class group to have students post messages sent out on a Listserv, set up virtual chat meetings with up to 10 participants, store and share files, and implement polls. There are other class management systems, such as Moodle, Desire to Learn, Edmodo, and Canvas, which we describe in chapter 6, related to conducting classroom discussions.

Students can also take courses available on iTunes U http://tinyurl.com/lbjbarh, Coursera https://www.coursera.org, Udacity https://www.udacity.com, MITOpen-Courseware http://tinyurl.com/kerepzm, and other university online course sites. You can use the iTunes U as a site for sharing your course materials—assignments, tutorials, readings, videos, images, podcasts, assessments, and so on. When students enter your iTunes U course, they see a bookshelf with your syllabus, keynote presentations, pages documents, PDFs, apps, assignments, topics, notes, and announcements on the left side. You can link to specific readings from the iBookstore, including iBooks, as well as videos from iTunes. In the Notes tab, you and your students can add and store notes from any texts or course. To create a course, you enroll in the iTunes U portal and then access the support site and the iTunes U Course Manager http://www.apple.com/support/itunes-u/course-manager, which provides tutorials on creating course materials.

Students are also increasingly enrolling in MOOCs despite some of the issues with students lacking the self-initiative to complete these courses, which may limit their applicability at the secondary level. However, there have been some noncredit MOOCs created by Verena Roberts (2013) for high school students such as Case of the Digital Footprint http://digifoot12.wikispaces.com, Beyond Facebook, and StudentHackEd, as well as the Creating an Open Classroom course for educators on K–12 technology integration. Students can also go to other courses at the Open Culture Links of 400 Free Online Courses From Top Universities http://www.openculture.com/freeonlinecourses.

There are a number of curriculum resource sites, such as Gooru, ReadWriteThink, Sophia, Share My Lesson, EdSitement, Curriki, Education World, and Thinkfinity, which include lesson plans and materials, including videos, that you can draw on for planning instruction (for links to these sites: http://tinyurl.com/ko6g9nx).

HOW CAN I ENGAGE STUDENTS IN PLANNING THEIR OWN LEARNING?

You can also engage your students in planning their learning by having them determine their goals and select those tools that will meet those goals to foster more self-directed, student-centered learning. In doing so, students are learning how to select those tools that will best achieve certain goals, something that they will eventually need to learn to do on their own.

To facilitate students' planning processes, you can provide them with a planning guide or heuristic. One example of such a heuristic is the iChoose http://iChooseTech. Weebly.com framework, which involves students determining their goals related to employing certain strategies based on Bloom's taxonomy (Bisson & Vazquez, 2013); for a conference presentation on use of iChoose, see http://tinyurl.com/mp245g2.

Students select a particular strategy: remember, understand, apply, analyze, evaluate, and create. They then respond to the following questions created with Google Forms:

1. What is your goal?

    Example: I will show the formula for the area of a right angle triangle.

2. Choose a digital tool.

    - Flipgrid
    - Google Drive
    - Show Me
    - Skitch
    - Subtext
    - Edmodo
    - Pic Collage
    - Popplet
    - Aurasma
    - Haiku Deck
    - I want to use something else.

3. What materials will you need?

    - Macbook (with camera)
    - HP Mini (with camera)
    - iPod
    - iPad

- digital camera
- ProScope
- desktop computer
- Flipcam
- paper/pencil
- other:

4. Which skill or skills will you use? You can choose more than one if you need to.

- remember
- understand
- apply
- analyze
- evaluate
- create

5. How will you show what you know?

Example: I will create a ShowMe to explain how to find the area of a triangle.

6. I will be working . . . [individually/collaboratively]

Once students complete a form in Google Forms and you know what devices or tools they are using, you can then group students according to certain tools that they will be using in their groups. You can also determine differences in students' selection and use of certain tools to differentiate your instruction when supporting students.

Giving students opportunities to frame their learning may result in their experiencing difficulties or failures, leading to their self-reflection and sharing of their feedback to teachers based on their expectations, something that enhances achievement (Hattie, 2011). For example, in using iPads in her classroom, Meg Wilson (2014) values her students making their own instructional decisions. She provides them with a list of apps, defined in terms of their general purposes. She then engages them in the following steps:

1. Divide my topics into important sub topics
2. Get the kids into groups (3s works best for me but 4 if I have to)
3. Pose a "driving question" to the class that doesn't have a specific "correct answer" e.g. "Should everyone contribute to the web?"
4. Offer supportive questions to spark the groups' conversations and give them areas to look at.
5. Get the groups into the habit of recording their discussions and discoveries in their favorite format. (Some group message, some audio record, some mind-map)

6. Have a shared class "success matrix" for every group to add to which outlines what would make a successful group product in general when covering the topic, answering the questions plus also product quality.

7. Challenge them to "AppSmash" their learning as a way of sharing with the class. "App-Smashing" is where content created in one app is used in a 2nd app. This forces a little more creative thinking in how to present their learning.

8. Most of the time we then upload, share and comment on other groups' creations. They will fail some of the time, but as far as what matters is concerned, these moments become the most important learning opportunities. Developing keen learners who see failure as opportunity must be our first target. This requires freedom and support from the teacher.

HOW CAN I USE BLENDED OR FLIPPED MODELS OF INSTRUCTION TO ENCOURAGE DIGITAL READING AND WRITING?

Fostering students' self-directed learning also involves alternative uses of classroom space and time through adoption of blended or flipped models of instruction (for more on flipped classrooms: http://tinyurl.com/m575ebc). In a blended or flipped model, you are combining face-to-face classroom time with online activities inside or outside class time with the goal of attempting to personalize instruction. In a flipped classroom model, rather than spending time during class imparting information to students through lectures or showing videos, you provide videos for students to view at home so that class time can then be devoted to students' hands-on work or discussion (Bergmann & Sams, 2012). A review of research on the use of the flipped classroom indicated that teachers perceive use of this approach as enhancing student learning and attitudes (Yarbro, Arfstrom, McKnight, & McKnight, 2014; Stansbury, 2013), with students preferring videos over alternative instructional resources (PBS/Grunwald Associates, 2010), or as providing them positive interactions with teachers and peers during class time, increased access to resources, the ability to work at their own pace, and more active learning (Driscoll, 2012).

Creating Videos for Blended/Flipped Learning

You can create your own videos using screencasting/video production tools, or you can select videos from YouTube or other video sites listed on the website http://tinyurl.com/lw4bo24. One useful resource for selecting and planning activities based on a flipped classroom model is the TED-Ed site http://ed.ted.com, which provides you with lesson-planning processes based on certain options (Bach & Watson, 2014). You can select a flipped lesson that has been previously developed, select a lesson and customize it for a particular class, or choose from videos on the site to create your own lesson. Or, you can have students create their own videos based on the topics or issues that you are studying—video production that requires not only a solid understanding of those topics or issues but also more ownership over the videos than if they were viewing videos available online.

To encourage students to go beyond simply viewing the videos without formulating responses, as part of the TED-Ed lesson template, you can add prompts to the screen— "Watch," "Think," "Dig Deeper," and "Discuss"—that serve to foster written interpretations of the videos that are then sent to the teacher (Bach & Watson, 2014, p. 109). For example, one lesson created by preservice teachers in a method class involved the following use of

> three different video interpretations of the scene in Macbeth when Macbeth hears of his wife's death. The lesson's questions encouraged students to first comprehend the events of the scene ("Think"), then compare and contrast the interpretations ("Dig Deeper"), finally ("Discuss") asking students to choose which interpretation was most effective in conveying the mood of the scene and why. (p. 110)

In describing his experience working with a flipped classroom (Ferlazzo, 2014), Troy Cockrum (2013), a middle school language arts teacher in Indianapolis and author of *Flipping Your English Class to Reach All Learners: Strategies and Lesson Plans*, notes the importance of being flexible in how and when to employ videos:

> An objective for a flipped classroom should be flexibility. The time and place the videos are viewed shouldn't limit the students learning. Although some have promoted the flipped classroom as a "video at home" approach, many teachers, myself included, allow students to watch videos in class. Students should be given option where (home vs. school) videos are viewed.
>
> Teachers should also be flexible in when the information is delivered. This is not the same "home vs. school" question, but rather when in the learning cycle. Some teachers prefer to front load the video content as an introduction to a concept. However, teachers should be flexible enough to recognize that placing the video later in the learning cycle after students have explored, thought critically, drew some inferences, and did their own research can help students better assimilate the material. (p. 2)

HOW DO I ACCOMMODATE FOR DIFFERENCES IN SPECIAL LEARNING NEEDS AND LANGUAGE DIFFERENCES?

It is also important to recognize individual differences in students' use of software/tool and device affordances given differences in their ability to employ certain social practices.

Struggling Readers and Writers

Struggling readers and writers often have difficulty contextualizing and defining connections among digital texts (Guthrie, Wigfield, & Perencevich, 2004). Some of these differences are due to gender differences. While males are more reluctant readers than females, middle school males who are reluctant readers value reading more than females after using e-readers (Miranda, Williams-Rossi, Johnson, & McKenzie, 2011), and male students express more positive attitudes toward recreational reading in digital settings (McKenna, Conradi, Lawrence, Jang, & Meyer, 2012), suggesting the value of using digital texts with struggling male readers.

Struggling readers benefit from using images or audio in reading digital texts. Providing struggling high school students with a digital video storytelling tool that included a short story being read aloud with subtitles and annotations (Malin, 2010) or digital book trailers (Gunter & Kenny, 2012) enhanced their engagement and comprehension. Students who have difficulty with reading further benefit from the use of audio recordings or text-to-speech tools for reading texts, as well as dictation or speech-to-text tools for producing texts (K. Garrison, 2010). They also benefit from using text-to-speech tools for listening to their own writing to assess the degree that it conveys their intended ideas or captures their voices.

Students With Learning Disabilities

Students with learning disabilities can benefit from the use of adaptive/assistive digital tools that provide individualized, supportive accommodations and instructional opportunities (Gordon, Proctor, & Dalton, 2012). Given the principles of universal design for learning, formulated by the National Center on Universal Design for Learning, you can identify students' abilities and needs evident in their individualized education plans to determine the use of tools to design learning activities consistent with these students' needs (King-Sears, Swanson, & Mainzer, 2011). For more on tools for special needs students: http://tinyurl.com/le9jzdq.

For students with visual learning issues, you can employ text-to-speech tools that provide these students with oral versions of texts, audio search tools, and screencasting tools to provide audio feedback to students' writing that combines the text with your oral comments. For students with hearing issues, you can employ subtitle/speech-to-text tools to provide them with text versions of audio. You can also draw on the resources available from the Center for Applied Special Technology (CAST), a leading organization that promotes planning according to universal design for learning. They have developed an online lesson plan development tool to assist teachers http://lessonbuilder.cast.org as well as a lesson plan exchange for sharing lessons based on universal design for learning http://udlexchange.cast.org/home. For other tools for working with special needs students: http://tinyurl.com/le9jzdq.

English-Language Learners

For working with English-language learners, you can employ tools that help students read web-based texts or websites that are only in English—for example, the IBM TradúceloAhora! (Translate Now!) software http://www.traduceloahora.org/en/home.html translates e-mails and webpages into Spanish. There are also numerous tools and apps designed for use in practicing language proficiency that scaffold students' language practice within social conversational contexts so that students practice their language use on their own but within a meaningful context facilitating language use. English-language learners benefit from opportunities to practice and employ English in purposeful, authentic reading/writing contexts in asynchronous online discussion forums to help them elaborate on the writing (AbuSeileek & Qatawneh, 2013). For more on tools for ELL students: http://tinyurl.com/lldfxb7.

Multimodal digital storytelling and audio production activities can also be used to support these students' reading and writing abilities (Hur & Suh, 2012). English-language learners posting fiction and receiving feedback on the FanFiction site http://www.fanfiction.net valued the collaborative exchange of responses to their fiction; female students used creative writing in ways that achieved identities that challenged the deficit identities often ascribed to them by their schools (R. W. Black, 2009a).

HOW DO I DETERMINE IF MY PLANNED ACTIVITIES ARE ACCOMPLISHING MY OBJECTIVES?

While it is often assumed that planning occurs prior to students engaging in an activity, it is important to recognize that planning is an ongoing, recursive process that occurs before, during, and after an activity. For example, as an activity is unfolding, you may recognize that your students are not engaged in the activity, leading to your revising the activity to adopt alternative tasks that may be more engaging.

One useful framework for reflecting on your planning is the "technology integration planning cycle" (Hutchison & Woodward, 2013). This model involves seven steps, as illustrated in Figure 2.1:

1. Ability to identify and adhere to a clear instructional goal when integrating digital technology.
2. Ability to identify an appropriate instructional approach for the instructional goal.
3. Ability to select appropriate digital or non-digital tools to support instruction.
4. Ability to foresee how the selected tool can contribute to the instructional goal.
5. Ability to identify the potential constraints of using the tool to determine whether they can be overcome.
6. Ability to understand how the instruction will need to be delivered or altered due to the use of the selected tool.
7. Ability to reflect on the resulting instruction and make changes/learn more about the instructional tools as needed.

What is central to this planning cycle is the need to consider constraints involved in students' use of tools—the fact that they lack knowledge on how to use a tool, are having difficulty employing the tool, are not clear about the purposes for using a tool, or have difficulty displaying the results of using the tool. In the planning cycle, if these difficulties are too challenging for students, you may decide that students need more assistance or that you need to select an alternative tool.

How Do I Cope With the Challenges of Using Technology?

This book would be incomplete without a treatment of some of the challenges with integrating Web 2.0 tools in the classrooms. Before we launch into the advantages and possibilities of these tools in creating rich, forward-looking educational environments, we want to suggest some ways to overcome these challenges so that you can progress in your use of digital tools in the classroom.

Technological Access and Use

Although schools have certainly improved in providing hardware necessary for use of these digital tools, issues of access remain a problem in many schools, particularly for schools in low-income areas that may lack the financial support for hardware and software and for students who may lack broadband access in their homes. Some schools still rely on use of classroom labs, which are often booked up, because they do not have the capacity for students to use laptops in their classrooms. This suggests the need to encourage students to explore alternative ways to gain access—for example, going to

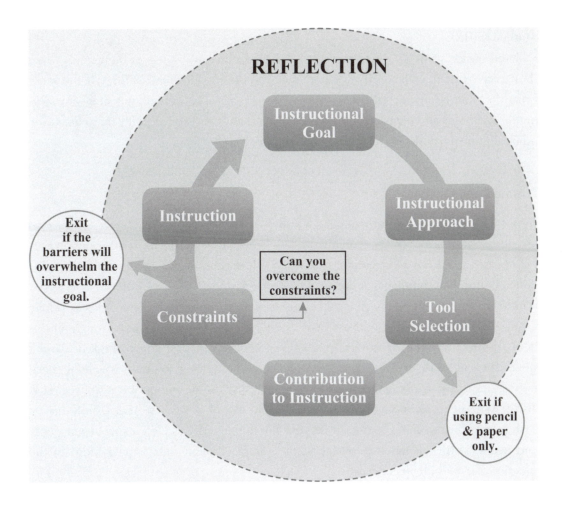

Figure 2.1.   Technology Integration Planning Cycle. *Source: From Hutchison, A., & Woodward, L. (2013). A planning cycle for integrating technology into literacy instruction. The Reading Teacher. Reprinted with permission of John Wiley and Sons, Inc. Copyright © International Reading Association.*

public libraries, which have now become popular places for adolescents to hang out after school. Schools can also employ "bring your own device" (BYOD) policies, where students use their personal devices in schools, although that raises issues of equity for students who do not own them.

Productive Uses of Devices

It is important to recognize the need to not assume that students will be using these devices in productive ways without some sense of how to use them to achieve certain outcomes. Analysis of students' perceptions of the degree to which iPads foster learning finds that it is important that students have a clear sense of purpose for using them given their potential for distracting options (W. Miller, 2012; Rossing, 2012) such that students end up using them for nonacademic purposes during class (Kinash, Brand, & Mathew, 2012).

Ninth-grade students were more likely to engage in on-task use of their iPads when they were working collaboratively on well-defined tasks (Hoffman, 2013). At the same time, they can be distracted by messaging, e-mail, or social networking sites—for academic and nonacademic social purposes, noting that they were more likely to use it for nonacademic purposes in classes in which they were not engaged.

Online Safety

In participating in social networking sites such as MySpace and Facebook, adolescents are often not aware of the potential risks of self-disclosure of personal information that can lead to unsafe or risky contacts by other adolescents or adults. To safeguard students, rather than simply block or restrict all access to Web 2.0 sites, you can discuss the ethical importance of taking personal responsibility for their online practices as public displays of behavior similar to those in any public space. As we reiterate throughout this book, this includes having students use only first names or pseudonyms, not disclosing their dates of birth or other private information, requiring log-ins for school social networking sites, avoiding spam on blogs, and using online netiquette practices. It is also important to promote students' responsible use of devices so that in interacting with peers, they assume the role of responsible digital citizens who respect their peers and avoid posting negative information or images of them online, as evident in the practice of cyberbullying or "sexting."

In one San Francisco high school, a student counselor, drawing on a curriculum developed by Common Sense Media at http://tinyurl.com/b557jm8, provides instruction on issues related to "disinhibition, reputation, anonymity" (Shahani, 2013). For example, the counselor addresses the problem of disinhibition as impulsive behavior lacking restraint that can result in aggressive online behavior leading to cyberbullying, as well as issues of privacy and trust associated with publicly sharing what could be considered private, confidential information.

All of this reflects the need for instruction on digital citizenship related to the need to engage in a respectful, responsible manner in online interactions. One useful resource for methods for fostering digital citizenship is the Digital ID project http://digital-id.wikispaces.com.

District Filtering/Blocking Policies

To address safety concerns, some districts have created filters or fire walls that block access to certain sites or software applications, often by contracting out to other companies to create these filters. Unfortunately, this can block access to useful Web 2.0 tools, in many cases, for arbitrary rather than educational reasons. As a result, students may not be able to use blogs, wikis, social networking sites, or podcasts in the classroom. You may therefore need to take an active role in working with and educating school administrators and technology support staff to establish policies related to students' public postings of writing and access to legitimate education sites (Willard, 2007).

Free Speech Legal Aspects of Online Reading and Writing

In crafting schools' "acceptable use" policies, it is important to honor First Amendment provisions that protect students' freedom of speech related to what students can write about or, in certain ways, with impunity, consistent with the requirements of the Children's Internet Protection Act of 2000 http://www.fcc.gov/cgb/consumerfacts/cipa.html.

Being Perceived as "the" Technology Expert

A major challenge that you face in employing Web 2.0 tools is the assumption that unless you are an "expert" in the use of a certain tool, you should not use that tool in the classroom. Although it is certainly important to know how a tool is being used in the classroom, you should not necessarily avoid using a tool if you believe that you are not highly "tech-savvy." In many cases, you can draw on the expertise of technology coordinators, media-center staff, colleagues, and even students to explain or demonstrate uses of a certain tool.

Based on use of the previously mentioned surveys or queries of students about their experiences with digital tools, you can ascertain the contributions that they as "teachers" could make in sharing their experience with the classroom. For example, if some students have expertise in blogging, they can talk to the class about why and how they are engaged with blogging, sharing specific examples of their posts and comments. Treating students as experts serves to bolster their senses of status and agency in the classroom, enhancing their sense of membership in the classroom community.

SUMMARY

In this chapter, we describe different strategies for planning instruction using digital reading and writing tools. Effective planning entails learning about your students' knowledge of and experience with digital tools, as well as their social practices and dispositions toward learning. Effective planning also entails creating activities that exploit the affordances of certain tools to foster use of certain social practices—for example, use of screencasting tools to share multimodal productions of learning. It also requires recognizing that many students still lack certain skills in use of digital tools while having students with those skills provide peer instruction in use of those tools. Effective planning requires making accommodations for students with learning disabilities or language differences through use of tools designed for these students, as well as establishing acceptable use policies regarding students becoming responsible digital citizens.

Chapters 2–9 describe the uses of specific digital reading and writing tools, beginning with accessing and assessing online information.

3

ACCESSING INFORMATION FOR CONSTRUCTING KNOWLEDGE

Searching for information is often seen as being antecedent to or isolated from the act of writing. With the development of digital searching, it has become clear that learning how to write is intertwined with the act of searching. Scanning, making decisions about what to hold on to and what to reject, and reading for the purpose of connecting someone else's ideas to your own are all important aspects of learning to write.

However, while 77% of writing teachers in one survey thought that students' use of digital search tools had a "mostly positive" impact on student research, 76% indicated that the use of search engines creates false expectations in students that they can readily find relevant information; 83% believed that the students are overwhelmed by too much information; and 71% believed that students do not access a range of different information sources (Purcell et al., 2012). This entails providing students with direct instruction on search strategies (Walraven, Brand-Gruwel, & Boshuizen, 2009).

In this chapter, we discuss the use of digital tools for constructing and carrying out a search for online information. Effective use of these tools relies on some important groundwork planning and recontextualizing their projects as students' work moves on. Helping students by contextualizing the task, while leaving them room to bring the project onto their own ground, will lead to successful searches. It also helps to build their uses of search tools over time, gradually increasing experience and expertise in using tools for correspondingly complex assignments.

INQUIRY-BASED LEARNING

It is useful to frame instruction in accessing online information for understanding and creating digital texts in terms of fostering inquiry-based learning (Beach & Myers, 2001; Bruce & Casey, 2012). Inquiry-based instruction shifts the focus of instruction from a transmission model of imparting information and knowledge to students to a constructivist model of having students learn to construct knowledge for engaging in research projects addressing specific questions, a primary Common Core writing standard (for more on inquiry-based learning, see http://tinyurl.com/mzgdj3h).

Common Core State Standard: Writing Standard 7

- Perform short, focused research projects as well as more sustained research in response to a focused research question, demonstrating understanding of the material under investigation.

Students can engage in inquiry-based learning through use of the inquiry cycle model of posing questions or problems, searching for information to address those questions or problems, investigating alternative solutions, creating new knowledge, and reflecting on newfound knowledge (Bruce & Bishop, 2002). This inquiry-based model of ask, investigate, create, discuss, and reflect is recursive in that as students are attempting to find information to construct knowledge when addressing their questions and problems, they recognize the need to pose new questions or problems requiring further investigations.

Inquiry-Based Instruction and Social Practices

Inquiry-based instruction also draws on the social practices identified in the last chapter, practices that we reference throughout this chapter. To pose questions or problems, students need to contextualize their questions or problems in terms of how and why they are reading or writing about a topic. If they are simply writing a report to summarize information related to addressing questions or identifying problems, that contextualization will be quite different than if they are writing an opinion paper or manifesto calling for action to address their questions or problems.

In gathering information from a range of different sources and texts, students are making connections among these texts to define consistent patterns or themes, leading to the ability to synthesize findings. Students will benefit from collaboratively assisting one another in accessing and evaluating information (Kiili, Laurinen, Marttunen, & Leu, 2012).

In accessing information, students need to adopt alternative perspectives to acquire an understanding of competing perspectives on a topic or issue to avoid a parochial understanding of it; acquiring alternative perspectives through discussion of their search results with peers leads to reflection on the limitations of their perspectives. By using different modes (e.g., images, audio, and video) to acquire information—for example, use of TED video presentations on a topic—students are expanding the scope of their learning.

Through adopting an inquiry-based stance on learning, students are also redefining their identities as active learners who, through their inquiry, can contribute knowledge to their peers and society. The use of digital tools can assist students in the use of these inquiry-based processes. Students learned to employ digital tools to ask, investigate, create, discuss, and reflect in addressing "how to make a banana split" by taking photos of their learning processes working in groups, then using those photos to create digital videos for sharing with a school audience (Bruce & Casey, 2012). Central to the success of this project was the teachers' continually framing and scaffolding of the inquiry processes, as well as the ability of students to engage in collaborative inquiry through adopting different roles—for example, note taker, photographer, and banana split maker.

Given the important social practices supporting inquiry-based processes, we organize this chapter around specific inquiry-based processes of accessing and evaluating information about students' problems or topics involved in accessing and constructing knowledge (Leu, Kinzer, Coiro, Castek, & Henry, 2013).

ACCESSING ONLINE INFORMATION

The ability to access or locate online information involves a number of "informational literacies" involving the use of social practices, literacies designed to meet the Common Core writing standard associated with gathering, assessing, and integrating information into one's writing. For a discussion of how information literacies are related to the Common Core, see November and Mull (2012) and http://tinyurl.com/movfep9.

Common Core State Standard: Writing Standard 8

- Gather relevant information from multiple print and digital sources, assess the credibility and accuracy of each source, and integrate and cite the information while avoiding plagiarism.

Identifying Specific Aspects of a Problem or Topic

The ability to identify a problem or topic depends on students' ability to contextualize their purpose and audience for reading or writing about said problem or topic. Students often have difficulty narrowing down their problem or topic to determine specific aspects of it to engage in online searches. For example, a student is creating a multimedia production on the negative effects of urban sprawl for her peers. Because this is a broad topic, she needs to narrow down her focus to specific aspects of urban sprawl to determine her search terms. To do so, she contextualizes her purpose and audience to identify what her peers, as her primary audience, may be most interested in learning about this problem.

Consistent with the social practice of adopting alternative perspectives, she also recognizes the need to define this issue based on consideration of both negative and positive perceptions of urban sprawl—that urban sprawl results in increased dependency on cars resulting in higher pollution, reduction of farmland, the need to build roads and sewer systems, and so on—developments that can also result in lower-cost housing. This leads her to consider specific different pro and con perspectives that would guide her searches for further information. Consistent with the social practice of adopting different modes for presenting information, she decides that she will include images illustrating the effects of urban sprawl—for example, images of large housing developments in what were formerly farmlands—leading to an expanded need to also search for relevant images.

Conducting Online Searches

Consistent with the importance of generating relevant information for use in writing, students need to know how to use digital tools to search for, access, and import online information from various databases or digital texts into their writing. This requires that they define specific, relevant search terms as well as access a range of different databases. However, students lack the ability to locate relevant texts or contextualize their searches based on their needs or purposes, as well as how to limit their searches to only familiar resources, such as Google or Wikipedia, as opposed to alternative resources (Head & Eisenberg, 2009, 2010, 2011). When asked to identify reasons for selecting certain search resources, college students noted that they preferred Google, Google Scholar, and Yahoo, in contrast to academic databases, sites that were perceived as easy to employ, that generate credible scholarly results, and that are easy to link to documents (Purdy, 2012). While these results do suggest that students perceive the need to acquire credible scholarly results, the fact that students perceive an engine such as Google as easier to use or as providing more credible scholarly results than academic databases suggests that students lack an understanding of how to employ academic databases, given their preference to obtain search results that are uncomplicated and straightforward (Grassian, 2006).

Students' lack of information literacies suggests the need for instruction in information literacies. Advanced-level college students who received extensive information literacy instruction, as compared with first-year college students who received some information literacy instruction, not only employed subject-specific databases but also had significantly more total citations, primary sources, and books and images to document their research than did the first-year students, who were more likely to cite newspapers and websites as scholarly resources and quotes from resources as filler in their reports (Samson, 2010).

Using Search Engines

Students can employ a range of different search engine platforms and apps listed on the website http://tinyurl.com/kn7mn76. Students can also employ RefSeek at http://www.refseek.com or iSeek Education at http://education.iseek.com/iseek/home.page, which focuses on academic results, thereby eliminating commercial or sponsored links. Students can also employ audio searches using speech recognition tools such as Siri for iPhones and iPads (2012 and later models).

Search Strategies

In using these search engines, students need to know how to enter specific terms relevant to their topics or questions; otherwise, their searches will generate thousands of irrelevant hits (for more on search strategies, see http://tinyurl.com/lt5ha4m). Effective searching requires that students strike a balance in identifying search terms that are not too broad or too specific. Because these search engines crawl the web for the most frequently accessed sites, their results often consist of sites that are not scholarly and those that are commercial and promote certain products. Students often rely on the results from some initial searches without recognizing the need to continue to search by entering in alternative search terms, requiring them to continue to revise their search terms to obtain alternative results.

Consistent with the social practice of contextualizing reading or writing tasks, equally important in engaging in online searches is students' ability to reframe a specific purpose, topic, or question that will guide their searches. If their purpose, topic, or question is too broad—for example, the effects of global warming on the environment—they may be overwhelmed with too many search results. If it is too narrow, they may generate insufficient results. Online tutorials such as those found at the Cooperative Library

Instruction site http://tinyurl.com/molx9fp can help students think about how to generate terms for a particular search. The Kimbel Library has made a series of videos on such topics as "Selecting the Right Number of Keywords" and made them available on Vimeo http://vimeo.com/12861706.

Students should also be aware of the fact that their search results are influenced by filter bubbles—that algorithms used by Google, Safari, Chrome, or Bing browsers filter their results based on their previous searches, preferences, and locations (Clark, 2013b). (For a TED talk by Eli Pariser on filter bubbles, see http://tinyurl.com/lzprgt4.) Students can test the effects of these filters by employing alternative search engines to determine if they can generate alternative results. They can also eliminate these filters by browsers by using the incognito mode in Chrome by going to File → New Incognito Window (Clark, 2013b).

You also need to model safe searching strategies related to avoiding access to objectionable or pornographic sites. While computers in schools have filters that block access to these sites, students find ways around these filters, and with "bring your own devices" policies, they can readily access these sites on their own. At the same time, schools can employ problematic filtering practices that unnecessarily block access to sites that may not contain objectionable material, resulting in a subtle form of censorship. However, the central theme for instruction in safe searching is that students need to assume responsibility for their own online actions (for more on safe searching, see http://tinyurl.com/k8837o6).

Using Google, Google Advanced Search, and Google Scholar

You can provide students with instruction and modeling of search strategies for Google and Google Scholar, two of the most frequently employed search engines (Purdy, 2012). Unfortunately, students do not take advantage of specific features of Google search. For a series of lessons on search strategies using Google, see http://sites.google.com/site/gwebsearcheducation/lessonplans and http://www.google.com/educators/p_websearch.html. Google has also launched the Google Search Education http://www.google.com/insidesearch/searcheducation resource site, which provides tutorials and professional development resources for employing Google Search.

Students can also use the Google Advanced Search for searching for more specific information, such as searching for pages that have "all these words," "this exact wording or phrase," "one or more of these words," "but don't show pages that have," or "any of these unwanted words." They can choose to obtain certain file types (doc, ppt, pdf, etc.), search within a domain, or use the timeline feature (selected after a search) to create a visual timeline based on information organized by years. They can further employ Google Scholar at http://scholar.google.com, which will provide them with more scholarly items than is the case with Google Search. You can also set up a Google Custom Search site for your class at http://www.google.com/cse for limiting and filtering searches to sites that you believe are most relevant and valid for the topics or issues that students are studying. Students can then share their search results directly to Google Docs.

You can demonstrate use of the following search strategy tips (Barseghian, 2011):

- Employ quotations around certain terms or phrases representing specific titles, such as the Beatles song "Yesterday."
- Use Control F function (or Command F on Macs) to find a word on the page that comes up in a search.
- Use "Define" and a word to obtain the word's definition.
- Enter years to focus on more current or older results.
- Learn to use the "Google's instant" function that predicts words one is typing to generate relevant optional search terms.
- Use the different tools in the left column related to "Images," "Videos," "Timeline," "Books," "Blogs," "News," "Discussions," and so on.

Using Academic Databases

The alternative to these commercial search engines involves the use of academic databases, which are available through school libraries' sites. These search engines include access to academic journals not available on search engines, although students can search for "open access" journals on search engines and journals listed in the Directory of Open Access Journals at http://www.doaj.org. They can also use the Library of Congress's Ask a Librarian at http://tinyurl.com/14ev or the IPL2 for Teens at http://www.ipl.org/div/teen to acquire information from academic databases.

Students need to be aware that many libraries are shifting toward metasearch tools that draw from various databases to pull up a variety of texts. At the University of Minnesota, this tool—which is now the default search box—is called MNCAT Discovery http://www.lib.umn.edu. At the University of Texas, a similar tool is called scoUT http://www.lib.utexas.edu. Such tools offer greater capability within a particular library system for filtering results (one can narrow the search field to only peer-reviewed articles) and for providing students the power to shape a large number of results more actively. To help students perform effective searches with such tools, it is necessary to teach them how to refine the search according to genre, date, and so on.

An especially important step beyond merely typing in search terms, then, becomes to teach students how to use the "Refine My Results" links at the side of the results page. A recent search on "renewable energy" gave a rather large number of hits, for example, but the "Refine My Results" menu broke this category down into more manageable numbers of sources based on type (articles, newspaper articles, reviews, legal documents, books), author, subject (renewable energy, sustainable development, energy industries, energy policy, climate change), date, language, source names, and journal titles. Students can learn to think about the various ways that such a topic has been written about and categorized from looking carefully at these menus. Importantly, students continue to recontextualize their topic as they search—an important piece to learning to write informed prose.

Students may also browse unsystematically without any sense of purpose or direction related to addressing their topic or issue. As they are browsing, students need to critically reflect on the information that they are acquiring so that they are purposefully making choices to select relevant links. "It's not just point and click. It's point, read, think, click" (Coiro, 2003, p. 459). Some of this unsystematic browsing is the result of not clearly identifying specific search categories or keywords. Students often have not formulated specific, relevant, mutually exclusive categories so that they then become lost in a sea of data.

Also, students may not know how to judge the value, sufficiency, relevancy, and validity of information they acquire. This requires self-monitoring and metacognitive awareness, a challenge for students with memory, attention-deficit, or spatial processing problems (McNabb, Thurber, Dibuz, McDermott, & Lee, 2006).

To help her students overcome these difficulties, Elizabeth Erdmann modeled search strategies for her students at Jefferson High School in Bloomington, Minnesota, by describing how she narrowed down her search by specifying certain key terms. She also had students work with media center resource people who assisted them in their searches of databases. For example, in studying the novel *Montana, 1948* (Watson, 1993), three of her students—Rachel Brummer, Claire Maccani, and Kyle Rusnacko—wrote their papers on the topic of "truth and lies," in response to Elizabeth's questions for focusing their topic:

> What does my topic mean (define the topic)? How does my topic apply to people in general? How have other authors presented this theme in their texts? How have teachers discussed these ideas in my classes? Which groups of people generally discuss, present, and/or defend issues related to my topic?

Rachel, Claire, and Kyle were engaged in an inquiry-based project addressing why people in the novel lie. They posed specific questions: "What really prompted these people to lie? What situations were they covering up, and how would their reputations be affected if people found out about these lies?"

Once Rachel, Claire, and Kyle specified their questions for writing about why people lie, they then needed to search for relevant information both in the novel and from outside sources that would address their questions. To access online information on research for why people lie, the three students went to a number of sites. In describing her search strategies, Rachel noted that she frequently begins with a Google search but then moves to specific databases available in the school media center:

> I start with Google and then I look for articles that I find and then I read those and then I refine my search. Then I go to databases like Gale Group and CQ Researcher, and I go to a lot of university websites. There was one at Cornell—I use that for Government. I have to write a paper on a Supreme Court case and I use that for a lot of law. I use a lot of advanced searches in databases because a lot of kids don't use them even though they are so helpful. They just go to Google, but it's not certified, but databases, they are.

For these searches, Rachel knows the importance of identifying specific keywords related to her questions: "I started out with 'why people lie?' And then, what is deception? Why do people deceive others?"

From her search, she "found a lot of information about how people lie to protect their reputation . . . that people lie to protect themselves."

> In the book, this kid's uncle was a rapist; he molested Native Americans. He deceived people with his character, like he was charming, but the kid's mom could see through it, but other people couldn't, so he was lying to the town with his character. But the family never told anyone because they wanted to protect his reputation.

She then "tied the information that we found to the situation when the people lied—evidence for what happened in real life."

PROVIDING INSTRUCTION IN THE USE OF SEARCH TOOLS

In planning to teach students to use search tools, showing how you and librarians view the search process and how it results in knowledge production can help students see themselves as participants. In addition to talking through expectations for a particular assignment, teaching students about how writers participate in the conversations that compel them to write can make the research process more engaging. In other words, students are helped by seeing how exploration through background reading and other forms of inspiration lead to a topic that then gets narrowed and in turn raises questions that lead to more focused searching for sources. The process continues with the evaluation of sources and the work of drafting and editing. Helping students picture this process and how search enters into each phase can help students see where their searching fits into the entire research "cycle" that leads back to more reading and writing. Some libraries, such as Capella University at http://tinyurl.com/k5boqo6 and Minneapolis Community and Technical College at http://tinyurl.com/n7sutvx, have good websites that explain and visualize the entire process.

As part of beginning a search, it can help to introduce students to the architecture of knowledge available on the web by teaching them how to put names to tools that they already use and by showing them more sophisticated strategies for using those tools. Teaching students the vocabulary of web search tools becomes important if they are to understand and make effective use of them. Rice University's Fondren Library offers a website at http://tinyurl.com/lgp52d2 that delineates differences among "subject direc-tories," "search engines," "meta-search engines," and "natural language engines." A metasearch engine, for example, takes a term entered and pulls from a number of different search engines. The results are then collected into a single list.

It is also important to be able to distinguish which information might be useful when using digital tools for the web. Another concern is to help students become aware of the domains that govern the information on the web. Some of the more important domains follow:

- *.edu*, educational
- *.com*, commercial
- *.org*, nonprofit organizations
- *.net*, network

Students need to know that domains are not always straightforward in what they prom-ise; CNN (cnn.com) and Yahoo (yahoo.com) report "news," for example, as they also sell various products to users. Students need to learn to read commercial screens for what might be useful as information for academic writing. Sponsored links may also "appear" as news, something that students need to be made aware of to choose good sources for their research. Helping students to understand the difference between such public sites and those that are paid for by libraries (e.g., Academic Index and ProQuest Newsstand) is crucial for gaining information that will be useful for academic projects. Students need to gain a view of the overall landscape of information available and begin to understand that the links that pop up in each site carry different purposes, only some of which will be helpful to them.

Teachers who have assigned research projects to students often comment on how students tend to take the first returns on a Google search to "fill out" their citations. To move forward with a project, students need to know that although information is widely available, it may take searching from a number of different angles to obtain valid and reliable information.

Students also need to know how to employ Boolean searches to broaden or narrow search results based on using AND (that both words are used in a search), OR (the either of two words are used in a search), and NOT (that one word and not another word is used in a search). For a useful tutorial on Boolean searches, see http://tinyurl.com/y8maxrm from the Colorado State University library.

Tools to Support Searches

The main challenge for working with digital searching is to help students navigate the many possible sources on the web and in library databases, then to develop a set of strategies to narrow the number of sources to a set that will help inform their topics. Some libraries have helpful online tools, including videos, such as those found at North Carolina State University Libraries at http://tinyurl.com/cwund8, that emphasize the back and forth of searching a topic, doing some reading, and adjusting that topic so that it will work for a paper or project.

Students also need to specify the focus of their searches. To do so, they can use the NoodleTools NoodleQuest tool http://www.noodletools.com/noodlequest, which helps students focus their searches using the following prompts with options to check off what will then provide students with some relevant sources:

I need to define my topic . . .
I need to find quality results . . .
I need to do research in a specific discipline . . .
The timeliness of information that I need is . . .
I need facts . . .
I need opinions and perspectives . . .
I need a specific type of media . . .
I have special search requirements . . .
I am (a kid, pretty new to the Internet, an Internet wizard)

Students can also use the Strategy Tutor tool at http://tinyurl.com/m2dzsbe developed by CAST for assisting students with learning disabilities with online searches.

For collecting information on certain topics, students need to know how to subscribe to news feeds using RSS feeds so that they receive information "pushed" to them rather than having to search out that information. As we discuss in detail in the next chapter, students can use sites with built-in RSS feed readers, such as NetVibes at http://www.netvibes.com. Or, they can use tools such as Reeder at http://tinyurl.com/ygzzavc, Feedly at http://tinyurl.com/3l9ffm5, or The Feed at http://tinyurl.com/353fk5a to select certain topics within these tools, which will then pull in material from a range of sources. (For more on creating and using RSS feeds http://tinyurl.com/kqmwype.)

Modeling Safe Search Strategies

In modeling search strategies, teachers need to demonstrate practices of safe searching related to objectionable or pornographic sites, as noted above. Rather than assuming that the problem can be solved simply by filtering content or censorship, it is important to take a proactive stance by addressing this issue as a matter of student behavior and attitudes—that students need to take responsibility for their behavior by adopting safe searching techniques.

In searching for information on the topic of why people lie as part of studying *Montana, 1948*, Jefferson High School student Rachel was aware of the need to continually assess the value and relevancy of the data that she is finding. She noted, "You get some weird stuff, but if sometimes if you scroll down enough, you find something good." She also noted the need to initially judge the scholarly nature of online material: "I read a little bit of it and if it's an article, then it'll be a little higher in ascendancy; if you get some really crazy, opinionated texts, those are fun to read, but not helpful." For example, Rachel felt comfortable about including quotes from one site in an article http://www.bbc.co.uk/dna/h2g2/A996942 that quoted Dr. John Busak, professor of psychiatry and director of the neuropsychiatry center at the University of New Delhi, because she believed that the BBC site was reputable and that Dr. Busak was connected to a university. The research that Rachel draws on was directly related to her thesis that the Hayden family deceptions were part of a family culture:

> Investigations have shown that there are those who are genetically predisposed towards lying and deceit. . . . Those who come from chaotic and dysfunctional families have a greater tendency to lie than those who grew up in a caring household. Busak hypothesizes that children from such families lie to change or modify reality to make life more tolerable.

Students may also not know that in their everyday lives, they practice many of the reading and search practices necessary for a successful academic search. Searching for music or movies with services such as iTunes, Zune Marketplace, and Rhapsody involves some of the same skimming and selection activities as those used for academic searching. Alvermann et al. (2012) report on one student's confidence in sifting through a lot of information on the web:

> Brad considered himself a discriminating (if not avid) reader and a selective user of web content. For example, when bombarded by multiple pieces of information online, Brad tended to focus on the middle of the screen where, experience had taught him, the important information could be found. He scanned captions before reading in-depth, and he attended carefully to a website's color-coding scheme, suspecting that it might provide a clue to where information was located. . . . Brad claimed that he

disliked reading books, although he said he enjoyed reading for "information" on various websites. When asked in one of the Saturday morning sessions if he ever got bored with the Internet, Brad replied, "Not really. Cause there's a lot of stuff to do. I hate to read books, but when I got to, I do. . . . I'd read [a book] online. It's easy. Somehow, it looks easier. If I'm reading something [online], I'm more focused. If I'm reading a book . . . I don't know." (p. 189)

Brad's online reading practices indicate how the time spent on the web outside of class has helped him gain useful skills and predilections that might bridge to academic tasks. Students do participate in everyday practices that translate well into educational ones (Merchant, 2007). Students therefore need to know that they already participate in "search" strategies and that they now need to take that everyday skill and redirect it toward new academic searching.

Creating Personal Learning Networks

Another everyday practice that students might translate into academic practices is the building of personal learning networks (mentioned in chapter 1) to build a network of online associations leading to the gathering of information. Personal learning networks combine digital tools with social connections to get work done, often in professional contexts (Rajagopal, Joosten-ten Brinke, Van Bruggen, & Sloep, 2012), by using the social practices of making connections among texts as well as working collaboratively. Similar to the give-and-take of information about particular bands or videos on social media such as Facebook, Google Plus, and Twitter, the academic version of this concept might be more formally and purposefully built through accessing information by subscribing to blogs, wikis, podcasts, Twitter, or social networking sites using an RSS reader such as Reeder http://reederapp.com to subscribe to specific tools that address their interests and needs.

Students can then use Facebook, Google Plus, or Twitter to access information from their peers or experts outside the classroom about something that students have expertise in, say, music. Following known experts on Twitter is another way to build a network that can become more global. Creating and promoting a blog is another way to begin to build the connections that are essential to developing information (see "Delighting in Writing" on WordPress, for example, http://tinyurl.com/krtgehp).

Schools or universities can also formalize personal learning networks through peer-assisted learning projects in which students assist their peers with instruction in acquiring search strategies. In the Library Research Assistance Technician program at California Polytechnic State University, San Luis Obispo, students provided informational literacies training sessions for their peers, resulting in highly positive evaluations from both faculty and peers (Bodemer, 2014). Having students serve as peer mentors/instructors also benefits these students, who gain expertise in informational literacies through serving as mentors or instructors.

SEARCHING AND CREATING NEW CONTEXTS

It also helps to introduce your students to the library and its digital resources gradually and then add more complex tasks to match more complex assignments. In Tom's class, this happens over a series of paper assignments that build on one another. Just as scaffolding is part of how the readings and writing in the course are imagined, experience with the online resources builds and deepens throughout the semester.

To help students gain familiarity with the web and searching for information in this new academic context, Tom's students are given assignments that connect readings about the course theme to the act of reading websites for the different kinds of knowledge that each offers. Within the course theme of consumer issues, for example, students are given a list of websites and then asked to name the site type (blog, website, online magazine article, etc.) and to write a sentence that gives an idea of what it is about. Finally, students are asked to write another sentence or two about what each website contributes to a many-sided understanding of consumption. In this exercise, an online *Forbes* magazine article reports different kinds of information than do individuals' stories about out-of-control spending on the Spenders Anonymous website. Students learn to distinguish among different kinds of information and how searches might distinguish among such sources.

A further exercise that comes a little later in the course asks students to make use of Google to find images relating to a course theme. Students work in pairs, finding familiar images of consumption, such as a McDonald's meal, and then writing an "uncooling" Word text, in the spirit of one of the readings by Kalle Lasn (1999), to accompany the image. Students gain experience in forming keywords that will produce a useful image, as well as learn to efficiently join an image to text in a basic Word file. They have also gone a step further by locating websites rather than merely reacting to a list given by the instructor.

A bit later in the semester, students are asked to become familiar with three academic indexes—Academic Search Premier, ProQuest Newsstand, and Ethnic Newswatch—offered through the University of Minnesota libraries, to complete a midterm paper. Significantly, students are taught at this stage to see their online searching as part of a broad range of options for obtaining sources. Students are then directed to course readings already assigned, an online skills inventory offered through the university, and basic information about careers searchable on the university's Career Resources Center website at http://www.career.umn.edu. As an exercise carried out in pairs in a computer classroom, students deepen their search experience by using a wider range of academic search tools with the support of classmates.

Given the need to direct students to particular sites, you may want to provide students with a list of possible indexes, web collections, and other source repositories that are tailored to your assigned projects, using tools such as Google Advanced Search or Scholar. If a goal is for students to make use of a particular kind of source such as an audio recording, students will do better searching if they have someplace to begin that search. The website History.com at http://history.com, for example, offers short audio clips of "famous speeches in American history," including many by U.S. presidents. Creating such a list of possible source sites, especially if particular kinds of sources are asked for in the assignment, is the first step toward helping students take an assignment into a manageable space of their own and begin to make it relevant for themselves.

A less directive approach but one that still gives students some guidance is to steer students toward particularly useful databases. Patty Fillipi, a first-year writing teaching specialist at the University of Minnesota, asks her students to begin their "inquiry paper" search with three databases accessed through the library system. Students branch off from these three as they deepen their searches, but having common starting points helps students establish a scholarly direction for their projects and gives them the opportunity to discuss the use of the search tools as they get going.

Using Pathfinders or Webquests

To assist students in searching for material, librarians have created pathfinders or web-quests that provide students with directions on how and where to search for topics or complete assignments (Dodge, 1995; Farkas, 2009); LibGuides at http://libguides.com/community.php and ipl2 at http://www.ipl.org/div/pf provide thousands of pathfinders organized by topic and discipline.

These pathfinders are designed to provide students with the same kind of support that a librarian would provide in a face-to-face interaction with a student, although they do not substitute for such individual help. The pathfinders contain information about keywords to use for searching, databases (usually limited to library subscribers), links, blogs, wikis, or experts to e-mail. They also begin with an initial description of a topic or issue that provides a context for students' research.

Teachers can create these webquests using websites, blogs, or wikis, as well as QuestGarden at http://questgarden.com for webquests or TrackStar at http://tinyurl.com/89vbgp8 for pathfinders. One limitation of pathfinders or webquests is that they can be overly prescriptive worksheets; they should therefore be designed more to support or model for students the research process, rather than do the work for them. In designing pathfinders or webquests, it is useful to keep them visually simple and appealing to reduce cognitive load demands, as well as to employ RSS feeds that serve to automatically update information sources (Kurt, 2012; for more on pathfinders or webquests, see http://tinyurl.com/lftkqvu).

DEVELOPING STRATEGIES FOR SEARCHING WITH DIGITAL TOOLS IN TOM'S FIRST-YEAR WRITING COURSE

Direct guidance of students as they work within an assigned suite of search tools is an effective strategy for helping students develop a search and locate sources for a writing task. Important to this process is to link the tools to students' development of their individual projects. In one of Tom's first-year writing classes, for example, students met in a computer lab at the stage of conducting research for a source-based paper. Given the assignment of writing a focused research paper within the wider semester-long themes of work and consumerism, students chose topics as diverse as "the history of tattooing," "student loan debt," and "the power of junk food addiction." Before tackling individual tools, students were led through a process of developing search strategies and plans within the context of their papers. They were also encouraged to make use of the search tools as they contemplated their topics.

One challenge in working with this framework was to get students to find common ground on which to form topics and discuss their projects. To respond to this challenge, the search process was integrated into the larger process of doing the paper. Discussions of assigned class readings earlier in the course, along with shorter papers written earlier in the semester, had given students this kind of class-based familiarity with some of the issues. At the point of writing a longer paper that demanded further research, Tom asked students to join the early stages of forming and refining a topic to the search process.

With the goal of getting students to begin to develop the ability to make choices in topic and research directions, Tom asked students to frame their searches by way of an in-class brainstorming exercise that resulted in tighter areas for a beginning search. Joining the task of narrowing a topic to the search process can help students gain direction for their project. Here is what the assignment looked like:

> Brainstorming for Paper 4
>
>   Please begin this assignment in class today and turn it in as homework for the next class. It's an assignment designed to help you think about choosing a topic for Paper 4. It should be useful to you as you prepare to write your topic proposal in class next time. Use the back of this sheet if necessary for writing your responses. Here are the steps:

1. Make a list of five course-related concerns that have come to you as we've done this course so far. These could come from former papers, or readings, or just things that have popped into your head. Examples could be, "Debt for college students" or "Working conditions for production of clothing."

2. Choose three of those five above topics and, for each, write down how each affects you personally. Examples: I am in debt due to my "cheap" Visa card. I buy clothing at the Gap.

3. Choose one of the above topics from either number 1 or number 2 and write down how this is a historical topic. I'm making the assumption here that everything happens in history and is, therefore, historical. Example: Credit cards were not always so easy to obtain. At some point, they became easier. The history is that credit appears easier to obtain, but I'm not sure how this came about. I could find this out.

4. Consider one of the above topics as one that might be important to someone. How could you approach this topic so that you made it important for fellow students and me (the principal audiences of this paper)? Example: Too many of my fellow students are in debt but don't think very carefully about the trade-offs of taking on this debt. My paper could give a good discussion of what is involved, culturally, economically, and personally in taking on debt while in school.

5. Write a question about your topic that you'd really like to get answered. Wait! Before writing that question, make sure it's one that is actually research-able. Example: What are some of the consequences of young people going into debt?

6. Write down as many search terms as you can think of for your topic. Use terms above that may be useful.

There are several advantages of using such an assignment as students begin to use online search tools for a project. First, students establish continuity with already-completed course activities and assignments. The "research paper" sometimes seems to appear on syllabi as something unrelated to anything else in an English or writing studies course. As they approach the act of searching, this step reminds students that they are starting with some knowledge and discussion about the overriding theme, as well as search experience from prior assignments.

Second, as students choose a topic, they are asked about personal investment that can lead to more persistent searching. Students chose topics that mattered to them. A few students chose to work with personal debt, for example, because of loans that they had had to take out. Another student had a plan of becoming a personal financial advisor. Motivations varied, but each student had the opportunity to establish a connection that motivated his or her work from this point forward.

Third, students began to juggle and reframe their topics as they were being formed—a way to begin the process of balancing their interests with the demands of the assignment. They also began to work with language, especially keyword search terms, about the topic that would make for an effective use of search tools.

Finally, since the class worked in a computer classroom with library and Internet access, the task was begun with the advantage of doing "exploratory" searches that helped them to arrive at a topic with some promise for finding materials. Tom observed students making use of search engines and library indexes, as they were encouraged to do, when writing their responses. Students were also able to talk informally with one another and the teacher about possible topics and how they might meet the criteria for the assignment.

After completing the brainstorming exercise, they then wrote a formal proposal in which they were asked for a working title, a paragraph that asked for a connection to discussions and assignments from earlier in the course, a paragraph that noted sources from their assigned readings that might be useful for the paper, and, finally, a paragraph that stated a plan for their continuing research on the project, paying special attention to the materials that they would seek and how they would go about finding them.

Brittany wrote a plan that included purposeful searching with a history database:

> In my paper, I plan to use articles, books, and possibly even a video that talks about this topic. I plan to check for articles on the U of M library page by searching through the Academic Search Premier and the Historical Abstracts databases. I want to check the Historical Abstract database because I want to see if our food has become healthier or unhealthier compared to the mid-20th Century when a lot of the food was homegrown. As for the book sources, I plan to search MNCAT on the U of M library page. I want to first check the video and media catalog on the U of M library page to see if I can find a video that talks about my topic, but if I can't find one then I will search for a reliable video on Google.

Jenna was able to build a topic by combining previous assigned sources with new ones that she was still finding:

> I will be using John Kenneth Galbraith's study titled "The Dependence Effect" to discuss why peoples' wants and needs are created by and more influenced by sexual advertisements than other types of advertisements. This way, it will provide a scholarly study to explain my thesis more in-depth. I also plan on using Kalle Lasn's article, "Culture Jamming," because it talks about wants and needs and about culture in American society. This will strengthen my argument because I plan to not only talk about people's habits, but why people have those habits. I plan on using many different sources for my paper. In addition to the readings from class, I plan to look at commercials, both current and from the past to see how they have changed over time. I also want to look into how consumer behaviors have changed over time as the types of advertisements have changed. I will most likely gather many articles from the web,

and I plan to look at the school's database and my local library for more sources. If I do decide to add visuals, I will most likely incorporate pictures of advertisements for products that will strengthen my argument.

Although less specific than Brittany, Jenna developed a strategy that involved combining familiar and less familiar avenues for obtaining sources. Significantly, since she was living at her parents' house this semester, she imagined working in the public library as well as using the university resources. Her subsequent use of the library tools was driven by a plan in which she had framed the project for herself.

Asking students to make explicit a plan, which they then shared in class with others in a small group, helped them to begin to frame a focused, well-considered search. Proposals were preliminary, of course, and the direction for some students changed as work continued, but each student had developed a plan and discussed it with other classmates and Tom.

EVALUATING SEARCH RESULTS

One of the central aspects of information literacy is the ability to judge the validity of information available on online sites (November, 2008). In contrast to information in peer-reviewed or edited journals, books, or news reports, there is often no editorial control over the information contained on many websites. Students may encounter websites or blogs created by groups with ideological agendas that present false information, as in the site http://www.martinlutherking.org, operated by white racists that contains racist misinformation about Martin Luther King.

To evaluate search results, students need to identify the source of the information on a site by attempting to identify the date or organization creating a site by locating the "about us" descriptor on a website. They can also use Whois at http://www.whois.sc to identify the domain name source (Barseghian, 2011) or the "Link: www.your websitename.com" to identify other sites that link to the original site to determine that sources of those other sites.

They can check on whether a site has been revised by checking the "updates" on posted articles to determine if corrections have been made to those articles (Barseghian, 2011). For further resources on assessing websites, see the Center for Digital Literacy: WebCHECK—The Website Evaluation Instrument at http://www.myweb check.net, the Berkeley Library Evaluating Websites http://tinyurl.com/p8im for analyzing website quality, November Learning: Information Literacies at http://nov emberlearning.com/resources/information-literacy-resources, or 21st Century Information Fluency at http://21cif.com/favorites.html. For more on evaluating websites: http://tinyurl.com/llamd3z.

Assessing Sites Through Comparison Across Sites

Assessing the validity or credibility of a text on a site involves corroboration of a text's claims relative to other texts through use of the social practice of making connections across texts. If in reading Text A, students are then willing to search for Texts B, C, and D on the same topic, they can then use those other texts to determine the validity or credibility of claims in Text A—analysis that is particularly important for reading research reports.

When college students were asked to read six documents on an issue, they attended to the source documentation within these documents, particularly those that had the strongest opposing perspectives, but they did not use intertextual comparisons among these documents to contrast the validity and credibility of claims by comparing the different document sources (Strømsø, Ivar Braten, Britte, & Ferguson, 2013). In attending to source references, they did not attend to information about the authors' credentials or document types. All of this suggests the need for instruction in helping students identify source information, through comparing the sources cited in different documents about the same topic. Students can also use the Sourcer's Apprentice site http://tinyurl.com/l645d7k to analyze uses of sources in history texts. This further suggests the need to teach students to adopt a skeptical stance towards material on the web by modeling critical analysis of problematic sites reported on monitoring sites such as http://snopes.com or http://lijit.com that identify misinformation on sites.

To engage in critical analysis of online content, students can also employ Roland Paris's CLEAR model at http://aix1.uottawa.ca/~rparis/critical.html, which focuses on the claims that the author is making, the logical structure of the argument, the evidence provided, the assumptions that the author makes, and the alternative arguments. For other resources on teaching critical analysis of online content, see Howard Reingold: Critical Thinking at http://critical-thinking.iste.wikispaces.net, Critical Thinking on the Web at http://austhink.com/critical, or University of British Columbia: Critical Thinking at http://learningcommons.ubc.ca/critical-thinking.

Michelle Luhtala, library department chair, New Canaan High School, New Canaan, Connecticut, has students analyze the following aspects of online digital texts (K. Schwartz, 2013).

> *Identifying features:* maps, graphs, documents, reprints etc.
> *Scope:* Is the source broad like an encyclopedia entry or does it go deeply into a subject? When researching, start broad and narrow along the way.
> *Sources:* Does the article references where the information came from?
> *Reliable:* What's a legitimate news source? Look for clues in layout, author biography, labels on the page that would indicate if it's opinion or reported work.

Currency: How recent is the work? Does that date matter for the purposes of the project?

Comparison: Can the information be compared to other sources?

Authority: Is the author really an expert? What clues from their bio would indicate if the author has a specific bias? Did he or she get paid to write the article? That can be a good indicator of bias.

Audience: Discern who the article is written for and that will help determine its purpose and perhaps its bias.

Viewpoint: Different viewpoints have varying degrees of validity. There are times when one viewpoint should perhaps be given more weight than another.

Purpose: Was it written to promote something?

Conclusion: What conclusions did the author draw?

Relevance: Is the source relevant to the research needs?

Using Wikipedia

Rather than dismiss online encyclopedias such as Wikipedia, however, we recognize its wide popular use and advocate making it a part of an overall search strategy. While not appropriate for most academic projects as cited sources, information from Wikipedia and variants of Wikimedia can be especially useful in early exploration of a topic. Unfortunately, students often do not realize that anyone can edit Wikipedia articles, nor are they familiar with the Wikipedia editing processes (Menchen-Trevino & Hargittai, 2011). When students do use Wikipedia to create articles, they often rely on copy-and-paste verbatim material from online source material without generating their own writing or citing sources (Sormunen & Lehtio, 2011).

This suggests that students need instruction on how to respond to and create Wikipedia articles, something that we discuss in detail in chapter 7. For analyzing Wikipedia entries, students can look at the revision histories on entries to note deletions and additions, as well as Talk Pages for discussions of misinformation (Jenkins, 2007). For working with younger students, we recommend use of the Qwiki app at http://tinyurl.com/3ed4ksw, which includes articles at a simpler readability level along with videos, images, graphs, and entries for millions of topics. You can also create study guides for use on studying topics linked to Wikipedia searches using the StudyGuideMe app at http://tinyurl.com/6mlzsfu.

Students can also learn by comparing Wikipedia entries to more reputable scholarly sources. Heidi Jacobs (2010) asked students to compare topical Wikipedia entries to Oxford Reference Online, and the activity opened up discussion of the advantages of Wikipedia's immediacy along with weaknesses over editorial authority. These assignments instill a habit of critical assessment of all sources, a crucial step in helping students become more critically aware information seekers (Elmborg, 2012).

To this end, Randall McClure (2011) has written of the need for students to move from "instinctive information behaviors" to "solid research skills." He recommends an eight-step process to help students navigate among general search engines such as Google and Wikipedia in this way:

1. Use Wikipedia to get a sense of the topic and identify additional search terms.
2. Use Google to get a broader sense of the topic as well as verify information and test out search terms you found in Wikipedia.
3. Search Google again using quotation marks around your "search terms" to manage the number of results and identify more useful search terms.
4. Search Google Scholar (scholar.google.com) to apply the search terms in an environment of mostly academic and professional resources.
5. Do a limited search of "recent results or "since 2000" on Google Scholar to manage the number of results and identify the most current resources.
6. Search your college's library research databases using your college library's web portal to apply the search terms in an environment of the most trusted academic and professional resources.
7. Focus your search within at least one general academic database such as Academic Search Premier, Proquest Complete, Lexis/Nexis Academic Universe, or CQ Researcher to apply the search terms in a trusted environment and manage the number of results.
8. Do a limited search by year and "full text" returns using the same general academic database(s) you used in step 7 to reduce the number of results and identify the most current resources. (p. 237)

Following such an ordered set of steps gives students a direction that is likely to produce a richer set of resources and knowledge for building a written project. In our view, these steps make the most sense when placed within the ideas about building social context discussed earlier.

News Literacy

Students also need to know how to critically analyze the credibility of and biases in news reports (P. Adams, 2014). For example, in his college journalism class at State University of New York, Stony Brook, Howard Schneider had his students read a news report with the headline "Girls Go 'Wild' for Booze, Sex," which was based on a survey indicating that 83% of young women noted that spring break involved heavy drinking and 74% indicated that there was extensive sexual activity during spring break (Finder, 2007). Schneider indicated to his class that the survey was challenged by polling experts who discovered that it was conducted online with volunteer participants, two-thirds of whom had never been on spring break—a violation of scientific polling procedures that employ a random sample of people who are directly engaged in a certain event. He noted that the fact that a newspaper published the report reflects a propensity of reporters or editors to print information that conforms to their beliefs, suggesting the need for both producers and readers of the news to be willing to be open to information that may challenge their presuppositions.

To foster students' awareness of the need to examine news reporters' factual documentation for their claims, you could provide students with examples similar to Schneider's survey—that is, articles with dubious evidence—and have them use the Factcheck.org site at http://www.factcheck.org to check on the accuracy of those reports (P. Adams, 2014).

Students could also determine who owns their local newspapers or radio/television stations in terms of how certain corporate interests may shape the content of news. To identify what companies own what news outlets, students can use the "Who Owns What" website at http://tinyurl.com/cyzk62, operated by the *Columbia Journalism Review*. For example, News Corp owns the *Wall Street Journal* and Fox News which has an influence on the editorial bias in those news outlets. Students also need to consider how the increased consolidation of media ownership to a small number of corporations—GE (NBC), News Corp (*Wall Street Journal*, Fox News, *New York Post*), Disney (ABC), Time Warner (CNN, Time), CBS (CBS News)—results in limited access to a range of different perspectives on the news.

The News Literacy Project at http://www.thenewsliteracyproject.org, the Center for News Literacy at http://www.centerfornewsliteracy.org, and the Pew Research Center Journalism Project at http://www.journalism.org provide useful resources related to news literacy instruction. For more on news literacy http://tinyurl.com/kxrvjjo.

SUMMARY

In this chapter, we describe a range of search strategies for accessing and evaluating online information in ways that employ certain social practices. Central to the effective use of these search strategies is students' ability to contextualize their purpose for accessing information relative to their eventual use of information for certain tasks and audiences. Students' searches can be enhanced through collaborative reading activities in which students support one another's understanding of search results. To assess the validity of search results, students make intertextual links among texts to contrast the validity of claims, as well as to recognize the need to be open to alternative perspectives evident in their search results. Once students access and assess online information, they then need to know how to organize, store, reflect on, and share information, which is the focus of our next chapter.

4

CURATING, ORGANIZING, AND SUMMARIZING INFORMATION

Once students have acquired their information, or texts, as described in chapter 3, they then need to synthesize, curate, and share that information with various audiences using different social practices that address the Common Core standards.

Common Core State Standard: Reading Standard 8

- Synthesize and apply information presented in diverse ways (e.g., through words, images, graphs, and video) in print and digital sources to answer questions, solve problems, or compare modes of presentation.

The ability to synthesize and apply information requires the ability to contextualize information relative to situation, audience, media, and genre. For example, a group of 12th graders were creating a multimodal orientation presentation on a website for incoming 9th graders about different features of their high school. In doing so, they recognized the need to employ a range of different media to appeal to their audience. So, they took photos and shot video of students engaged in different extracurricular activities, school organizations, classes, sports, and special events to include on their website, along with their own commentary.

This activity required that they synthesize this material in a manner consistent with a defined purpose to convey positive as well as problematic perceptions of the different aspects of their school; they did not want to be perceived by the 9th graders as sugar-coating some of the realities of the school culture.

DIGITAL CONTENT CURATION TOOLS

Given the amount of information that is readily available, employing digital content curation tools can serve to access, store, organize, categorize, aggregate, and display information. Just as museum curators have to consider how to effectively store, organize, categorize, and display artwork, students learn to use these tools in curating information to access and present information based on their senses of purpose and audience. For example, for use in storing and organizing material from the web, students can use Pocket for Mac http://tinyurl.com/l6oqgne, Windows/Chrome http://tinyurl.com/mcfcvjj, iOS http://tinyurl.com/mwhndpu, or Android http://tinyurl.com/88gjxal as well as Instapaper for Mac http://www.instapaper.com, iOS http://tinyurl.com/7ptqg7w, or Android http://tinyurl.com/7ptqg7w to add bookmarklets to their browser bar to then store links to websites and tag those links based on certain categories.

Many of these curation tools function as "push tools" that provide students with information relevant to certain topics, thereby reducing students' need to have to search for information by subscribing to RSS readers such as Feedly. English teacher Hauna Zaich (2012) noted,

> One day I was looking at all of the materials, connections, blogs, publications, and information online . . . and realized that I could use curation to sort through them, organize them, and make them more accessible to my students from a single platform.

For a lesson on plagiarism, she collected material on writers who had been accused of plagiarism, then organized it in an online bulletin board to share with students.

It is also important for students to synthesize not only information but also multimodal images, audio, and video texts that serve to communicate information and ideas, as noted in a Common Core speaking and listening standard.

Common Core State Standard: Speaking and Listening Standard 2

- Integrate and evaluate information from multiple oral, visual, or multimodal sources in order to answer questions, solve problems, or build knowledge.

Drawing on the idea of the Cornell boxes as collections of disparate items, Geoff Sirc (2004) describes ways in which students in his writing classes function as curators who collect a range of digital texts to create "box logic" exhibits or "arcades projects" about different aspects of hip-hop culture (p. 112). His students begin by searching academic databases and sites related to the topic of hip-hop and rap. Students then take notes on the material they find. Sirc responds to these notes by posing inquiry questions about their topic or suggesting other links and resources. Then, by examining how museums present their physical and digital exhibits, students mount their own arcades project. They are then using digital writing as

> a compelling medium and genre with which to re-arrange textual material—both original and appropriated—in order to have those materials speak the student's own voice and concerns, allowing them to come up with something obscure, perhaps, yet promising illumination. (p. 113)

As curators combining print and images, audio, and/or video texts, Sirc's students were employing the social practice of defining connections among texts to infer consistent thematic patterns, a practice that addresses the Common Core reading standard of inferring relationships among texts.

Common Core State Standard: Reading Standard 9

- Analyze how two or more texts address similar themes or topics in order to build knowledge or to compare the approaches the authors take.

Sirc encourages his students to continually reflect on how the connections and combinations of texts serve as

> a vehicle of reverie, an object that would enrich the imagination of the viewer. The model of college writing, then, becomes the contemporary DVD—a compendium of "finished" text, commentary, selected features, interviews, alternative versions, sections initially deleted . . . our new classroom genre might best be called a diary, journal, repository, laboratory, picture gallery, museum, sanctuary, observatory, key . . . inviting us to see things in a light in which we do not know them, but which turns out to be almost one in which we hoped one day to see them bathed. (p. 146)

In creating their "box logic" presentations, students needed to consider how they were combining or remixing digital texts in ways that would be visually or aesthetically appealing to their audiences by addressing the social practice of adopting different modes, a practice that addresses the Common Core speaking and listening standards associated with multimodal presentations.

Common Core State Standard: Speaking and Listening Standards

2. Integrate and evaluate information from multiple oral, visual, or multimodal sources in order to answer questions, solve problems, or build knowledge.
4. Present information, evidence, and reasoning in a clear and well-structured way appropriate to purpose and audience.
5. Make strategic use of digital media and visual displays of data to express information and enhance understanding.

CHANGES IN HOW AND WHERE STUDENTS ACQUIRE INFORMATION

The use of these curation tools represents a shift in how users acquire information that in turn shapes the ways in which information is generated and edited. Given the mobility of devices, students can acquire this information across a range of different devices and locations—for example, between their iPad and iPhone so that they can access their iPhone while waiting in a coffee shop line. In the past, people acquired information provided for them by the media; now people can personalize the types of information that they are receiving depending on their needs, interests, and location. Tim Carmody (2011) quotes Flipboard founder Mike McCue's description of his use of Flipboard:

> It's a mix of what's going on in the world and what's going on in your world, fused together. And it might seem weird that I'm looking at a picture of my daughters, and then the next flip I'm reading a story about Iran. But to me as a reader, when I'm standing in line waiting to get my coffee, those things are what I care about.

Carmody also posits that the use of curation tools changes how media producers define the context for access and analyzing information. Rather than simply perceiving context as providing background information for a story or media, producers now perceive context in terms of five factors: medium, location, time, social, and identity.

Producers consider the effect of the *medium*, the size and capabilities of a device's screen—for example, the fact that an iPhone has a small screen. They also consider *location*, how users will be using a device to access information relevant to being in a location—for example, shopping in a specific section of a store or traveling in a certain city. In addition, they consider *time* in terms of the time of day that a user is accessing the information and how much time that a user may have to obtain that information. They are also recognizing the *social* aspects of how users share, recommend, and comment on stories for their social networks, sharing that may then be picked up by other users for further sharing on other networks. In the case of making choices about what and for whom they are sharing information, users are constructing an online *identity* within these networks—for example, that they may want to be perceived as an expert on a certain topic that they are sharing with others.

In applying the social practices to curation, it is important to recognize the need to go beyond simply collecting materials, to contextualizing materials based on a goal for students' learning through use of the materials (White, 2012). Related to the social practice of making connections, in modeling the role of a curator, you are contextualizing materials to engage students in defining intertextual connections among the different texts that you share with them. For example, you may create a Pinterest board with book cover images of the different texts that your students are reading in your class (for an example, see http://tinyurl.com/pumyzdb). You can then ask students to not only determine how each cover captured the story line, genre, media, or themes in these texts but also how the connections across the different texts reflect certain story lines, genre, media, or themes. You can also contextualize the content, again as do museum curators, by providing your own additional comments or tags to the material related to your overall goal.

Then, when you ask students to curate their own collection, you can have them contextualize that collection based on *their* conception of goals, audience, situations, genre, and media consistent with the MAPS heuristic—media, audience, purpose, and situation (T. Hicks, 2009). Students could engage in collaborative construction of collections consistent with the social practice of collaboration. In doing so, they may add their own alternative perspectives to the same texts, resulting in different interpretations of those texts.

DIFFERENT TYPES OF CURATION TOOLS

To engage your students in collecting digital texts and creating curation presentations, there is a range of different types of curation tools that you and your students can use for collecting, organizing, and sharing digital content tools that we discuss throughout this book. For example, students can store content on websites, blogs, or wikis or on DropBox, Google Drive, Diigo, or Evernote (for more on digital storage and content curation tools: http://tinyurl.com/n8oj6n5).

Aggregation Dashboards

One type of curation tool consists of an aggregation dashboard that pulls information from different news outlets, blogs, and other information sites into one composite page, often a browser's front page (Vincenzini, 2013). These include NetVibes http://netvibes.com, Symbaloo http://symbaloo.com, Feedly http://feedly.com, ProtoPage http://protopage.com, iFlow https://iflow.com, and Individurls.com http://individurls.com. Central to students' successful use of these aggregation dashboards is the ability to identify key terms and categories related to their interests and needs, categories that serve as the basis for acquiring relevant information.

Pinboard Curation Tools

There are also curation tools that are particularly useful for curation purposes given how they present information in appealing visual layouts—for example, pinboard curation tools listed on the website for searching and then posting, or "pinning," online content onto a virtual pinboard/bulletin board, along with text or tags to describe the online context (for iOS and Android pinboard apps: http://tinyurl.com/l7to3th). Students can add buttons from these tools to their browser bars so that when they find relevant material, they can click on the button to add material to that tool. As is the case with search strategies described in chapter 3, students need to be able to clearly define those topics and related search terms or tags for acquiring feeds related to those terms or tags. For example, if students select a topic such as "climate change," they may be overwhelmed with material, as opposed to the topic of "future changes in sea levels." Students working in small groups reading different texts can share online information and their responses within and across these groups (for suggested activities for Pinterest: http://tinyurl.com/meejhbn and http://tinyurl.com/cz6hf9a; for an example of sharing books read in Steven Bickmore's adolescent literature class: http://www.pinterest.com/steven_bickmore/texts-for-english-7542-fall-2011).

An analysis of the use of Pinterest to create a multimedia online resource in an introductory college anthropology course found that students responded positively to the use of Pinterest for organizing and grouping information by topic (Pearce & Learmonth, 2013). One student noted,

> The nice thing about Pinterest is that the information is grouped. With YouTube, it's all videos and they are meshed together which can be quite confusing. The nice thing about Pinterest is that you can group them by topic. You can then add anything; article, photos, videos or whatever you want.

School administrators Eric Sheninger: https://www.pinterest.com/esheninger, Kristen Hernandez: https://www.pinterest.com/techgirllsu/administrators, and Kimberly Franck: https://www.pinterest.com/kimberlyfrank/school-principal are also using Pinterest to share relevant resources with other administrators, teachers, and parents (Devaney, 2013).

Another useful educational curation tool is eduClipper https://www.educlipper.net. You and your students can use eduClipper to add "clips" as image files, Google Drive files, links to videos, PowerPoints, PDFs, and so on, along with comments to "boards" as instructional units based on certain topics or themes. You can also provide students with access codes to join these "boards."

Magazine/News Curation Tools: Using RSS Feeds

There is a range of different magazine/news curation tools, such as Zite, Flipboard, Pearltrees, and Zinio (for these tools: http://tinyurl.com/mml6h73). These tools draw on relevant material to curate that material to create magazine-like layouts according to topics or themes. Students can select those topics according to the information that they want, as well as to share information on Facebook or Twitter.

These tools rely on the use of RSS feeds to pull news stories from a range of sources. Students can employ RSS feeds to subscribe to various magazine/news sites and then create their own curation folders to store RSS feeds from news sites—for example, using Safari http://macmost.com/macmost-new-668-combining-rss-feeds-in-safari.html.

To do so, students

- Create a curation folder on their bookmarks bar to add RSS feed URLs to their folder by finding RSS feed icons (usually orange) on various news sites.
- Go to that folder and find items to insert into their curation sites. When they find a news site, for example, the *New York Times*, they click on the RSS feed icon next to the refresh icon within the URL box.
- Go to their Bookmarks link to save that feed URL to their folder. They can also add other news outlets' RSS feeds to their folder. When they open that folder, they can search for items using the options in the right column. Students can also use browser curation tools such as NetVibes to collect material.

One advantage of using these online content creation tools is that most of them are cross-platform so that students can access or share the content on their smartphones, tablets, or computers. For example, students can use two of the more popular news curation tools, Zite and Flipboard, to select topics for accessing current stories or news items based on those topics, as well as to add their own links to other content sources, such as Facebook, Twitter, or blogs. Students can also create their own photo magazine based on examples such as found on Zite and Flipboard that organize stories around phtoso of current events issues. To create collage magazines based on collections of images, students could use the iOS InstaMag-Magazine http://tinyurl.com/qxf2njl or

Android InstaMag http://tinyurl.com/m3fynzo apps that include large collections of images.

Classroom Curation Cloud Storage Sites

There are a number of cloud storage sites, such as iCloud, Google Drive, DropBox, Wiggio, OneDrive (Microsoft), and Evernote (listed on the website http://tinyurl.com/k74t9dg), which can be used by students to store and share files within a classroom.

One heavily used cloud storage site is Google Drive https://drive.google.com. Students can use Google Drive to

- Store up to 15 GB of images, videos, and text files.
- Use a range of tools, such as Docs, Presentations, Sheets, Forms, Drawings, Scripts, and Mind.
- Use mapping or WeVideo.
- Sync their files across different desktop, laptop, table, and smartphone devices.
- Save digital texts to Drive using the Chrome browser "Save to Drive" extension.
- Engage in chat when working on document.
- Share documents with Google+ members or while participating on a Google Hangout.
- Use the Research menu options under Tools on Google Docs to access related topics.
- Use Forms to create surveys.
- Use Sheets to create Forms using the Form option under "Create."
- Use the iOS: http://tinyurl.com/lqgxu2d and Android: http://tinyurl.com/mhesykz Quickoffice apps to read or edit Office files that can then be uploaded to Google Drive (Chartier, 2014). For more in use of forms and spreadsheets: http://tinyurl.com/nxt2dgp.

Another popular cloud curation tool is the note-taking Evernote tool http://evernote.com (described in more detail in the next chapter), which allows students to store their notes, files, images, and videos in the "notebook" folders. You can also create assignments within Evernote as well as respond to students' work in it.

One major advantage of these cloud storage sites is that all of a students' work can be stored on them so that both you and your students can choose to share their work with selected peers or with an entire class, reducing instances in which students lose or misplace paper texts. Students can also create folders for organizing their files according to topics. Students then no longer need to be concerned about having to save files on the school's computers or a flash drive because they can access those files from the cloud. They can also access these files from their computers, tablets, or smartphones.

However, there are potential security issues in terms of who may have access to these files, so students need to know that they should not share their personal identification information on these sites. Sites that provide limited storage space may fill up quickly, particularly for storage of video files. When students begin to create their electronic portfolios, as discussed in chapter 11, they can then readily move their writing into their portfolios based on their categories. In using these storage tools, it is important that they label, categorize, or tag their texts so that they can later readily search for and identify the content of those texts.

Archival Curation Sites

In addition to the library databases described in the previous chapter, you or your students can access archives created by organizations that include collections of different types of texts (for a list of archival curation sites: http://tinyurl.com/lcef8za).

One of the more useful curation archives is the Library of Congress Digital Collections http://tinyurl.com/2knoku (for the iOS app: http://tinyurl.com/lwztuy9), which contains news articles, songs, images, political cartoons, advertisements, photographs, and so on, as well as a resource section for teachers http://tinyurl.com/72swu4b on the uses of primary resources in the classroom. Ashley Watkins (2012) describes a number of ways that teachers have used the collections for teaching literature:

- For teaching *The Great Gatsby* (Fitzgerald, 1992), students find examples of photos, advertisements, and magazine articles from the 1920s http://tinyurl.com/klzkp4x.
- For teaching poetry writing, students find narratives from the "American Life Histories: Manuscripts From the Federal Writers' Project" to then write poems based on their responses to these narratives http://tinyurl.com/mjaauls.
- For teaching Karen Hesse's (1999) *Out of the Dust*, a teacher shares images of the Dust Bowl period with the students. Students then select free-verse passages from the novel and find images from "America From the Great Depression to World War II: Photographs From the FSA and OWI, ca. 1935–1945" that illustrate the passages, and they use the collection to find an image that embodies an important element of the poem http://tinyurl.com/ksrs3gz.

Students can also create their own archives of websites as part of the K12 Web Archiving Program http://www.archive-it.org/k12, developed by the Internet Archive and the Library of Congress. Students employ the Archive-It http://www.archive-it.org service to curate content, create collections as time capsules, and provide descriptions of the content of these capsules.

To effectively access information in these archives, students need to have a clear sense of their purpose related to identifying key search terms. They also need to define their research questions so that they can use those questions for analyzing the information, documents, and images they acquire. For example, if students are engaged in place-based writing about the historical development of their town or city and they acquire a set of images portraying changes in their town or city over time, they need to know how they will use those images to define related patterns or themes—for example, that the images portray a shift from a manufacturing economic base to a medical/technology economic base. For strategies for using primary documents, the Historical Scene Investigation site http://web.wm.edu/hsi/index.html created by the College of William & Mary School of Education includes some historical cases involving students using documents to address questions related to analyzing these cases.

Students can also access online literary texts using literary archive sites listed on the website http://tinyurl.com/kxx276v. In using these sites, Allen Webb (2009) recommends having students create their own literature anthologies annotated according to information about authors, movements, traditions; cut and paste texts to create hypertexts; and add commentary on characters or themes.

Because students often have difficulty selecting fiction texts geared for younger readers without an understanding of the content of the books, authors, genres, or readers' evaluations/reviews, they can benefit from going to sites such as Subtext http://www.subtext.com or HereBeFiction http://www.herebefiction.org linked to school libraries or Project Gutenberg http://www.gutenberg.org. For example, Subtext includes responses and recommendations by readers of all ages, as well as discussion forums. The HereBeFiction site provides school librarians and teachers with a means for sharing their reviews and recommendations on the site as well as on Twitter, Facebook, and Pinterest (C. Harris, 2013). Students can also access and share responses to young adult literature on the TeenReads site http://www.teenreads.com. Teachers can also use the Actively Learn site http://www.activelylearn.com to access online literary texts, add questions linked to the Common Core (including related background material or images/videos), and have students share responses and annotations.

Padlet http://padlet.com is another curation tool for posting sticky notes on a "wall," notes that can include information or links (for video tutorials on Padlet by Jesse Black-Allen: http://tinyurl.com/nt25mvx and by Richard Byrne: http://tinyurl.com/ks3nnf8). For examples of Padlets created in Jackie van Geest's English class at South St. Paul High School, see the following:

Leilani Serrata-Ramos, Made With Love: http://padlet.com/wall/by5lj1sg2n
Karla Sanchez, Ravenna: http://padlet.com/wall/o047x74n4k

Josh Koehler, Grendel's Story: http://padlet.com/wall/ia4zab8x92

Students' Participation in "Argument Curation"

In her 12th-grade composition classes at Rose High School, Greenville, North Carolina, Ashley Hutchison (2013) has her students engage in an "argument curation" research project associated with her school's Project Connect http://tinyurl.com/lty2ng8 activity for seniors. In that project, students identify a topic or issue that interests them. They then investigate the topic or issue by making connections with peers, parents, community members, and teachers to learn about it, consistent with the social practice of making connections. They then share their findings with peers, parents, community members, and teachers through their e-portfolio website.

To help her students complete their research project, Ashley has students create a website using Google Sites to collect and store resources. Students are required to find at least three resources on five argument topics related to their larger topic or issue; students then have to summarize the conflicting perspectives evident in the resources, an activity consistent with the social practice of adopting alternative perspectives. By doing this project, students often change their attitudes on their topic or issue, as evident in one student, who was opposed to gay marriage but, after reading his 15 resources, changed his attitude and argued in his report that gay marriage should be legalized.

Students then receive feedback from peers about their reports as a means of acquiring others' perspectives on their work. Then, in addition to including their reports in their e-portfolios, as part of the school's Project Connect activity, students make a short presentation of their work to an assembly at the end of each semester—an event that students, teachers, parents, and townspeople attend. Students are also encouraged to consider ways in which they can draw on their work to make changes in their school or community.

This argument curation project highlights the importance of students going beyond the familiar, often uninspiring "research project" to engage students in curation based on topics or issues that interest them, so that they acquire alternative, often competing perspectives by collecting a number of resources and by interacting with peers, parents, community members, and teachers to gain their alternative perspectives on their topic or issue.

Using Storify in a First-Year Composition Course

Storify (for a video introduction: http://tinyurl.com/kpflecd) can be used to access stories derived from social media on current news topics, issues, or events, as well as for creating reports on books that students are reading to share with a class. Rebecca Harris used Storify for her first-year composition course at Florida Southwestern State College to engage in multimodal writing based on the following personal narrative assignment:

> The Storify essay bears similarity to a collage or inspiration board in that it requires you to collect important items and arrange them visually and textually. For the purposes of this assignment, you will need to collect, link to, and/or discuss four of the following elements in your narrative: a quotation, video clip, audio clip, photograph, news story, meme, song, website, or an item from a social networking site.
>
> Other items may be added to your Storify essay as you see fit. You will collect your items and turn them into a coherent essay about critical inspiration. The key to this project is to uncover connections between the items we find motivating, inspiring, or comforting. Over the course of the project, we should ask ourselves the following questions for reflective critical thinking:
>
> What do these materials have in common?
> In what ways are they different?
> How do they appeal to us? Through emotion? Logic? Ethics? Morality?
> In what particular ways do these items inspire us?
> How can reflecting about these objects help us in our writing process?
> Your essay should
>
> - Be approximately 500 words of text
> - Include a minimum of four items from the list above
> - Illustrate connections between your items and critical thinking about those connections
> - Illustrate a coherent and critical reflective narrative
> - Answer some or all the questions for reflection listed above or answer questions you have generated yourself
> - Provide evidence of critical thinking and analysis of materials
> - Be presented in a visually appealing and organized way
> - Demonstrate the ability to transition among your materials
> - Create and tell a story of critical inspiration

In reflecting on her students' use of Storify, Rebecca noted in a blog post (R. Harris, 2013),

> The bulk of my students liked being able to integrate "their" stuff, Facebook photos, songs, or YouTube videos, into their essays, which included a personal narrative and a definition essay. . . . Using Storify allowed them to think of themselves as already being writers and so therefore lessened their anxiety about graded writing and being "perfect" for the professor. . . . Multimedia writing feels more organic to most of my

students than writing traditional papers, thus it seemed that multimedia writing also encouraged more experimentation from them in terms of the genre of their writing.

At the same time, she noted that while they were familiar with using sites such as Facebook, they were less familiar with using a site such as Storify to create their essays within an academic context. For future use of this assignment, she will

> devote an entire week of class to the site itself, talking about what it can do for them personally and academically, making my pedagogy transparent, discussing the similarities and differences between academic and non-academic essay composition, and acknowledging anxiety about using a familiar thing—social media—in an unfamiliar context.

Consistent with the social practice of connectivity, Mihailidis and Cohen (2013) perceive curation as the use of storytelling to engage in problem solving as critical media literacy. They cite the example of students using Storify to create curated stories to retell certain events by accessing and organizing different images, texts, tweets, and posts. To do so, students had to address the following questions:

- When is a story complete online?
- What does authority mean in storytelling?
- How are mainstream media reports different from peer-to-peer reports?
- Can social media be effective in helping to tell a story?
- How many different voices are needed for a story to be deemed complete?
- How do social media enhance a story? What do they take away?

Students also had to justify the use of certain sources to create their stories as well as address issues of the credibility of the sources from Facebook, Twitter, and blogs. In using certain sources, they had to critique the biases and ideological assumptions inherent in the reporting involved in their sources.

Using Word Clouds

Curation can also occur by creating word clouds, such as Wordle http://www.wordle.net or Tagxedo http://tinyurl.com/n2cmzmv, which display the words in text of different sizes based on the frequency of use of these words—the larger the word, the more frequently it was used. Or word clouds can be revised using different patterns, colors, and designs (for Adam Bellow's video on use of Tagxedo: http://tinyurl.com/ln5aujc).

Students can also use Wordle to study poems, stories, speeches, blogs, or websites to determine word frequency as a reflection of the thematic focus of these texts—for example, the fact that the word *dream* is frequently used in Martin Luther King's "I

Have a Dream" speech. As demonstrated in her video, Marley Silvestri http://tinyurl.com/lmezp6e uses Wordle to determine uses of words or phrases in her writing and students' writing to give feedback to students' writing. For example, Melissa Baralt had her Spanish-speaking students at Florida International University input the first draft of their essays written in Spanish into Wordle, resulting in their noting repetition in their use of certain words (Waycott, Sheard, Thompson, & Clerehan, 2013, p. 95). After rewriting their essays three times, they began to employ more diverse vocabulary.

Online Polling or Surveys

While Google Forms can be used to conduct polls or surveys, there are other tools, such as Survey Monkey or Poll Everywhere, specifically designed for creating and conducting online polls or surveys http://tinyurl.com/lrfqkm9, most of which are free. You can also use "clicker apps," such as the combination Socrative Teacher Clicker http://tinyurl.com/7t4whre and Socrative Student Clicker http://tinyurl.com/72n6edj, to have students respond to survey prompts. These survey tools can then generate results that can be exported into spreadsheets or used to analyze results for creating graphs or charts (for more on online polling or surveys: http://tinyurl.com/lrfqkm9).

You can also use online surveys to have students respond to opinions or attitudes regarding certain issues, current events, or characters' actions as data that can then be used to initiate discussions. For example, in studying *Of Mice and Men* (Steinbeck, 1993), students can respond to the statement "Curley is justified in killing Lennie at the end of the novel: agree or disagree." To obtain responses to questions or prompts, you can employ The Answer Pad http://theanswerpad.com Go Interactive tool as a clicker device to elicit students' responses to questions or prompts.

Spreadsheets

Another digital tool for collecting and organizing information is the spreadsheet tool, such as Microsoft's Excel http://office.microsoft.com/en-us/excel and Excel for Mac http://www.microsoft.com/mac/excel and the 2013 Excel Web App http://tinyurl.com/ma7l7l8, which can be stored on OneDrive, Google Drive Speadsheets, or Zoho Sheet as part of the Zoho suite. While students may typically use spreadsheets in math and science for inputting quantitative data for calculations and generation of graphs and charts, students in English language arts can use them in their own research to analyze results of survey data.

VISUAL REPRESENTATIONS AND COMMUNICATION OF INFORMATION AND IDEAS

Students need to learn how to understand and create digital texts associated with the visual representation and communication of information and ideas through use of charts/graphs, infographics, and concept maps. Visual or graphic representations are particularly helpful for supporting struggling students or students with disabilities (Dexter, Park, & Hughes, 2011). Likewise, any learner who is having trouble understanding concepts can benefit from the explicit displays of various terms and ways in which these are interrelated. Clearly, if students understand vocabulary and the concepts represented by it, this knowledge enables the comprehension of difficult texts in various subject areas.

Audiences can more easily comprehend information or ideas through visual representations as evident in the use of infographics in newspapers and online reports. However, the challenge in use of visual representations of complex data or information is that they can oversimplify or distort that data or information, requiring that students learn to critically analyze the ways in which the data or information is being presented in a chart/graph, infographic, or concept map.

Charts and Graphs

Students can create charts or graphs http://tinyurl.com/lv77z3b to present numerical data as a primary focus in math, science, and social sciences using tools such as Google Charts http://tinyurl.com/pbplxcz to create a range of different types of charts/graphs http://tinyurl.com/c7sodtl—for example, a pie chart, line chart, column chart, bar graph, scatter graph, table, or geography chart. Charts are a convenient way to analyze spreadsheet data visually, and they are built into Google Docs. To create charts, students draw on data from a spreadsheet by selecting the following:

- The data cells they want to include under "Edit" on the spreadsheet
- "Chart" from the Insert menu
- The range of data to include
- The type of chart under "Charts"
- Creating labels for the Title, Layout, Horizontal, and Vertical
- "Preview" to edit the chart and finalize the chart

They can also use the EduWidgets tool http://tinyurl.com/kkhxfue, created by the Virginia Department of Education for creating graphs, timelines, and interactive images (for more on graphs and charts: http://tinyurl.com/ouj2xh8).

They can also employ graphic organizers such as argument vee diagrams to identify arguments and counterarguments by putting pro arguments on the left side of the V, counterarguments on the right side of the V, and potential conclusions at the bottom (Nussbaum & Schraw, 2007).

Infographics

Students also use infographic tools such as Visual.ly or Easel.ly http://tinyurl.com/ ouj2xh8 to create visual representations of large amounts of information that combine graphs, charts, or figures in an appealing manner (Porcaro, 2013). For a YouTube video on the value of visual information presented with infographics: http://tinyurl.com/ ltmrz5u and descriptions of infographics: http://mnli.org/mnli13/infographics and http:// infographiclabs.com/news/what-is-an-infographic; for 46 tools for infographics: http:// www.teachthought.com/technology/46-tools-to-make-infographics-in-the-classroom and Kathy Schrock's infographics workshop: http://tinyurl.com/llj7ue8.

One advantage of infographics is that, like charts or graphs, they help audiences readily synthesize certain patterns or trends through an appealing visual summary of data or information about certain topics or phenomena. To examine examples of different infographics, students can use the Infographics app http://tinyurl.com/7t7gqof to study different ways to present data. For example, Carl Anderson, a teacher at the Perpich Center Fine Arts High School, Golden Valley, Minnesota, describes his use of infographics:

> I think it was David Warlick who I once heard say that with new technologies, "first we do old things in old ways, then we do old things in new ways, and then we do new things in new ways." Students in my Digital Foundations class at the Perpich Center Fine Arts High School in Golden Valley, MN are asked to approach digital arts in this manner, first learning how to use image editing software to paint and edit photos, then exploring how the computational power of the machine can be utilized to visualize data, and finally to explore new art forms not possible before tools like social media and video game engines were available to artists. When these students explore the use of the computer for data visualization, they are asked to produce infographics that help the viewer arrive at a misunderstanding of the data they convey.
>
> Infographics are a hot topic right now. We see them everywhere from magazine articles, to Internet memes, to billboards. Infographics are basically just the coupling of data with images and graphics to help convey the meaning behind the numbers. However, these designs can be harmful and misleading. Through the juxtaposition of imagery and the context in which all design elements are placed, the infographic designer can infuse data with a feeling or emotion; they can tip the viewer into misinterpretations.

I began this unit by introducing students to Marshall McLuhan's "Medium is the Message/Massage" concept where he argues that it matters less what content is conveyed than the medium it is conveyed with. In this argument McLuhan also states that the dominant medium in any culture and time carries with it a bias that people use to measure truth. I also read them a passage from Neil Postman's (1985) book *Amusing Ourselves to Death* where, drawing on McLuhan's work, he talks about how at points in human history we had vastly differing sources of truth. "'Seeing is believing,' 'reading is believing,' 'counting is believing,' 'deducing is believing,' and 'feeling is believing' are others that have risen or fallen in importance as cultures have undergone media change. As a culture moves from orality to writing to printing to televising, its ideas of truth move with it." I use these two texts then to engage students in a discussion about why data and statistics are held in such high regard in terms of ascertaining the truth today.

After discussing McLuhan and Postman, I have students study propaganda techniques used in marketing. I also have them look at ways in which a person can make a graph or chart that is misleading such as failing to include important aspects of the data set, not using a full range to make comparisons seem more drastic, changing the width of items in a vertical bar graph to make a statistic seem bigger or smaller than it really is, etc. I then have students critically analyze examples of infographics looking for ways they might be misleading.

The third day of this unit I share some data visualization tools. As a digital arts teacher I tell my students that I don't teach software, I teach concepts. Software changes at a rapid rate and I believe it is more important for them to learn how to use a variety of digital tools. Therefore, when I give an assignment I do not restrict them to just using Adobe Photoshop or Illustrator but provide them with a digital toolbox full of different types of tools. By the time students reach the infographic lesson they have already become familiar with digital tools for photo editing and digital painting. For this assignment I start with demonstrating how you can create different types of graphs and charts using spreadsheet software like Microsoft Excel and how you can copy and paste your charts and graphs into an image editor to further customize its appearance. I also share online tools like ManyEyes http://www-958.ibm.com/software/data/cognos/manyeyes, Gapminder http://www.gapminder.org, and Picktochart http://piktochart.com. I have them spend some time playing around with these tools, getting comfortable with them and exploring their capabilities and limitations.

At the end of the third day of this unit I give them their unit assignment: Find a piece of data or statistic from a credible source using design and visual rhetoric, and produce an infographic that easily leads viewers to misinterpretations. Make numbers tell a lie! I also provide students with a few sample data sets that they may use if they have difficulty finding a reliable data set on their own. The work they produce show how aesthetics can be more powerful than data.

The students then shared their infographics with one another. Emma Eubanks created an infographic on childhood obesity (Figure 4.1), and Emma Wood created an infographic on the use of DNA testing related to criminal justice (Figure 4.2). Anderson's students' work demonstrates how students can share their concerns about certain issues based on data to support their issues through the use of visually appealing infographics.

QR Codes

You or your students can also create QR (Quick Response) codes, which are barcode images representing any web-based text—a URL link, bookmark, e-mail, text, and so on—that can be scanned by a tablet or smartphone to access the link. To do so, you or your students can employ QR code scanners and reader tools listed on the website http://tinyurl.com/knnbwnu. You or your students enter a URL into one of these sites to create a QR image to provide students access to texts. See Richard Byrne's QR Codes Explained and Ideas for Classroom Use: http://tinyurl.com/d4jcrrk.

QR code images can also be added to e-book textbooks or files or cut out and pasted into print textbooks or handouts to provide students with additional resources or activities; students can also add their own images to their blogs, websites, or reports. You can use QR codes for differentiated instructions to provide students with tasks or resources—for example, having groups of students study different aspects of the same topic or issue (Burns, 2013). And you can use QR codes to create scavenger hunts in

Figure 4.1.   Emma Eubanks: Childhood Obesity. *Source: Screenshot of Child Obesity used with permission of Emma Eubanks.*

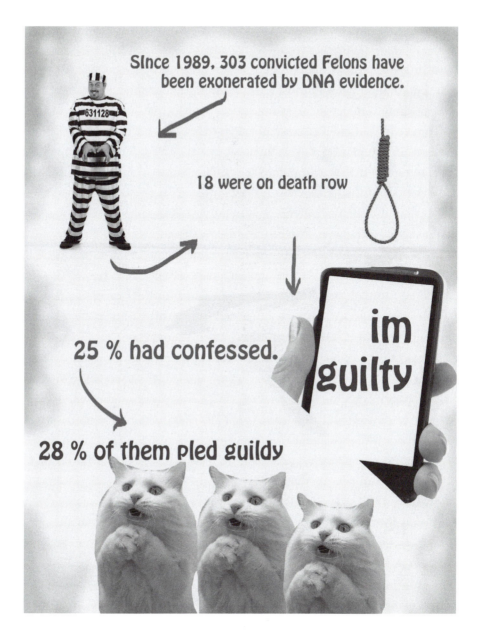

Figure 4.2.   Emma Wood: DNA Evidence. *Source: Screenshot of DNA Evidence used with permission of Emma Wood.*

conjunction with the SCVNGR Android app http://tinyurl.com/jwho43y or iOS app http://tinyurl.com/lstxeeq for information that leads to solving a problem or formulating an answer (Hertz, 2011).

Outlining Tools and Apps

Students can employ outlining tools and apps listed on the website http://tinyurl.com/ kb8nkks for organizing and planning writing or presentations through listing ideas or topics and determining the logical and hierarchical relationships among these ideas or topics. One major advantage of digital outlining tools is that they can provide students with ways to visually scaffold or organize topics so that they perceive the logical relationships between their topics, as well as how some topics function as subtopics to major topics. For some tools, they can color code their topics to determine how they may clump. It is important that students use these outlining tools several times so that they gain a sense of comfort in using them for generating and organizing their ideas.

Students may initially have difficulty learning to employ an outlining tool, but over time as they become accustomed to using it, they may then be more proficient in using it. Analysis of ninth graders using an outlining tool found that they benefited from repeated use of the tool; initial use of the tool had no effect on the quality of their writing, while repeated use of the tool resulted in improvements in their organization and reduced mental effort (De Smet, Brand-Gruwel, Broekkamp, & Kirschner, 2012).

One advantage of outlining is that rather than attempting to generate an organized, readable draft from scratch, students can plan out their ideas or topics without concern for organization or readability because they are the audience for their outlines. As with freewriting or brainstorming, this means that they can cognitively focus just on idea generation and not be concerned about structure or expression (Galbraith et al., 2005). They need not be prematurely concerned about the linear organization of ideas or topics because they can reorder their ideas or topics later.

While it was often assumed that students should begin their work by creating an outline that will serve to guide their writing or presentation, one problem is that they may not have developed ideas or topics to create an outline, suggesting that they need to first engage in some freewriting or brainstorming to create ideas or topics (Elbow, 1973). Moreover, if they first create an outline prior to drafting, they may believe that they are then obligated to follow their outline without making changes in their draft. A more productive and realistic approach to outlining is for students to engage in it throughout the development of their ideas or topics through some initial freewriting or brainstorming; they can even draft some text and then step back and create an outline to help them structure what they have written as an unfolding blueprint or framework that guides their thinking while continuing to revise their outline as they generate new ideas or topics.

Digital Mapping Tools

Consistent with the digital practice of defining connections among texts, another important set of visual tools consists of digital mapping tools listed on the website http://tinyurl.com/m73ue5r. In using these tools, students are creating visual representations of the intertextual and logical connections among certain topics, issues, or components of a text, event, presentation, or project. To do so, they identify key words or ideas as nodes to insert into circles or boxes and then draw lines between the circles or boxes to define the logical relationships among words or ideas, for example, whether a subtopic serves as an illustrative example of a major topic. Maps may also include color coding so that students can use different colors to represent different nodes as well as include images or links in lieu of words for their nodes (Beach & O'Brien, 2014).

By sharing the same digital maps, a group of students working on the same project can visually represent their thinking for one another so that they are literally and figuratively "on the same page." Students can then pose questions to one another based on their maps—for example, questions about the need to further expand their topics perceived to be lacking information on their maps.

Students can also use their maps to define an overall focus for their projects. While students' maps may begin with a focus on certain topics, as they develop their maps, students may note that their focus has shifted when they begin to develop other sections of their maps, signaling the need to alter their overall focus.

Digital mapping helps students to expand and elaborate on concepts and ideas through defining connections between these concepts and ideas. For example, the digital map in Figure 4.3, created using bubbl.us https://bubbl.us, describes different types of digital tools described in this book and the relationships among the use of these tools.

To create maps, students can simply draw their own maps on a whiteboard or use drawing tools (for uses of whiteboards for drawing or mapping: http://tinyurl.com/manrtgd). For example, for responding to *The Great Gatsby* (Fitzgerald, 1992), students created mind maps http://tinyurl.com/myck49x to portray the relationships between different characters and themes in the novel (Weinstein, 2012).

One of the more robust mapping tools is the desktop and iOS Inspiration tool http://www.inspiration.com, which is free for creating up to five maps, but costs $9.99 for the iOS app and $9.00 a month for the desktop version, which is relatively expensive when there are a lot of free alternatives. However, Inspiration does include a range of different components. Students can import files, links, and images into their maps and then share their maps on Pages, iTunes, or Dropbox. They can also move between a "Diagram" (map) and an "Outline" perspective so that they can use the material from their maps in their essay writing.

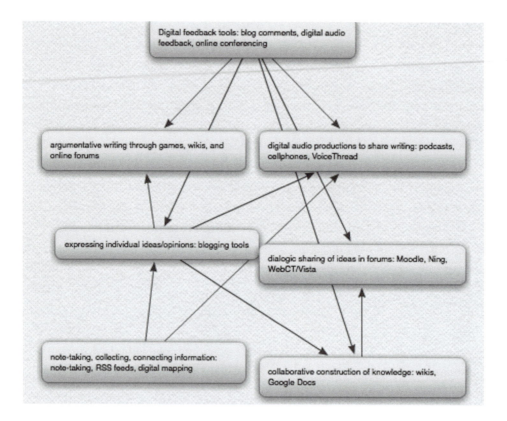

Figure 4.3. Map of Different Digital Tools

Michael Hasapopoulos describes his use of Inspiration for writing about *Hamlet* in his 12th-grade literature class at Armstrong High School, Robbinsdale, Minnesota:

> In my 12th grade AP Literature class, the students have been tackling the text that seems to be the ultimate challenge for readers—*Hamlet*. Needless to say, the classic revenge tragedy is regarded as Shakespeare's finest (if not most popular and produced) tragedy, and over the course of six years of teaching *Hamlet* to the Advanced Placement student, I have discovered that the challenges the play presents to students lie along two main lines: the myriad convolutions of plot and the myriad characters that come and go throughout the protagonist's experience. Over the course of shaping a curriculum for Hamlet that addresses student discussion, interaction with the text via journaling and student dramatic presentations, and soliloquy analysis, the challenges have persisted.
>
> Not one to accept academic defeat easily, I used some aspects of a previous curriculum devised for a research project on the use of technology in the high school classroom. Coincidentally (or perhaps not due to this teacher's love of Shakespearean tragedy), the technology-based unit centered on *Macbeth*. For the *Macbeth* unit, students read, journaled, discussed, and tested entirely via the technology of the comput-

er and of the Internet. I had created a website specifically for the class and the project, where students would go for assignments, readings, and download any activities involved with the play. Much of what we did as a class centered on student-directed searches and student-directed on-line discussions (via a specialized discussion site: http://www.proboards.com). The results of the study returned quite favorably, with the main conclusion that most of the students in our particular demographic had considerable technology savvy, which acted as a motivator to learn and interact with the text.

I thought that this would be a good way in which to augment the students' journal assignment, which was to journal each act of Hamlet focusing specifically on character development, use of language (literary and rhetorical terms), and a passage analysis (their choice). Here's the journal assignment:

Conduct your Act III journal using Inspiration. Remember to focus on character development/depth, plot nuances, language use (literary and rhetorical terms), and your passage analysis. You may use any kind of organizational structure that fits your fancy. I think it is a good way of breaking down, say, a soliloquy for passage analysis, analyzing character and character traits, breaking through to the subtext of character speech, commenting on literary devices and setting, etc. Be creative!

Students were able to use the Inspiration software to interact in any way they saw fit with the text; the software is particularly effective when isolating the requirements of the journal assignment: the character study, language analysis, passage analysis.

The software significantly aided in students' ability to place the text in a manageable format in which to break it down into patterns and to make interpretive leaps from the analysis. By having the information presented in one clear, colorful, creative manner, I believe, also aided in the engagement that students demonstrated in the assignment.

Another robust mapping tool is MindMeister http://tinyurl.com/n9sxoqk for both desktops and iPads/Chromebooks. As with Inspiration, students can import files, links, and images into their maps as well as export their maps as PDF, image, Word, or PowerPoint files. They can employ different colors, icons, and themes to generate visually appealing maps.

Students can also use mind maps to portray ideas, questions, or topics that emerge during brainstorming or discussions to create a visual depiction of their ideas, questions, or topics. They can revise their maps as the discussion evolves to portray shifts in their formulation of ideas, questions, or topics. For example, in participating in an online role-play described in the preface, students created "argument maps" projected on a screen for viewing while they were caucusing in their classroom groups to identify the different roles related to their pro/con positions on the issue as well as lines among these roles to portray allegiances.

Another interesting mapping tool is the myHistro tool http://www.myhistro.com for viewing or creating stories as timelines that are displayed on a geographical map that can include images, videos, or text. For example, students can create myHistro maps to create a narrative timeline of their family history to portray different places that their previous family generations inhabited.

Use of Digital Geographic Maps

Students can also employ geographic mapping tools listed on the website http://tinyurl. com/m73ue5r for use in writing about topics or issues requiring an understanding of certain geographic places. Students can connect to databases of information about a region so that they perceive, add, or remove different features or topics (often represented by pins) on a map—for example, icons representing historical sites.

For engaging in place-based writing about specific locations or for writing about the impact of climate change on specific regions of the world, students can use Google Maps, Google Earth, or Apple Maps to capture images to include in their writing. For studying literature, students can use Google Lit Trips http://www.googlelittrips.com/ GoogleLit/Home.html, which portray writers' geographic locations related to their texts. For writing about past events, students can employ the WhatWasThere http:// tinyurl.com/7so8jx6, It Happened Here http://tinyurl.com/7cvvjea, or HistoryPin http:// tinyurl.com/6qw9apg tools to access historical photos and information about historical events with images that can provide information about changes over time of the same site.

SUMMARY

In this chapter, we describe the use of a range of different tools for curating information and texts for use in understanding and creating texts. Use of these tools helps students organize often complex information in ways that enhance their understanding of issues or ideas, as well as communicate information in visually appealing ways to their audiences.

In the next chapter, we describe the use of tools for students to formulate responses to texts through note-taking, sharing annotation responses to texts on social bookmarking sites, and responding to texts using social networking sites.

5

NETWORKING AND CONNECTING THROUGH NOTE-TAKING, SOCIAL BOOKMARKING, AND SOCIAL MEDIA

For teaching his English classes, Nicholas Provenzano (2012) organizes his instruction around the use of Evernote notebooks:

> For my classes, I created four different notebooks to separate the different notes and information. I created notebooks for assignments, notes, handouts and stories. These notebooks house all of the information my students will need over the course of the school year. These are notebooks I create and share with them. It has really helped organize my class and provide the best information for my students.

He also uses Evernote for easy sharing with his students through e-mail or by sharing a link to an Evernote notebook on a class website:

> Since I use Evernote for lesson planning, most of the time I copy the homework from the lesson plan and paste it into a new note in the assignment notebook. I love this quick and easy homework sharing method. I used to spend hours every week updating my school website and making copies of assignment sheets. I can now make one edit in my Evernote notebooks and all 150 of my students have instant access to the assignment. Very few programs offer that type of immediate information sharing. Using the assignments' notebook, I am able to upload documents, rubrics and other information that my students can access from home or on their mobile device.

He also scans writing into Evernote to share on his Shared Notebook (Provenzano, 2013). In addition, he can e-mail documents directly into his notebooks. He then uses the Evernote Clearly feature to highlight parts of articles or reports, as well as record audio notes using the Audio Notes features. Provenzano's use of the Evernote note-taking tool demonstrates how digital note-taking tools can be used for fostering writing and organizing instruction.

Related Common Core State Standards

- *Grades 6–8:* Use technology, including the Internet, to produce, publish, and update individual or shared writing products in response to ongoing feedback, including new arguments or information.
- *Grades 6–12:* Use technology, interact and collaborate with others.
- *Grade 7:* Use technology, including the Internet, to produce and publish writing and present the relationships between information and ideas clearly and efficiently.

In this chapter, given the importance of students formulating their responses to reading in their own words, we describe the use of digital reading and writing tools for sharing information and responses to texts using notes and annotations through note-taking and social bookmarking tools, as well as participating in social media/networking sites. The primary focus of the chapter is on helping students to formulate their responses to texts to develop ideas through collaborative sharing of digital notes or annotations, as well as participating with others through social networking. We also describe the use of discussion tools in the next chapter, as well as other collaborative writing tools in chapter 7.

Much of this chapter revolves around addressing the social practices of connectivity, interactivity, and collaboration—social practices associated with the use of the affordances of digital tools to mediate these practices related to the Common Core State Standards (Council of Chief State School Officers and the National Governors Association, 2010).

DIGITAL NOTE-TAKING TOOLS

A major tool for both understanding and creating texts involves the use of digital note-taking tools listed on the website http://tinyurl.com/kjuwa2r. By taking notes in response to a text, students are more likely to focus their attention on that text, leading them to formulate their own responses to a text, presentation, or video. Rather than just copying text verbatim, in taking notes students need to reformulate or translate the text in their own words so that they are integrating the information and ideas according to their own prior knowledge or beliefs. To help students go beyond just regurgitating text, you can have them employ dual-entry note-taking where in one section of the page, they may copy/paste in or restate/summarize the text. Then, in another section, they formulate their own interpretations or reflections about that text, an approach that encourages them to go beyond restating text to reflecting on and interpreting that text. You can also model your own note-taking to the class by modeling how you reformulate ideas.

One advantage of using digital note-taking is that students can take notes and import texts or images to add to their notes—for example, copying/pasting sections of their reading and then adding their notes to that reading. While many note-taking tools such as Evernote have their own storage process, students can easily store their notes on Dropbox, iCloud, OneDrive, or Google Drive as well as move them directly into Word, Pages, iAWriter, or Google Docs for developing their drafts.

Challenges in Taking Notes

Students indicate that they often have difficulty taking notes in terms of capturing key ideas in a lecture or text and contextualizing those ideas relevant to their purposes for learning (Boyle, 2011). Because less able readers have difficulty inferring key ideas, they simply copy or regurgitate a presenter's language or quote from a text without generating their own summaries (Ramsay & Sperling, 2011). You can therefore support this contextualization by assisting students in clarifying their purposes for studying or writing about a topic. For example, students are writing a paper on the topic of family conflicts as portrayed in literature. You can assist students by determining whether they have a clear sense of purpose for writing their paper. Then, when they are taking notes, they are thinking about how they will be using those notes in formulating their thesis and supporting reasons.

Mayer's (2008) SOR model of learning a note-taking strategy can help students contextualize their note-taking by focusing on the following:

Selection: attending to the relevancy of the information in terms of the purposes for learning or subsequent writing.

Organization: organizing the information according to a coherent mental representation by making connections between the information.

Relating: determining how the information relates to current prior knowledge of a topic.

Students can also use the CUES strategy: cluster (recording three to six key points), use (listening for cues from the teacher on how to organize information), enter (add in notes about the key point), and summarize (use keywords to categorize the key points)

(Boyle, 2011). Middle school students who employed this strategy generated more notes and more key points than students not employing this strategy (Boyle, 2011).

While students may have difficulty going beyond copying texts to using notes to summarize their interpretations of presentations or texts, that does not necessarily mean that students are not learning from completing notes. One study found that simply copying a sentence from each paragraph from a text may be just as productive as summarizing paragraphs in that knowing which sentence to copy to capture the main idea of a paragraph entails some level of interpretation of the main idea in that para-graph (Horney et al., 2009).

Another challenge has to do with how quickly students take notes. If they take notes too slowly, they may miss certain key ideas, but if they take notes too quickly, they may not be reflecting on the ideas to translate them into their own words (Boyle, 2011). This suggests providing time for students during your own or their peers' presentations to pause to allow time for students to reflect on the presentation through their note-taking.

Students' ability to take notes is also influenced by their prior knowledge about a certain topic (Gil, Ávila, & Ferrer, 2011; Wetzels, Kester, van Merriënboer, & Broers, 2011). High school students who had low prior knowledge of a topic had to exert much higher mental effort and had less efficiency in keeping notes than students with high prior knowledge. This suggests having students use their note-taking to develop their own questions based on their prior knowledge, which they can use to extract relevant information and ideas from texts to construct their own knowledge.

Different Note-Taking Strategies

Jim Burke identifies a range of different types of note-taking strategies http://tinyurl.com/jqk7r that vary according to formatting or organization. One familiar note-taking system is the Cornell system, which involves the five R's of recording information or facts, reducing or summarizing that information or meaningful facts down to main ideas, reciting the key concept or ideas, reflecting on one's personal perspectives on these concepts or ideas, and reviewing to determine how to employ what one has learned for further writing or presentations. You can use Google Docs templates to create a template to scaffold students' use of these five strategies (for an example, see http://tinyurl.com/n2xauw3).

Students can also use the Cornell Notes PDF Generator http://www.cornell-notes.com (R. Stewart, 2013) to scaffold their note-taking based on the traditional Cornell method of dividing up a page to put their notes on the right side, keywords and ques-tions on the left side, and summaries at the bottom of the page.

Handwritten/"Sketch" Notes

There are also tools for use in creating handwritten digital notes, as opposed to typing notes, by using a stylus with a tablet and a note-taking or drawing tool. One advantage of using handwritten notes is that students may not have access to a keyboard for typing their notes. Students may also actually prefer to employ handwritten notes because they can also draw pictures, diagrams, or doodles as part of their note-taking. Evernote http://www.evernote.com can be used to combine photos of handwritten notes with typed notes or audio notes so that students can create their typed or audio notes in response to a picture of notes (Holland, 2013a). For example, eighth-grade students took handwritten notes on paper, typed a summary of those notes in Evernote along with a picture of their handwritten notes, and then added those notes to a shared Evernote classroom notebook for the teacher to review (Holland, 2013a). Students can also use Skitch http://tinyurl.com/7zdk8rb for drawing on images saved in Evernote to add arrows, drawing, figures, and so on, to an image.

Students can also add photos of whiteboard notes or PowerPoint slides as well as images to their notes. For example, Vancouver teacher Brad Ovenell-Carter employs a stylus with the iPad Paper app on his iPad to create "sketch-notes" that can then be saved to Evernote or Google Drive (Glader, 2013). He posits that the use of "visual note-taking," "sketch-notes," or "sketchnoting"

> inverts the traditional note-taking process. . . . You are not trying to capture everything. You are looking for high-level ideas. I never write any piece of trivial knowledge down that I can look up later. . . . When I come away from a conference, I have a better idea of what the speaker was trying to say.

In his class, he has some students assume the role of note-takers while others assume roles of students drawing on the whiteboard; students then take photos of notes to add to class files on Storify (Glader, 2013).

Wendi Pillars (2013) describes how she uses sketchnoting to model her creation of visual depictions or metaphors of her thinking. She suggests that for students who are intimidated by sketching to focus simply on capturing the idea without being concerned with the artistic quality of a sketch.

Students can use sketchnoting to portray their visual responses to their reading through creating visual images, charts, or graphs. In responding to literature, in addition to or in relationship with their notes, they can use handwritten notes to draw their portrayals of characters, events, settings, or themes—for example, drawing figures to represent chapters and mapping connections among these characters (Schmidt, 2013). Based on the idea of students' uses of visual representations to portray their interpretations, you could assess their sketchnoting using the following questions:

- How does the student identify plot?
- What design choices does the student make?
- How does the student display understanding of the reading?
- Does anything in the response identify misunderstanding?
- What do I like about this response as an assessor? (Schmidt, 2013, p. 56)

Using Audio Dictation Note-Taking

Another approach to taking notes involves the use of audio dictation note-taking tools listed on http://tinyurl.com/kd6oura including Google Voice (to record on Chromebooks), Siri (to record into Pages), Dragon NaturallySpeaking (Windows only), OneNote (Windows only) http://tinyurl.com/ys5wou, Dragon Dictate for Mac or MacSpeech Scribe http://tinyurl.com/4qkh5dr, or Dragon Dictation http://tinyurl.com/ylgqctp. Students can often record audio notes in a more spontaneous manner, resulting in more extensive notes than with written notes.

Students can also employ recording note-taking pens such as Livescribe at http://www.livescribe.com (for a video on the use of Livescribe pens in schools, see http://tinyurl.com/pwr7mlu and http://tinyurl.com/ockouou). Use of these pens allow students to handwrite their notes as well as drawings that are then synced with a tablet or computer using the Lifescribe+ App at http://tinyurl.com/nwhz93u, as well as record their own or others' audio that is synced to their written notes. In addition to the Livescribe 3 or Smartpen, there are a number of other note-taking pens—the Mobile Notes Pro, Sky Wifi Smartpen, Echo Smartpen, Staedtler Pen 990, Wacom Inkling, IRISNotes 2 Executive and IRISNotes 1 for Smartphones, LogiPen Notes, Capturx for OneNote, and DigiMemo—as well as pens with built-in microphones that record audio and video cameras that can record video. Some also employ tablet apps or paper that students can use to access audio associated with certain notes when they tap on those notes. In addition to using recording pens or audio notes apps, students can employ digital voice recorders produced by Apple, M-Audio, Olympus, Panasonic, RCA, Samson, or Sony to record their own notes, along with interviews, lectures, or presentations (Ash, 2009).

One advantage of recording notes is that students can record not only their own thoughts but also interviews, discussions, or lectures to have a stored record of audio files for use in reviewing or recalling later. For example, students engaged in oral history projects can record interviews along with their verbal observations of certain people and places (Ash, 2009). They can then sync their audio with their written notes so that, for example, in recording a lecture, they can connect their written notes to the lecture.

Use of these audio note-taking tools can be supportive of students who are struggling with or are apprehensive about writing, particularly students who are learning disabled as well as English-language learners. These students can record their notes about what they learned in a class for later review. Because these students may be more proficient with their speech than with their writing, they can dictate their thoughts to create a transcript and then use that transcript to revise their writing. The fact that they are recording their thoughts means that they often voice ideas in a spontaneous manner, which reduces their apprehension about expressing their ideas.

For students who have difficulty reading texts to take notes, students can use the Speak Selection feature on iPads; students can highlight a text and have it read to them (to turn on the Speak Selection feature, select Settings → General → Accessibility → Speak Selection, then slide the Speak Selection option to On) (Kelly, 2013).

Students may be more comfortable in dictating their thoughts when they are talking with others. So, students could pair up and dictate their thoughts to each other, with Student B simply providing positive reactions or questions to encourage Student A to continue talking. Students could then review each other's transcripts and assist each other in making further revisions. As they become more comfortable using audio note-taking, students may then gain confidence in their verbal expression of ideas, leading to developing a sense of voice (Beach & O'Brien, 2014).

Modeling Note-Taking Through Sharing Notes

One advantage of the use of note-taking tools is that you can model the use of social practices involved in sharing your notes or outlines on the whiteboard, overhead, or computer. You can connect your own or students' tablets wirelessly to a projector to model note-taking practices projected on a large screen or whiteboard. To wirelessly connect students' tablets or Chromebooks to a whiteboard, you can employ iPad apps such as Doceri Interactive Whiteboard http://doceri.com, Idea Flight http://tinyurl.com/n4jcwyp, SyncSpace http://tinyurl.com/ls7g97s, Jot Whiteboard http://tinyurl.com/l5bfs7t, Splashtop Whiteboard http://tinyurl.com/kh5w38v, Stage http://tinyurl.com/k5popvz, Android apps such as SyncSpace http://tinyurl.com/n62z34s, or Splashtop Whiteboard http://tinyurl.com/mxm262u. Or you can use a class Twitter or back-channel tools, such as TodaysMeet http://todaysmeet.com, for sharing responses to presentations or videos on one screen next to another screen showing a video.

In sharing note-taking, you and your students can then orally reflect on the processes employed in creating their notes or outlines, discussing the challenges in doing so. The fact that students then have a shared written record of notes from class presentations or discussions can serve to foster further reflection about what they have learned in a class. Students can also create "exit reflection" notes at the end of a class regarding what they learned for a particular class meeting to share verbally or online, reflections that can provide you with insights into students' learning in that class.

SOCIAL BOOKMARKING TOOLS

A second set of tools that we include in this chapter consist of social bookmarking tools listed on the website http://tinyurl.com/mbu5qfv. Social bookmarking involves collecting websites, storing them on a social bookmarking site, and adding tags to those links. Students can then share their collections of websites with peers for collaboratively constructing knowledge about certain topics or issues.

You can then create groups for students to share their links with members of an entire class or within subgroups of students working on specific group projects. For example, a group of students working together to generate a report may use social bookmarking to share links to sites on that topic, along with adding tags on pages related to that topic (for more on social bookmarking and tagging sites: http://tinyurl.com/mbu5qfv).

One widely used social bookmarking tool is Diigo for desktops at http://diigo.com to add to a desktop browser, or the Diigo Browser tool for iPad or iPhone at http://tinyurl.com/43nfl8t, Diigo Web Collector at http://tinyurl.com/lzrwh9k, or Diigo Android app at http://tinyurl.com/mggqmgu to add to a browser for bookmarking certain sites. You can use Diigo to set up special Educator accounts to add students to a class "group" account along with privacy settings (see http://www.diigo.com/education) for sharing bookmarks with members of that group.

One important aspect of bookmarking sites involves adding keyword tags to identify topics addressed in a web page/site. As we noted in terms of search strategies in chapter 3 and curation in chapter 4, the ability to effectively tag pages/sites in terms of their overall thematic focus is an important reading strategy. Keyword tags are also central to the use of Twitter hashtags and image searches using Flickr and Google Images.

Annotating Digital Texts

A key component of social bookmarking tools involves annotating digital texts. Annotations have been used since the medieval period to share responses to texts (Jackson, 2001). Students can use Diigo and other social bookmarking tools to add "sticky note" annotations to online texts to share with the entire class or with members of subgroups, annotations that can serve as the basis for discussions about a text. In using Diigo, students highlight a section of a text and add a sticky note annotation that pops up when others click on a sticky note icon. By doing so, they engage in collaborative discussions on a topic fueled by sharing of questions or alternative perspectives.

In addition to using social bookmarking tools, students can employ web and PDF annotation tools listed on the website http://tinyurl.com/jvhbs6z to add annotations or comments to a website or PFD file. Middle school students in a Bay Area school used Diigo and DocAS apps for adding annotations to readings in their science classes (Castek & Beach, 2013). Seventh-grade students read articles on the pros and cons of wind energy related to the use of wind turbines and then used Diigo on their iPads to add annotations to these articles. Students posed questions such as "How much does the wind turbine cost?" and "How many birds does the wind turbine kill in a year?" (Castek & Beach, 2013, p. 559). These questions served to prompt other students to respond to those questions. For example, when one student posed the question "Why are they complaining about the turbines? It doesn't even look bad," another responded with "That's what you think, but have you actually been near a wind turbine or lived around one?" (p. 559). Students also built on one another's annotations to extend their interactions, noting that "wind energy is free and keeps the air clean instead of polluting the air," "people could install wind turbines to generate energy," "coal isn't a good source of energy," and "wind power has many advantages that we could use" (p. 559).

Based on a review of these annotations as a form of prewriting, students then drew on them to generate their own essays, essays that reflected the competing perspectives voiced in these annotations. One student's essay on the pros and cons of wind energy drew on the competing perspectives derived from the annotations:

> Everything has something bad about it, wind energy is renewable but sometimes it is a waste of energy. In my opinion, it's a bad thing because if one of the wind turbines is broken, there's no law for that company to fix them. Yes, some people might say its renewable and causes no pollution. Wind energy has some things that are good about it but overall it's a waste of space and money to build. (p. 560)

This student noted the positive aspects of wind energy as something that was renewable, as well as the problems with wind energy by drawing on the class's annotations.

In two sixth-grade science classes in the same school in which students were studying climate change, students were reading essays about the Mauna Loa observatory to collect data on carbon dioxide levels related to climate change (Castek, Beach, et al., in press).

As illustrated in Figure 5.1, students added Diigo annotations to these essays, resulting in discussions about the issues. Analysis of the students' annotations indicated that students were responding to one another in a dialogic manner as opposed to simply responding to the text. They were posing and responding to questions, stating claims, summarizing what the text or other students shared, disagreeing with or challenging peers, extending peers' ideas with more evidence, and clarifying ideas when misinformation or a misunderstanding was shared.

In focus group discussions, students indicated that they preferred the use of Diigo to handwritten annotations given the ease of use in adding annotations. They also noted that attaching sticky notes to specific places in the text encouraged them to focus on details in the text. Because students were receiving annotations from members of two different classes, they were exposed to a wide range of perspectives that fostered collaborative argumentative writing. The students' teacher noted that sharing different annotations meant that the students were exposed to a range of different perspectives that they would not have formulated on their own.

Annotations can also be used to support reading instruction. For example, they can be used to help students reflect on how their purposes for reading can shape their focus and interpretations. One teacher had students annotate a description of contents in a house as perceived by a thief and a real estate agent based on differences among their own purpose for reading, the purpose of the thief, and the purpose of the real estate agent; they used different highlighting colors to show how these different purposes would focus on certain words in the text, highlighting that reflects the students' metacognitive thinking that can be used to assess their learning (Brahier, 2006).

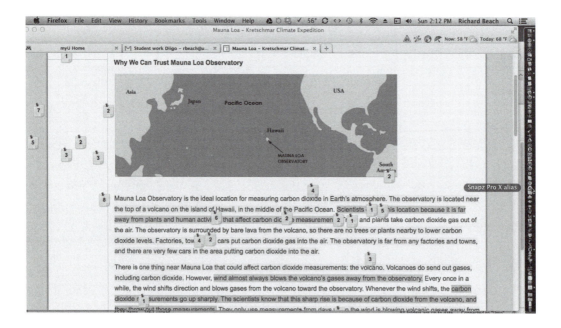

Figure 5.1.   Students' Use of Diigo Sticky Notes. *Source: Screenshot of students' use of Diigo as part of a research study approved by Portland State University.*

SOCIAL MEDIA/NETWORKING TOOLS

As noted in the preface, students are increasingly using a range of social media/networking tools—Twitter, Facebook, Pinterest, Instagram, Google Plus, Snapchat, Vine—for social interaction with their peers and family members (Gover & Selleck, 2013). They devote an average of 5 hours a day in online activities, with 90% engaging in some form of social networking and 75% maintaining their own page within social networks (Common Sense Media, 2012). Thirty-three percent prefer texting; 7%, use of a social networking site; and only 4%, talking on their phones (Common Sense Media, 2012). As of 2013, 24% of adolescents use Twitter, up from 16% in 2011; the typical Facebook user has 300 friends; and 90% share photos on social networking sites (Madden et al., 2013). They are increasingly aware of issues of privacy associated with uses of social networking—for example, the extent to which they share private information or problematic photos on their Facebook pages (Lenhart et al., 2011).

Given this extensive use of social networking tools outside of school, teachers are increasingly using these tools within schools. Sixty percent of junior high schools employ social networking/media tools at least twice a week (Van Vooren & Corey, 2013). The challenge remains as to how to harness use of these tools for academic purposes (Barnes, 2012).

Facebook

The most widely used social networking site is Facebook. As previously noted, while there are indications of a decline in the use of Facebook by young people, given a corresponding increase in the number of adults using Facebook (Duggan & Brenner, 2013), many adolescents and college students continue to employ Facebook, particularly in terms of affiliations with certain groups. One major change in Facebook is that students 13 to 17 years old can post status updates, videos, and images for public consumption, as opposed to just their friends, a move perceived as providing marketing people with information to target advertising to students (Goel, 2013). However, because Facebook requires that they post this material under their actual identities, they then are more reluctant to post problematic comments.

Given its use as a tool for creating social relationships in a public arena, one major issue in using Facebook in the classroom is the challenge of merging students' informal social experiences with formal academic learning while maintaining distinctions between a teacher's and a student's roles (Aydin, 2012). At one university, faculty members were more reluctant than students to use Facebook for instructional purposes (Roblyer, McDaniel, Webb, Herman, & Witty, 2010). All of this reflects an ambiguous stance toward the use of Facebook in the classroom. Allen (2012) notes,

> Any use of Facebook will necessarily confront both teachers and students with the fact that, in an online environment which is so closely entwined with real identities, real places and persistent communication, they are always explicitly negotiating the boundaries between formal and informal. In other words, Facebook does not allow us to separate formal and informal uses in education. Its design and social affordances are all about confusion and overlap, while its computer-mediated format also trumps the traditional use of time and place as a means of enforcing the separations between people based on role and function. (p. 224)

Dana Boyd (2014) also indicates the further challenge of coping with what she defines as "context collapse" associated with the blurring of private and public so that in sharing writing on social networking sites, students have difficulty identifying their audience to contextualize their writing in terms of their purpose. While students may assume that, for example, on Facebook, their "friends" are their audience, they can also sense that there are invisible audiences reading their postings. Not knowing who is reading their postings creates the "context collapse" challenge where students do not have a clear sense of the rhetorical context given multiple potential audiences.

Given that they are writing for largely invisible audiences on Facebook, students may be unsure or anxious about adopting a critical stance to share with their peers (Pangrazio, 2013). Publicly sharing critical analysis on Facebook also entails students critiquing of their own participation on a site on which they are already actively participating.

One topic for analysis has to do with whether students construct their identities on Facebook according to expectations created by the Facebook world. An analysis of 13- to 14-year-old girls' interview discussions of their use of Facebook indicated that they experienced a lot of pressure to construct an identity that was consistent with the norms for what constitutes an ideal Facebook identity:

> Through both subtle and overt means, Facebook encourages an identity that is extroverted, outgoing and even sometimes narcissistic; most importantly, one that would be approved by their peer group. The pursuit of such an identity made it difficult for the participants to critically engage with the site, as they become immersed in the social reality of Facebook. While the participants may have had some degree of critical awareness of the site, they were unable to maintain this critical approach as they set out to achieve the 'ideal' self, set out in their personal profile. (Pangrazio, 2013, p. 43)

This potential blurring of the private and public suggests that for use of Facebook in the classroom, we recommend that you create a separate Facebook class account just for your students so that their postings are shared only within your class. Or, students may simply use Facebook on their own to create closed study groups to assist one another in completing class assignments without having any formal classroom Facebook group

(Estus, 2010). Doing so then distinguishes between their academic use of Facebook and their own personal, social use of Facebook.

One benefit of using Facebook in the classroom is that students are acquiring the use of the social practices described in chapter 2—the ability to interact online with others, work collaboratively within groups, or construct online identities. In one survey, 83% of parents perceive the benefits of their children acquiring use of these practices through sites such as Facebook as outweighing the potential dangers, with more than half believing that participation on social networking sites makes their children more open-minded (McClatchy-Tribune Information, 2012).

Another potential benefit is that students may be more willing to write about personal issues using Facebook, something that may be particularly important for students who may be reluctant to self-disclose personal matters, while recognizing the challenges of sharing personal issues with peers (Simmons, 2013). College students preferred Facebook as a more informal, supportive context for sharing ideas as compared with Moodle, which is perceived as a more controlled, formal, instructor-driven space (Waycott, Deng, & Tavares, 2013).

Students' use of Facebook also serves to enhance their social capital in terms of bridging connections based on weak ties or bonding with others based on strong ties, particularly for students with low self-esteem who might be reluctant to make face-to-face connections (Ellison, Lampe, Steinfield, & Vitak, 2010). An analysis of 2,368 college students' use of Facebook found that higher users did devote more time to participation in campus activities; their high use was not related to time devoted to studying (Junco, 2012).

You can also have students reflect on their uses of Facebook. In his first-year college writing classes, David Coad (2013) has his students write about how they use Facebook versus how Facebook influences them in terms of the rhetorical practices they employ. Or, students could observe a peer's participation on Facebook and write a paper analyzing his or her persona or ethos (Balzhiser et al., 2011). The assignment prompt included the following:

> In other words, if we knew nothing about this person other than what appears in this space, how might you characterize this person? In concluding, use what you know or what you have researched about such spaces and college students' uses of them in order to speculate about how this person's persona or use of the space compares with others or about technology generally.

From observing a peer's posting, photos, friend lists, connections, and group memberships, students were asked to identify certain patterns related to the peer's relationships, friendships, power, beliefs, personal attributes, and so on, that suggest the persona or ethos the peer is constructing on Facebook:

What do you think this person's persona or ethos represents culturally? Do you find "ethnic," "class," "national," or other similar significances? How reliable or valid are your arguments? In what areas of your analysis are you most/least confident? Could others come to different conclusions by looking at the same information? How might the person being analyzed respond to your analysis? What additional information would you need to make more accurate and thorough analyses?

Students then engaged in peer reviews with the peers they were writing about to provide feedback about the validity of their observations.

This assignment provides students with a useful focus on an understanding of how writers construct personae or ethos on Facebook through their postings and images, as well as for use of their writing to gain their audience's positive identification. At the same time, in using this assignment with students, it would be important to stress the need to avoid making negative judgments about peers based on some netiquette guidelines that you share with your students.

Twitter

Twitter is a popular microblogging social networking tool that can be used for a variety of purposes (for tools involving use of Twitter: http://tinyurl.com/ldnplxr). There has been increased use of Twitter by young adults since 2010 and a related decline in use of Facebook by younger users (Duggan & Brenner, 2013; Ingber, 2013; A. Smith & Brenner, 2012).

Use of Twitter fosters the social practice of interactivity and connectivity in that users typically include links to sites as well as hashtags with keywords that assist users in searching for or connecting with topics. Users also select certain other users to follow based on their expertise or popularity. Use of Twitter involves the social practice of constructing identities through asserting oneself as part of a larger community dialogue (Murthy, 2012).

In addition to the primary Twitter app, a number of other related Twitter apps provide different formats for organizing and structuring tweet feeds listed on the website. There are other related resources for use in supporting Twitter, such as Twitdoc http://twitdoc.com for sharing documents and images on Twitter, TweetWallPro http://www.tweetwallpro.com for projecting tweets on a screen, GroupTweet http://www.grouptweet.com/ for creating a single Twitter account for members of a group to share their tweets, and TwtPol http://twtpoll.com to create surveys on Twitter.

To use Twitter, students need to complete their bios, as well as know how to "follow" not only students in your class but also people who are experts on certain topics of interest to students. Students can then share their links in their tweets or "retweet" others' tweets by repeating those tweets—for example, RT @rbeach. Students can also send tweets to specific people by using @ before that person's Twitter handle, as in @rbeach. And they can retweet others' tweets by hovering over a tweet, clicking on the "Retweet" link, confirming the selection of that tweet, and then clicking on the "Retweet" button. To add commentary to a retweet, students can copy/paste a tweet into their own message, add the letters "RT," "Retweet," or "retweeted" along with the author's @username, and then add a comment before the retweeted message.

To use Twitter in your classroom, you can first set up a Twitter class account or create a Twitter hashtag for a particular class—for example, #smithEnglish233pd4. You can then send out notices about assignments and deadline reminders to your students; in one study, this led to higher tests scores for eighth-grade students receiving tweets on Twitter compared to students who did not receive messages (Van Vooren, & Corey, 2013).

Students can share Tweets as part of the Do Now weekly activity sponsored by the PBS station KQED http://tinyurl.com/ke4f4ub. Students are given questions each week on current issues, science, or popular culture at the Do Now site http://kqed.org/donow. They can then respond on the site itself or by using Twitter using their own Twitter accounts.

Google+

Another social networking site is Google+. While it has not achieved the usage of a Facebook or Twitter, it does have some advantages for use in the classroom (for LiveBinders resources on use of Google+, see http://tinyurl.com/kjj3fpf created by Steven Anderson, 2013). One advantage of Google+ is the use of Circles, consisting of members of a group who may focus on and share responses to particular topics. For general social networking use, you can add people to your Google+ as "friends," "family," "acquaintances," or people you are following (to add people to Circles, see http://tinyurl.com/m4q9cgr). You can therefore create a Circle consisting of members of an entire class or create subgroup Circles based on specific topics or issues that you are discussing in your class. Your students can then share responses or resources to their peers within these Circles.

You or your students can also join public or private Communities organized around topics. For example, for acquiring and sharing information about technology integration, you can join the Google Apps for Education Community http://tinyurl.com/n6m1979, EdTech Community http://tinyurl.com/pzuu4019, or Connected Learning Community http://tinyurl.com/kfg4k25. Or, as with Circles, you can create a classroom Community by following these steps at http://tinyurl.com/mv5ztvc (Kharbach, 2012). For instructions on how students can sign up for Google+, see http://wiobyrne.com/signing-up-for-and-using-google-and-communities (O'Bryne, 2013).

Another advantage of Google+ is that you can then easily incorporate the use of other Google tools, such as Google Docs, Blogger, Forms, and Presentations, into use with Circles. For example, to share their analysis of a certain topic, students could use Google Forms to share information organized according to certain categories.

Social Networking Sites Designed for School Use

A large number of social networking sites are designed for use in schools, sites such as Edmodo, Schoology, Ning, eduClipper, Canvas, Lore, HaikuLearning, and Gaggle (for links to these and other sites: http://tinyurl.com/443pqj2). These sites, which we refer to throughout this book, can function as course management systems in that they include discussion forums and tools for collecting and sharing students' work.

Another social networking site is Youth Voices at http://youthvoices.net, which was launched in 2003 by teachers associated with the National Writing Project and the Teachers Teaching Teachers podcast at http://tinyurl.com/lb6wh4p to create a site that provides students with a sense of ownership in contributing material associated with their interests, needs, and issues. On this site, students from schools throughout the United States share their writing. A related site is sponsored by TakingITGlobal, GlobalKids, and the Asia Society, called Ymex.org (Youth Media Exchange) http://ymex.org, where students can share media and discussions addressing certain global issues. And students can participate on the Teens in Tech site http://teensintech.com to share and obtain information about technology.

Affordances of Social Networking Tools

Academic benefits of using social networking tools can be considered in terms of their affordances. Dana Boyd (2010) identifies four affordances of social networking tools: persistence, replicability, scalability, and searchability. Helping students use these tools for academic purposes entails helping them learn how to exploit use of these affordances.

Using these tools fosters persistence in that interactions are recorded and archived so that, in contrast to everyday oral conversations, there is a permanent record for users to return to for further responses or development. For example, students using Twitter can search back through tweets shared on a class Twitter account to find relevant tweets on a certain topic for use in writing a report. Replicability has to do with the fact that material on sites can be easily copied and transformed for a range of other uses—for example, incorporating material from a Tumblr blog post into a report.

Scalability has to do with the fact that the content being shared can be readily disseminated without vetting, resulting in a range of differences in the quality and validity of the content (Boyd, 2010). In their book on "spreadability" of online content as related to scalability, Jenkins, Ford, and Green (2013) note that the degree to which content is readily spread online often has to do with the degree to which it attracts audience attention by users, which means that users, as opposed to news or media institutions, now assume a larger role in determining which content received attention. Some of this content may garner considerable attention, while much of it garners little attention, all of which requires attention-transacting practices to promote certain content. This requires that in using social networking sites for research, students need to know how to judge the validity of content based on academic criteria, as opposed to popularity.

The affordance of searchability means that people can readily locate people and information in ways that influence their actions and attitudes. This means that students can search for people or organizations with expertise on certain topics to then access information.

This leads to the question of the social practices that students learn through participation using social networking tools. Knobel (2013) argues that through participation on academically oriented sites, students acquire what Gee (2013a) describes as "premium digital literacy" practices associated with learning the uses of academic/disciplinary languages employed on certain social networking sites. Knobel cites the example of a Reddit social networking site, AskHistorians http://www.reddit.com/r/AskHistorians, where users post content consisting of questions such as "Why did world population growth slow in 1959 and 1960?" (p. 5) and answers related to historical facts and then vote up or down on the historical accuracy and validity of the submitted content. These criteria reflect the use of discourses, standards, and norms valued by historians, such as "being factually correct," "presenting strong arguments," "no sweeping generalizations," or "no speculation." Knobel posits that participation on this site requires knowing how to engage in substantive discussions on a certain topic or post; respond to questions; and analyze different, competing arguments.

At the same time, some students can experience an addiction to having to be continually connected to social networking sites, related to the need to recognize the value of momentarily abstaining from a dependency on social media/networking (Moeller et al., 2012). Engaging in social networking can also involve multitasking that can serve to distract students from focusing their attention on completing learning tasks (Rosen, Carrier, & Cheever, 2013). In one study, multitasking was related to reduced performance on recall and recognition of information (Srivastava, 2013).

One approach to discourage compulsive use of social networking sites involves the use of Study Boost https://studyboost.com, which helps students focus their attention on studying through sharing questions on IM or SMS (Byrne, 2013d). Students can link their Study Boost accounts to their IM or SMS and then create questions to share with peers to then answer those questions, leading to feedback from peers.

Students could also reflect on their social interactions with others on these social networking sites by addressing the following questions:

- How has electronic media changed the way we communicate in general?
- How is your communication pattern different from when you weren't texting or using Facebook, MySpace, and/or Twitter?
- How has the way you communicate on social media sites changed the way you communicate when you're off-line?
- How are our public and private personas different? Why? For what purposes?
- What deliberate choices have you made in crafting your online persona? Why? (Swartz, 2011, p. 6)

SUMMARY

In this chapter, we describe the uses of note-taking, social bookmarking, and social networking tools for understanding and creating digital texts. Students use note-taking tools to formulate their responses to texts and topics as well as share their notes with peers. They use social bookmarking tools to collect, categorize/tag, and store online material for use in their work, as well as annotate texts. And they use social networking tools for interacting with you and their peers, something that we describe in more detail in the next chapter, on online discussions.

6

ENGAGING IN ONLINE DISCUSSIONS

In this chapter, we turn our focus to ways that you can use digital discussion environments to enhance writing instruction and student engagement. By *digital discussion environments*, we mean Internet environments designed for conversation and collaboration. Other terms associated with digital discussion environments include computer-supported learning environments, virtual learning environments, and online collaborative learning environments. The explosion of social media and popular use of Web 2.0 tools have made online discussions more popular than ever before. As Kathleen Blake Yancey (2009) reports, "today, in the 21st century, people write as never before—in print and online" (p. 4). Web 2.0 tools—blogs, wikis, instant messaging (IMing), and chats—all support digital discussion environments, as do tried-and-true discussion technologies such as e-mail Listservs and online bulletin boards. Videoconferencing tools such as Skype and Google Hangouts add video and audio capabilities that enhance text-only discussions. Virtual environments such as Second Life and MOO (multiuser dimensions, object oriented) offer a multimedia experience and the opportunity to literally build a virtual discussion environment. Along similar lines, gaming environments offer yet another tool for digital discussions that incorporates visual as well as verbal elements. These environments may vary in terms of purpose, number of participants, software, and design, but they have several common elements: they are highly interactive, they require writing, and they encourage student-centered learning. For these reasons, students find digital discussions engaging and even fun. And, when used wisely by instructors, digital discussions can help ground rhetorical concepts of audience, purpose, voice, and tone in interesting and engaging ways.

Fostering digital discussions also relates to the Common Core Speaking and Listening standards regarding one-to-one and group discussions, in which students employ multimodal sources and visual media to share information and build knowledge by evaluating contributors' alternative perspectives.

Common Core State Standards: Speaking and Listening Standards

1. Participate effectively in a range of interactions (one-on-one and in groups), exchanging information to advance a discussion and to build on the input of others.
2. Integrate and evaluate information from multiple oral, visual, or multimodal sources in order to answer questions, solve problems, or build knowledge.
3. Evaluate the speaker's point of view, reasoning, and use of evidence and rhetoric.
4. Present information, evidence, and reasoning in a clear and well-structured way appropriate to purpose and audience.
5. Make strategic use of digital media and visual displays of data to express information and enhance understanding.
6. Adapt speech to a variety of contexts and communicative tasks, demonstrating a command of formal English when indicated or appropriate.

While online discussions have become more common in writing classrooms, it is important to note that not all online discussions are engaging. In fact, results from a national survey of online writing teachers acknowledge that students often feel fatigued by online discussions in online writing courses due to the sheer volume of posts that students must read and write for a given course (CCCC Committee for Best Practices in Online Writing Instruction, 2011, p. 6). Several others acknowledge the difficulty of keeping students engaged in online discussions, for reasons including the high reading load required to respond, the lack of motivation to contribute beyond course requirements, and the lack of direction regarding how to write quality responses (Brunk-Chavez & Miller, 2006, 2007; Uzuner & Mehta, 2010; Yena & Waggoner, 2003; Stedman, 2000). Other studies raise more questions about online discussions. A joint study by the National Writing Project and the Pew Research Center, "The Impact of Digital Tools on Student Writing" (Purcell, Buchanan, & Friedrich, 2013a), suggests that while the increased use of digital writing encourages collaboration and revision opportunities, teachers note "an increasingly ambiguous line between 'formal' and 'informal' writing" as well as students' tendencies to think of writing in "truncated forms" (p. 2).

Indeed, the growing prevalence of digital technologies requires us to carefully consider the ways that we integrate digital discussions in our classrooms. Kathleen Yancey (2009) makes this point well as she talks about "twenty-first century literacies": "We thus face three challenges that are also opportunities: developing *new models of writ-*

ing; designing a *new curriculum* supporting those models; and creating *models for teaching* that curriculum" (p. 4, emphasis hers). In response, this chapter articulates a rationale for using digital discussions, synchronous and asynchronous methods and tools for supporting them, and suggestions for managing their use in the classroom.

WHY BOTHER WITH DIGITAL DISCUSSIONS?

There are several good reasons to integrate digital discussion environments into writing classes. One is that digital discussions reinforce regular writing practice. We know that students are already writing in digital environments, using tools such as Facebook, Twitter, text messages, IMing, wikis, and blogs. A Pew Internet & American Life Project survey (Lenhart, 2012) found that 75% of adolescents 12 to 17 years old engage in texting, with 63% texting daily. Students are already using these media to create verbal and visual messages, to share and discuss ideas, and to develop social relationships. By integrating these media into writing classrooms, we can build common ground and increase student engagement and interest in writing.

Another good reason to use digital discussions is that they encourage students to learn from one another by sharing and building on one another's ideas. Said differently, digital discussion environments support constructivist learning theories—the idea that knowledge is an active, experiential, and collaborative process. In *Engaging the Online Learner*, Conrad and Donaldson (2004) suggest that constructivist learning and online learning environments go hand in hand: "Activities that require student interaction and encourage a sharing of ideas promote a deeper level of thought" (p. 5). Many scholars, in fact, argue that online learning succeeds when it is engaging and represents constructivist learning assumptions (Brooks & Brooks, 1993; Palloff & Pratt, 2001).

Some of these assumptions include the idea that students are not mere receptacles for learning but that they actively participate in their learning process. Some scholars add that constructivist learning benefits from guidance provided by students' teachers (Kirschner, Sweller, & Clark, 2006). Constructivist learning theories have gained important traction in connection with digital discussion tools. Technologies that afford conversations among colleagues, students, and instructors help build community in ways that enhance learning. Some have made connections between constructive learning and "personal learning networks" (PLNs) suggesting that we learn best from the connections that we make with other people and the materials that we share with one another (Anders, Duin, & Moses, 2013; Gruenbaum, 2010). Personal learning networks, for example, highlight "networked learning" and are associated with connectivism, open-source platforms, situated learning approaches, and social pedagogies (Anders et al., 2013). Networked learning approaches might also involve social networking capabilities for discussions through tools such as Ning, Edmodo, and Collaborize, all of which build on the idea that students share information and ideas with one another through social and digital channels. Given these constructivist notions of education, digital discussion environments are not only a useful activity but perhaps a central activity for promoting engagement and strengthening community in a classroom.

Another important reason to use digital discussions is that students write to learn as they compose messages and reflect on course material. Students can post summaries of course material; they can find related stories, articles, or links on a particular topic; they can respond to specific prompts created by the instructor; and they can respond thoughtfully to other students. These and similar activities require students to think critically about course material and articulate what they understand about it. Students consequently immerse themselves in writing, constantly composing and reading texts. Cathie English (2007) explains that she used online discussions to help students synthesize and compare ideas on literary texts in ways that she could not do in a traditional classroom:

> How many students will be able to answer these questions in a large-group discussion? . . . When students receive writing prompts in an online discussion, each student must respond to one of the writing prompts and cite the text to support his or her thesis. (p. 57)

She explained that online discussions became an "extension of our classroom" (p. 58). In a similar vein, others have argued that because students are continually engaged in online writing environments outside and inside the classroom, they are learning to use writing to be heard by others, practice with writing that can improve their writing over time (M. Harris & Pemberton, 1995).

Digital discussion environments also help students understand audience and purpose more concretely. Because digital discussion environments are public, students understand that they have a ready audience consisting of other students in class and the teacher. Gordon Brune, a fifth-grade teacher who uses blogs, reports,

> My students no longer see themselves writing for a teacher or a bulletin board but for a real audience. Many times, my students have excitedly and incredulously stated things like, "Man, people all the way from China are reading my stuff!" (Curtis, 2006, p. 25)

Digital discussion environments can include students from other schools—even other countries—thus broadening awareness of multiple layers of audience in writing tasks.

The implications of a real audience are powerful: Students may have more motivation to write and may take more time thinking about and preparing their messages. The

Pew Research Center (Purcell et al., 2013a) confirms as well that digital technologies help reinforce a broader sense of audience: In a survey of over 2,000 middle and high school teachers, "96% agree (including 52% who strongly agree) that digital technologies allow students to share their work with a wider and more varied audience" (p. 2). This stronger sense of audience can help students craft messages with sharper focus and purpose than traditional paper-based assignments. We as teachers also benefit from increased awareness of audience. We can read our students' entries and have a clear sense of the ways in which students comprehend course material and ways that they need help. Ultimately, digital discussion environments help us stay in tune with our students as writers.

SYNCHRONOUS DISCUSSIONS

Synchronous forms of online discussion are described as "real-time" discussions, meaning that discussion participants are on the computer at the same time and are typing messages or speaking to one another via the Internet. Synchronous discussions can take the form of text, audio, video, or some combination. In text-based discussions, participants type messages to one another synchronously, and the resulting discussion appears as a written transcript, with contributions labeled according to participant names. In audio or video synchronous discussions, participants talk to one another much like they would on the phone. Many audio and video synchronous tools have additional features, such as a text-based chat, screen sharing, or the ability to send private messages. Synchronous discussions also occur in gaming contexts, where multiple participants contribute to story lines and scenarios, thinking through various audience roles. Synchronous discussions can be closed or open discussions. Open discussions are often sponsored by web-based providers such as Google or Yahoo, while closed discussions must be set up by someone and are often a feature of a web-based program that houses multiple discussion or web features, such as Blackboard, Moodle, or Drupal. As we describe here, synchronous discussions can be used for a variety of educational purposes.

Using Synchronous Discussion to Connect With People Across Distance

Synchronous discussions are an excellent way to connect people across time and distance; for example, synchronous discussions are often used for businesspeople to "meet" online, even though they might be sitting in different time zones around the world. Video chats allow students to both talk and type with others, sometimes even sharing the same screen.

You can employ the Skype for Educators http://www.skypeforeducators.com/educators.htm service to match up with other teachers around the world and match your students with other students throughout the world. These discussions can be focused around problem-solving situations and real-life experiences. For example, one writer describes a project called "Mystery Skype," in which students connected with a classroom somewhere else in the world and they had to use maps and other clues to solve the mystery location (A. Schwartz, 2013; http://tinyurl.com/mgwjtd5). In another example, Silvia Rosenthal Tolisano developed a program called "Globally Connected Learning," in which Skype is used by instructors to connect participating classrooms around the world http://aroundtheworldwith80schools.net. These discussions can be focused on a variety of topics; Tolisano described one project in which third graders Skyped with classes in Missouri, Indonesia, Prague, Argentina, and New Zealand to explore learning about different communities, including rural and metropolitan areas. In a blog reflection about the activity, she notes,

> The latest connection was with Anna Faridaku, a teacher and children's book author from Indonesia. Students took turns speaking with Anna, who was just amazing in connecting (via the screen) to the kids, answering and asking questions. She engaged them and pushed them to deeper thinking about similarities and differences about our communities. ("Learning About Communities," http://aroundtheworldwith80schools.net)

Tolisano argues that the ability to talk with others around the world is an important and valuable skill that Skype facilitates; she provides a helpful model for Skype conversation that includes progression from "ping pong" conversation to "free flowing conversation" ("Taxonomy of a Skype Conversation," http://aroundtheworldwith80schools.net; see also http://www.scribd.com/doc/81291959/Get-Started-With-Skype). Programs such as Global Learning Communities make use of the free Skype technology to help teachers create thoughtful and engaging discussions with other students.

Synchronous discussions can happen with resident students also, for purposes of connecting students with others. Google+ Hangouts video chat can be used for up to 15 students participating in school-sponsored chats. In using Hangouts, you can also project the Hangouts chat to the entire class on a screen, use the screenshare feature to share documents using Google Docs, and record the video chat to create a video for later sharing with your class. Hangouts is particularly useful for small groups in that membership can be limited to certain students. Teachers can also use Hangouts to bring in guest speakers, hold teacher or peer writing conferences, interact with students if they are ill, schedule parent conferences, create shows similar to podcasts, or have meetings with colleagues (Ady, 2013). Students can also participate in "virtual field trips" using Hangouts, in which classes can visit museums, zoos, aquariums, or organizations' buildings, such as the Seattle Aquarium, Minnesota Zoo, or Philadelphia Museum of Art (see http://connectedclassrooms.withgoogle.com).

Using Synchronous Discussions to Build Community

Another common reason to use synchronous discussions is to build a sense of community among students in the class. Synchronous chats bring a sense of fun and engagement; students sometimes feel more relaxed contributing to these chats because they can be informal and experiment with language as a way to foster online social relationships. In the textbox, students from Sara's literature class engaged in an evening chat on Tappedin.org (note: Tappedin.org ended service in 2014). Sara notes that in her students' exchanges, verbal "fooling around . . . actually helps to foster a chat environment that is more open and fun, and thus more engaging overall."

Chat Discussion 1

Kansas: hey yall

Montana: okay . . . hmmm. I suppse that being in nature (to me) is sort of peaceful and relaxing, but super scary at the same time (this is also assuming that it is all of a sudden NIGHT time and i'm in the middle of nowhere hearing wolves) okay, i'm kidding

Pennsylvania: hey what are we supposed to read for Wednesday

Pennsylvania: did she run away?

Montana: haha probably

SaraWi: Okay, you need to be though page 23 for TOMORROW. The day after today.

Ohio: i like being in the nature i think its relaxing too! nature brings you intouch with yourself and takes all the outside stuff your used to

Pennsylvania: then what for wednesday i wont be there tomorrow

Hawaii: I like nature, in the summer

Montana: you should've stayed after class Pennsylvania

Montana: bah, HA

Ohio: yea i cant wait till summer

SaraWi: through page 46 for Wednesday

Pennsylvania: i left after 4th hour

Hawaii: I wouldnt want to be living off the land in the middle of winter, in alaska, that would be too much nature for me

Hawaii: yeah, me too

Pennsylvania: i didnt think i was not gonna be ther tomorrow

Oklahoma: yes the java download worked

Pennsylvania: thnax mrs w

Ohio: ok enough pennsylvania lets talk

Pennsylvania: lol

Hawaii: ha

Hawaii: thems be fightin words

Ohio: yup

Wyoming: Sry I am late

Oklahoma: sweet, we should do this often, i like doing this at home

SaraWi: Okay, okay, KENNEL.

Ohio: get out your late

Wyoming: frowns

Kansas: lol ur silly

Hawaii: ha . . . mrs. W . . . new Q

In the exchange, it could be argued that the students are totally "off task." However, through engaging in this online verbal play, they are establishing social connections critical to forming a sense of community. Another word for the kinds of interactions seen in these chats is "back channel" or a kind of "check-in" from various group members about what has been said or assigned. These kinds of comments are important in establishing a community that shares digital discussions. In an interview with Sara, one student contrasted face-to-face classroom discussions with their online discussions:

Jim (student): Um, I really think that those out-of-class in the evening online discussions. . . . Those were really fun. . . . I had fun doing those. I seemed really loose and it was a comfortable environment because we were at our house—I don't know if that makes you think better or what, but there were a lot of different, like, good answers on those, like ones you wouldn't see in class.

Sara: So, you think it was because people were more relaxed that they were then able to think more clearly about what the book is actually saying?

Jim: Yeah, and they can be more themselves and say what they really think.

Many scholars agree that helping students become comfortable in an online environment is a critical first step in using any digital discussion environment. For example, Rita Conrad and Anna Donaldson (2004) articulate a strategy called "phases of engagement," in which they suggest four gradual phases of increased engagement. They suggest that in Phase 1, the student plays the role of a "newcomer," and the instructor plays the role of "social negotiator." The goal of this phase is simply to help students get to know one another in the online space. Activities recommended for this phase are "icebreakers, individual introductions, discussions concerning community issues such as Netiquette rules in a virtual lounge" (p. 29).

As students become more comfortable in digital discussion environments, you can design interactive activities that are more challenging. Conrad and Donaldson (2004) encourage thinking about digital discussion environments in terms of a continuum through which you can engage students at increased levels of engagement. For example, Conrad and Donaldson suggest that in Phase 2, students play the role of "cooperator" and teachers play the role of "structural engineer." In this phase, the "instructor forms dyads of learners and provides activities that require critical thinking, reflection, and sharing of ideas" (p. 29). Phases 3 and 4 require increased participation from students: Phase 3 requires students to collaborate more fully, such as through jigsaw exercises, and Phase 4 requires students to initiate exercises in the class and take leadership roles. The "phases of engagement" approach can be a useful guide for teachers planning to integrate digital discussions purposefully. It augments the idea that online instruction thrives when we purposefully involve students in their learning.

Using Synchronous Discussions to Stimulate Critical Thinking

To push the idea of an "engagement continuum" further, we can return to our class example. In the textbox, Sara uses the chat function of Tappedin.org with her same students for a different purpose. Here, she exemplifies Phase 2 of Conrad and Donaldson's (2004) approach by modeling how to frame questions to help students think critically. In this case, students are discussing Jon Krakauer's (2009) *Into the Wild*, a story that recounts the experiences of Christopher McCandless, a college graduate who attempted to survive on his own in the Alaska wilds, only to starve to death.

Chat Discussion 2

SaraWi: So, what is your first impression of this kid throwing off the life of privilege (being rich) to live off the land, alone, without material possessions? Is he foolish? Crazy? Brave? A genius?

Hawaii: I do think he's kind of foolish

Sara Wi: Why?

Ohio: well I think that its smart to go and find yourself do what you really want instead of following the crowd hes doing what hes always dreamed not just dreaming about it

Hawaii: obviously if he ends up dying he wasn't prepared for how harsh the Alaskan winters are

Montana: right on Hawaii

Kansas: cause he could have had a great successful life

Pennsylvania: true

Hawaii: the local that drove him to the woods or whatever even told him that hes going to freeze

Hawaii: he didnt even have warm boots

Montana: no, he didnt

Oklahoma: he wasnt prepared, but that dosent mean it was the right choice, it was his choice, period

Kansas: that sux i hate cold toes

Ohio: yea me too I hate being cold

Ohio: I think the "last adventure" before college got away from him

Wyoming: But you can still have a great life if you dont have any worldy possessions (Money, cars, ect…)

Montana: HA

Hawaii: I think he maybe should have looked into it a little more, like the dangers, and the risks he could be taking

Pennsylvania: yea he should have

Kansas: yea lots of risks

Montana: but then it wouldn't have been spontanious

SaraWi: Why would anyone be so extreme in throwing off society and the material world?

Oklahoma: in life people need to make there own decisions, or their life wont be fully complete he wouldent have been able to feel complete without this journey, it was a life journey, he was finding himself, how can you live life not knowing who you are, he needed this trip

Ohio: i think that if you really want something your not going to look at all the consequences your gunna just do it

Oklahoma: because the material world is fake

Oklahoma: he hated that

Wyoming: Maybe they werent happy with their life so they decided to go and try something new.

Kansas: thats a good? I dont get it

> *Montana:* but was it worth dying over?
>
> *Pennsylvania:* because he probably wants to adventure a new life thanx extreme
>
> *Wyoming:* He didnt mean to die
>
> *Montana:* i understand, but he DID

Sara starts the discussion with a question about the students' general impression of McCandless, providing students with initial means of formulating some opinion about him. When Hawaii states that he is "foolish," Sara poses a *why* question to encourage him to support his claim. Later in the conversation, she poses another question related to explaining McCandless's motives: "Why would anyone be so extreme in throwing off society and the material world?"—a question that leads some students to focus on the limitations of the larger world itself as "fake." Through posing these questions, Sara is modeling the inquiry process in exploring a person's motivation, leading her students to expand on their thinking.

Cautions on Synchronous Chats

While using synchronous chats to engage students in role-play can be a useful creative exercise, there are some cautions to consider. Considerable concern has been expressed about people posing or passing for someone that they are not on chat sites to establish relationships or solicit sex (Burbules & Callister, 2000; Dreyfus, 2001). Given the anonymity of the web, people can adopt virtual identities that may bear little relationship to the selves that they adopt in lived worlds. In chat rooms, they can pretend to be identities for the purposes of attracting others in an attempt to create actual live-world relationships (Donath, 1996). To avoid these concerns, we recommend that you use chat sites that are password protected, where participation is limited to students and teacher, or where participants require teacher permission to join the room (see Fryer, "Safe Digital Social Networking (DSN) or Proactive Approaches to Address Cyberbullying and Digital Social Networking," http://teachdigital.pbworks.com/w/page/19791115/safedsn).

ASYNCHRONOUS DISCUSSIONS

Asynchronous online discussions can be best described as "delayed time" discussions, in which participants write separate messages at different times and send them to one another via the Internet. The messages then are stored in a server, and participants must log in to that server through an e-mail account or website password to retrieve their messages. A standard example of asynchronous discussions is e-mail. A person may send an e-mail message at whatever time is convenient for him or her, but because the recipient retrieves the message when he or she chooses, the recipient may not reply to that message instantly. Time lapses between discussion contributions by hours, days, or even weeks (hence, "delayed time"). Other forms of asynchronous discussions include Listservs (e-mail groups with distinct membership), discussion boards hosted by websites (e.g., Moodle, Drupal, and Blackboard), social networking sites for education (e.g., Ning, Edmodo, Collaborize Classroom), blogs (web-based journals written by individuals), microblogs (blogs with short character limits, such as Twitter), and wikis (collaboratively authored websites). Of these options, social networking discussions have become extremely popular, especially the mircoblogging "status bar" ("What's on your mind today?") as well as the ability to connect with others by responding to or "liking"/"disliking" comments in microblog formats. We also add to this list texting or IMing, in which individuals send messages to one another via the Internet, often by phone or other mobile devices. Texting or IMing is often thought of as synchronous because participants often respond very quickly to one another, but, technically, texting and IMing are asynchronous because responses are sent separately across time and distance.

Basically, all asynchronous discussions appear as a kind of written transcript of conversational turns in an ongoing discussion. Depending on the technology, the turns can appear together in the same transcript (as in blogs, which archive contributions in reverse chronological order); they can occur as separate messages, organized into categories or "threads" of discussion topics (as in discussion boards, e-mails, and Listservs); or they can be separated by hypertext links (blogs and wikis allow for links to comments and outside websites). Social networking sites might show comments in microblog form, sharing each (short) contribution in a reverse chronological order (most recent first).

In any case, asynchronous discussions are supportive of students' frequent writing. However, they are challenging because responding to these discussions requires a lot of reading for students and instructors, which may lead to fatigue (CCCC Committee for Best Practice in Online Writing Instruction, 2011, p. 6). Many scholars have commented on the challenges of keeping students engaged in asynchronous discussions (Brunk-Chavez & Miller, 2007; Stedman, 2000). Some methods for using asynchronous discussions to keep students engaged include reflecting on course material, collaborating in large or small groups, engaging in global exchanges, and encouraging blog and microblog activities. In "Three Ways to Increase the Quality of Students' Discussion Board Comments" (2010), Sedef Uzuner and Ruchi Mehta http://tinyurl.com/mx5jpa3 emphasize "educationally valuable talk" in which students critically engage with subject matter in digital discussions. They suggest that when students simply fulfill requirements of responding to material and posting to another student, they are not always critically engaging with the text. Uzuner and Mehta offer three suggestions: (1) Have the class create guidelines for meaningful discussions; (2) use Grice's maxims, such as quantity, quality, relation, and manner; and (3) have students engage in self-evaluation regarding their posts. The authors suggest that these strategies help students see themselves as collaborators in the discussion, rather than simply writing to fulfill a requirement (par. 8, http://tinyurl.com/mx5jpa3).

Like synchronous discussions, asynchronous discussions can be used for a variety of educational purposes, as we describe in the sections below.

Using Texting to Expand Notions of Writing

Adolescents are continually using texting for engaging in their own personal or social discussions. In 2011, 63% of adolescents texted daily, as opposed to 39% calling on cell phones, 35% socializing face-to-face, 29% sending messages through social networking sites, 22% IMing, and 6% e-mailing (Lenhart, 2012). For adolescents who text, the median number of texts sent daily was 60, with the heaviest texters (more than 100 a day) also engaging in the highest talking on phones (Lenhart, 2012).

While texting combines features of both oral and written language use, there are a number of advantages to the use of texting as writing over phone calls as oral communication (Wood, Kemp, & Plester, 2013). Talking on the phone requires that users are both available to talk, while that is not the case with texting. Texting creates a written communication record not accessible with talk. In texting, users also have more time to reflect on their intended message, while talkers have less time to reflect, so that users can revise their messages (Kasesniemi & Rautianinen, 2002). For users who are less comfortable in face-to-face social interactions, texting provides them with a safer space for communication (Reid & Reid, 2007). Adolescents' use of IMing has a positive effect on the development of off-line friendships (Koutamanis, Vossen, Jochen, & Valkenburg, 2013). At the same time, given the blurring of oral and written features of texting, users often do not perceive texting as a form of writing in that texts can be sent and responded to immediately in a conversational mode (Roschke, 2008).

As the amount of texting increased, major concerns were expressed in the media about the negative effects of "textspeak" language use on students' writing—that students would draw on their texting experience in their writing, resulting in the deterioration of students' writing quality (Wood et al., 2013). However, research on students' use of texting and their writing quality finds low correlations between students' level of texting and errors in their writing, as well as positive correlations with language use and reading ability (Durkin, Conti-Ramsden, & Walker, 2011; Plester, Wood, & Bell, 2008; Plester, Wood, & Joshi, 2009). A study of younger children found a positive correlation between their texting and their reading, spelling, and phonological processing (Wood, Jackson, Hart, Plester, & Wilde, 2011). Students also learn to code-switch between use of texting for informal social purposes and their formal academic writing (Rowan, 2011).

Analysis of college students' use of IMing exchanges found that students were employing certain paralinguistic features as a hybrid mixture of oral and written language—the use of "eye dialect," slang, emoticons, and metamarkings that served as cues providing readers with how to interpret their texts (Haas, Takayoshi, Carr, Hudson, & Pollock, 2011). For example, in the following exchange, the use of metamarking such as ;-) or the use of asterisks to imply intent serves to clarify meanings:

Aaron: u're place or mine;-)

Aaron: (hoping u'll say yours

Aaron: cuz mine's disgusting)*hint (p. 397)

While some research suggests that use of texting that flouts grammatical rules has a negative relationship with students' use of syntax (Cingel & Sundar, 2012), one issue in that research is whether or not students' use of syntax in their writing is related to their inability to correct their writing, as opposed to being related to their use of texting (Wood et al., 2013).

Given students' high use of texting/IMing, you may use texting tools to communicate with students about assignments, deadlines, and resources, as well as invite students to text you with their questions. At the same time, you also need to establish some guidelines regarding this use of texting for academic purposes—for example, whether you want to have parents texting you.

In addition to a number of different texting tools, there are also school-based messaging systems designed for use in schools for communicating with students and parents—such as Class Parrot, Kikutext, WeTxt, Remind101, Sendhub, and Class Pager—or Tom's Messenger to record audio messages for students related to assignments, reminders, and announcements. One advantage of using texting/IMing is that many students—particularly students in developing countries who only have access to a cell phone, as opposed to a computer or smartphone—can receive messages, particularly if a school has a "bring your own device" policy, where students can use their cell phones in school. One study of students' use of the Whatsapp app in a South African university found that use of the app enhanced communication, collaboration, and engagement for students, particularly those in geographically remote areas of South Africa (Rambe & Bere, 2013).

All of this raises the question as to whether and how you can use texting to foster classroom discussions within or outside the physical classroom setting. You can build activities around an analysis of students' use of texting in which they discuss examples of differences between their use of language in their texting versus use of language in their writing, differences involving code-switching practices. They may note differences in their use of "textspeak" related to abbreviations, acronyms, emoticons, alternative spellings, syntax, and what Haas et al. (2011) define as "eye dialect" and "metamarkings" versus their formal written language, as well as translating their "textspeak" into formal written language and their formal written language into "textspeak." For example, students can examine creative alternative spellings or acronyms for words used in texts in terms of whether they can identify those words. They can also create skit scripts or stories based on dialogue consisting of text exchanges among characters to develop identities or conflicts among characters.

However, one negative effect of the use of texting is that during classes, students frequently do engage in using their mobile devices, particularly for texting, which can serve as a distraction. One study of 777 college students found that 90% admitted to using their devices for nonclass activities during class times, with 27% using their devices 4 to 10 times; 16%, 11 to 30 times; and 15%, more than 30 times—with 86% of the students engaging in texting (Jaschik, 2013), with texting and Facebook during class negatively related to overall grade point average (Junco, 2014). While it may be difficult to ban the use of mobile devices during class, 54% of students indicated that it may be helpful for teachers to institute some policies regarding the use of devices during classes given that such multitasking can distract students from engaging in a focused manner.

Using Asynchronous Discussions to Reflect on Course Material

One of the great benefits of using asynchronous discussions, as opposed to synchronous discussions, is that the delayed-time nature of asynchronous technologies allows students more time to reflect on course material. In this way, asynchronous discussions can be used for creative, reflective assignments and can be tailored to address all phases of engagement, as suggested by Conrad and Donaldson (2004). For example, to introduce students to a digital discussion environment (Conrad and Donaldson's Phase 1), you could create a prompt in a discussion board in which students post messages and respond to other students to become familiar with the online space. The textbox includes a specific example of a Phase 1 asynchronous exercise.

"Favorite Place on Earth"

Use discussion board technology, and have students write about their favorite (physical) place on earth. Have students put the name of the place in the subject line of their message. In the content of the message, have students write one paragraph in which they describe this place and explain why they like it. Then have students reply to at least one other student in class about that student's favorite place. A simple exercise such as this could accomplish many goals: It introduces students to the digital discussion environment; it encourages them to respond to other students in the environment; it requires them to craft a coherent paragraph; and it requires them to use descriptive language.

Asynchronous environments can also be used to help students reflect on course material, an often-cited advantage of asynchronous environments. Alison Black (2005) explains, "A reflective response involves critical thinking and focuses on what students in the classroom may have learned" (p. 6). Asynchronous discussions could be created to have students talk about readings, answer thought-provoking questions about course material, or even explore related topics and bring those back to the class discussion (English, 2007). In her study of "e-lit groups," or electronic literacy group discussions, Dena Beeghly (2005) reports that students wrote short responses about assigned literature readings and then used those responses to stimulate discussion. Beeghly found that using asynchronous discussions allowed students to have more time to think about their responses to readings, thus stimulating critical thinking while also creating a learning community (p. 16). Similarly, in a study of middle school classrooms that used threaded discussion groups for a literature course, Grisham and Wolsey (2006) found that asynchronous discussions fostered deeper responses to the literature than did paper journal writing or face-to-face discussions.

Using Asynchronous Discussions for Collaboration

Whereas reflective discussions often involve individual student responses to questions, collaborative/group discussions involve a community-based approach to discussions in which students share information with one another. In one interesting study of college student writers, Andrew Virtue (2013) examined the use of virtual group discussions rather than individual contributions to large class discussions. In the virtual groups, a leader role was assigned and rotated on a regular basis, and the leader generated prompts for discussion. He discovered that in comparison to a class that used individual response approaches, the group discussions approach maintained engagement in discussions for a longer period. They also gained important moderating skills. This approach required students to take active roles in group work and to carry responsibility for those roles throughout a course.

Indeed, one of the strongest predictors of online course success is the potential for computer-supported collaborative learning. However, online instructors struggle to engage students in successful online collaboration. Successful collaboration creates a community in which learners experience a sense of belonging and a perception that personal contributions are valued.

Using Asynchronous Discussions for National and Global Exchanges

You can also have students from different classes writing to and for one another. Teachers from these different classes could take turns providing discussion prompts. As students respond, they can read replies from students in both classes. Besides partnerships, you could also tap into national web projects with an interactive component—the GoNorth http://tinyurl.com/nwgjnnq, Polar Husky http://polarhusky.com, or Earth Education http://tinyurl.com/k5udkhp projects sponsored by the Learning Technologies Media Lab, University of Minnesota. These sites offer dynamic curricula that chronicle the journeys of explorers in different locations around the world. Explorers write about their journeys or send videos, and students can write to explorers, asking questions or offering comments and observations about the explorations. Discussions that occur in environments like these involve students around the world and provide a wonderful way for students to understand how writing is a critical vehicle for communication.

Students can also engage in online writing with students throughout the world using tools such as ePals http://www.epals.com, a site with 5 million students and teachers from 191 countries, which includes e-mail and blogs, as well as ePals Mentoring for students to interact with local community experts or businesses. These tools include multilingual translation tools so that students can interact with other students who speak different languages. ePal writing can be particularly valuable when students are working with others from different countries so that students learn about lives across different social and cultural contexts. In one project, second-grade American students engaged in a joint writing project with British students in designing a unique monster (Rowen, 2005). The American students sent their written descriptions of their monsters to the British students, who then drew the monsters, scanned their drawings, and returned them to the American students. This led to further online discussions about differences in these students' lives, language use, and weather (for more on use of online pen-pals sites: http://tinyurl.com/m7n7jo6).

TOOLS FOR FOSTERING DISCUSSIONS

While the quality of your classroom discussions often depends more on your use of an engaging prompt or the quality of your preparation for the discussion than the nature of the tool employed in conducting the discussion, there are tools that we have found to be particularly effective for fostering discussion. The following course management systems offer synchronous and asynchronous discussion capabilities: Moodle, Desire2Learn, Angel, Brainhoney, Blackboard Mobile Learn, Blackboard Illuminate, Pearson's PowerTeacher 2.0, LanSchool, Collaborize Classroom, Schoology, Edmodo, and Canvas. The following social networking tools can also be used for both asynchronous and synchronous discussions: Facebook, Twitter, Google+, Ning, and Grou.ps (for more on use of tools for fostering discussions: http://tinyurl.com/9vufs7h). Here we highlight a few notes about using course management systems, social networking tools, and interactive presentation tools to foster online discussions.

Course Management Systems: Discussion Tools

Moodle.org is an open-source program and course management system for creating online courses. Moodle includes discussion boards and other discussion features, such as blogs, "dialogues," and "workshops," which can facilitate a variety of activities. Moodle provides templates for a syllabus, calendar, deadlines, and forums; you and your students then have access to these courses within your school. Moodle.org also has 50 "language packs" that can be used in working with English-language learners. You can also use Moodle's built-in wiki to have students engage in collaborative writing (see chapter 7). In contrast to Ning or Nicenet.org, which are housed on their own servers, Moodle does require some technology support staff to set up a Moodle site on a school's server (for an example of use of Moodle in the Hopkins, Minnesota, school district: http://courseweb.hopkins.k12.mn.us; for a description of use of Moodle in the classroom: http://www.wtvi.com/teks/moodle).

For focusing written discussions, Collaborize Classroom http://www.collaborizeclassroom.com and its Collaborize Classroom Pro iOS app http://tinyurl.com/mk4t36w are particularly effective for scaffolding discussions. For example, Collaborize provides students with information about different roles that they can adopt in a discussion—the "silent moderator," who poses questions without participating in the discussion, or the "involved participant," who facilitates discussion. It also provides students with tools for conducting surveys or polls to determine their attitudes on topics or issues, results that can be used to foster further discussions. English teacher Catlin Tucker reports that she uses Collaborize in her 9th- and 10th-grade classes to post different types of questions about readings in class (Kessler, 2010). Using Collaborize, she is able to set up different formats for responses, such as agreeing or disagreeing, responding to multiple choice questions, or posting responses. She stopped "filtering" the discussions and reported that the students respond to discussion questions as much as they do on a social networking site, learning from one another. She finds that Collaborize supports students' social tendencies, noting that for most students, "it's natural to have conversations online" (Kessler, 2010).

We also recommend course management systems such as Edmodo https:// www.edmodo.com or Schoology https://www.schoology.com/home.php for use in supporting classroom discussions. Because you may be using one of these systems as your overall classroom platform for use of their other features—assignments, calendar, blogging, evaluation, etc.—using one of these systems means that you don't need to have students employ a whole separate discussion platform.

Social Networking Discussion Tools

You can also employ a classroom Facebook account for discussions, using Facebook apps such as SocialBox to engage in synchronous chat with Facebook friends, Filefly to share files, or Facebook Opinion Polls for polling "friends" about topics or issues. Students can share their responses to literature by creating profiles for characters who then post messages related to their thoughts and actions from the text. For example, as they are reading *To Kill a Mockingbird* (Lee, 1988), students could assume the roles of Scout, Atticus, and other characters to engage in a virtual interaction.

Using a classroom Twitter account or class hashtag, students can share tweets on certain topics, issues, news items, or responses to texts—for example, #HungerGames to describe the *Hunger Games* books and movies (Gover & Selleck, 2013). You can also use Twitter for back-channel discussion responses to presentations or videos by projecting a Twitter feed on a whiteboard/screen so that students can respond during a presentation or video. As noted in the last chapter, students also use keyword hashtags to participate in groups organized around discussion of topics—for example, #ipad or #android for discussion of iPads and Android apps.

Students can also create fictional dialogues using tweets. Students in a 9th-grade American studies class adopted the roles of soldier characters from *The Things They Carried* (T. O'Brien, 2009), operating in groups of five soldiers engaged in the Vietnam War (Eidman-Aadahl et al., 2013). Students had to imagine these soldiers' thoughts and tweet those thoughts to other "soldiers" in their group. Students then used material from these tweets as well as lines from the book to create poems about war.

Another social networking tool that can be used for discussions is the app Subtext http://www.subtext.com. Subtext supports students' selection and reading of books as an e-reader, as well as their sharing of responses to books and being exposed to readers' reviews. It provides access to free public domain books available as .epub files (this excludes Kindle books) and paid books using Google Play, as well as articles and blog posts, including PDFs that you can add to the site using the "Save to Subtext" feature.

To use Subtext, you create a class group or specific book club groups so that students can then access books or PDFs for discussions. You can then add notes to texts in which you can pose discussion questions or prompts, as well as have students submit replies to just yourself, submit replies before viewing others' replies, or share their replies with their peers. Students can also add their thumbs-up/thumbs-down responses and their own notes for their peers for each chapter in a book and reply to their peers' notes, which, as we noted with annotations, serves as a means for discussions about a text. Subtext also provides students with text-to-speech audio readings of text, which is particularly useful for struggling readers. Students can then compare the audio with the print version of a text.

Julie Walthour, a teacher at West Junior High School, Hopkins, Minnesota, describes how she uses Subtext:

> Subtext has brought my reading instruction into the digital world. What I most appreciate about Subtext is that I can use all the instructional strategies I used before, but when they are embedded in the text, everything is simpler. My students and I are no longer juggling the text, sticky notes, a notebook, the white board and a Moodle reflection because all of those functions are available in Subtext. I use Subtext as a digital think aloud—I can be in the pages of the text with my students without physically being next to them. I'm able to enhance instruction by including pictures, video or maps; I can remind students of their purpose for reading and give students hints about what they should be noticing. Students love to answer polls—Who's rooting for Team Peeta? Team Gale? Kids can engage in discussions prompted by me or by each other without leaving the app. Scaffolding and differentiation can be done without drawing attention to differences. Online discussions can get off track but when students realize the teacher is a part of the discussion group and sees everything they post, that quickly ends.
>
> This year we're using Subtext to roll out our all-school advisory informational text reading initiative. To get our students engaged with the text, with their peers and with their advisory teachers, we've chosen high interest articles—a report on how poop transplants are used to treat intestinal disorders, a study showing that Oreos are as addictive as drugs, a look at the sport of coleo where cowboys flip bulls by the tail. We have achieved engagement!
>
> My colleague and her students read *The Hunger Games* in Subtext. One of the themes they highlighted throughout the text had to do with what is happening in American society (reality television, emphasis on looks, individual freedom vs. the group, etc.). Because students highlighted and tagged examples using Subtext, they were able to have rich discussions where they could go back to the text to find exam-

ples to support their claims. The highlighting and tagged text then was exported to a Google Doc where they wrote a paper on the theme. Student discussion and papers were much stronger—and text based—because of features in Subtext.

I'm anxious to start setting up students in their own independent reading groups using Subtext. Students can access books from the public library or on Overdrive from the school collection. Voracious readers love to share and kids love to interact digitally— what a fabulous way to make that work.

As with Subtext, LitPick http://litpick.com includes free adolescent literature texts as well as opportunities for students to share responses and reviews of these texts, along with forums with authors and reviewers.

Interactive Presentations Tools and Mobile Devices

Interactive presentation tools can be used with students' mobile devices to foster discussions based on students' interactive written responses to presentations. As you or your students are making presentations, you can use the LiveSlide https://atlaslearning. net presentation tool to have students respond to your writing prompts or questions on their mobile devices (for video demonstrations: http://tinyurl.com/m7hnoye; for a description of the use of LiveSlide on the TechEducator Podcast: http://techedu catorpodcast.com/40). You can also employ other interactive presentations apps, such as iOS Doceri http://tinyurl.com/kmmnkyw), iOS http://tinyurl.com/mnsh8mk, and Android http://tinyurl.com/mjjuuqq, Celly apps, Socrative iOS http://tinyurl.com/n4vgbym, and Android apps, or MimeoMobile http://tinyurl.com/lj2zom2.

For example, you can upload your PowerPoint or Keynote presentation that includes slides with open-ended prompts to LiveSlide, which are then projected to the students' devices and the classroom screen. Students can then enter their responses to share with just you or the entire class as projected on a screen, creating a collaborative discussion.

Other Audio/Video Discussion Tools

There are other tools for use in creating synchronous audio and video discussions—for example, Share Board, Fring: Video Calls + Chat, BT Chat HD, ooVoo Video Chat, Vtok: Google Talk Video, FaceTime, Chat for GoogleTalk, ClickMe Online Meetings, GoToMeeting, and Adobe Connect for iOS. Students can also use the Groupboard app and SyncPad apps to share a collaborative whiteboard for drawing and chatting simultaneously, as well as the ability to upload photos (for more on videoconferencing tools: http://tinyurl.com/lyem98y).

To foster discussions in his high school English classes, Matthew Gillipsie (2013) has his students go to the Neat Chat site http://www.neatchat.com to create a new chat that then creates a URL to share with a small group or the entire class. He also uses Neat Chat along with TodaysMeet http://todaysmeet.com to have students post questions or comments during his own or others' presentations.

Students can also use The Over the Line? http://tinyurl.com/mmbs6sv iOS app to discuss personal issues related to their social relationships, bullying, sexting, use of social media, competitiveness, pressures, and so on, by submitting stories and responding to or rating those stories anonymously. Students can also access programs that provide assistance for addressing these issues—for example, the National Teen Dating Abuse Hotline and the National Suicide Prevention Hotline.

Finally, students can use the Flipgrid http://tinyurl.com/m52e9ck iOS app to create video clip responses limited to 90 seconds from students to grids as collections of questions addressing a topic or theme. Collections of these students' responses along with photo images of each student can then be posted on class blogs or websites.

PLANNING DIGITAL DISCUSSION ENVIRONMENTS

Of course, digital tools themselves do not create powerful learning experiences; what you do with them makes them effective. This idea has been expressed in the popular mantra "Pedagogy must drive technology," which means that you need to first articulate your goals for using technology and not let tools drive your choices and actions. Clearly articulating goals allows us to justify and defend the use of technology in the classroom, and it helps us explain how and what students are learning through technology integration (Hawisher, Selfe, Moraski, & Pearson, 2004; R. Selfe, 2005). Thus far, we have discussed several reasons why you might consider using synchronous or asynchronous discussions in your writing classroom:

- Engaging students in productive collaboration and response
- Helping students write concretely for audience and purpose
- Exploring, constructing, and maintaining online identities
- Developing and creating a learning community
- Reflecting on course material
- Exchanging ideas with other students
- Corresponding with students across distance
- Offering critical review of peer work

Of course, these are but a few pedagogical goals that might drive digital discussion environments, and they are not necessarily mutually exclusive. In fact, your decision to integrate digital discussion environments might include overlapping goals. For example,

Grisham and Wolsey (2006) articulate the multiple goals that they had for using threaded discussion groups:

> We wanted to build group coherence among students. We wanted to share informa-
> tion about the readings with them and have them share information with one another.
> We wanted students to process ideas about the reading. We envisioned that we might
> do some tutoring online, refine students' communication skills, and also provide feed-
> back to students. (p. 652)

Whether your goals are single or multiple, the important thing is to go through the exercise of articulating what you want to do with digital discussion environments and let those goals guide your activities. In doing do, you will ensure that your pedagogy is driving your use of technology. So, as you begin thinking about your own goals, consider the ways that students read and write in your class. How might synchronous or asynchronous discussions enhance learning?

In addition to articulating overall goals for using online discussion, you might consider ways to scaffold digital discussion environments to help students build writing and critical thinking skills. Earlier we discussed one technique for scaffolding, which was to use "phases of engagement" as you plan for digital discussion environments. Another way to scaffold is to offer several different forms of online discussion in an online environment, keeping in mind that different technologies work best for different activities. To illustrate, Grady and Davis (2005) suggest the following strategies for scaffolding online: (1) develop a personal home page for each student as a way to initiate discussion and interaction; (2) establish a class Listserv and personal e-mail as a way for instructors to make announcements and connect with students (and for students to make their presence known as well); (3) schedule synchronous chats weekly for 1 hour to supplement course material and assignments and use a planned agenda and discussion moderator for chats; (4) create online discussion boards organized according to discussion topic to further discussion on ideas mentioned in other forums (pp. 116–118). Offering multiple discussion forums may reinforce concepts and give students the chance to reflect in a variety of meaningful ways.

Managing Digital Discussion Environments

As you become more experienced with digital discussion environments, you might notice nuances of online communication that emerge that require your guidance. Does one student dominate digital discussion? Do some entries include inappropriate language? Are some students avoiding the digital discussion environment? These are examples of issues that can arise in a digital discussion environment when facilitating online discussions (for more on strategies for fostering online discussions: http://tinyurl.com/9bcopuq).

While these environments are designed to be student centered, there are moments when teacher guidance is necessary and helpful. An important question about asynchronous discussions is how participation can be regulated. While discussion boards serve as spaces for delayed-time reflection, they also foster participation from all students. Perhaps for this reason, discussion boards have been characterized as a solution to "equalizing" class participation.

In the early 1990s, several scholars made the claim that online discussions "equalized" student populations by allowing everyone to contribute to class, unencumbered by impressions of race, gender, or class. Students who may have felt "silenced" in a face-to-face classroom setting could contribute more freely in an online environment (C. L. Selfe & Hawisher, 2002). However, many of the arguments about equalizing and democratizing online discussions have since faded, especially given that teachers have found that online discussions can create new divisions among students, based on such factors as typing speed. But the appeal of discussion boards cannot be denied: certainly, if participation is required, discussion boards can "equalize" discussion, or at the very least, they can easily demonstrate patterns of discussion and domination in the classroom.

Another management issue in digital discussions involves politeness, or "netiquette," in online environments (for more on online netiquette, http://tinyurl.com/kpffjht). This issue arises when students use acronyms, abbreviations, or symbols to shortcut communication. Such conventions might be acceptable and familiar to many students—but most likely, this is not true for all students. Before committing to digital discussion environments, you might want to poll your students about their access to technology outside the classroom. Such a poll might reveal that some students have access to a high-speed Internet connection at home or that they participate in other personal digital discussion environments on a regular basis. You will also learn through a poll which students do not have access or do not care to participate in digital discussions. Having this information might help you better understand patterns of communication that emerge in your digital discussion environment. You can give your students a short survey along with Figure 6.1 about their experience with digital discussion environments.

Sample Student Poll of Technology Access and Use

1. What forms of online discussion have you used?
2. What are your favorite forms of discussion?
3. Which online discussions do you use in school?

4. Which online discussions do you use outside school?

Use the table in the figure to answer Questions 1–4. Place an *X* in the boxes that apply.

At the very least, this survey will start a discussion between you and your students about technology. You might learn about access issues, their favorite technologies, and even about "lingo" that they use to talk about technology. Survey results will also help you make appropriate design choices and ensure better chances that students will engage in discussion environments.

Politeness could also emerge as an issue when students "hog the floor," or dominate digital discussions, or when they use inappropriate language. These issues are more prevalent in a chat environment than an asynchronous environment, when participation might rely on typing speed. Strategies can get around these obstacles, such as formalizing a discussion by acting as a discussion leader or assigning a student facilitator to lead the conversation with discussion questions. Another strategy is to monitor turn taking

	Favorite discussion environments	Discussion environments you use in school	Discussion environments you use outside school
Bulletin Board			
Email			
Blogs			
Instant Messenger			
MySpace			
Chat rooms			
MOOs or MUDs			
Wikis			
Interactive gaming environments			
FanFiction			
Text messages			
Other			

Figure 6.1.   Students' Use of Different Discussion Tools

through visual symbols that create etiquette online. For example, Craig Smith (2006) proposes that chat participants use simple symbols to indicate turn taking: (1) an exclamation point! or question mark? is used to indicate when someone wants to make a contribution or raise a question, the equivalent of raising a hand in discussion; (2) three forward slash marks /// are used to indicate the end of a contribution. Smith suggests that participants follow these rules and wait to see participant contributions unfold before jumping in the discussion; participants felt that the technique worked well to manage discussion and create a more coherent conversation.

To evaluate students' discussion participation, you could develop a rubric based on valuing collaborative sharing with peers. For example, Howard Rheingold (2014) employs the following rubric for assessing students' posts:

> *4 points* = The posting(s) integrates multiple viewpoints and weaves both class readings and other participants' postings into their discussion of the subject.
>
> *3 points* = The posting(s) builds upon the ideas of another participant or two, and digs deeper into the question(s) posed by the instructor.
>
> *2 points* = A single posting that does not interact with or incorporate the ideas of other participants' comments.
>
> *1 point* = A simple "me too" comment that neither expands the conversation nor demonstrates any degree of reflection by the student.
>
> *0 points* = No comment.

SUMMARY

In this chapter, we suggest that digital discussion environments encourage students to practice writing, to build community, and to enhance learning. We review various synchronous and asynchronous technologies that can support digital discussion environments, and we suggest strategies for scaffolding discussions and helping students participate through reflection and increased critical thinking. These digital discussions can then continue when they begin to consider how to present their writing on blogs and wikis, the subjects of our next chapter.

7

CO-CONSTRUCTING KNOWLEDGE THROUGH COLLABORATIVE WRITING

One primary affordance of digital tools is that they serve to mediate collaboration in that students can work together virtually on the same text without having to be physically present through face-to-face interaction. Students using Google Docs or a wiki can each contribute to and revise the same text.

In this chapter, we focus on the social practice of students' collaboration in understanding and creating digital texts. However, as we argue, given the emphasis in schools on evaluating students for their individual, autonomous performance, students need extensive instruction and support to help them engage in productive collaboration. Effecting collaboration can serve to enhance learning depending on students' having a clear sense of purpose, knowing how to engage in cooperative learning, defining roles and responsibilities, having a sense of interdependence, and on teachers' monitoring and evaluating student learning (D. W. Johnson & Johnson, 2009).

DIGITAL WRITING TOOLS FOSTERING COLLABORATIVE WRITING

Schools and universities are increasingly using collaborative digital writing tools listed on the website http://tinyurl.com/lpwks68, such as Hackpad https://hackpad.com, Titan-Pad http://titanpad.com, or PrimaryPad http://primarypad.com, which employ color codes to indicate different writers' contributions. For a description of students using different collaborative writing tools designed for a student audience, see M. Barton and Klint (2011): http://tinyurl.com/l3j4wlg.

Students can also use the MixedInk http://tinyurl.com/k7pxmb7 platform, which supports different students creating text that is then combined into one remixed composite text (for a video demonstration: http://vimeo.com/10468404). Students can rate one another's writing and then draw on one another's texts. Students can then engage in further revisions and another round of ratings that serve to generate a final composite text based on those ratings.

Using Google Docs and Forms

Of these different available collaborative writing tools, students are frequently using Google Docs (Kumar, Liu, & Black, 2012) as one of the Google Drive apps for use with browsers, or they are using the iOS Google Drive app http://tinyurl.com/ckuvapt or Google Docs for Android http://tinyurl.com/m2z9h4c or the Android MyDocs app http://tinyurl.com/m2z9h4capps.

Students can upload their Word or Pages files to Google Docs or download them as a Word, PDF, or HTML file. To collaborate with peers, they click on "Share" and submit their peers' e-mail addresses so that their peers' names are listed as coeditors. Students can also access different versions of their drafts using "Revisions." For useful tips on using Google Docs, see http://tinyurl.com/nj77dd2.

In using Google Docs, as a teacher you can download the Read&Write for Google™ http://tinyurl.com/o29vc2k add-on extension for use with a Chrome browser (for the free educator registration: http://tinyurl.com/ofqgeq9). This tool assists students through audio productions of the color-highlighted text on Docs, including audio translations; audio and image word definition; predictions of alternative words in creating text; and tools for collecting, annotating, and navigating texts. This tool would therefore be particularly useful for struggling readers or writers, as well as English-language learners.

Teachers are also increasingly using Google Forms http://tinyurl.com/pahen25 to create open-ended questions or survey questions to have students share their responses to the same questions to compare answers. For creating questions for use by respondents on a Form, you or your students select from a range of different types of prompts/questions, such as whether respondents provide short versus longer answers, multiple choice, checkboxes, selections from a list, rating scale, or grid. You can view respondents' answers on a form as a summary of responses, as a spreadsheet, or as a downloaded CSV file.

Students at Minnetonka High School, Minnetonka, Minnesota, have used Google Forms for a range of different purposes http://goo.gl/Zr2VD (for a video by Ben Stanerson, a technology coordinator in the Minnetonka Public Schools, on making Google Forms: http://tinyurl.com/n33qwv2). For use in her English class at Minnetonka High School, Sara Martinson has students use Forms for a class review of *Romeo and Juliet* http://tinyurl.com/ld4buj2 (see Figure 7.1).

For giving feedback on students' formulation of thesis statements about short stories feedback http://tinyurl.com/ld4buj2, see Figure 7.2.

Type your thesis statement here. Please put the literary device you plan to discuss in CAPITAL LETTERS	Type your topic sentence for Body Paragraph ONE here.	Type your topic sentence for Body Paragraph TWO here.	Feedback
Pride can cause people to make reckless decisions and cause great harm. (THE SCARLET IBIS & TO BUILD A FIRE) - Lesson learned by the protagonist.	Compare: how they both make reckless decisions. The man choosing to hunt alone and brother choosing to push doodle to his limits.	Contrast: the harmful affects of their pride. The man dies because of his pride, while brother's pride causes the death of someone else.	I'd put something either in the thesis or the link that identifies your lit term.
LESSONS LEARNED BY THE PROTAGONIST: The value of family is interpreted differently by Swamp Boy and Brother, which causes their regrets later in life. (Swamp Boy and The Scarlet Ibis)	Contrasting the value of family according to Swamp Boy and Brother	Comparing the regrets each of them experience later in their lives	I'm not sure about that first provable part. Are you going to write that one values family less than the other? I'm not sure that's accurate...
SYMBOLICALLY speaking, To Build A Fire and The Scarlet Ibis are very similar in showing life and death.	Comparing fire (the man's life) and the ibis (life)	Comparing death through the cold weather and the Doodle's coffin	How do you plan to connect the paragraphs if you aren't using the same symbols? It seems like your paragraphs will be separate entities rather than interconnected. You'll need to figure this out.
THEME As shown in To Build a Fire and Scarlet Ibis, pride can lead to good consequences, as well as bad ones.	Contrast Doodle learning to walk and Man's cruel treatment of dog.	Compare Doodle's death and Man's death.	It's not clear in your thesis that you'll be writing a compare / contrast essay. Can you find a way to make that more clear to your audience?

Figure 7.1.   Use of Google Forms to Share Students' Thesis Topics. *Source: Screenshot of use of Google Forms used with permission of Sara Martinson.*

Brian Turnbaugh (2010) used Google Forms to survey his students' media uses, including the time that they devoted to use of different kinds of media (for a copy of the survey: http://tiny.cc/SyKoT). In his survey of students' number of hours devoted daily to watching TV, surfing the web, participating in social networks, sending text messages, reading, or playing video games, he found that for surfing the web, 29% devoted 0 hours; 43%, 0–1 hours; 20%, 1–2 hours; and 8%, 2–3 hours.

For working collaboratively on a Google Form, you or your students can add individual collaborators to give them editing privileges. You can select from a range of different templates to create Forms specific to your needs, and you or your students can also create a Form using data from a Google spreadsheet, as well as add images or videos to a Form. Other alternatives to Google Forms for open-ended responses include Learnclick http://www.learnclick.com, JotForm (can be used with DropBox: http://www.jotform.com, Webanketa http://webanketa.com, and Webform http://webform.com).

CHALLENGES OF ENGAGING STUDENTS IN COLLABORATIVE DIGITAL WRITING

There are a number of challenges associated with engaging students in collaborative writing. One major challenge is that students are predisposed to an individualistic, competitive mode of writing on their own and being evaluated for their own work. Therefore, they are often reluctant to engage in collaborative writing when they assume

Original Text & Citation	Explicated Text	Context / Significance / Explanation	Literary Terms you could use with this passage
I pray the, good Mercutio, let's retire./The day is hot, the Capels are abroad,/And if we meet we shall not scape' the brawl,/For, now, these hot days, is the mad blood stirring. (3.1.1-4)	1. Please Mercutio, let's go home 2. The day is hot in temperature as well as temper, and the Capulets are out in about 3. If we should happen to run into them, we most definitely will get into a fight 4. For the tension between us is so high that there surely will be blood.	Benvolio just what's to keep peace and doesn't want get into trouble. This shows the readers that he is a peaceful man and wants to keep peace between the two families.	Characterization Mood (shows that there is tension-blood stirring, hot tempers)
But love thee better than thou canst devise Till thou shalt know the reason of my love. (3.1.70-3.1.71)	I love you more than you can think Even though you don't know why I love you.	This is Romeo expressing his newfound love for tybalt because he is his cousin, and it is dramatic irony because Romeo and the reader know Romeo is married to Juliet, but no one else knows the connection.	Dramatic irony
Romeo! The love I bear thee can afford hate / No better term than this: Thou art a villain! (3.1.61-3.1.62)	Romeo, I have so little love for you. The only thing I can say is this: you are a villain!	Mercutio and tybalt are about to fight. Then Romeo shows up to try to talk them down. He tries to show his love to tybalt, but tybalt only shows his anger and hatred to Romeo for ruining his party.	Rising action: this leads to their fight, and then mercutio's death. Conflict: Romeo vs tybalt
A plague o' both your houses! They have made worms meat of me. (3.1.111-3.1.112)	O, the houses are so bad, Because of them, I am dying.	Because the reader knows how lighthearted mercutio usually is, by him being so serious about this situation, the reader realizes how bad the feud is.	Conflict: the Anger between the families

Figure 7.2.   Use of Google Forms to Provide Feedback to Students' Thesis Topics. *Source: Screenshot of use of Google Forms used with permission of Sara Martinson.*

that their grades will be based on their own writing. Even if a teacher assesses a group's efforts, students may be concerned about the validity of such an assessment when some members contribute more than others in generating writing (for strategies on fostering collaboration: http://tinyurl.com/kklqfpd).

Students in one study (Brunk-Chavez & Miller, 2007) noted difficulties in collaborative wiki writing in groups because of the following:

- They do not believe that knowledge is socially constructed.
- They dislike groups in which there is a leader and followers.
- They distrust their peers as having less knowledge or writing ability than their teacher.
- They believe that they are not capable of helping their peers.
- They perceive little value in shared talk to improve their writing.
- They disagree with their peers' beliefs, leading to struggles in sharing ideas.
- They respond negatively to poorly designed collaborative groups and assignments.
- They become frustrated with peers who do not contribute.

This suggests the need to develop procedures for fostering and assessing students' collaborative writing based on the degree to which each member of a group contributes to the collaboration, procedures that would include students' self-assessment of their own and their peers' contributions. You can also access the revision history data on collaborative writing sites such as Google Docs or wikis to obtain information about individual students' specific contributions in revising a text.

A related challenge is whether students can effectively work together in a collaborative manner. Students are more likely to engage in productive collaboration when each member of a group can define his or her particular roles and responsibilities for contribution to the group's work. For example, in working collaboratively on a research project studying problems in funding of their school's athletic programs based on gender equity differences, a group of students could divide up their tasks according to sports programs in their school to identity differences in the funding of those programs.

Another challenge has to do with instances in which students have difficulty coming to consensus on a certain topic or issue given the differences in their perspectives or beliefs within a group, particularly if members of a group are friends. Addressing and reconciling these differences requires some careful negotiations, whereby students voice reasons for their differences given their alternative perspectives or beliefs.

To address these challenges, students could devise a written agreement or contract that specifies goals and norms constituting a particular collaborative effort (Ingalls, 2011). In this agreement or contract, students identify their instructor's expectations in terms of their purpose, genre, style, audience, voice, research, length, deadlines, and so on, as well as how members plan to communicate with one another, make decisions, adhere to deadlines, and address potential conflicts. Members also define what each perceives to be criteria for a high-quality final product and then determine how to successfully complete the project. During the collaboration, students should continually refer back to the agreement or contract if revisions of the goals, expectations, deadlines, and criteria need to be revised, as well as determine if members are each adhering to the agreement or contract (Ingalls, 2011).

Students could also address some of the following questions related to expectations regarding roles and participation in a group:

- What are some of the roles that people are likely to fall into (e.g., Newcomer, Wrapper, Lurker, Aggregator, etc.)?
- How likely is it that participants will stick with the project? If you expect many participants to leave, how will this effect the group and the outcome?
- Do you envision new people joining the group as time goes by? If so, what features are you designing that will support their integration into an existing flow?
- Will the project work if people dip in and out? If so, what features support that? If not, how will people stay focused?
- What social objective, or "product" if any, is the project aiming to achieve?
- What do you expect the group to do, from the moment it convenes, to the end of its life-span, to create the specific outcome that will exist at the conclusion of its last meeting?
- How much of a time commitment do you expect from participants? Is this kind of commitment realistic for members of your group?

- Does everyone need to participate equally? How might non-equal participation play out for participants down the line? (G. Johnson & Corneli, 2014, pp. 98–100)

Another factor influencing collaboration is the design of classroom spaces. The physical aspects of classroom spaces have been transformed so that students can more readily interact with one another face-to-face as opposed to sitting in straight rows—for example,

> Case Western recently installed an "active collaboration room." The room has a large TelePresence screen at the front of the room, but also an interactive whiteboard (IWB) on the wall, other projection screens, and collaborative tables that seat from three to six students. There are three cameras, and when a student or instructor is speaking, or if the instructor is writing on the board, one of the cameras pans to this person automatically. (Nastu, 2012)

BLOGGING

Another primary tool for engaging students in collaborative writing is blogging. Students can create their individual blogs and interact with other students' blogs using comments, or they can contribute to a composite class blog. In setting up blogs, you face the choice of having each student have his or her own blog as opposed to having students all contribute to one classroom blog (for steps on setting up a class blog from Edublog: http://tinyurl.com/l6fsvlq).

Blog Platforms

There is a range of blogging platforms available for classroom use, as well as a number of different types of blogs and uses of blogs http://tinyurl.com/mdnjgmf. The most frequently used web-based blogging platforms in schools are Blogger, WordPress, Edublogs (hosted by WordPress), and KidBlog. For microblogging of short posts, students can use Tumblr http://www.tumblr.com. One advantage of EduBlog and KidBlog is that they are designed primarily for use in schools and therefore have a lot of useful privacy features related to limiting access to only students within your class.

Course management systems such as Moodle, Blackboard, Edmodo, Schoology, SumTotalSystems, Desire2Learn, or Collaborize Classroom as well as social networking tools such as Ning have built-in blogging features. Even if they do not, you can link a class blog into your course management system or class website. For a video by Ann Murphy on how she uses blogs in her world literature class using the blog feature in

Blackboard, see http://www.screencast.com/t/HGpy4V8OztoS; here are some blog posts by her ninth-grade students: http://blogs.acpsk12.org/weread/sample-page.

For blogging on iOS devices, students can use apps for the blogger tools noted above as well as apps such as BlogPress, Tumblr for iPad, or Blogsy on iPads, or Blogger-droid Tumblr, Weebly, LiveJournal, or Bloglovin on Android devices. Students can use these apps to export blog posts to blog platforms such as Blogger, Wordpress, EduBlog, KidBlog, Tumblr, or Squarespace. So, students can create a post on their device and then export it to different desktop blogging platforms, something that can be useful for students who prefer to type on desktop or laptop computers. You can also create a classroom blog as an iOS or Android app using the Educators App http://educatorsapp.com by e-mailing the blog's URL to Educators App; you can then distribute the blog as an app for students or parents (Beach & O'Brien, 2014).

Using these blog platforms allows students to present their writing in a physically appealing, multimodal layout through the use of templates, embedded images, video clips, and hyperlinks to other blog posts, connections consistent with the social practice of making connections with their peers as well as audiences outside their classroom. Through linking to others' posts and posting comments on blogs, students are adopting alternative perspectives through restating these ideas or positions objectively and then raising questions about those ideas or positions to formulate counterarguments or citing examples to refute these ideas or positions.

In creating their blogs, students need to be familiar with the different components of a blog (Gunelius, 2012, pp. 50–63):

- *Home page* that portrays a blog's overall topical or thematic focus, typically organized using two-to-three column layout, with a header containing a blog's title, images, and/or description of the blog that appears on all pages.
- *Template* for a blog's layout and design provided by a blogging platform students can draw on to create their blog.
- *Profile or about page* that provides readers with a description of the student biographical information and the focus of the blog.
- *Posts* that consist of entries with a title and content often including links to one's own or other posts; post titles that are also listed in a sidebar.
- *Comments* that readers compose at the end of a post in response to that post; you can assign students' to be "journal buddies" to insure that all students receive comments.
- *Tags* that identify topics covered in posts that are listed in a sidebar to assist in searching for those topics addressed in posts; these tags typically appear as a word cloud with more frequent topics appearing in larger font.
- *Blogroll* that lists other blogs a student may be following.
- *Archives* that include links to past posts.

- *Footer* that includes contact information, copyright statement, and/or links to social networking sites.

Setting up individual blogs is relatively simple. For setting up a Blogger blog, students use their Gmail/Google account to sign into Blogger on Google Drive; create a name/URL for their blog http://XXX.blogspot.com; select from different template options for the layout, font, and color options; create a post entry with a title; and add information about themselves on the profile page. For instructions on how to set up Blogger (Curran & Wetherbee, 2012), see http://tinyurl.com/ld9qzhc.

Individual Versus Class Blogs

In using blogs in the classroom, you can opt to have students have their own blogs, or you can create a class blog to which all students contribute posts. One advantage for using individual blogs is that students may experience a greater degree of ownership of their blog, leading to more self-initiated writing than what might be the case with a classroom blog. The major disadvantage to individual blogs is that students may encounter difficulties setting up their blogs and require additional assistance, suggesting the need to select a blog platform that is relatively easy to use. Students' use of individual blogs also needs to be monitored to ensure that their blogs are password protected and that they are not disclosing private information in their profiles or posts or being attacked by spammers. As a teacher, you also need to keep track of and monitor a large number of different blogs.

One advantage of using a class blog is that all posts submitted to the blog can be monitored so that only teacher-approved posts end up being published. Another advantage is that, because they are exposed to their peers' posts, students are more likely to read and provide comments on one another's posts with class blogs than when each student has his or her own blog. Class blogs are particularly useful in teaching an online course because they serve to centralize students' writing in one place, as is the case with online forums.

Purposes for Using Blogs

In contrast to use of wikis (discussed later in this chapter) for the purpose of organizing and sharing of information, blogs are often used to voice positions about certain topics or issues of interest to a blog's subscribers, creating a collaborative interaction around these positions, a focus on argumentative writing that is central to the Common Core standards for English language arts writing.

Kristen Hicks (2013a, 2013b) identifies a number of benefits of blogging for students: Blogging contributes to enhanced student interaction with course materials and interaction with peers and instructors through adding comments, sharing of resources, taking ownership of their ideas in ways that enhance their self-confidence and sense of voice, practice of writing, and increased student engagement. Because blogs can extend beyond the classroom to a public audience, students also adopt a public voice in framing their positions. Dana Boyd (2006) uses the metaphor of the soapbox speaker in a community square to describe the process of adopting a public voice. She quotes one blogger, Jennifer, who noted the following:

> You're basically standing on a soapbox and reading something out loud only with a blog it feels like there's a big community square and everyone's got a soapbox and they're about the same height and everyone's reading at the same time. So it's a matter of people going and listening to one and oh, I don't like what you're saying and blogging with someone else and listening to what they're saying until you happen to find someone who is saying something interesting or you happen to know where your friend is on his soapbox saying something. (p. 3)

Boyd notes that Jennifer perceives herself as "speaking, performing her thoughts to a conceptualized audience" (p. 3). This focus on voicing positions to an audience leads to readers posting comments or to other bloggers responding to blog posts in their own blogs by agreeing or disagreeing with these posts, suggesting that the blogosphere itself constitutes a collaborative forum. This suggests the importance of having students read one another's posts to provide comments or responses in their own posts to foster such collaborative interaction. By expressing their opinions in a forceful manner, they are more likely to receive comments from their peers.

However, bloggers may often voice their positions without providing adequate reasons or evidence to support those positions. Given the emphasis in the Common Core argumentative writing standards on the need to provide supporting evidence for one's positions, in creating their blog posts, students need to conduct research on their topics or issues to provide such supporting evidence.

In her American literature class at Edina High School in Minnesota, Kathleen West was frustrated with her classroom discussions of literature. Many of her students were not sharing their responses, and when they did, they just offered cursory interpretations, disconnected from other students' ideas. She recognized that the usual teacher-led classroom discussion just was not working. She decided to set up a blog as an optional tool to foster more engaged interaction among students:

> I hoped that blogging would change the dynamics of our large-group interactions in positive ways. On their blogs, students would not necessarily be referring to a teacher-

generated question based on a particular reading assignment. Instead, they could feel
free to offer thoughts and opinions on different sections of the book in their asynchronous electronic conversations, which would "level the playing field" in terms of ability
and motivation to complete reading assignments.

In writing their posts on Kathleen's class blog, students were mutually sharing their
responses to literature. Kristina's post elicited two responses from her peers, which in
turn encouraged her to make some further responses to *The Great Gatsby* (Fitzgerald,
1992).

> *Kim:* I don't really think that being on separate islands meant that Gatsby and Daisy
> were doomed not to get together. Gatsby moved across from her on purpose.
>
> *Kristina:* He did? Where did it say that? And did Fitzgerald say why he wanted to be
> across the bay from her? I think it would make more sense if they lived on the same
> island, since he was doing everything he could to get close to her.
>
> *Axeman:* Thank you for your thoughts [Kristina], and I have a question for you: How
> does Gatsby know its her light? He would of had to sneak around her house and find
> out that she has a green dock light which is on 24/7. Isn't that kind of creepy?
>
> *Kristina:* I don't think that he would even have needed to know that it was specifical-
> ly her dock where the light resided, because the symbolic significance would still be
> there. I think that the point was that the light was on the other egg where she lived
> and in that way, by seeing it he could feel closer to her.

Students shifted to a more informal language style because they were now writing to
peer and web audiences. Kathleen noted that her students were expressing their responses to literature as part of conversing with peers:

> I found that students come to see through their blogs that their individual responses to
> class texts matter and are worthy of an audience of peers. As such, they're written in
> language that is meant to appeal to that audience, peppered with sarcasm, pop-culture
> references, and abbreviations that invite age-mates in. I found that blogs are a safe
> virtual space to bring students "outside" identities and literacies into the classroom.

While, ideally, students will generate their own topics or issues to address in their blogs,
some students—particularly those who are apprehensive about writing—may need engaging, open-ended prompts that encourage them to write. To encourage students to
generate their own topics, you can have students pose questions about a topic or issue
that interests them. For example, Paul Allison (2009) notes how his students formulate
critical inquiry questions for sharing with others on the site Youth Voices:

I ask my students to find a question or a set of questions that they develop in their own speculative writing, and eventually they do online research about their questions, connecting with others who have published on the Internet, and critically interpreting the welter of information available to them there. Students grow their blogs over a semester of working with other students and teachers who share their social network, Youth Voices. (p. 89)

He also poses questions for his students to consider in their blogging:

- What are you passionate about and how do these interests fit with other students' big questions?
- What voices or sources of information do you think are important to include in your search for answers?
- How do you become an effective online networker and get people with shared interests to value your voice online? (p. 89)

Teachers Recognizing the Value of Blogging through Blogging

It is also useful for teachers themselves to engage in blogging so that they understand the specific practices involved in it and how to model these practices for their students. Kristin Wallace, an English teacher at Westonka High School, Mound, Minnesota, draws on her experience in keeping her own blog, Writeonwallace, http://write onwallace.blogspot.com, to foster blogging in her classroom:

After writing my own blog for a year, I had the confidence to integrate blogging into my classroom. This process has evolved tremendously over the past two years. When I first introduced blogging to my students, they had very little control over their content. Each week, I provided them a topic or question and they responded. The result was little more than an online journal. Technology was only a substitution for traditional writing and not the transformation that I wanted.

After only a semester, I realized in order to transform students' writing their blogs needed to be more authentic. So I gave over control to the students and allowed them to create a blog around topics of their choice. We began our new blog by exploring what our passions were and then selecting one of these as a theme for the blog. Students began writing about video games, soccer, longboarding, music and ballet. I was amazed at how quickly the blogs began to develop simply by shifting the ownership to the students. Students began to see their blogs as a reflection of themselves. They became excited about the design and content of their blogs and were even motivated to share these electronic self-portraits with others. And most importantly, the blogging motivated many of my reluctant writers. Armed with their own passion, writing was no longer a daunting task, but rather a method of self expression and discovery.

Over the past two years, integrating blogs into my classroom has transformed my curriculum more than any other technology or tool. Blogging has allowed my students to develop as writers, thinkers and learners.

Let's be clear, blogging has not been easy. Writing is hard whether it is on paper or online. The difference is the students are writing for a real audience and about topics which inspire them. It doesn't matter if their passion is politics, snowboarding, or Disney, they all have something to say when it is a subject they choose. As I look to the future, my hope is students will be blogging with other students in other schools by this time next year.

Blogging also helps or, more accurately, forces me to reflect on my teaching. Self reflection is key to the development of any skill. Writing about my successes and my challenges helps me to sort out what works and what doesn't, but more importantly, it asks me to reflect on why. Teaching isn't a job; teaching is a craft and as any craftsman will tell you, skills are forged over a lifetime. It is easy to be swept up in the business of teaching (attendance, meetings, budgets, data), but blogging forces me to slow down my pace, reflect on my practice, and hone my craft.

Writing About Relevant Topics or Issues

One crucial aspect in using blogs is finding topics or issues that students will perceive as engaging, particularly topics or issues that are relevant to their everyday lives. In her first-year college composition course at Arizona Western College, located near the Arizona/Mexico border, Bree McGregor used a class blog based on a Wordpress platform to have her students collaboratively write about issues facing their campus. These topics included navigability/design of campus parking, on-campus housing, the dining facilities, campus safety, the Math Center, the Game Room, and bus service to/from campus. Groups of students selected one issue; gathered information about it; and interviewed peers, faculty, staff, and administration about their perceptions of the issue. By doing so, her students were writing for actual audiences—for some tangible purpose—to improve the quality of their campus life. Students then wrote drafts, received feedback, made further revisions, and engaged in some Wordpress blogging tutorials. Students then created blog posts that included hyperlinks as well as photos or videos; they also made oral presentations to their class based on their blog posts to further emphasize the importance of a peer audience.

Bree noted that her students faced a number of challenges in writing their blogs. Because her students were quite familiar with the issues of campus life they were addressing and because they already had certain opinions regarding these issues, in conducting research on these issues, she anticipated that they would have difficulty adopting an impartial stance on these issues. She was also concerned that given their familiarity with these issues, they may assume that they do not need to conduct further research and simply write about their own recollection of an issue, failing to use their research and writing as a tool for gaining new insights into that issue.

Another challenge had to do with her emphasis on the value of collaboration. Many of her students had job or family obligations, which limited the amount of time that they had for engaging in collaboration outside of class time. Given these time constrictions, she "created project components that can be completed by group members individually—without actually meeting as a group outside of class." Where collaboration was required, she "allotted class time to at least complete 50% of that component" (personal communication).

She knew that her students needed to recognize the difference between writing traditional essays and creating blog posts in terms of layout, white space, links, images, and video, requiring alternative formatting consistent with blogging:

> Students may want to format this post differently than they would a traditional essay. For example, long, uninterrupted paragraphs of text are not especially reader-friendly for blog design. I prefer students use block format, adding white space and photos and videos between paragraphs to break up large chunks of text. (personal communication)

In evaluating her students, 60% of their grade related to the quality of the content, which stemmed from students' ability to effectively collaborate; 10%, to use of links; 10%, to use of images; 10%, to use of video; and 10%, to their oral presentations.

In their blog posts, students described the services provided by the Arizona Western College's Math Center, including the tutoring that helped students in their math classes http://tinyurl.com/oa8nhnb; their Writing Center http://tinyurl.com/qc566n6; their international program http://tinyurl.com/o3ksuwb; the college's Game Room http://tinyurl.com/pfptkr7; their bus transit system http://tinyurl.com/nbd4zrk; the financial aid program http://tinyurl.com/oyqu9n3; a learning center located in the town of San Luis, Arizona, that can be used by students in lieu of having to drive to the Arizona Western College main campus located 45 minutes away in Yuma, Arizona, http://tinyurl.com/ncwom5u; their academic advising program http://tinyurl.com/psruwmg; vending machines on campus http://tinyurl.com/qjm6mf6; the importance of diversity http://tinyurl.com/oejewjq; issues of parking on campus http://tinyurl.com/oejewjq; the importance of teachers http://tinyurl.com/owocz7v; a "freshman survival guide," with tips on how to be a successful student http://tinyurl.com/ocq3d9t; and different places and resources on the college's main campus http://tinyurl.com/pvlx5hh. For each of the different posts, students shared their posts with one another for comments, creating a sense of audience.

Reading Blogs to Prepare for Writing Blogs

A critical step in using blogs is to have students read blogs to become familiar with their different features and conventions, as well as learning to add comments to them. As part of college foreign language classes, students read blogs written in French and German (Ducate & Lomicka, 2008). They were asked to read posts on these blogs once a week and note new vocabulary words, along with reporting on what they learned about the blogger's identity and cultural context. Students compared their own interest and cultural experiences with those of selected bloggers. Then, they created their own blogs to write posts in French or German along with adding comments to one another's posts. Students noted that they benefited from reading blogs in another language to assist them in their own language learning as well as their learning the conventions of blogging—learning that enhanced their own blogging.

To foster blog writing across countries and cultures, the QuadBlogging http:// quadblogging.net project connects students from throughout the world. In this project, four teachers from different schools in different locations or countries have students from one school create blog posts for one week while students from three other schools add comments, followed by students from another school for the next week receiving comments, so that after one month, all students receive comments (Boss, 2012). After receiving comments from students from these different locations, they were exposed to a range of alternative cultural perspectives.

Journal Writing Tools

As with blogs, students may employ journal/diary writing tools listed on the website http://tinyurl.com/m3anowg. Students can use these tools to engage in informal writing to record their perceptions of readings or events, keep field notes, describe autobiographical experiences, or reflect on what they learned in a class. To engage in collaborative journal writing across different platforms, students can employ the Clib http:// tinyurl.com/6sf4w94 tool.

Students may reflect about their reading or observations, employing "dual-entry" journal formats in which they put their responses to their reading or observations on one side of a page and then their reflections about those responses or observations on the other side of the page. Some journal apps, such as Taposé http://tinyurl.com/ ck83l9d, also allow students to view their writing on one side of the screen and a web search browser on the other side of the screen.

Using Comments With Blogs or Journals

Students also connect with one another by making and receiving comments on one another's blogs or journal posts—often, the more comments they receive, the higher their level of engagement in blogging or journaling. One advantage of using "blog partners" is to ensure that students receive at least some comments. Knowing that they can anticipate some response to their post may then help them formulate it in a certain manner.

"Comment starters" can be used to prompt student comments (Davis, 2007), "starters" such as "This made me think about . . . ," "I wonder why . . . ," "Your writing made me form an opinion about . . . ," "This post is relevant because . . . ," "Your writing made me think that we should . . . ," "I wish I understood why . . . ," "This is important because . . . ," "Another thing to consider is . . . ," "I can relate to this . . . ," "This makes me think of . . . ," "I discovered . . . ," "I don't understand . . . ," "I was reminded that . . . ," or "I found myself wondering . . ." Students also need to invite comments from their peers as well as react to comments to encourage further conversation by asking questions such as "Do you agree?"

Learning to make effective comments as well as creating their own posts in response to others' posts requires students to go beyond simply restating what their peers are *saying* to interpreting what their peers are *doing* in writing their posts—their purposes, agendas, and strategies. Joseph Harris (2006) describes different dialogic moves that students could adopt in their blogging: "coming to terms," "forwarding," "countering," and "taking an approach." In "coming to terms," students are summarizing a topic or issue by defining the purpose or need to address that topic or issue as well as citing others' voices from their peers or published blogs. In "forwarding," students are recontextualizing these other voices to reframe the topic or issue into different or new situations. For example, in a class blog discussion about the issue of cyberbullying, a student may cite peers' examples of their own experience with cyberbullying in their school and then analyze what might happen had their school adopted some strict guidelines regarding the use of cyberbullying. In "countering," a student may adopt an alternative perspective or way of thinking about a topic or issue to challenge status quo perspectives or ways of thinking. "Taking an approach" applies the ideas and positions shared on a class blog to a new topic or issue.

In having students post comments, it is also important that students follow netiquette guidelines associated with avoiding negative judgments, obscene language, or name-calling (M. Stewart, 2011). All of this means that it is important to make sure that you set up procedures that do not allow unknown people to contact your students. This would include having students do the following:

- Only use first names and not disclose personal information in profiles on their blogs—for example, their addresses, e-mail, or phone numbers.
- Use only blogs that are secure and password protected so that the only people who can make comments are you and peers in a class; one advantage to a classroom blog is that you have more control over access than when students have individual blogs, particularly for limiting spam.
- Be aware of issues of privacy and disclosure of personal information on the web, as well as issues of access to their blog.
- Avoid language, personal attacks, and flaming that would cause harm to other students or compromise their privacy.

Adopting "Acceptable Use Policies" for Blogging

Because students will be including material and links from the web on their blogs, administrators and parents are concerned about students accessing and importing inappropriate or "adult" material on their blogs. Schools are also required by the Child Internet Protection Act to filter out such content, as well as to formulate a policy regarding their students' protection from such material. However, such filtering often does not block certain content, and it may block out other material that may be beneficial. Then, students do not have access to material for legitimate academic purposes. If they are doing an assignment on certain topics related to sexuality, violence, terrorism, gambling, and so on, they may find that access to sites on these topics has been blocked, leading them to use "circumventor" sites to skirt blocking or filters.

All of this suggests the need for schools to develop proactive policies regarding online access to share with students and parents as opposed to punitive policies limiting students' web access. Schools may be rightfully concerned about the costs of potential litigation if they have to address problems with blog use. However, in attempting to ban blog use, particularly if that use occurs outside school property or in the home, they could face legal challenges related to free speech rights.

To encourage students to adhere to these practices, schools adopt "acceptable use policies" that students would sign indicating their agreement with following these procedures. For use in his school, Bud Hunt (2006) has drafted an acceptable use policy:

1. Students using blogs are expected to treat blogspaces as classroom spaces. Speech that is inappropriate for class is not appropriate for your blog. While we encourage you to engage in debate and conversation with other bloggers, we also expect that you will conduct yourself in a manner reflective of a representative of this school.
2. Students who violate the agreements here shall forfeit their right to school Internet access and will face other sanctions deemed appropriate by the administration.

3. Student blogs are to be a forum for student expression. However, they are first and foremost a tool for learning, and as such will sometimes be constrained by the various requirements and rules of classroom teachers. Students are welcome to post on any school-appropriate subject (this one might be hard to define. With blogging having such a personal emphasis, I wonder how we balance school and personal lives) at any time, outside of their classroom requirements.

You can also send letters to parents informing them about how and why blogs are being used in the classroom, a rationale for using them in terms of teaching writing, the protections related to privacy and access, and a request that they grant permission for their child to participate in using blogs in your classroom.

Because blogs are public spaces, students may have difficulty knowing where to draw the line in terms of sharing private, confidential information or criticisms of peers, teachers, administrators, public officials, or parents. They need to realize that sharing private, confidential information or criticisms of others to an unknown public can have serious consequences, in some cases, even legal charges of libel. Although the courts have recently protected journalists' use of blogs to voice criticisms under the free speech amendment, students still need to be cautious about what they share if they do not know who will be reading their blogs.

Creating Multimodal Posts

In creating their posts, students need to go beyond simply composing print-based essays to exploit the multimodal affordances of blogging through insertion of visual images, audio, and video, something we discuss in more detail in chapter 8. To do so, they can employ the infographic tools described in chapter 5, such as Infogr.am http://infogr.am to insert charts, graphs, or infographics; ThingLink http://www.thinglink.com to insert interactive images with links to images, audio, and video; SoundCloud https://soundcloud.com to create audio clips to embed in a post; or the YouTube mobile app for iOS http://tinyurl.com/cqc85sm or Android http://tinyurl.com/cqc85sm to record videos with their laptop/Chromebook camcorders using the YouTube editor to insert a video clip into their posts (Byrne, 2013c).

To add images, videos, or links to their posts, students click on one of the relevant icons in the "Post Editor" toolbar; they can then search for images/videos—for example, from Flickr Creation Commons or YouTube—to add to their posts. Students also need to know that if they create content for their Blogger or WordPress blog using Word or Pages to then transfer to their blog, they should not copy/paste that content into the Blogger "Compose" editor or the WordPress "Visual" editor, because they are also transferring the Word or Pages code, which will change how the text appears in a blog post; this is not an issue when using text from Google Docs (Byrne, 2013f). They should instead paste their content into the "HTML" editor that will then reveal any additional code; then that code should be deleted, as well as inserting *br/* in angle brackets between paragraphs if necessary to preserve paragraph spacing. They can then check on the formatting by going to "Compose" or Visual" prior to going to "Publish."

To allow you or other readers to subscribe to their blog and receive post updates, students can create RSS feeds for their blog using Feedburner http://feedburner. google.com. For instructions on creating a RSS feed for Blogger http://tinyurl.com/ krbgfde; Edublogs automatically creates feeds http://yourblog.edublogs.org/feed. To subscribe to a blog, readers can then use feed readers such as Feedly http://feedly.com, Digg RSS Reader http://digg.com, Netvibes http://www.netvibes.com, FeedDemon http://www.feeddemon.com, or Pulse https://www.pulse.me to read blog updates; they can also use RSS feeds to subscribe to a blog and receive updates on their e-mail, as well as add the "Follow by e-mail" gadget available under "Layout" to the blog.

Multigenre Student Blogs

For her 10th-grade class at Waconia High School, Waconia, Minnesota, Katie Keogh had her students engage in a multigenre writing project to generate texts that they shared on both Schoology and Google Drive to receive feedback and then on their blogs (for the complete assignment: http://tinyurl.com/m68sd7x). The students' posts reflect the use of multimodal blogging in that they had to create seven texts from different genres: letter, song, poem, obituary, alternate story or novel ending, character diary, editorial/opinion piece, or long-form interview transcript.

The following are some of the blog posts based on certain themes created by students in Katie's class; these blogs are also included on the website http://tinyurl.com/ lfll2z2. Because the students were reading *All Quiet on the Western Front* (Remarque, 1996), students built their blogs around aspects of war and the experiences of the novel's main character, Paul, who dies in World War I. Many of the students created a letter from Paul to his parents describing his coping with war.

Dana Hatfield: bravery and camaraderie http://danahatfieldblog.blogspot.com
Elle Fischer: sadness and depression caused by war http://ellefischerblog.blogspot. com
Emily Rolf: death caused by war http://emilyrolfblog3.blogspot.com
Taylor Liebsch: death caused by war http://taylorliebschblog.blogspot.com
Madi McCabe: companionship http://madimccabe.blogspot.com
Michael Weible: suffering http://michaelweibleblog.blogspot.com
Margaret Brose: the effects of war http://margaretbroseblog.blogspot.com
Caitlyn Hanson: sacrifice http://caitlynhansonblog.blogspot.com

Christina Sawvel: consequences of war and understanding death/grief http://
christinasawvelblog.blogspot.com

Gabbie Brakemeier: consequences of war http://gabbibrakemeierblog.blogspot.com

Kaylah Pask: fear of dying http://kaylahpask.blogspot.com

Modeling Blogging for Students

By sharing their blog posts with students, teachers are modeling blogging practices for students. In a national study of teachers' blogging as a means of communicating with students, parents, and the community, as well as a form of instructional practice, Jeffrey Felix (2008) found that teacher blogging increased peer interaction among students, teacher interaction with the students, and sharing of ideas, as well as fostered more positive student attitudes toward learning. Those teachers who reported posting daily to their blogs indicated that they post writing assignments 60% of the time on their blogs. Teachers also reported that students were motivated by their modeling to communicate with peers within and outside their classrooms.

This suggests the value of teachers fostering students' sharing their blog posts, along with reflections on blogging strategies. Students in Emily Wender's (2013) first-year British literature college course on literary criticism blogged to engage in collaborative sharing of responses to literature. Students posted responses to a classroom blog once a week and had to respond weekly to least one other student's post.

Wender also wrote her own posts to model different types of writing on a "Sample Blog" that students were required to read and add comments to. She found that in their posts, students adopted a tentative, exploratory stance associated with suspending closure, being tolerant of ambiguity and uncertainty, and taking risks.

Fictional Blogs

Students can also employ blogs to adopt fictional voices as part of constructing a narrative in a manner similar to the use of Facebook or Twitter to create fictional characters who interact with one another (for information on collaborative fiction writing: http://tinyurl.com/lbydts5).

Students could create a series of posts in narrative sequence, blogs that employ a lot of hyperlinks and features to create a narrative, blogs to tell a partial story linked to fan fiction sites, role-playing blogs, character diary blogs, or blogs used for publishing literary texts or for commercial purposes (Thomas, 2006). One example of a collaborative fiction-writing and role-playing site is the New Worlds Project http://rpgnewworlds.net, which is based on a science fiction world in which participants grapple with issues of peace in the midst of a world war in 2051. Within this site is a Creative Writing Project in which participants collaborate on stories about their experiences in the world war.

Consistent with the idea of the serial novel, one popular type of fictional blog consists of diary accounts of one or more protagonists containing extensive links to other posts or sites. When readers provide comments, the writer then uses material from these comments in later episodes. In adopting these hybrid styles in their blogs, students are experimenting with shifts in voice and style. They could reflect on how their use of voice in their blogs serves to define their personae as writers across different contexts.

Similar to the online role-play described in the preface, in responding to the novel *Montana 1948* (Watson, 1993), which portrays the effects of racism toward Native Americans in a small Montana town in 1948, students in Elizabeth Erdmann's class assumed the roles of different characters in the novel as well as actual persons (the owner of the Washington Redskins, Louise Erdrich, Russell Means [Native American activist], etc.) to debate the issue of whether the University of North Dakota "Fighting Sioux" mascot should be abolished on a class blog (Beach, Doerr-Stevens, & Boeser, 2011). In their roles, some students argued that the mascot was offensive to Native Americans in the same manner as the racism portrayed in the novel, while other students argued that the mascot should not necessarily be perceived as offensive. Drawing on the novel to adopt these different roles helped students connect relatively contemporary, lived-world aspects of racism to the novel.

In another role-play in Elizabeth's class, students used a blog http://schooledthewriteway.blogspot.com to create the roles of fictional high school students coping with the issues facing adolescents portrayed in Laurie Halse Anderson's (2006) *Speak* and Stephen Chbosky's (1999) *The Perks of Being a Wallflower* (for directions: http://tinyurl.com/mvxfb8t). The students then used their roles to write letters to Charlie, the main character in *The Perks of Being a Wallflower*, providing him with advice as to how to cope with the difficulties of being a social outsider in his own high school.

In working with sixth graders at Cary Academy, Cary, North Carolina, Meredith Stewart (2011) had her students read one of three dystopian novels by Lois Lowry: *The Giver, Gathering Blue*, and *Messenger*. Students then worked collaboratively to create their own utopian world through blog posts consisting of letters, recipes, photos, and songs that portrayed challenges associated with creating a utopian world in setting up a government, social structure, and an economic system (for more on collaborative fiction and role-play: http://tinyurl.com/lbydts5).

Audio/Video Blogs

Students can also create audio blogs using tools such as Voxopop http://www.voxopop. com or Evoca http://www.evoca.com using cell phones to record audio to post to a blog, creating an asynchronous oral interaction in which they interact in collaborative groups in a discussion format. Use of audio blogs are particularly helpful for working with English-language learners to enhance their oral language use (Hsu, Wang, & Comac, 2008; Huang, 2013). You can also have students create video blogs or vlogs in which they record themselves using their computer's camcorder talking about certain topics, as well as showing audiences certain artifacts. Vlogs can be used in the beginning of a class to have students introduce themselves to one another as a group process activity.

WIKIS

Students can also employ wikis to engage in collaborative writing. Wikis are websites that allow different users to add or edit content to the same site, so they serve to mediate collaboration. While the focus of blogs is on voicing opinions, the focus of wikis is on collaboratively creating shared repositories of information (for more on resources for using wikis on the website http://tinyurl.com/lzb7d42).

Wikis foster collaboration by serving to centralize work on a single site, providing a record of users' revisions, including links among pages within a wiki, integrating complex sharing of ideas, creating a historical record of work over time, fostering transparency for participants to view one another's contributions, and supporting networking of ideas (Barondeau, 2014).

Students can therefore add new information to course wikis across different classes—for example, creating study guides for a course to assist new students beginning the course. Students in first-year composition classes at St. Cloud State University add new information to a wiki textbook, *Rhetoric & Composition* http://en.wikibooks. org/wiki/Rhetoric_and_Composition, about different aspects of learning to write.

You can use a number of wiki platforms, such as Wikispaces (for a tutorial on use of Wikispaces: http://awikispacetutorial.wikispaces.com), PBworks http://pbworks.com (for a tutorial on use of PBworks: http://tinyurl.com/l89uuxz), and MediaWiki. There are also a number of iOS and Android apps for creating wikis, apps that students can sync across different devices so that they can collaborate using different devices—for example, moving their notes taken on a smartphone to a desktop or tablet.

In using these wiki platforms, students select the edit mode to revise text. To edit a page, students should have to sign in with an account and password to avoid persons outside of class making edits to a class wiki. As with blogs and websites, students can insert links and images. Once they have completed their revisions, they then select "Save" to read their revised texts.

Because wikis include a revisions history for a document, you can determine which students in a group made what revisions, data that you can use to assess students' collaboration based on which students are contributing what material. You can use this revision history feature to demonstrate the value of revision by showing students how subsequent revisions improved a text. With his social studies middle school students, Clarence Fisher (2007) shows students different versions of the same text on a class projector and has them discuss how and why their revisions improved their writing. He subscribes his wiki to his Bloglines [discontinued tool] so that he can receive notices of revisions; he then gives students credit for making certain revisions in texts. Fisher finds that

> some kids are not fact checkers and spelling editors. These kids are more often contributing pieces of new information about a topic to a page. Other kids are adding little that is new, but are carefully following through the pages, checking the spelling on them, editing for grammatical errors, etc. (p. 2)

Critical to the success of wikis is the creation of a clearly defined, transparent organization based on a specific set of categories listed in a sidebar. For example, for sharing responses to a novel, students can organize those responses according to categories of characters, setting, key events, themes, information about the author, reviews/critical analysis, and so on. Then, within those categories, they can create subcategories—for example, within characters, characters who are changing and those who are not. Or, a wiki could be organized based on responses to separate chapters of a book, as is the case with this book's wiki http://digitalwriting.pbworks.com with each chapter containing links and further reading.

Challenges in Using Wikis

There are a number of challenges associated with using wikis to foster collaborative writing. One study of the use of wikis in schools found that they were often used by teachers to share content with students or by students to individually complete assignments, as opposed to their use for classwide collaboration of shared knowledge (Reich, Murnane, & Willett, 2012). As a result, students perceived little purpose in using wikis because they engaged in little collaborative revision. This suggests the need for you to provide students with some sense of purpose for using a wiki in terms of fostering collaboration.

Using Wikis to Enhance Reading Ability

We believe that wikis can also be used to improve students' reading ability, particularly middle school or junior high students who as "struggling readers" are often intimidated by texts. When they encounter a wiki, students may be less intimidated than if they are reading a print text because they know that they can revise or change a wiki text. As a result, they are responding to a wiki text not only as readers but also as writers who are thinking about how they might revise or improve a text.

Knowing that they can revise a text requires students' ability to infer a writer's intended meaning to make the appropriate revisions that build on that intended meaning. In working with his junior high students, Andrew Rummel, West Junior High School, Minnetonka, Minnesota, describes how he uses wiki writing to not only help students share their writing but also improve their reading skills:

> I look at wiki as a new type of text. It is a community text that can evolve in a way that a traditional paper isn't able to. In my seventh grade language arts class, the students use the wiki to explore a few different subjects. At the beginning of the year, the students create wikis that represent the interests and backgrounds of the students in our class. They begin by selecting an aspect of their lives that is interesting, such as fashion, gaming, reading, music, movies, travel, etc. They then develop ways to get information from each other about this interest. As they interview each other online and in person, they present the information they find. Then, the wiki first lets them display the information in hypertext. This allows them to express their findings through multimedia production, including text, images, sound, and links to websites. This first part of the assignment facilitates a number of interesting conversations around these questions:
>
> How do you represent other people's views in a respectful way even if you disagree with their tastes or opinions?
>
> How do you clearly present information on a website?
>
> How do you best balance images, sound, links to other sources, and text?
>
> Because they have created wikis, it allows them to read and respond to the discoveries about the class as a group of people with a rich base of interests, experiences, and knowledge. They have the opportunity to expand on the topics and comment on the writers' representations of their responses.

At the same time, in contemplating revisions in others' texts, students need to be respectful of others' work so that they are not altering or deleting it in ways that change their peers' intended meanings. Rummel encouraged his students to reflect on the problems with altering their peers' work by having them reflect on the following questions:

- How do you change text created by another person in a way that still validates the work they have done?
- How do you add to another person's creation in order to expand on the topic in a way that holds true to their vision and organization?
- What rules of conduct apply to people working in this context?

Rummel notes how his students learn to respect each other's work:

> Because they need to agree as a group how to present the contradicting information, they need to both examine their sources and defend the validity of their information. The wiki serves as an evolving text that allows the students to return to it, evaluate the information for clarity and validity in the context of a growing understanding of the subject. The students have the opportunity to continually change the organization and content of their pages based on discoveries made along the way.

Wikis can also be used to enhance students' collaborative development of literary interpretations. For sharing their responses to the novel *The Kite Runner* (Hosseini, 2004), Theresa Haider's high school students worked collaboratively in groups to conduct research on background aspects of the novel related to the history, religion, and culture of Afghanistan and the Taliban, information that served to enhance their interpretation of the novel. To assist her students in writing essays about *Montana 1948* (Watson, 1993) based on the previously mentioned online role-play about the "Fighting Sioux" mascot, Elizabeth Erdmann used a wiki http://jhscollegewritingmontana.pbwiki.com for groups of students to collaboratively share information about the setting, characters, timeline, comparisons to outside sources/topics, and the use of Native American mascots related to the online role-play. Elizabeth had her student groups initially define what and how each member would contribute. In an interview with Richard, Katie Nelson described her strategy for collaborating with another student on their paper on the knowledge and wisdom in the novel:

> We wrote notes to each other about what I thought the paper was about, and I bolded the stuff that was important because if we're writing two different papers, it's not the same. It was hard because we never saw each other . . . but he was a smart guy so that he knew where I was going. We made the outline very detailed and then we divided up who was doing what paragraphs.

Katie identified some of the affordances in a wiki that fostered their collaboration:

> It was easier to organize. I learn better what things are visual. This way was very clear—whom you could click on. You can also easily delete something and adjust it; its very flexible as far as multiple authors and multiple things that you're trying to do at

once because it wasn't just a paper; it was organizing notes, and reading the book and collecting information; so it's multifaceted in meeting our needs.

In describing his collaboration with two other students on a paper about power in *Montana 1948*, Josh Hiben described the processes of collaboration:

It was cool to have a couple of people from different classes that I didn't really know too well to see what they got out of it and their perspectives; we mailed blogs and wikis back and forth, and we came to a compromise as to what we wanted and I learned twice as much as I wanted because of their perspectives.

Navigating Links on Wikis as Hypertexts

One challenge in reading wikis as hypertexts is that students need to navigate across different links, requiring them to determine their purpose for selecting certain links over others based on defined purposes for responding to texts. Having students create their own literary texts as hypertexts can help students learn to navigate links. For example, college students created poems using wikis by adding to and revising one another's language, which enhanced their ability to interpret poems as hypertexts (Dymoke & Hughes, 2009).

As in "choose your own adventure" stories, literary hypertexts also contain alternative subplots that readers select as they move through a text—for example, alternative endings to a story. Having students create their own literary hypertexts based on alternative subplots helps them learn to purposefully select certain subplots. To engage college students in revising an Alice Munro story, Teresa Dobson (2006) put a selection of the story on a wiki. As illustrated in Figure 7.3, her students then added their own mini-narratives to specific parts of the story as a form of remix of the original story—for example, elaborating on a specific exchange between characters or on an aspect of the setting. From adding in their subplots, students not only learned the conventions of hypertext literary texts but also enjoyed reading each other's additions.

Responding to and Creating Wikipedia Articles

Students can also respond to and collaboratively create Wikipedia articles. As we noted in chapter 3, Wikipedia has emerged as a primary open-access information source based on adherence to certain standards and editorial vetting of contributions (for information on responding to and creating Wikipedia articles on the website: http://tinyurl.com/k6uxhwp).

Students can create Wikipedia articles on their school, a town/suburb/city, a novel/play that they are reading in a literature class, an historical event/figure or issue that

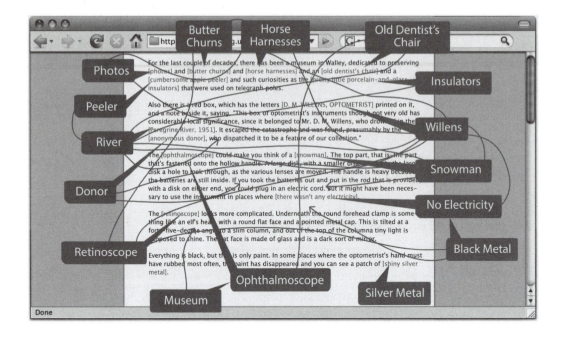

Figure 7.3. Students' Use of a Wiki to Respond to a Short Story. *Source: Screenshot of image from Teresa Dobson, "The Love of a Good Narrative: Textuality and Digitality."* **English Teaching: Practice and Critique, 5(2), 2006, used with permission of the Editors and Teresa Dobson. Copyright © Teresa Dobson.**

they are studying in a social studies class, a species or phenomenon that they are studying in science class, and so on. By doing so, they are learning to critically evaluate articles, search for and apply relevant research, perceive the value of Wikipedia as a resource, and learn to work collaboratively with others on a task that serves to benefit the larger community. You can obtain resources for use in having students edit and create articles compiled by Konieczny (2012) http://tinyurl.com/okb76lh.

Central to editing and creating Wikipedia articles is the ability to determine the validity and reliability of cited sources consistent with the Wikipedia guidelines http://en.wikipedia.org/wiki/Wikipedia:Identifying_reliable_sources given that Wikipedia is considered to a source for accurate, scholarly knowledge. Because its articles can be created by contributors who may not be experts on certain topics, resulting in controversy about the validity of the articles, comparisons of similar *Encyclopedia Britannica* and Wikipedia articles found no difference in the accuracy of those articles (Giles, 2005), although instructors may still recommend treating it as a secondary versus primary source (Eijkman, 2010).

To help students understand the importance of the use of reliable sources, 240 students at the University of Sydney worked in collaborative groups to examine articles based on a topic that interested them identified as "Wikipedia articles needing factual verification" http://en.wikipedia.org/wiki/Category:Wikipedia_articles_needing_factual_verification. Students took screenshots of the pages identifying unverified facts to then conduct research on their university's library databases and then edited the articles to correct the articles (Di Lauro & Shetler, 2013).

In addition to use of Wikipedia, students can access information on other wikis, such as the Wikimedia Commons http://commons.wikimedia.org, which contains digital media; Wikiversity http://en.wikiversity.org, which contains access to learning resources; Wikisource http://en.wikisource.org, which contains almost 300,000 texts; or Wikibooks http://www.wikibooks.org, which is designed to foster collaborative book writing as well as access to books.

SUMMARY

This chapter describes the use of tools such as Google Docs, blogs, and wikis to help students engage in collaborative writing. Effective use of these tools requires instruction and support for collaboration in terms of students determining their roles and responsibilities within groups, creating engaging assignments that provide a sense of purpose and audience, modeling effective collaboration, fostering use of multimodal features and links, and emphasizing the importance of adherence to valid and reliable sources.

8

COMPOSING MULTIMODAL TEXTS THROUGH USE OF IMAGES, AUDIO, AND VIDEO

In this chapter, we describe ways of understanding and creating multimodal digital texts in terms of three basic components: images, audio, and video. In doing so, we recognize that these three components are often seamlessly meshed in multimodal texts, so discussing them as separate categories is somewhat artificial. After we describe tools related to understanding images, audio, and video, we conclude the chapter with a description of ways to combine the three components in producing texts such as digital stories or poetry.

THE CENTRALITY OF MULTIMODALITY

As previously argued, multimodal texts are central to communication in the 21st century, in which people rely on showing versus telling to convey their ideas (Kress, 2009). This requires understanding and creating texts based on principles of design. For example, in creating a digital video, students need to know how to create a script and storyboard based on a design for effective use of cinematic techniques to engage audiences. A focus on design includes considering the aesthetic aspects of images, audio, and video related to their social and cultural meanings.

A number of Common Core State Standards (Council of Chief State School Officers & National Governors Association, 2010) involve employing images, audio, and video to learn to do the following:

- "Synthesize and apply information presented in diverse ways (e.g., through words, images, graphs, and video) via print and digital sources to answer questions, solve problems, or compare modes of presentation (reading standard)" (p. 39).

- "Integrate and evaluate information from multiple oral, visual, or multimodal sources to answer questions, solve problems, or build knowledge (speaking and listening standard)."
- "Use technology, including the Internet, to produce, publish, and interact with others about writing (writing standard)."
- "Gather relevant information from multiple print and digital sources, assess the credibility and accuracy of each source, and integrate and cite the information while avoiding plagiarism (writing standard)" (p. 42).
- "Make strategic use of digital media and visual displays of data to express information and enhance understanding (speaking and listening standard)" (p. 49).

IMAGES

In this first section, we discuss a range of different tools students can use to access, create, display, and analyze images.

Image Repository Sites

One primary image repository site for accessing images is Yahoo Flickr http://www.flickr.com, also available as iOS http://tinyurl.com/dycxr59 and Android http://tinyurl.com/6r8bekk apps (see Flickr for Educators http://tinyurl.com/kp7rhc8 for uses of Flickr in the classroom). Students can find images at a number of image repository sites listed on the website http://tinyurl.com/kw74d6q.

To search for images on Flickr, students enter keywords as tags that Flickr users have added to their images. These tags represent the use of "folksonomy" keywords because they were created by members, as opposed to the use of a database or library taxonomies. Students can also search for images based on Groups who share a common interest in images about a certain topic—for example, images about a certain place/city, hobby, or type of artwork.

Students can also find images on Google Images http://www.google.com/imghp or use the ImageSearch Pro http://tinyurl.com/6vtlw9c app to search on Google Images as well as Picasa http://picasa.google.com to upload, organize, and edit their own photos.

Using Copyrighted Images

In using copyrighted images, students need to be aware of "fair use" provisions of the copyright law that allow for uses of copyrighted images for educational purposes associated with transforming an image for purpose of critical analysis, parody, or remix

(Hobbs, 2010); see also the *Code of Best Practices in Fair Use for Media Literacy Education* (Center for Media & Social Impact, 2012). The following are some guidelines to provide students in determining whether or not they are violating copyright with the classroom context governed by fair use of copyrighted material. The fair use of a copyrighted work for purposes such as criticism, comment, news reporting, teaching (including multiple copies for classroom use), scholarship, or research is not an infringement of copyright. A key consideration in determining fair use has to with the degree to which use of an image or text represents a *transformation* of the original image or text.

In determining whether the use made of a copyrighted work in any particular case is a fair use, consider the following:

- Purpose and character of the use, including whether such use is of a commercial nature or is for nonprofit educational purposes
- Nature of the copyrighted work
- Amount and substantiality of the portion used in relation to the copyrighted work as a whole
- Effect of the use on the potential market for or value of the copyrighted work

Briefly, these indicate these three issues:

1. The use must not attempt to "supersede the objects" of the original but rather be educational or critical.
2. The less of the original that is used in relation to the whole indicates more likely that use is fair, although the importance of the specific portion is also considered.
3. The use must not infringe on the copyright owner's ability to exploit the original work (for instance, by acting as a direct market substitute for the original work) but not through criticism or parody.

> *Text:* Brief attributed quotations of copyrighted text are used to illustrate a point, establish context, or attribute a point of view or idea that may be used under fair use.
>
> *Images:* There are a few blanket categories, but the rule of thumb seems to be to use them "in good faith."
>
> *Audio clips:* Brief song clips (under 30 seconds) may be used. Spoken word audio clips of historical events, such as speeches by public figures, may be used when attributed to the speaker.

In using Google Images, students should select the "Usage Rights" menu to identify the different copyright options for using images. In using Flickr, it is important that students recognize that many of the images on Flickr are copyrighted, so use of those images requires permissions or even payments. They should use the "Creative Commons copyright search" option http://www.flickr.com/creativecommons to find images whose producers have assigned their images a Creative Commons copyright, which means that students can use them without having to seek permission from the producer; students will still need to provide attribution information in using the images. See http://tinyurl.com/k5m46d6 for an infographic from Foter (2012) on different Creative Commons copyright options.

IMAGE CREATION TOOLS

Students can also create their own images using their smartphones or tablets along with the many photo tools for editing their images. In using the iPhone or iPad, students can use the bundled Camera app to take still images and videos and then use image-editing tools listed on the website http://tinyurl.com/kw74db9. For example, students can use Adobe Photoshop Express to rotate, crop, flip, or straighten their photos; change or alter colors, including black-and-white or tint; add filters of Soft Focus, Sharpen, or Sketch; add special effects such as Border, Rainbow, Vibrant, or White Glow; and add borders.

In a high school class of 16 female students of color entitled "Sistahs," students used photography and poetry to create web-based visual autobiographies for sharing with others http://www.urbanedjournal.org/archive/Issue3/notes/notes0006.html (Wissman, 2008). Rather than perceiving photography as simply a means to represent reality, these students used photography as a social practice to portray their identities in the social contexts of their lives.

> Envisioning photography as a social practice recognizes that the images produced are not simply a transparent recording of reality; rather, the images encapsulate a particular framing of that reality that is highly intentional and unique to the individual photographer. Envisioning photography as a social practice also entails considering the social context in which images are produced and received and considering the shaping influence of those contexts on the images and interpretations of those images. (p. 14)

Students can also create photologs in which they share their photos along with commentaries on sites such as Jux https://jux.com as a desktop or iOS tool. For examples, see Fotolog http://www.fotolog.com, Photoblogs http://www.photoblogs.org, or TextAmerica http://www.textamerica.com. They can also submit photos or videos directly to their blogs using cell phones—what is described as moblogging. In moblogging, they are sending a picture or video to an e-mail account that then posts it to their blog (to create moblogs for Blogger: http://www.blogger.com/mobile-start.g).

Instagram/Snapchat

Two popular tools for taking and sharing photo images are the iOS http://tinyurl.com/3gtb4hz and Android http://tinyurl.com/c79oqws Instagram apps and the iOS http://tinyurl.com/ar63ctm and Android http://tinyurl.com/aayfp4z Snapchat apps. While these have become popular social media tools for sharing images with peers—for example, the use of Snapchat to create "selfies" (self-portrait images) http://tinyurl.com/k9bchv4—they can also be used in the classroom by creating a private classroom account, which means that only students in the class would be creating/accessing images. These tools can be used for engaging in photojournalism or digital storytelling in which students take photos about a certain event, topic, or issue in their school or community to share with their peers—for example, a sporting event or school election (Spencer, 2012). Or, students could share photos of their art/project work; field trip experiences; famous people, characters, or authors whom they are studying; book covers of recommended books; or science experiments (Hudson, 2013).

VoiceThread

One popular tool for collecting and commenting on images is VoiceThread http://voicethread.com (for a webinar on using VoiceThread as well as integrating VoiceThread into Moodle: http://tinyurl.com/km5jgt5). Students can import images into VoiceThread from Flickr or other image repository sites to then add audio or written comments about these images. One major advantage of VoiceThread is that peers and teachers/parents can share their comments to the same image, fostering a collaborative interaction about the meaning of any image (Beach & O'Brien, 2013). For example, junior high students took photos of different places in their school to upload to VoiceThread and then added their comments about these images, resulting in sharing of perspectives on the meaning of different places in their school (D. O'Brien, Beach, & Scharber, 2007). Because their comments involved responses to images, students were more likely to employ concrete, descriptive language, and the reluctant-writer students benefited from having the option of employing audio comments.

In another project as part of a larger unit on climate change, sixth-grade students were studying the topic of photosynthesis related to the creation of carbon dioxide emission climate change in two science classes (Beach & O'Brien, 2014; Castek, Beach, et al., in press). Working in groups of two or three, the students used VoiceThread to select and upload Flickr Creative Commons copyrighted images portraying the process of carbon dioxide photosynthesis. Using VoiceThread fostered the social practice of student collaboration by focusing their joint attention on the same images.

Students also employed the doodle line feature in VoiceThread to focus their audience's attention on particular aspects of an image, reflecting their awareness of their audience. For example, a student used the image of the number 350 as a key index of an excessive level of CO_2, to draw a doodle line around the number 350 to then state in an annotation that humans would die when the CO_2 level exceeds 350 (Beach & O'Brien, 2014). In focus group perceptions, students noted the benefit of being able to collaboratively view and comment on the same images, as well as actively challenging one another's claims about those images, leading to further revision of their ideas.

Students also used VoiceThread to engage in critical analysis of the images through recontextualizing (Van Leeuwen, 2008) the intended meanings of images. One student used the image of smoke emitted from a Ford Mustang, an image associated in popular culture with power and speed, to note that the Mustang was releasing combustion (Beach & O'Brien, 2014). In doing so, she is recontextualizing the positive popular cultural association of the Ford Mustang image to convey an alternative, critical perspective on that image of a car creating combustion.

Marqueed

Another related tool is Marqueed http://www.marqueed.com, which students can use to add comments with or next to images that they import or drag into the Marqueed site for sharing with others (for a video demonstration: http://tinyurl.com/k7xrzwc). Marqueed is particularly useful for working collaboratively on a project that involves selecting and analyzing images—for example, choosing among a large repository of images to create a presentation or to add illustrations to an infographic or book.

ThingLink

Another related tool is ThingLink http://www.thinglink.com, which allows students to add links within images to other images or websites. For example, students can create an infographic as described in chapter 4 and then insert an icon into the infographic that then opens up to another image or website.

Glogster

Another popular tool, Glogster EDU http://edu.glogster.com, can be used in collecting and combining visual images to create a "Glog" for posting visual posters to the class. As part of a media literacy unit in which students were studying movie posters, seventh-grade students used Glogster to create a Glog movie poster based on a fictional movie in which they play starring roles (De Abreu, 2010). Students had to determine their film's genre, create a name, include a picture of themselves, and provide background text and images to capture the genre and story line; students then shared their Glog movie posters with their entire class.

Haiku Deck

Another popular tool is Haiku Deck for desktop http://tinyurl.com/k2ty5ed and iPad http://tinyurl.com/jw3jb3t. Haiku Deck is a presentation tool that emphasizes the importance of using images to create presentations, as opposed to the overuse of text. Students can readily import images from Flickr, Google Images, and other sites as well as edit images to enhance their presentations.

Comics Creation Tools

Students can also use images to create comics or graphic novels (Hissey, 2011). One of the most popular comics creation tools is Comic Life for Mac and Windows http://tinyurl.com/n3rnnnq and for iPads http://tinyurl.com/aff67h7. Students can import images/photos into Comic Life pages and then select from a range of different templates, fonts, colors, balloons, and so on, to generate their comics. While there is a 30-day free trial, unfortunately, a single license for Comic Life is $19.95 and $4.95 for the iPad app. Other less expensive options to Comic Life include the Android Comic Strip It! app http://tinyurl.com/lfg7sjo, the iOS Comic Book app http://tinyurl.com/a9ec6aw, or Comic and Meme Creator http://tinyurl.com/mccyn9j (for comics creation and reading tools: http://tinyurl.com/lkgkf4c).

Based on reading of the autobiographical novels *Night* (Wiesel, 1982) and *Persepolis: The Story of a Childhood* (Satrapi, 2004), Elizabeth Erdmann's 10th-grade students created Comic Life autobiographical memoirs portraying a particular significant event in their lives. Based on their reading of these texts, students had to identify certain images and characters' reactions to key events in the texts that portrayed the significance of these events in terms of the main characters' identities. They then found and reflected on photos about their own lives or families to describe the setting for the photos, people in the photos, events surrounding the photos, who and why certain people may have been missing from the photos, thoughts that could be attributed to people in the photos, and their recollections associated with the photos. Students then created their own memoirs using these photos imported into Comic Life, along with added-in captions and speech bubbles.

For example, one student, Yasmin Ahmed, created a comic entitled "Understanding Islam," in which she describes her experience growing up "in a conservative Muslim family" in a largely White suburb and only later realizing in junior high school that her peers began to perceive her as distinct given stereotypical media representations of Muslims as terrorists. In her comic, as illustrated in Figure 8.1, she employs visual images to convey her story.

After showing examples of media images of Muslims as terrorists, at the end of her comic, she "decided that I didn't like the image that people had of Islam." So, in a block with a peace sign, she adds the caption, "I decided to spread the word that Islam is about peace, not war."

Drawing/Painting Images

Students can also draw or paint their own images using apps such as Paper http://tinyurl.com/d793uvt, Sketchbook Pro http://tinyurl.com/3j6ndda, Doodle Buddy http://tinyurl.com/3cnygow, or iDraw http://tinyurl.com/6pujdkb, which include different brush and pencil tools for drawing using a range of different color options. Students can use these tools to create images for use in their presentations, comics, blogs, websites, digital stories/poetry, or e-books.

RESPONDING TO IMAGES

To help students formulate their responses to images, you can have them employ the critical response protocol "What are you noticing? What did you see that makes you say that? What does it remind you of? How do you feel? What questions does the image raise for you? and What did you learn?" (Beach, Campano, Edmiston, & Borgmann, 2010, p. 47) as well as the visual thinking strategies model (Housen, 2007) that includes the questions "What's going on in this image? What emotions do you associate with this image? What in the image made you think X? What are you seeing that suggests X? and What's missing or left out of this picture?" Or, students can employ these activities to respond to images:

1. Jot down a word or phrase that comes to mind for each of the images.
2. Write one connecting emotion or mood that the image conveys or that you feel.
3. Describe what the photo, movie clip, etc. represents.
4. Think of a sound or melody that might accompany the visual.
5. Ask probing questions: What is the intended message? How is meaning conveyed in the image (e.g., gender, ethnicity/race, setting, social class, national identity)? Who do you think is the author? Why did the author choose this particular genre, mode, medium, color, spatiality?
6. Tell the story that one image evokes for you. (Rowsell, McLean & Hamilton, 2012. p. 446)

Figure 8.1.   A Student's Use of Comic Life: Selection From "Understanding Islam." *Source: Screenshot of image from "Understanding Islam" used with permission of Yasmin Ahmed.*

Students can also critique instances of stereotypical representations of gender, ethnicity/race, and class by collecting a number of different images about the same phenomena to then note certain consistent patterns across these images that reflect certain stereotypical representations. In his digital writing class, Richard asked his students to collect images, video, and/or texts about a certain topic or issue; look for consistent relationships or patterns in the material that suggested certain groupings or categories; and then reflect in a blog post about their findings. The students in the class then created and shared their own collections http://tinyurl.com/ko76pbf. One student, Gina Nelson, analyzed representations of homelessness in the media, noting that the media often portray the homeless as drug addicts, panhandlers, or "beggars" living on the streets in urban areas. She then included clips, such as a trailer for *The Pursuit of Happyness* that portrays an employed male wearing a suit who is homeless, as well as material portraying rural families or children as homeless, noting that "after having watched *Pursuit of Happyness*, I became increasingly aware of my own judgments and bias about people who are homeless. Most of my preconceived notions of homelessness come from either the media or seeing men panhandling on the streets."

Another student, Nicole Kronzer, examined the portrayals of sisters in media, poetry, and literature. She found that sisters were portrayed in a binary way, either as "best friends" evident in Barbie doll sisters or as "enemies," with little alternative variation associated with her relationships with her own sisters.

AUDIO

A second major mode involves audio associated with creating audio essays or podcasts. While it may be assumed that focusing on audio production may detract from students engaging in writing, in creating these productions, students are writing and revising scripts. In creating these audio productions, students are relying on their voice as the primary means of communication by focusing on the "sound" of the language in their scripts (Comstock & Hocks, 2006). Attending to the "sound" of their writing encourages students to experiment in their writing on adopting different voices that engage audiences through the use of shorter sentences with "punch," pauses or silences, and a sense of rhythm (for resources on audio productions and podcasting: http://tinyurl.com/l7b8mfo).

For example, for her first-year composition students at Metropolitan State College of Denver, Elizabeth Kleinfeld (2013) had her students create audio essays based on the *This I Believe* radio program and project.

> I hoped that the immediacy and physicality of the audio essays would help students
> understand how readers/listeners make sense of a text. Second, I wanted students to

be able to understand how they could use their authorial voices more consciously and deliberately.

Students listened to 5 of the 18,000 audio essays on the *This I Believe* website http://thisibelieve.org to identify the qualities of effective audio production. Students then composed and revised scripts, practiced reading those scripts, and then recorded audio files using Audacity http://audacity.sourceforge.net to create MP3 files to post to a class blog for peers, friends, and parents to access.

Students can also create radio productions similar to those on National Public Radio. For example, junior high students listened to stories about the town of Lake Wobegon on Garrison Keillor's *Prairie Home Companion* to create their own audio stories using GarageBand (D. O'Brien et al., 2007). Because they had created their own fictional town populated by characters, they then created a radio play podcast based on stories about their characters in this fictional town using GarageBand to add sound effects to their production.

In an oral history project, students recorded interviews with seniors about their recollections of certain historical events or periods (Shriver, 2012). Central to the success of the project were the students' reflections in group discussions and journal writing on their interviewees' reactions to their questions, prompts that were particularly effective, memories that were most vivid, unexpected information, and comparisons between their own and their interviewees' experiences.

Students can also perform a readers' theater production http://podtheatre.pbwiki.com/Background, based on existing scripts in the public domain http://www.teachingheart.net/readerstheater.htm, by creating a 10-minute play http://www.10-minute-plays.com/index.html, or by creating their own scripts based on issues they face in their lives.

Using Digital Tools in Speech Classes

One major focus of the Common Core State Standards is on public speaking activities that require both use of a script and effective oral presentation skills. Students benefit from practicing their speeches privately prior to public delivery. In working with his students in his high school public speaking class, Matthew Gillispie (2013) used the iPad Camera Roll to have his students record their practice speeches to critique their presentations to prepare for their classroom presentations. He also had them work on their oral delivery skills by recording their reading aloud famous speeches using the QuickVoice Recorder http://tinyurl.com/l97z56z and the iOS app (for the QuickVoice Recorder Android app http://tinyurl.com/c9ypxrf) to then self-assess their use of pitch, rate, and volume to then e-mail to him. He then had students use their iPads to record one another's actual presentations to provide written peer feedback. After his students gave their speeches, he had them share their feedback using the back-channel tool TodaysMeet http://todaysmeet.com.

Creating Podcasts

To prepare for creating podcasts, students should first listen to podcasts, which are MP3 audio files typically produced on a regular basis that audiences can subscribe to using an RSS feed (for directions on creating podcasts http://blog.teachercast.net/podcastingforeducators and http://tinyurl.com/m2f67xx).

The use of podcasts has transformed instruction in that students can listen to recorded lectures of not only their own instructors but also from universities throughout the world available on sites such as iTunes U http://tinyurl.com/lbjbarh. And teachers can listen to podcasts related to their teaching on the EdReach http://edreach.us, Ed-TechTalk http://www.edtechtalk.com, or TeacherCast http://teachercast.net channel shows.

Students can create podcasts as talk shows, including Skype interviews with invited guests recorded using Audacity http://tinyurl.com/4t7vc, Audio Hyjack Pro http://tinyurl.com/6km4h, Piezo http://rogueamoeba.com/piezo, or Skype Auto Recorder (for Windows http://tinyurl.com/6km4h); oral interpretations of literary texts; news broadcasts about school events similar to the CNN student news http://www.cnn.com/education; role-play skit/drama productions about events in their own lives or historical events; guided tours of certain places or exhibits; and so on. In her ninth-grade social studies class at South View Middle School in Edina, Minnesota, Gina Nelson created a role-play on the Constitutional Convention of 1787. She asked her students to adopt the roles of five different delegates to the convention—George Washington, James Madison, Benjamin Franklin, Governor Morris, and Alexander Hamilton—and, working as a group, to create a podcast based on these participants' conversations.

Students create these podcasts by using the same processes involved in recording MP3 files. Students can use their iPhone or iPad to record audio; in fact, they can achieve a higher-quality recording by using an external USB mic and connecting it to the iPad Apple Connection Kit normally used with cameras (Mallery, 2011), as well as using headphones to listen to their recordings.

One challenge in creating podcasts involves finding a place to store MP3 audio files, which can be sizable. Students can now store audio as well as video files on Google Docs within their Google Drive as well as use Podbean http://www.podbean.com, Podcast Garden http://www.podcastgarden.com/h/en, Hipcast http://www.hipcast.com, or Libsyn https://www.libsyn.com.

In using GarageBand for Mac http://tinyurl.com/lemswvx or iPad or iPhone http://tinyurl.com/9jexo6t to record and edit their audio files, students

- choose "Track," then the "New Track" option, and then select the option "Real Instrument," because they are recording using their voice;
- click "Record" to record their podcast and click on "Record" again to stop recording—they can edit their recording to remove certain sections, raise or lower the sound, and add "loops" as sound effects, jingles, or music; and
- export their file to iTunes by going to "Show Podcast Track" and then "Share to Send Podcast to iTunes."

To use Audacity http://tinyurl.com/4t7vc, they

- set up their preferences in "Edit Preferences" by selecting "Audio I/O" (Input/Output)—with "Output" as their sound card and "Input" as their microphone option;
- under "File," select "Save Project" and give their file a name;
- under "Project," select "New Audio Track," and a grey-colored track will appear;
- click on the red "Record" button to start to record their voice and hear how they sound on playback—they can then record, and their voice appears as a blue waveform;
- use the "Selection" tool to move their cursor over the blue waveform to highlight a section that they want to edit; and
- under the "Edit" menu, select "Cut" to delete the section (or "Delete" in Mac or "Backspace" in Windows) or "Copy" to move the section elsewhere using "Paste."

To transform these MP3 audio files into a podcast to distribute them as a podcast on their blog or on iTunes so that audiences can subscribe to that podcast, they need to create an RSS feed as an XML file using Feedburner http://Feedburner.com, FeedForAll http://www.feedforall.com, or Podomatic http://podomatic.com. To add a feed to a Blogger blog, they first add their MP3 file to their blog by going to "Posting-Create," add a title and show notes, and then add a link to the file and publish—creating a URL link. They then go to "Setting-Site Feed" to obtain a feed address—which is in Atom. To convert their Atom feed to an RSS 2.0 feed, they go to Feedburner and paste in the Atom feed URL to create an RSS feed for inclusion in iTunes (for directions on submitting podcast feeds to iTunes: http://tinyurl.com/672arbs).

VIDEO

The use of video in the classroom has transformed classroom instruction, as evident in teachers and students accessing and creating videos to communicate their ideas, as well as in the "flipped classroom" model. Videos allow students to experience engaging presentations, portrayals of historical events, literary adaptations, and science demonstrations, as well as create their own videos. Much of this transformation has to do with readily available videos as well as the ease of creating and editing videos (for resources on accessing and producing digital videos on the website http://tinyurl.com/87pyqkf). An increasing number of videos have been created for instructional purposes—for example, videos created by Flowcabulary http://www.flowcabulary.com consisting of videos about academic content based on hip-hop rap lyrics and animations, including videos about literary texts.

Accessing Videos

Students can access online videos from a range of different sites. The largest sites for videos are YouTube http://www.youtube.com and the iOS http://tinyurl.com/8ey7y3j and Android YouTube apps http://tinyurl.com/cqc85sm. YouTube apps are often perceived as not having educational value or as including extraneous material, so they are frequently blocked in schools (you can employ Subscriptions http://tinyurl.com/89bqb3u or browser extensions such as A Cleaner Internet http://clea.nr to remove extraneous material from YouTube).

Given this issue, one option is YouTube EDU http://www.youtube.com/education, which includes free educational videos from universities, PBS, TED, and other educational sites, as well as playlists organized by subject and grade level. You can also use the YouTube for Schools service http://www.youtube.com/schools (for an introductory video: http://www.youtube.com/teachers), which provides schools with controls over which videos are viewable within a school by creating their own YouTube video network within their school. Schools can sign up as Partners so that you can log in to preview videos from YouTube EDU, but students cannot log in. And because YouTube is incorporated in the Google Apps, you can create a separate classroom YouTube available just for specific classroom use http://tinyurl.com/mnj749x, as described by Mark Garrison (2013), Hopkins School District Minnesota Google Summit. In winter 2014, YouTube also launched the YouTube Nation site http://tinyurl.com/m6flqbf, which includes selected videos organized by certain topics or issues. For storing videos and organizing videos, you can use MediaCore http://mediacore.com. Students can log in to this site to access certain videos, and you can then keep track of the videos they are viewing.

Annotating Videos

To foster specific responses to the use of cinematic techniques in these videos, as well as reactions to the topics and issues portrayed in videos, you can have students use video annotation tools such as YouTube Annotations to add annotations to specific shots in a YouTube video. To activate the annotations feature, students click the arrow next to "Upload" at the top of a YouTube page, select "Video Manager," click the down arrow to the right of the "Edit" button, select "Annotations," click the "Add" annotation button on the right, and then, once the annotations have been added, click "Publish" http://tinyurl.com/mvh2abn. Students can also use VideoAnt http://ant.umn.edu to add annotations to any online video by inserting the video's URL into the site to then add annotations that appear next to each shot.

Given the increased popularity of the "flipped classroom" approach, you can create lessons based on videos using the EDpuzzle http://edpuzzle.com tool, which allows you to search for and select videos, upload your own videos, crop videos, add annotations or voice-over questions or comments within a video, or embed quizzes. Similarly, you can use the VideoAnt http://ant.umn.edu or Google Video annotations http://tinyurl.com/m3rl8de to also add questions or prompts to foster students' responses. Students can use the Movie NotePad http://tinyurl.com/7nug56b app in which they import videos into the video player and then take notes on specific aspects of the video.

When having students respond to videos, you could have them identify specific uses of engaging digital video techniques as described in the PBS documentary *Side by Side* http://sidebysidethemovie.com/production-notes. To encourage her students to respond to aspects of videos that engage them, Elizabeth Barniskis has her students select certain YouTube videos and describe how that video portrays activities they engage in or beliefs to which they subscribe:

> At the start of each year, I have each student submit a video from YouTube that fits some aspect of their personality. I call it this activity "What is Your YouTube?" They need to select a video that is representative of an activity they love or a belief they hold to be true. For the first two weeks of class we begin each day watching two or three of the videos. The kids come in excited to share their own videos and experience new videos. There is a brief writing component; I use it to introduce the idea of writing for an authentic peer audience.

Creating and Editing Videos

Students can create videos using their mobile devices to then upload to video production and editing tools listed on the website http://tinyurl.com/lf7r42w. Through creating videos, students are learning to use video as a powerful tool for communicating their ideas and concerns (for tutorials on creating videos: http://tinyurl.com/lbuhak7; for more on digital video production: http://tinyurl.com/lf7r42w). Students can create videos as movie trailers (for movie trailer templates, see iMovie for Mac http://tinyurl.com/nslxsww or for iOS devices, see http://tinyurl.com/9y2gab4), trailers to recommend books, short story adaptations, or documentaries about an issue facing their school or community.

Producing engaging videos requires careful planning through the creation of a script using ScriptWrite http://tinyurl.com/6pnvtxw or Storyist http://tinyurl.com/7cse948 apps and a storyboard using Storyboards http://tinyurl.com/852zj9l or Storyboard Composer http://tinyurl.com/yjxqpoz apps. They can also use some of the previously mentioned comics apps to plan out the length of time for certain scenes or shots, the selection of certain types of shots (close-ups, midshots, establishing) or angles, the use of sound effects or music and lighting, and story line development, in which they can recognize the need to portray their story or topic without attempting a lot of experimental techniques.

In creating videos, students need to realize that they do not necessarily need to go out and shoot video footage. They can simply import their own or others' online images or video clips to create video using editing tools listed on the website http://tinyurl.com/lf7r42w. They can also use YouTube to record videos on a webcam and upload them directly into YouTube using the YouTube Quick Capture. They need to go to "Upload videos" and then select "Use Quick Capture" and then click "Record," to then share their videos on your own class YouTube Channel, assuming that YouTube is not blocked in your school, or the AwesomenessTV Channel http://tinyurl.com/csg72oe, which consists of videos produced by adolescents largely about adolescents.

For his video production classes at West Junior High School, Hopkins, Minnesota, Kevin Kos perceives his role as teaching students to critically analyze videos through video production:

> We need to teach students how and why a video works; we need to analyze what we use in teaching for perspective and bias; we need to show them how to tell a story visually for emotional effect; and we need to provide the time for students to create and share their own learning with video projects. This involves a dedicated Movie Lab cart with 15 laptops and 15 Flip Cameras (purchased through a grant). All filming projects are in groups of two to four.
>
> Also, understand that without realizing it, the digital video world is already in your classroom. Every device has a high definition camera with editing software built into it, and many students have been creating media for years. They just lack instruction in basic techniques. Those students who know how can help teach you and the rest of the class and then you are off. Make sure everyone has access in some way with groups and from there the progression to iMovie and Final Cut is not far off.

He recommends beginning with having students focus on certain particular cinematography techniques using the "show us" technique:

> Begin by teaching one aspect of any video you show in the classroom with basic film terminology. What choices did the director or editor make? Why? How? Then add short projects that take 20–30 minutes. Whenever you have an extension activity, give students the option of a short seven second video in 20 minutes through Vine.

He also uses the "show us" phrase to have students identify topics for creating their videos:

> I've done this for Allegory of the Cave, irony, or euphemism in a video. I also have assigned to them vocabulary words. Other teachers have used this for just about anything from how the Earth revolves around the sun to a language concept to photosynthesis. "Show us . . ." Those two words have amazing powers. They span anything we can do in a school.

In his video production class, students engage in the following activities:

Film Clip Analysis Assignment: Analyze a clip from a movie or TV show and discuss the shots used and the reason why in front of class.

Practice Boot Camp Editing: We film a scene for class that all students must edit individually in the computer lab.

Camera Use through Conversation Assignment: Students will learn how to frame shots and use a camera for filming.

Film a Task Assignment: On the first project, the students will film a simple task in a creative way using no zooms and at least five close-ups. Tasks include getting a drink of water, checking out a book etc. This assignment is graded P/F.

Action/Reaction: With this one the students are to film a series of reactions to something shocking or outrageous.

Movie Review: Students must watch a movie or film outside of class and analyze it technically in about 200 words.

Clip Remix Assignment: Film a scene you have analyzed in the Film Clip Assignment.

Copyright/Documentary Assignment: Demonstrate an understanding of copyright law by making a documentary.

Final Film Project: Students will work in a group of three people to complete a video of their choosing. It must be 3–4 minutes long and contain a variety of shots and angles. The editing must be polished and the film needs to contain titles and music.

Final Digital Editing Test: Students will be given a scene and a song and asked to show what they have learned by editing this in the most professional way pos-sible.

He also uses video as the basis for a range of different projects:

- Ask students to make a storyboard of a paper they are about to write. I tell them to show it in six frames. They may use drawings, clip art, or actual pictures from an electronic device, and then edit it on iMovie.
- Make a video about their paper. After a student has written a paper, I may have them make a video of it. Put them in groups and have them decide how they will film it, then let them do it. This will take three days and I've done this for narratives as well as a video on "How to Write a Paper."
- Advertisements/Propaganda Films (and in foreign languages)
- Political Ads
- Summarize the key lines in a chapter or play.
- Creation of short plays and dialogs.

Creating Video to Influence Audiences

One critical factor in creating videos consistent with the social practice of contextualiz-ing digital texts in terms of purpose and audience has to do with having some defined purpose for creating a video in terms of having some rhetorical effect or uptake on one's audiences.

Demonstrating some of the ways that video tools can be used purposefully, one of Tom's writing studies classes made videos to accompany and extend a study of the written manifesto form (Baepler & Reynolds, in press). One of the decisions that Tom made when developing the assignment was to build a context in which students were making decisions for their videos that would allow them to choose their topics from their own interests but also from within the contours of the course goals. In this case, the course was designed to teach students about writing that brings about cultural and social change through use of videos.

Tom was interested in students making use of "everyday" technologies to carry out their projects, partly because of their increased ubiquity and partly because of a recent Pew study reporting that students had more experience in consuming media than in producing it (Baepler & Reynolds, in press). With shrinking budgets, he was also inter-ested in students producing video with minimal noninstructor technical support.

Among the goals in forming the assignment, Tom wanted his students to write a compelling digital text that included video; to argue effectively with available technologies; and to develop a vocabulary for discussing the choices made among visual, written, and audio modes. Students were asked to produce written text along with the video.

Using their smartphones and a classroom set of flipcams for creating videos, students imagined how to approach their topics based on these tools and free editing software, such as Movie Maker, iMovie, and Jaycut http://jaycut.com.

To obtain a more fine-grained understanding of students' levels of experience with producing media, Tom surveyed the class and found that students indeed had little experience with creating videos or making use of mobile technologies for academic projects. Nevertheless, they were open to the idea and, by the end of the project, had developed confidence and skill in video production. In a postproject survey, students reported a 45% gain to the statement "I am confident that I can edit a video clip" and a 57% gain to the comment "I am confident I know when to select video, text, and still images to effectively convey what I mean" (Baepler & Reynolds, in press).

Students were assigned to read manifestos by Marx, Marinetti, and Malcolm X, among others, commenting in Moodle discussion forums as well as in class. They were then asked to create a "digital manifesto" that updated the written form for our time. In small groups, students discussed and chose topics that were urgent and important to them. While some students chose more global concerns, such as global warming, some of the best projects were local ones based in campus concerns.

The Student Union Video

One such project by Ana, Simone, and Philip advocated for saving student-painted murals in the student union multicultural center's space described in chapter 2. This student union video was successful in most ways and informative for thinking about how to teach such projects. After preliminary brainstorming in class, students were shown storyboarding websites and then asked to produce a storyboard for their own projects. As an important step for how to "write" the video, students delineated the sections of their video, drew rough sketches of their planned shots, and made assignments of who would carry out the filming. The student union group decided to make use of the camera to conduct interviews with students who had a stake in saving the murals.

After creating rough cuts of their videos, students viewed and commented on two other projects using the video annotation tool VideoAnt http://ant.umn.edu. Much like a peer-review process with drafts of papers, students were able to annotate for particular items determined by Tom as well as the group. For example, students looked for the ways that manifesto strategies, such as the use of repetition for effect, were employed, and they commented on their effectiveness. Then each group was able to view its own videos with comments at the points where the comments appeared.

A sign that students made the project "their own" was when they began to adjust and make decisions once they realized the possibilities and affordances of the technologies. In the editing phase of the project, the group decided that it wanted to provide a wider focus—namely, to advocate for the power of murals for people to express themselves in public spaces that were too often dominated by commercial images. This was especially appropriate given that the murals were to be replaced with university-branded images and sculptures. Learning that their editing program Movie Maker allowed still images to be included along with original video, they shaped their video into two sections: a video montage of commercial images juxtaposed with images of graffiti and murals in urban spaces. These images prepared the audience for an engagement with their main concern of advocating for the student union murals.

A postproject reflection showed that this group was effective in thinking about the relationship of making meaning through careful multimodal writing. The group wrote on decisions that it made with positive statements such as "We explored graffiti as a specific art form in public spaces" and

> As a transition into discussing murals as public expression of personal and cultural identities, we portrayed three images of Kenyan political murals; we focused on the importance of murals at the University of Minnesota for students who are about to lose their murals, and our film concluded with interviews from students speaking to the importance of murals to their cultural center.

With regard to their accompanying written manifesto, they wrote, "We utilized text only to frame our visual representations of our manifesto when we felt that our argument might not otherwise be completely understood." In short, students were wrestling with the challenging choices implicit in multimodal production. Such choices present teachers with challenges that are not always resolved, as when the union group, toward the end of its project, chose a piece of music to play over its images that seemed to Tom to undo some of the sharp commentary of their visual and written modes. In the end, it was a matter of how the music was perceived by different audiences (in this case, the students as one and Tom as the other).

As a final step, the students contemplated bringing the video to administrators but in the end ran out of time. Nevertheless, the relationships that they had formed with one another and with the stakeholders in the union debate indicated a successful engagement with the writing and technology. Not only were they carrying out their assignment, but they were also involved. In a postreflection, Ana reported that it still "raised her blood pressure" to think of the murals being destroyed in the union.

As part of teaching the digital manifesto assignment, Tom made it clear to students what they would be graded on. He developed a grading rubric that was handed out with the assignment sheet to point students in directions consistent with the course goals.

Students were relieved to learn that this was not an assignment that rewarded especially high-end film production, for example, but that application of manifesto principles discussed in class held great importance for the project. In the end, the project was aimed at a better understanding of writing and how it is used to effect cultural change.

Challenges in Doing Video Work

However, despite the high level of student engagement, Tom encountered a number of challenges in having students create videos. Students in a "regular" writing class sometimes expressed a lack of confidence and skill in carrying out what they perceive to be a monumental task; one student reported, "I am not very artistic."

Teaching students about some basic uses of cameras and editing can help them build confidence and give them ideas for their work. Tom did this in two ways: First, a research associate in the Office of Technology, Paul Baepler, created a quick video introduction to the use of the cameras and posted it on the class Moodle site. Then, students were directed to Vimeo http://vimeo.com/videoschool, where they were able to access basic filming and editing instructional videos.

Additionally, in class students were shown clips of videos from YouTube that advocated for social or cultural change, such as "Save the Gulf" with Sophia Bush and Austin Nichols http://www.youtube.com/watch?v=25jfWXWoXZg. Discussions were aimed not only at the content but also at how each video got its point across through pacing, choice of shots, and camera uses. To prepare for these discussions, students were first asked to annotate the video using VideoAnt. By joining written commentary to the viewing experience, students developed a practice and perspective that was useful for producing their own videos. Given the class focus on writing, the treatment here was to have students to think about how to express themselves effectively with tools that they were already using.

Student reactions to the project were overwhelmingly positive. Students reported that the project made the class more engaging, that they considered the technological skills useful for future employment, that the project gave them a better understanding of the manifesto as a written form, and that the project helped them learn more in the course (Baepler & Reynolds, in press).

Creating Video Screencasts or Vlogs

You or your students can also create video screencasts or vlogs (video blog posts), often designed as talking-head presentations or demonstrations on a certain topic, issue, or phenomenon. While screencasts or vlogs are increasingly used by teachers with the "flipped classroom" model, students can also create their own screencasts or vlogs to share their knowledge with their peers, a sharing that enhances their sense of agency as coteachers.

To create these screencasts or vlogs, you or your students can simply create a recording using an iPad, iPhone, or computer/Chromebook with a webcam. To record the use of a desktop screen—for example, how to employ desktop software tools—you or your students can use Jing http://tinyurl.com/ln3oy2a, Camtastia Studio http://tinyurl.com/6nvnr3f, Screenr http://www.screenr.com, ScreenFlow for Mac http://tinyurl.com/mjok3ma, or Screencast-o-matic http://tinyurl.com/k5yxruy. You or your students can use these screencasting tools to create demonstration videos on the use of various technology tools that students are using for their work. For example, you can have students use the Explain a Website http://tinyurl.com/kmg9mjw, an iOS app used to create a screencast analyzing specific useful features of a website.

You or your students can also employ screencasting tools such as ShowMe http://tinyurl.com/cfqothz, Explain Everything http://tinyurl.com/mev4trl, ScreenChomp http://tinyurl.com/llhm5hd, or EdCreations http://tinyurl.com/ml7chpc (for tips on creating screencasts: http://tinyurl.com/n4vsb4f). For example, students in a seventh-grade science class working in pairs used ShowMe to create videos on the topic of genetics (Castek & Beach, 2013). They first created storyboards, then drew stick figures to portray their ideas about genetics, and then added their voice-over comments. For example, two students created a ShowMe presentation on the dominance of certain traits influencing a baby's eye color, in which they drew stick figures of parents and a baby to illustrate genetic inheritance of different eye color http://tinyurl.com/lagok8h. The students recorded the following voice-over commentary:

> "If a brown eyed and a blue eyed parent had a baby, what color eyes would the baby have?" They then drew two parents, "Bob" with blue eyes and "Suzy" with brown eyes, along with the couple's baby. . . . They added a question mark next to the baby to illustrate that they were posing a question related to the dominance of a certain trait. They then created a drawing showing that "this is the child and the child's eyes are brown because brown was dominant." (p. 561)

Creating vlog posts can be engaging for those students who prefer to convey their ideas in a more multimodal format. Students can best learn about vlogs by viewing them on vlog directories such as Mefeedia http://mefeedia.com, FireAnt http://fireant.tv, or VlogDir http://www.vlogdir.com (for tutorials on vlogging: http://digitalwriting.pbwiki.com/Vlog+production+tutorials and http://projectnml.org/examplars/06vlog).

Animation Videos

Another option for creating videos of live action includes animation videos. One advantage to creating animation videos is that students have relatively more control over the content in that they are creating it as opposed to having to shoot live action, which requires dealing with a lot of logistics.

We list tools for creating stop-motion/claymation, image/drawing, and puppet animation videos on the website http://tinyurl.com/lf7r42w. To create stop-motion videos, students can simply move objects or artifacts to create their videos (for examples of stop-motion animation videos, the National Film Board of Canada http://www.nfb.ca/playlists/stopmostudio). To create image/drawing videos, students can import images or their own drawings. And to create puppet animations, students create a script for their puppet characters and record their dialogue to coincide with movements of their puppets.

CREATING DIGITAL STORYTELLING AND POETRY AS MULTIMODAL PRODUCTIONS

Students can employ images, audio, and video tools to create digital poems or stories as multimodal productions that combine images, audio, and video to engage their audiences. Through these productions, students who are unengaged or marginalized in school can experience a sense of purpose and agency. For example, analysis of seventh- and eighth-grade African American youths' creation of podcasts and videos in the Digital Youth Network http://digitalyouthnetwork.org found increases in measures of creative production for personal expression, subject matter learning, the ability to communicate with larger audiences, and acquisition of digital literacies, particularly when students created productions for an authentic rhetorical purpose and audience (Barron, 2006; Barron & Gomez, 2009; for more on digital storytelling and poetry: http://tinyurl.com/lhyglfh).

Digital Storytelling

Students can engage in digital storytelling that typically consists of 2- to 5-minute digital videos that combine a narrated piece of personal writing, photographic images, and a musical soundtrack (Alexander, 2011; Lambert, 2012; Ohler, 2013; for resources: Center for Digital Storytelling http://www.storycenter.org and Digital Storytelling with the iPad http://tinyurl.com/4oxkb7z). Ohler (2013) recommends having students develop their stories around characters' change or growth in coping with challenges, leading to transformation in characters' lives by creating a story map for use in creating a story-board or script for a digital video production.

Students can use Storybuilder http://tinyurl.com/mmwb7pt to post notes in planning their story; Story Map http://tinyurl.com/ykqgbob to identify setting, characters, conflict, and resolution; Storyboard That http://www.storyboardthat.com or Storyboard Generator http://tinyurl.com/7uvars5 to create a storyboard; as well as Inklewriter http://www.inklestudios.com/inklewriter, Storybird http://storybird.com, or Storyrobe http://storyrobe.com to generate narratives. Students can also employ the iBooks Author http://www.apple.com/ibooks-author or Book Creator http://digitalvaults.org tools to create their digital stories.

One useful tool for creating digital stories is the free iOS Adobe Voice app http://tinyurl.com/lmmmlh5 for iPad. To use this app, students

- select a template for their story based on the options of Explain Something, Follow a Hero's Journey, Promote and Idea, Tell What Happened, or the open-ended Make Up My Own template;
- upload images from the site as well as their own images or photos, as well as icons or text options;
- record their own commentary as well as music about those images to create a video; and
- publish their video using e-mail, Facebook, Apple Message, Twitter, or Adobe's cloud.

To create stories based on historical events or persons, students can access the Digital Vaults site of the National Archives http://digitalvaults.org. Students can also study examples of digital stories, such as *Inanimate Alice* http://www.inanimatealice.com, which combines audio, text messages, images, music, video, cell phone calls, and language portraying the development of a female main character, Alice, over time (Botzakis, 2013).

Storyspace http://www.eastgate.com/Storyspace.html is one tool used to create hypertext stories in which readers select optional storyline paths similar to choose-your-adventure stories (for examples of hypertext stories: http://www.eastgate.com/catalog/Fiction.html; for a teacher-narrated story about how Storyspace has been used in high school, see "Lindsay's Story": http://eastgate.com/storyspace/art/Taylor.html).

Additionally, students can create videos based on their analysis of the previously described visual techniques employed in comics and graphic novels. For the course "Cinema, Comics, and Cameras" at West Junior High, Kevin Kos has students analyze the narrative techniques employed in films. His students analyze the use of the same visual narrative techniques as employed in comics and graphic novels. Students then create storyboards that serve as the basis of their own video productions.

Digital Poetry

Students can also create digital poems. They can access digital poems on sites such as PowerPoetry http://www.powerpoetry.org, the Electronic Literature Association collections http://collection.eliterature.org/1 and http://collection.eliterature.org/2, PBS Poetry Everywhere http://tinyurl.com/cpa299, the Electronic Poetry Center http://epc.buffalo.edu/e-poetry/e-authors.html, or Moving Poems poetry videos http://movingpoems.com.

Students can use sites such as Slide.ly http://slide.ly to make image videos. To model use of Slide.ly, Jaclyn van Geest, an English teacher at South Saint Paul High School, South Saint Paul, Minnesota, created a poem using Slide.ly about an immigrant worker who dies in a New York City fire http://tinyurl.com/kr3epwr. They can also use the Away With Words app http://tinyurl.com/kngxuyq in which students attach words in a free-association manner to images.

In his high school English class, Jerrod Nelson, Wayzata High School, Wayzata, Minnesota, had his students create digital poems using their own choice of digital tools—Prezi, VoiceThread, iMovie, and so on. He had his students focus on the following features in creating their digital poems:

Animation: Moving words or pictures around can create meaning and engage readers.

Audio: Hearing words can have a profound effect on the listener and convey meaning not otherwise attainable through written words.

Video: Even more than audio, video of the poem or video that goes alongside the poem can create new levels of meaning and engagement for the reader.

Nonlinearity: When reading a poem on the page, the reader has to read it in a certain way. With digital poetry, it does not need to move in a certain direction at a certain speed. It can move in different directions, go back and forth, and really do whatever you want.

Reader Choice: Like nonlinearity, you could give readers a choice on how they move through the poem. For example, if readers click on a certain button, they see one part of the poem, and by clicking on another button, they see a different part of the poem. Or maybe they even get to insert text into the poem to create meaning for themselves.

Two students, Lexie Nelson and Chad Snorek, created a digital poem http://youtuber/E5-ZTt1QlVY using the Minecraft animation tool Mineimator http://www.stuffbydavid.

com/mineimator about a man, Steve, who creates a clone who then turns on Steve. Cinnamon Manuel created a poem, "The First Summer Day," http://tinyurl.com/lngm4wu using the GoAnimate http://goanimate.com animation tool.

Remixed Texts

Students can also respond to and create remixed texts by taking parts or snippets of texts, referred to as "supercuts" http://www.supercut.org, from different sources and creating new texts that often parody the meanings of the original source texts (Navas, 2012); for a video, see "Everything Is a Remix" (Ferguson, 2012) http://vimeo.com/14912890. For example, one popular YouTube video "I'm Not Here to Make Friends" http://tinyurl.com/ly8blqs (Juzwiak, 2009), consists of 52 clips from different reality TV shows in which participants assert that they were not participating on these shows to make friends (Burwell, 2013). One useful tool for creating remixed documents is Mozilla Popcorn https://popcorn.webmaker.org for accessing and combining different online texts (Parker & O'Byrne, 2013). Students can also use the Dragontape http://tinyurl.com/7vuv4z9 app to create remixes of YouTube videos, as well as the Media Breaker site with examples of "Lamplatoon" remixes of ads to parody or critique those ads using clips from television ads—parodies and critiques covered under fair use of copyrighted material.

To foster discussion about remix in her classroom, Catherine Burwell (2013) had her high school students respond to the video remix "Buffy vs. Edward: Twilight Remixed" http://tinyurl.com/q4fm8av, consisting of clips from *Buffy the Vampire Slayer* and the first film in the *Twilight* series, in which Edward's stalking is challenged by Buffy. Students discussed the producer's argumentative stance, portrayals of gender representations, changes in the characters from their original programs, use of humor, and other aspects of the remix process. In a discussion with his college students, Tom's students examined issues of copyright associated with creating remixes related to fair use copyright law associated with the use of critical analysis and parody involved in transforming the original texts.

Students can also take some of the canonical texts that they are reading and create a remixed digital version of those texts, as was the case with a remixed version of *Moby Dick* (Jenkins & Kelley, 2013). Students can also access the My Pop Studio site http://mypopstudio.com for remixing images, texts, and music from celebrity magazines, reality television, and popular music to foster critical analysis of media representation of females.

ASSESSING STUDENTS' VIDEO PRODUCTIONS

To assess students' video productions, you can employ rubrics such as one used by Elizabeth Erdmann, which involved ratings from 1 to 4 for the following features:

- Script/storyboard: the degree of planning and development of detailed descriptions of shots, movement, narration, and dialogue.
- Video: the degree to which the camera was always in focus and steady, the variety of planned shots and angles, and effective use of composition based on the rule of thirds.
- Audio: the clarity of sound and use of silence.
- Lighting: the use of sufficient lighting to eliminate shadows and glare.
- Editing cuts: the degree to which cuts are used to eliminate unnecessary slack time.
- Transitions: the appropriate use of transitions to create a smooth flow between scenes.
- Titles: the inclusion of clearly displayed titles that enhance the story/content.
- Pacing/continuity: use of steadily paced clips to maintain audience interest.
- Music/sound: use of well-balanced music/sound that enhances the mood and pacing.
- Graphics/animation: clear graphics/animation that enhance the topic and mood.
- Content: the extent to which the video tells a compelling story with a connected structure.
- Creativity: the use of imaginative creativity suitable to the content. (Beach & Swiss, 2010, p. 317)

Students also wrote "artist statements" in which they had to answer the following questions:

- To what extent does the completed work fulfill your artistic intent?
- What are its strengths and weaknesses?
- How did feedback affect the development of the work?
- Give at least two examples of technical problems you encountered.
- Explain how these problems were resolved in the creation of the piece. (Beach & Swiss, 2010, p. 317)

To assess students' digital storytelling, Kevin Hodgson employed these criteria http://www.umass.edu/wmwp/DigitalStorytelling/Rubric%20Assessment.htm:

- Story development through well-integrated uses of images, video, audio, and text.
- Fostering audience engagement and reflection through appropriate pacing and editing.
- Use of variation in pacing, tempo, and editing speed to engage audiences.

- Effective use of music choices and voice-over appropriate to the content.
- Selective use of video versus still images.
- Quality of self-narration that employs an authentic, conversational style and pauses.

SUMMARY

In this chapter, we described the use of image, audio, and video tools to create multimodal digital texts. We argued that understanding how to effectively use these tools to employ visual/auditory rhetorical strategies to engage audiences requires the ability to interpret images and audio/video texts to determine producers' uses of these tools. We also argued that students need to know how to draw on popular culture/media texts to make connections with their audiences.

9

DESIGNING AND EDITING DIGITAL TEXTS FOR AUDIENCES

Consider the image in Figure 9.1, from Tom's magazine seminar.

The student who took the photograph, Samantha Lee, created the image as part of a process to solve a design problem. In short, her group had written individual articles that had been joined into a magazine. She was charged with creating an image that

Figure 9.1.   Magazine Cover Image from Tom's Magazine Class. *Source: Photo of magazine cover created by Samantha Lee used with permission of Samantha Lee.*

would somehow crystallize these pieces and form a "cover" image. Knowing that her classmates had written with a theme of campus activities available to first-year students, she took this photo, suggesting the many activities that occur on campus. She took the photo against the background of one of the main buildings on campus, one that her audience (next year's freshmen) would surely recognize. Smartly, she also knew that leaving neutral space in the image, as well as taking the photograph in black and white, would allow a title to be overwritten in the e-book authoring software that her class was using.

In this chapter, we focus on understanding and creating texts for their design. This focus shifts students' attention to the effective use of digital formatting, organization, language, and visual rhetoric. It also entails recognizing how aspects of design require choices specific to their rhetorical situation. As the Digital Rhetoric (Digirhet.org, 2006) group notes,

> writing today means weaving text, images, sound, and video—working within and across multiple media, often for delivery within and across digital spaces. And, perhaps now more so than ever before, writing requires a deep attention to context, audience, and meaning-making across the multiple tools and media available to us as writers. (p. 241)

Selecting, combining, formatting, and editing text, images, videos, and sound serves to create "an *ethos* that requires, encourages, or even discourages different kinds of inter-activity for that audience" (Hocks, 2003, p. 632). Students therefore need a clear sense of purpose and audience associated with making choices about optional text, images, audio, and video to engage in visual rhetoric (for more on visual rhetoric: http://tinyurl.com/l364297). This focus on the use of digital tools within a rhetorical context is empha-sized in the Common Core speaking and listening standards.

Related Common Core State Standards

- *Speaking and Listening 4:* Present information, findings, and supporting evidence such that listeners can follow the line of reasoning, and the organization, development, and style are appropriate to the task, purpose, and audience.
- *Speaking and Listening 5:* Make strategic use of digital media and visual displays of data to express information and enhance understanding of presentations.

ANALYZING DIGITAL DESIGN

A first step in helping students attend to digital design is to have them consider how the use of different formats or designs serves to communicate different meanings to audiences. To focus her students' attention on design features, Anne Wysocki (2004a) has her students complete some writing in crayon as opposed to the keyboard—something that they find to be challenging. Students then discuss the differences in what they wrote, how they wrote it, and how they thought their audiences would respond to their writing. They recognize that their writing with crayons projects a certain persona that differs from that with texts written with word processing.

Students then analyze design features of specific examples of blogs, wikis, websites, and other digital texts in terms of how easily and quickly they can comprehend the material and use it to navigate to other pages or links (for more on visual design of blogs, wikis, and websites: http://tinyurl.com/kql4bcm).

As we note in chapter 1, students can think about their rhetorical contexts based on the five components or MAPS: mode (genre), media (forms), audience, purpose, and situation (T. Hicks, 2009). In this context, students learn the craft of designing and formatting digital texts through choosing particular features. In designing websites or creating blog posts and presentations, they attend to typography, layout, templates, color, graphics, images, and user navigation; in creating audio and video, they attend to use of sound, music, voice, camera techniques, editing, framing, voice-over, and so on (T. Hicks, 2013; for more on visual design: http://tinyurl.com/lmmtdwy).

Print Versus Online Reading Processes

In analyzing aspects of digital design, students can reflect on differences between how they process print versus online texts. One of the differences has to do with their purposes for reading online texts. When audiences go online, they are often seeking certain information—the latest news reports about a political campaign, movie ratings, sports scores, book purchases, and so on. As previously noted, in contrast to reading print texts, in which readers' eyes move from left to right in processing information in a linear manner, in reading online texts, readers' eyes focus initially on whatever information is most relevant in terms of their purpose or needs (Kress, 2003). If they are shopping for inexpensive cameras, they may first focus on the camera prices.

This means that writers of online texts need to consider how to foster a sense of relevance for their readers through use of design features (Mattewson, Donatone, & Fishel, 2013). By recognizing that their readers are seeking information most relevant to their needs, students can design texts that help readers quickly and efficiently locate relevant information or ideas. Too much text information, information located in too many different font sizes, or misuse of banners or columns can detract users from easily locating relevant information.

Another difference between print and digital texts is that, in contrast to reading print texts, readers of digital texts are quickly scanning pages without reading every word. Eye-tracking research on how readers read news sites found that they initially scan for headlines, summaries, and captions; when they read the articles, they only read 75% of them (Petersen, Torkelson, & Torkelson, 2002). Given this "scan, select, and move on" reading process (Redish, 2007), students need to consider how to highlight items as well as how to slow down their readers so that they actually attend to certain key bits of information. To do so, they can, for example, provide readers with lists of items rather than sentences or paragraphs to summarize important information for quick scanning while slowing down the reader who is attempting to skip over information (Petersen et al., 2002).

Given the scan-and-skip processing, students also need to front-load key information in the beginning of their text. In the traditional essay, students learn to begin with an introductory paragraph that provides background context for a topic or thesis articulated later in the essay. In contrast, in writing in their blog or wiki, writers employ an "inverted pyramid" organizational structure by beginning with their overall topic summary in the beginning of their text.

Readers of digital texts also benefit from having an initial schema for organizing their reading of texts (Redish, 2007). Students can also use titles or headings to provide readers with an overall organizational schema for understanding the logical relationships among different sections of a text. It is also important that the titles or subheads be retained in the same place across different pages so that audiences know how to determine a page's content.

Students need to limit the amount of information they provide. One problem with websites or PowerPoint pages is that there can be too much information for readers to process at any one time. Students need to recognize that the amount of information available is related to how much information is available on a screen—something that differs from reading print texts. In reading screens, readers want to see the front page captured within their initial screen space to avoid scrolling down to find needed information.

Students can also analyze and use different fonts or typefaces to convey different meanings—for example, using larger font size for titles of more significant stories and smaller font size for less significant stories. Wysocki (2004a) distinguishes between the use of font as "decorative"—used as stand-alone header, title, or advertising slogan—as opposed to use of typeface "for extended reading" as part of the regular text (p. 127). She finds that certain fonts are used as "decorative" typeface: script, gothic, postmodern, or fonts which are associated with certain art movements. For extended texts, she identifies a range of categories of font: "Roman," "Modern," and "Sans serif," which are associated with different levels of formality.

Another readability principle has to do with guiding readers' expectations for navigating across different pages. Because readers want to quickly navigate pages, they need a clear idea as to where links will take them so that they do not become lost in an endless maze of pages. Readers also need a clear understanding of the content of a link so that they know whether or not to click on that link to acquire certain information. To guide readers' expectations, students need to clearly identify their hotlinks using specific words or phrases to summarize the content of the linked material.

Reading texts on e-reader devices as well as on tools such as Subtext http://www. subtext.com differs from reading them as print texts in that students can share highlights of sections of texts, add annotations, and search for key words. For example, in her instruction, Meg Griswold (2013) projects her Kindle App from her laptop to her classroom screen so that students can focus on the same text for close reading of that text. She notes,

> When reading *Fahrenheit 451*, we engaged in frequent collective close readings of passages projected onto the screen. When a student introduced a passage or quote for discussion, I quickly typed a few words from that passage into the search bar, clicked the link in the results, and projected that page. (p. 103)

Analyzing Document Design

For students to learn to design and edit digital texts, they need to learn to analyze specific aspects of document design. To help them, you can have students respond to examples of both well-designed and poorly designed websites http://webpagesthatsuch. com based on their own reactions to a site in terms of ease of use; appeal and engagement; structural organization by categories; use of navigational icons or cues to move to other pages; and understanding the site's representation of an organization, school, group, or community's purpose.

In responding to these websites, students could also analyze the ways in which images and words are aligned on a page. If there is too much information or if it is difficult to determine the function of certain parts of a page or site, then they have more difficulty processing that information. Students can analyze alignment by perceiving a page according to a grid whose sections are organized or chunked according to columns or vertical sections. In this grid, the top vertical sections assume more importance than those images or words on the bottom section.

For example, the Youth Voices website http://youthvoices.net (Figure 9.2) is designed to appeal to a youth audience given its purpose for fostering students' sharing of their writing on this site.

Its "About" page states the following:

> We are a site for conversations. We invite youth of all ages to voice their thoughts about their passions, to explain things they understand well, to wonder about things they have just begun to understand, and to share discussion posts with other young people using as many different genres and media as they can imagine!

To attract students' attention, the image of the *Catching Fire: Hunger Games* movie based on the *Hunger Games* book appears on the left side, an image linked to Adrita's writing about the theme of teamwork http://tinyurl.com/logjj7a:

> A theme in the book is "take one for the team." This is shown throughout the book a lot where people have to work together in order to survive. One example would be Mags: She is a very old winner from the games and even though there were people who were keeping her alive, she killed herself through the stuff that the game's stadium was releasing. She did this in order to let all the other players be able to run away from the poisonous gas rather than get held back because they were helping her. This is an important theme because everyone is able to connect to it and learn from it.

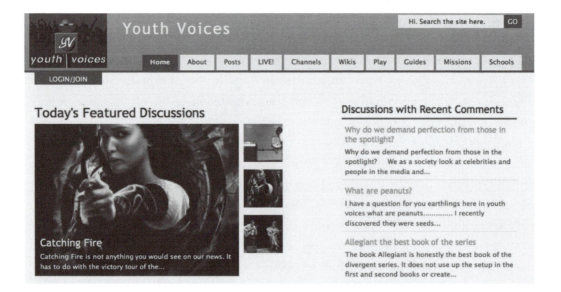

Figure 9.2. Youth Voices Site. *Source: Screenshot of YouthVoices (youthvoices.net) site used with permission by Paul Allison.*

In addition to this particular writing, users can access Adrita's other writing on the site http://tinyurl.com/ltec3bq.

To foster reactions to the discussion topics, a list of topics appears on the right side of the page. The front-page categories for different content on the top provides students with choices for navigating the site. For example, the Channels page http://youthvoices.net/channels includes different categories for submitting writing: "argument," "arts and entertainment," "booktalk," "connected research," and so on. The Schools page http://youthvoices.net/schools includes a map indicating the location of the different schools throughout the United States whose students are participating on the site.

Students could pair up and share think-aloud responses to how they comprehend pages on websites such as Youth Voices in response to the following questions:

- "What do I notice first on the page? What do I notice next?"
- "What specific images, icons, font size, color, and sections draw my attention to what things on the page?"
- "How quickly and easily can I find things on this page?"
- "How engaged am I in reading this page?"
- "If I want more information, what do I do next? If I want to go to another page, do I know what to click on and where I will be going?"

Students can also analyze effective use of design features by studying the template options provided by blog, website, or presentation platforms in terms of use of images, color, font, layout, alignment, and navigation options. For example, students can go to the Blogger site to set up a blog and then consider the different template options http://tinyurl.com/kfj3em5.

Then, working in pairs, students select those templates and color options that they believe would best serve their purposes and best represent the persona or ethos they wish to project on their blog. They then discuss how different images, language, layout, and color on the blog templates have different appeal for their audiences by addressing the following questions:

- What are the specific images and words in this template?
- What is the relative size of the images and words?
- What kinds of information are located on a page—are they easy or difficult to find?
- How are these images and words arranged or aligned on the page in the template?
- What is the relationship of images and words in the template?
- What icons, buttons, or words are used to help you navigate the template?

In identifying these different design features of a text, students then consider how the features are being used rhetorically to communicate to different audiences and why they selected certain features over others. To engage in this analysis, students could address these questions:

- Who is the audience for this blog?
- What is the message or idea that is communicated to the audience in this blog?
- How are the images and words used to convey this message or idea?
- How are the size, arrangement, and alignment of images conveying this message or idea?

Students could then review actual blogs, as well as other sites, to share their reactions to how the design features and layout serve to convey the intended messages or content. Students could also reflect on the use of these features in creating websites using Google Page Maker http://pages.google.com/-/about.html (for more on blog/wiki/website design http://tinyurl.com/kql4bcm).

Based on their analysis of aspects of digital design and readability, students can then create their own digital texts, such as presentation texts, websites, e-books, and literary texts. Consistent with the social practice of collaboration, they can then share their responses to one another's texts to reflect on instances of effective use of design and readability as both producers and consumers of these texts (for more on readability formulas: http://tinyurl.com/n23gpql).

PRESENTATION TOOLS

Students are familiar with using presentation texts created with PowerPoint http://tinyurl.com/2f6woro, Keynote http://tinyurl.com/mzf99z9, Prezi http://prezi.com, Google Slides (on Google Drive) http://tinyurl.com/l3zxkyd, or ZoHo Show http://tinyurl.com/keyvc6o (for more on presentation tools http://tinyurl.com/l7vuc7x).

One increasingly popular presentation tool is Prezi, a cloud-based tool that can be used across different devices or edited on an iPad using the Prezi Viewer app http://tinyurl.com/bz95szk, which can also play Prezi presentations on iPads at different stations in a classroom or science lab. While students can download PowerPoint files into Prezi, Prezi differs from PowerPoint and Keynote in that, rather than a series of separate slides, the information is contained within a rhetorical space that can serve to engage audiences. In viewing Prezi presentations online audiences can zoom in and out according to their need to focus on certain information (for a Prezi presentation on the attributes of Prezi for engaging audiences: http://tinyurl.com/m78x4fk). For example, students at Mount Pleasant High School, Mount Pleasant, Michigan, created a Prezi presentation http://goo.gl/3c8xq addressing the question "How does Lady Macbeth defy gender conventions of her time?" which included images and videos to engage audiences in multimodal ways (T. Hicks, 2013, p. 75).

Students can use Slideshare http://www.slideshare.net or Sliderocket http://tinyurl.com/mjwronp to upload Keynote or PowerPoint to create online presentations, as well as Vcasmo http://www.vcasmo.com, Present.me http://present.me, Slidesiz http://tinyurl.com/mutaoxp, or Authorstream http://www.authorstream.com to create video presentations. And for their narrated presentations, students can use the screencasting tools described in chapter 8—ShowMe, Explain Everything, or VoiceThread.

You can also use Whiteboard apps such as Jot! http://tinyurl.com/qzuqj63, ZigZag http://tinyurl.com/l3lcecp, or Doceri http://tinyurl.com/kmmnkyw to create an interactive whiteboard so that what you or your students draw or write on iPads appears on it, along with projecting PowerPoint or Keynote presentations (Glikmans, 2013).

Creating Effective Presentations

One major limitation of many presentations using these tools is that presenters include too much information on each slide. As a result, audiences often listen to presenters reading text from slides rather than seeing ideas represented more dynamically in images. Creating effective presentations therefore involves knowing how to employ images, charts, graphs, images, and websites in place of, or in conjunction with, print. Haiku Deck http://tinyurl.com/mxuvphf and Animoby https://www.animoby.com are particularly conducive to creating these visually focused presentations in that they are designed to easily import images; they also include templates and tools that limit the amount of text used in presentations.

It is also important to recognize that presentation texts can be used to go beyond simply presenting information to creating multimodal argumentative texts. Students can import clip art, photos, and video clips to their slides by going to sites such as Empressr http://www.empressr.com or Toufee http://toufee.com as well as the image or video sites described in chapter 8. When importing clip art and photos, they need to adjust the size of or crop the image so that it fits on a slide along with any captions or other language. Because the memory size of digital photos is often large, slowing down loading time, the images need to be optimized by using the "Compress Pictures" option under "Format."

Students can also add audio or video clips to their presentation by embedding an audio or video file in the presentation or by linking to a file in the computer's hard drive, ideally stored in a folder with other files for that presentation. In adding audio to a slide, students select "Sounds" under "Insert" and then choose whether they are using sound from a gallery, file, or CD, or recording their own sound. They then select whether they want the sound played automatically when they reach a slide or when they click on a speaker icon on a slide. When importing a video file, students select "Movie Insert" and then, as with audio, determine if the video is played when they reach a slide or when they click on the video icon. They can also have the video fill up the full screen by selecting "Play Full Screen."

For example, four African American eighth-grade girls constructed a multimodal PowerPoint presentation to portray alternative images of poverty and homelessness in their community (Mahiri, 2006). They wrote material based on their perceptions of homeless people in their neighborhood, including some digital photos. To add music to their photos, they accessed songs from sites, including http://www.aaliyah.com and http://www.kirkfranklin.com, where they found some background music, such as the song "I CARE 4 U," by Aaliyah, as well as gospel music, which, as one student noted, "leaves you with a spiritual feeling" (p. 59) (Beach & O'Brien, 2014, p. 185).

These presentation tools can also be used to create literary texts. The Empressr http://www.empressr.com tool and iOS Perspective http://tinyurl.com/kpvopgv app are particularly useful for supporting story creation. In Jerrod Nelson's English class at Wayzata High School (referred to in chapter 8), Sarah Bangan used PowerPoint to create a poem about the different seasons of the year http://tinyurl.com/kwhvlo3.

Students in Jacqui van Geest's English class at South St. Paul High School, South St. Paul, Minnesota, were studying point of view in their literature class. Students then created Google Presentations in which they had to adopt a villain's perceptions of story events. Stephanie Bukowski adopted the perspective of the phantom in *Phantom of the Opera* http://tinyurl.com/nxuu8fa, and Claire Ravn adopted the perspective of the evil stepsister in *Cinderella* http://tinyurl.com/lqnorxr.

Students are more likely to generate effective presentations if they engage in some careful planning prior to their presentations. As with video productions, students can use storyboards to plan out their presentations, determining which selected images they are using to convey certain information or ideas (Fryer, 2013a).

Interactive Presentations

Another limitation in the use of presentation tools is that they position audiences in a passive role as receptacles of information. Redesigning presentations to make them more interactive serves to engage audiences. This includes students not rushing through their slides to allow time for audiences to reflect on the information presented and even posing questions, as well as including questions on their slides or blank slides on a handout for peers to engage in freewriting or images and video clips to prompt discussion.

To foster interaction, you or your students can use interactive presentation tools such as SlideIdea, GoSoapBox, Socrative Teacher Clicker, eClicker, iResponse, or SRN Response listed on the website http://tinyurl.com/l7vuc7x for embedding prompts or voting options for smartphone or clicker polling to garner students' perceptions or attitudes on certain topics or issues for display to the class. For example, you or your students can use the 2ScreensRemote http://tinyurl.com/csknx3n using an iPhone as a remote or Presentation Pal http://tinyurl.com/km2t3ze using an Android phone as a remote, as well as to project images, documents, PDFs, and websites in a whiteboard-like frame. You can also use the iOS PowerPresenter http://tinyurl.com/mtk5oog app to draw on the iPad screen for projecting on the screen. And you can use the NearPod http://tinyurl.com/lkzmjau or Idea Flight http://tinyurl.com/ky4vdpe apps to display your presentations directly on your students' iPads as opposed to an overhead screen.

In working with her 10th-grade students in a communications class, Heather Johnson, of North High School, North St. Paul, Minnesota, used an online PowerPoint presentation to foster students' blog responses to the novel *The Secret Life of Bees*:

> The required Communications course that I teach is a comprehensive course that covers public speaking, interpersonal skills, nonverbal skills, conflict resolution, listening skills, etc. That trimester, I decided to create a blog for my students as a forum for this course where they can go and share examples of how to and how not to communicate. I kept the specifications quite broad to start, telling them to keep it related to Communications. In doing this, the blog has become a forum not only for the examples, but also for the students to share ideas for upcoming speech topics, inquiries on how to write the outline, etc.
>
> For a required blogging assignment I gave to my English 10 students, I set up a time for us all to go the computer lab, and students participated individually in an interactive PowerPoint presentation that I found online, created by Mr. Harrington, Mrs. Scott, and Mrs. Thompson, Normal Community West High School, Normal, Illinois.
>
> Students accessed the presentation (and the follow-up blog) at my teacher page website.
>
> This PowerPoint is an interactive tool that explores various aspects of Sue Monk Kidd's novel, *The Secret Life of Bees*. The three teachers created a fantastic PowerPoint, five pages in length, providing many fascinating links leading to aspects of the book that will help students understand the novel on a deeper level. For example, the PowerPoint links to an interactive beehive; the animated movie-like beehive details bee behavior, feeding habits, mating, and fun facts.
>
> The students absolutely loved this interactive component of the PowerPoint. Additionally, the novel opens at a crucial time in American history, 1964. Understanding the timeline and having a historical context is critical when reading this particular

novel, and the PowerPoint led students to various timelines and calendars for exploring the history of this era.

Creating a PowerPoint with active links is something that I would like to do with the novels I teach in the future. The students seemed to truly have a valuable experience, as they reported in their online blog. Once they were done with the PowerPoint, they were required to post a response on their class blog, discussing what they learned from the PowerPoint, what they liked, and any overall reactions to the new information and how it may relate to the novel. I required the responses be at least three–four sentences in length.

As the following excerpts from their blog posts about the novel suggests, the PowerPoint help students interpret the novel: *AJ Swanson: The PowerPoint helped to explain more about the time period and what the main character is going through. I thought it was interesting learning about the actual life of bees in the interactive hive.*

Students at times did not even seem to notice that they were learning; they were so excited to blog and explore online on their own. I have rarely seen such a level of excitement for a novel and I plan to continue activities such as these in the future. Digital writing has opened up new opportunities in my classroom and I look forward expanding on this new form of writing in my English and Communications classes. It was a "virtual" field trip of sorts, and the follow-up blogging piece added a productive way to share student ideas and responses.

To help students assess their work on their presentations, you can provide them with some criteria formulated by Troy Hicks (2013):

- Emphasize salient points by focusing on key ideas through choices in font and color, limited amounts of text, and the inclusion of a visual metaphor.
- Integrate appropriate (with regard to both content and length) multimedia and visual displays as a coherent part of a broader presentation. . . .
- Clarify information by using appropriate multimedia effects such as panning, zooming, and highlighting, or otherwise animating limited selections.
- Strengthen claims by providing a variety of evidence that meets the criteria of given contexts. . . .
- Add interest by periodically using transitions, a black screen, or slides with an alternative background or image in conjunction with verbal cues that signal the audience to pay attention. (p. 76)

CREATING E-BOOKS

Both teachers and students are increasingly creating their own e-books that range from short reports to replacements for often expensive, heavy textbooks. These e-books can be designed for a course or a school's specific curriculum, as well as updated to address changes in that curriculum (for more on creating e-books on the website http://tinyurl.com/l8f8nej).

As with any digital text, one benefit of creating e-books is that you can add links, images, videos, or presentations. For example, Al Gore's *Our Choice* http://tinyurl.com/9dw9nym is a highly interactive, visual e-book portraying the effects of climate change on the earth's environment.

Teachers and students can also self-publish e-books to sell on Amazon Kindle and the Apple Store or through Smash Books. For example, seventh-grade students at Woodlawn Beach Middle School, Woodlawn Beach, Florida, created an e-book that was converted into an app entitled *Creatures, Plants, and More!* http://tinyurl.com/kfyv5v5, which is for sale on the iBooks bookstore (for a presentation by Wesley Fryer on self-publishing books: http://tinyurl.com/lljtw2g).

Platforms for Creating E-books

There are several different platforms that you or your students can use to create e-books, including iBooks Author, Adobe Reader PDF files, Scrivner, Calibre, and others listed on the website http://tinyurl.com/l8f8nej to create MOBI or EPUB files (Luke, 2012). The simplest option for use in your classroom is to create a PDF file, which precludes some of the interactive or video features available through iBooks Author or Calibre for selling on Amazon. You or your students can create a text in Word or Pages and then use "Save As" in Word or "Export" in Pages to create a PDF file to then add to the "Books Library" in iTunes.

The iBooks Author http://tinyurl.com/6wj3po7 app involves

- Downloading the software and creating an e-book on a Mac (Gruman, 2012; Langer, 2012 http://tinyurl.com/9hs5pl4; McKesson & Witwer, 2012 http://tinyurl.com/82q6ko4).
- Importing Word or Pages files into iBooks Author for further editing—for example, attending to the beginning or ending of chapters.
- Using editing widgets to add presentations created in Keynote or video.
- Creating a PDF file for use in a classroom or having it available for free or for a price on the Apple Store (for further information: http://www.apple.com/support/ibooksauthor).

For creating e-books for reading on Kindles or other e-reader devices, you or your students need to create EPUB or MOBI (for Kindles) files based on HTML code. You or your students can use Pages to save a file as an EPUB file. Creating an EPUB or MOBI file using Word involves saving the file as a Web page (HTML) and then using the Calibre software program http://calibre-ebook.com for Mac or PC to convert that file into either an EPUB or MOBI file for previewing on a e-reader device (Luke, 2012).

Or, you or your students can use Scrivner http://tinyurl.com/2wuxsbu, Zinepal http://www.zinepal.com, or Aerbook http://aerbook.com/site for writing and editing files that can then be used to create EPUB or MOBI files. Finally, students can also use iOS Book Creator http://tinyurl.com/c4akzv6, eBook Creator http://tinyurl.com/lm64r7l, or Scribblepress http://tinyurl.com/axj4wqz apps or the Android eBook Maker http://tinyurl.com/lz4kud2 app to create e-books.

Creating Digital Literary Texts

You or your students can also create digital literary texts that, as with digital storytelling or poetry described in the last chapter, include images, photos, videos, drawings, music/sound effects, and alternative templates. Students can use the tools listed on the website http://tinyurl.com/lsok3s6 for creating multimodal children's books to share with young students. To create engaging children's books, they could first study examples of high-quality children's books, particularly those with artistic illustrations, and then create their own books or take an existing story to add illustrations to the story.

ONLINE SITES FOR SHARING WRITING

Students can also share their literary writing on sites such as FanFiction.net, Figment, or Wattpad, sites listed on the website http://tinyurl.com/mpyqctf. For example, on the FanFiction site http://www.fanfiction.net, students receive helpful feedback on their submissions from a highly collaborative community. When female English-language learners shared their writing on this site, they received positive feedback about it in ways that enhanced their self-perceptions and challenged the deficit identities often ascribed to them by their schools (R. W. Black, 2009a).

Students can also use tools such as Joomag https://edshelf.com/tool/joomag, Scoop-it https://edshelf.com/tool/scoop-it, UniFlip http://www.uniflip.com, OpenZine http://www.openzine.com/aspx, Calameo http://www.openzine.com/aspx, or Themeefy https://edshelf.com/tool/themeefy to create a classroom, sports team, or school magazines, as did Tom's students (described in chapter 3). And students can create digital scrapbooks or photo albums using iPhoto or Shutterfly Studio (free download from Shutterfly), Clipmarks, Plum, or Tabblo (for more on creating digital scrapbooks: http://tinyurl.com/78h4828). Judy Annan (2006) created an activity http://tinyurl.com/24tyx39 in which students identified certain topics and themes based on their reading of the online version of *The Adventures of Huckleberry Finn* http://ww3.telerama.com/~joseph/finn/finntitl.html. Students

- Viewed an example of a digital scrapbook in the form of a PowerPoint presentation about Mark Twain—*Mark Twain, An American Icon* http://tinyurl.com/lhq2ntm.
- Reviewed sites related to the topics and themes portrayed in the novel, found images that conveyed their interpretations of these topics and themes, saved these images in folders, and then copied and pasted the images into PowerPoint, saving the URLs on the Landmark Project's Citation Machine http://citationmachine.net.
- Reflected on their work, based on the criteria that they needed to collect at least 10 "scraps" of information imported to their PowerPoint.
- Shared their presentations with their class, which were evaluated according to a rubric on content, design, variety of material, citing of source information, mechanics, understanding of the topic, topic focus, and quality of the final presentation.

Creating Online Newspapers or Newsletters

Students could also analyze and produce online classroom newspapers or newsletters. In a program sponsored by the American Society of Newspaper Editors, 470 schools now publish online editions available at myhighschooljournalism.org; see also, the Write Site http://www.writesite.org, designed for middle school students. This includes analyzing the use of layout in the school newspaper in terms of how stories are blocked out on pages, as well as the effective use of font size, titles, columns, white space, and use of images in, for example, the award-winning newspaper *Paly Voice* of Palo Alto High School, Palo Alto, California http://voice.paly.net.

To create online newspapers or newsletters, students can simply use word-processing tools, blogs, or a website meshed with newspaper templates from Build a Newspaper http://www.buildanewspaper.com, as well as use the Printing Press http://tinyurl.com/ajr8s7a or Issuu http://issuu.com to create these newspapers or newsletters (for more on classroom newspapers/newsletters: http://tinyurl.com/lstew4c).

In his journalism class at Edina High School, Edina, Minnesota, Jim Hatten has his students analyze the school newspaper to then create their own classroom newspaper:

> I decided to create an online newspaper for my Intro to Journalism class http://edinajournalism.googlepages.com/gazette, which was linked to the class website. I wanted to create an online newspaper for this class because the class had no direct link with the school newspaper, and I wanted my students to have the real experience of

being published. Creating an online newspaper allows them the opportunity to have both an audience of their classroom peers, and a real world audience that extends far beyond the classroom walls (including to their parents).

It is my hope that my Introduction to Journalism class's newspaper will become as widely read as the school newspaper, if not more so. The stories that students wrote were electronically submitted to me, and a student editor and I copied and pasted them into a new Google Page which was hyperlinked to the class newspaper page. I feel students "owned" their articles more than classes without a means of publication because they knew their work would be on the website for all to see. Students also discussed in class which student should have the lead story on the website and why. Discussions revolved around news judgment, writing abilities and audience analysis. Through discussing which story would appear in which part of the online newspaper and which stories would be more prominently featured, the class applied nearly every aspect of the course goals in a collaborative culminating activity.

Online newspapers create an inexpensive mass medium for students to experience real world application of the skills and efforts they develop in class. Because the audience is open-ended and public, students tend to self-edit better, challenge themselves in their own writing, and think critically when given another student's work to read. It is easier for me as a teacher to manage student homework and monitor missing assignments. Students value their work more and take ownership of their own abilities and downfalls as writers. For each of these reasons (and so many more) digital literacy resources are infinitely valuable to my journalism classes.

LEARNING TO CODE

Underlying any digital text is a coding system. While students do not need to know these systems to create digital texts, there is an increased interest in providing them with instruction on computer programming, as evident in the Hour of Code http://code.org/educate/hoc campaign launched in 2013 to provide at least 1 hour of computer coding instruction in December 2013. To justify giving his sixth-grade students coding instruction, Kevin Hodgson (2014) argues that while he does not expect his students to master programming languages or become software programmers, he believes that understanding how technology works in their lives requires some understanding of coding so that they can influence how digital tools can be used to enhance their lives. He also believes that coding is a form of composition:

> So, yes, coding is composition, and reading and writing programming languages on even a very basic level belong in the writing classroom as much as in the computer science class. Is there any doubt that the workforce that my sixth graders will enter in a

decade or so will be highly technical and that those who understand the technology will have a leg up on those who don't? I have no doubts whatsoever.

Students can learn coding from participation on sites such as Codeacademy http://www.codecademy.com or Code School https://www.codeschool.com, which provides interactive lessons. There are a number of apps that can be used to teach coding listed on the website http://tinyurl.com/lotrmw7—for example, Scratch, GameStar Mechanic, Hopscotch, and Codea.

Creating Apps

In addition to learning to code, you or your students may also want to engage in creating apps. You can submit your class website to the Educators Apps site https://educatorsapp.com to create iOS or Android apps free for up to six classes. There are also online courses on creating apps listed on the Open Culture site http://www.openculture.com/computer_science_free_courses, whose resources you can access even if you are not taking the courses.

There are also a number of apps that can be used to create apps—for example, Appear http://appmakr.com, TouchAppCreator http://tinyurl.com/cwfdmop, iOS http://tinyurl.com/kd6xthv, Android http://tinyurl.com/ku6gy56, Chrome OS App Press, App Inventor http://appinventor.mit.edu/explore, Android SDK for Mac http://tinyurl.com/cczsh7v, Microsoft Touch Develop http://tinyurl.com/msrdttw, or Conduit Mobile http://mobile.conduit.com/Mobile-apps.aspx. To use these apps, students can insert text, images, videos, audio, or links to create pages within their app and then publish their app for use on devices.

ANALYZING READABILITY OF DIGITAL TEXTS

Another key factor influencing digital design has to do with the ease of comprehension of a digital text or its readability—how easy texts are to comprehend given readers' search for relevant information on a site (Kress, 2003). Readability is often defined in terms of the level of difficulty of words or sentences (i.e., the number of syllables) or in terms of sentence length (i.e., number of words in a sentence). Students can use Word to obtain a readability score for their Word documents or employ online readability tools (for more on readability formulas http://tinyurl.com/n23gpql).

However, it is important to note that determining readability simply in terms of words and sentence difficulty does not capture a number of other factors that contribute to an audience's ease of understanding of digital texts. Reading and navigating texts on a screen differs from reading print texts. For example, online users need a lot more white space on a screen to orient their attention than what is the case with print texts. It is therefore important to consider a number of other principles of readability contributing to audience comprehension unique to processing digital texts.

One key factor shaping readability is what Charles Bazerman (2014) describes as cohesive devices that provide readers with a sense of coherence:

- Text markers, section identifiers, predictors of the reasoning or steps coming up, or summative passages tying together where one has been in previous sections, to launch the next stage.
- Transitional words and phrases that explain the connective logic between sentences or paragraphs, such as "therefore," "afterwards," or "as a consequence of."
- Compound and complex sentences that put several topics in relation.
- Even simple sentences can tie together multiple prior topics of discussion and launch new topics from previous ones.
- Pronouns that refer back to prior subjects, keep them alive, and provide continuity, but the reference must be clear. . . .
- Precise use of verb tense to identify the time locations of specific actions and their relation to each other. . . .
- Repetition of exact words or core roots—what is known as *lexical cohesion*.
- Using synonymous or related terms, to establish a limited domain of meanings and familiar relationships (or semantic domain), helping the reader make sense of the text. (pp. 127–128)

Editing Tools for Document and Text Files

As we discuss in the next chapter, students can engage in peer editing using Comments in Word to provide feedback to specific highlighted sections of a document, resulting in editing revisions recorded using Track Changes. Students can also read aloud their text to one another or employ some text-to-speech tools as well as use the Natural Readers http://www.naturalreaders.com tool to listen to their drafts so that they can hear the need for needed changes to enhance readability.

Word .docx files are formatted so that text fonts and organization appear ready for publication. In contrast, text files with .txt or .rft are created by a text editor using tools such as ASCII to represent letters or numbers. One advantage of text files is that they can be used across any platform, while document files are limited to use with a particular platform or word-processing program.

While in most cases students are not using text files, students may use these files in creating their own websites that are constructed by using text files meshed with HTML tags. To edit text files, students can use a number of different editing tools listed on the website http://tinyurl.com/kxx4yzy for use with both document and text files that include what is known as the Markdown feature with text files that add code for use in publishing online. With Markdown, students can edit their texts to automatically add code to those texts for online publishing.

Grammar/Spelling Checkers

Another important set of digital tools for editing are grammar and spell-checkers—for example, those in Word or AbiWord that identify grammar and spelling errors (for more on grammar/spell-checkers: http://tinyurl.com/l8479w3).

These tools are particularly valuable for students who are prone to making a lot of errors. One study found that middle school students who were having spelling difficulties were much more likely to correct spelling errors when using a spell-checker than not (MacArthur, Graham, Haynes, & De La Paz, 1996; for more on grammar and spelling checkers: http://tinyurl.com/l8479w3).

At the same time, as part of editing instruction, students need to know how to employ grammar and spelling for actually correcting errors identified by the checkers. This includes having students frame the context for errors so that they make corrections with that context in mind as well as some of the principles of readability previously mentioned. For example, students may be writing a lot of sentences such as "The ball went over the fence. John threw the ball." The first sentence violates the given/new or prior-knowledge principle; a reader does not have a reference for the ball, so they ask, "What ball?" By combining these sentences and referring to the fact that the ball was the ball that John threw, a reader then has a referent for the ball, as in "The ball that John threw went over the fence." This suggests having students work in editing groups so that, as audiences, they can pose questions such as "What ball?" to help students address issues of given/new or prior knowledge.

Students also need to recognize some of the limitations of grammar and spelling checkers (MacArthur, 2006). Although grammar or style checkers may flag errors, they may be based on erroneous assumptions about language use. These checkers often incorrectly identify grammar errors, particularly the use of subject-verb agreement and use of the passive voice (Kies, 2012). For example, use of passive constructions may be noted as problematic when in fact the use of the passive is appropriate. Writers may use the passive when they want to deflect attention away from the agent as actor, as in "Company employees were fired by the CEO," as opposed to "The CEO fired company employees." Grammar checkers may also identity problems of usage as grammar errors. Students therefore need to understand differences between grammar as syntax and usage as how language is used, particularly in terms of addressing issues of dialect differences.

Students also have difficulty correcting grammar issues because they lack the vocabulary to explore alternative sentence structures or to avoid repetition. To find appropriate vocabulary, students can employ online thesauruses, such as Roget's thesaurus http://www.bartleby.com/thesauri, Thesaurus.com http://thesaurus.reference.com, or Wiki-Saurus http://en.wiktionary.org/wiki/WikiSaurus, for generating synonyms for replacing repetitive words (Montgomery & Marks, 2006). To help students address grammar errors, students can go to various online editing resource sites http://tinyurl.com/mddtw5q created by university online writing centers.

There are also problems with spell-checkers. They may simply not identify misspellings, or they may identify proper nouns as misspelled, as well as words that have not been entered into a spelling dictionary; if the spell-checker provides a list of optional spellings, students may not be able to select the correct option (Montgomery, Karlan, & Coutinho, 2001). Montgomery and Marks (2006) suggest using an "InSPECT" approach for coping with spelling errors: "In the document, Start the spell checker, Pick correct alternatives, Correct additional errors, Type in your corrections" (p. 35). They also suggest using games or worksheets that provide alternative spellings, as well as having students work together in editing conferences to correct one another's errors. Students could also sound out difficult syllables, such as "ence" versus "ance" in "independence," or associate problem words with certain topics (Dobie, 2007). For example, to note that "cemetery" uses *e*'s, a student could associate that word with "eerie." Students can also use grammar-checking tools such as Grammarly http://www.grammarly.com to check on their grammar.

Using Word Clouds For Editing

Students can also employ word cloud tools such as Wordle http://www.wordle.net or Tagxedo http://www.tagxedo.com to insert their texts and identify repetition of certain words that appear larger than other words. By editing a text and resubmitting it to a word cloud site, students can perceive the benefits of editing their texts. M. E. Garber (2012) describes his use of Wordle to assist him in editing a story:

> I copied and pasted a story that I'd recently spiffed up and before I submitted it, I ran it through Wordle. My protagonist's name was largest, equal in size to her partner's name. Well, that made sense. Much smaller, yet clearly the next level of importance, came five words. Two made sense. Three were troubling: Voice, Eyes and Looked. . . . After changing these words and phrasings, I ran the story again. Viola! Clean story, with the themes showing largest (after the names). Off the story went, vastly improved.

CITING MATERIAL

Students need to document any reference to, or paraphrase of, a writer's article, chapter, book, or website, regardless of whether they quote that writer or not, including recognizing the differences between direct quotes and paraphrasing a writer's text (for more on citations/reference styles http://tinyurl.com/kg6u9wr). Students also need to know how to employ the different types of reference styles—the Modern Language Association and Chicago styles, typically used in literature or the arts, and the American Psychological Association style, typically used in social sciences.

When citing online sources, students should realize the value of citing sources—that they are also providing readers with a service by including a current correct URL with the reference. Students should therefore include, if possible, the authors, the title, the date that the student retrieved the document, and the URL. For example, for access to the sixth edition of the American Psychology Association's publication manual, the author of the site would be noted as American Psychological Association; the date is the copyright date on the website, 2014; the name of the site is APA Style; the date of retrieval is July 1, 2014; and the URL is http://www.apastyle.org resulting in the following reference: American Psychological Association. (2014, July 1). APA style [web log post]. Retrieved from http://www.apastyle.org.

Using Reference Software

Students can also use reference or citation management software, such as Bibme http://www.bibme.org, Easybib http://www.easybib.com, Write-and-cite (for RefWorks) http://tinyurl.com/2fkafqy, and Citation Machine http://tinyurl.com/yfxdgyd, which collects references and then formats them using different styles to create a bibliography (EdTechTeacher, 2013; for more on reference and citation tools http://tinyurl.com/kwzvpsz).

One advantage of this software is that students can create their own reference database or library for use in writing different papers. Thus, whenever they need to add references to their papers, they can go to their databases for these references rather than having to hunt them down. This software also formats their citations as they are writing their papers and then adds references according to a selected citation style.

The two dominant commercial citation management software programs are EndNote and RefWorks. RefWorks, which is housed only on the web, is typically sold as site licenses to schools and universities and is less expensive than EndNote. A similar service, CiteULike http://www.citeulike.org, as well as Scribe 2.5, Wikindx, or JabRef, can be used to organize notes according to citations, to automatically link a citation in the text to a reference list, to format references in Modern Language Association or

American Psychological Association style, and to create reference lists. For CiteULike, because citations are stored on a server, students can access it from any computer and share their library with others.

Because students in K–12 classrooms may be using only a limited number of references, they could then turn to free citation software programs, such as the Citation Machine http://tinyurl.com/yfxdgyd, the program most suited to K–12, and select their choice of style format, type in the source, and create citations in a relatively straightforward manner.

Issues of Plagiarism

There is much fear among teachers and administrators that the Internet has caused an "epidemic" of plagiarism. Students can download entire papers and turn them in as their own. They can cut text from Internet sources and paste it into their papers without attribution, in an attempt to make their work seem more sophisticated. And they can splice together entire papers from multiple sources without doing much more than creating transitions and making sure that the font is the same. Under these circumstances, teachers' suspicions have grown, often to the point that they suspect some degree of plagiarism in a class of students.

Instances of plagiarism can be detected by entering a "familiar," suspicious line from a student's paper into Google and seeing if a close match results. You can also use plagiarism checker tools, such as TurnItIn http://turnitin.com (for more on plagiarism detection http://tinyurl.com/kdj5wor).

Before deciding whether to subscribe to a plagiarism detection service (which can be done at the course level or across an entire school or university), it is important to know how these services work and why there may be more principled ways to subvert plagiarism than submit student writing to computer detection systems (Anson, 2008). For example, TurnItIn works by matching the text in papers submitted to its search engine against a large database of existing work written by students and professionals.

The technology produces what the company calls a "customized originality report" that provides an index of how much in a student's paper is copied from another source. The text of the paper is shown in a left frame; in the right frame are any sources that match the text in the left frame. For a highlighted passage, the program retrieves the original passage that appears to match the student's. In addition to looking at published sources for matches, TurnItIn's search engine scans all student essays that have been submitted before. Even if a paper submitted to TurnItIn from one class is plagiarized, any future student can never use that same paper because the system will find it.

Several aspects of technologies such as TurnItIn have led many educators—and whole campuses or schools—to avoid subscribing to it or to drop their subscriptions

(Anson, 2008). First, students must submit their work to the system, which then stores the papers in its database forever. Although the company will argue that the original papers are turned into a "code" that in some ways protects each student's copyright, this code is still a version of the students' work. Forcing students to send their work to a company that in some sense "owns" and stores it is at least ethically questionable. In one case, at McGill University, a student won a suit on the moral and ethical grounds that he was the owner of his work and could not be forced to submit it to TurnItIn.

Second, most teachers using plagiarism detection software require at the start of a course that their students submit all their graded work to the system. Even though no one has yet committed plagiarism, it is already assumed that the entire class is potentially guilty. This can have the effect of signaling to students that they may not be trusted not to plagiarize, which alone can work against establishing an atmosphere of respect and collaboration.

Finally, there have been a number of cases in which students have been falsely accused of plagiarism because a computerized detection system discovered some percentage of their work was not original. Chris Anson (2008) corresponded at length with a student who was suspended from a special honors program because a small percentage of a difficult paper she wrote was flagged as plagiarized by a plagiarism detection system. The students were not told that their papers were being submitted; furthermore, they received no support at all from the teacher for writing their papers, which were assigned at the beginning of the course and collected at the end. The student had dutifully cited all her sources with parenthetical references following each instance of a quoted source but neglected to put quotation marks around the sentences themselves. The computer has no way to consider such cases—it does not bring the complexities of human judgment to bear on what it sees. The teacher and administrators, trusting the computer's judgment, also failed to consider the context of the so-called plagiarism and simply rejected the student's appeals. It took filing a lawsuit to force the university to perceive the issue from more than one perspective. Computers cannot "read" or understand text, and as a result, there will be mistakes in the way that they detect plagiarism. If a student's career can be affected by such mistakes, we ought to approach their use with considerable caution.

Much has been published about plagiarism, but there is growing educational consensus that teachers need to do their part to provide a context in which it is difficult to plagiarize and in which students are not motivated to do so—for example, by creating unique, interesting, engaging assignments instead of dull, "canned" assignments on which dozens or hundreds of papers have already been written. The Council of Writing Program Administrators (2003) has created a "best practices" document that advocates these and many other useful and principled strategies. The council cautions that the availability of computerized plagiarism detection services "should never be used to justify the avoidance of responsible teaching methods" (p. 7).

SUMMARY

Learning to employ digital design involves creating digital texts that are engaging and easy to read based on principles of readability and digital layout. By analyzing their own engagement and comprehension of texts, students then recognize how specific aspects of layout, white space, font, and images, as well as grammar and spelling, can enhance engagement and comprehension. And they can apply design principles to create inter-active presentations for engaging their audiences. Students also need to know how to effectively employ grammar/spelling checkers and citation software.

10

USING NEW TECHNOLOGIES FOR FORMATIVE RESPONSE TO WRITING

From her well-known longitudinal study of student writing at Harvard, Nancy Sommers concluded that feedback to student writing, particularly for first-year students, is critical to improving their writing as well as their future success as college students (Walk, 2000). Sommers notes that "freshmen use feedback to understand what it means to think in more complex and sophisticated ways" (p. 2). One student in the study noted that the "comments showed me other possibilities to consider and what it would mean to go deeper into a subject" (p. 2). In the study, those students who received the most initial frequent feedback had the largest gains in writing quality in their first year of college. That feedback provided them with a sense of belonging and connection to instructors in what can seem to students as an impersonal university.

Typically, teachers place themselves at the center of this process: Students submit papers and other written projects, and then, over the next few days (and with an often heroic effort), the teacher offers the students individual comments and suggestions to help them improve as thinkers, researchers, writers, and producers of digital texts. This process teaches students about principles of writing in the context of their own work, which requires careful reading, learner-centered commentary, and considerable time.

A number of digital tools, however, are now providing opportunities for teachers (as well as peers) to provide responses not just more easily or quickly but in ways that are more helpful to students' development as writers and for the thoughtful revision of their work in progress as well as their final projects. Anne Beaton, a high school English teacher at Armstrong High School, Robbinsdale, Minnesota, had this to say about her decision to use digital tools in word-processing programs to provide feedback on her students' papers:

> I needed to find a way to better utilize their face-to-face time in the classroom. In
> addition, reading papers and writing feedback by hand had become taxing and frus-

trating—I never felt as though I was able to fully communicate my thinking to the writer. I found myself leaning on catch phrases like, "nice" or "??" or "unclear" rather than taking the time to fully explain myself in the margin. Time spent commenting was replaced by rubrics that served as a quick easy way to distribute comments to the masses. I could simply place an "X" in the box and let the student decipher why their effort fell there.

But X's do not teach. I was determined to find a better way to reach my students. . . . I had used the "Track Changes" and "Insert Comment" tools in MS Word with my own writing, but had not considered their effect with my students. Jumping directly into a text to rewrite a sentence or attach a comment to their work was intriguing. I was curious about how my ability to offer direction and feedback to students might be augmented with the help of these tools. How refreshing to truly show a student a variety of word choices instead of jotting "w/c" or reconstructing a sentence to show a grammatically correct version or place the period inside the quotation marks. I realized that with the help of electronic feedback, I could provide visual examples that served as mini lessons tailored to each student.

In this chapter, we examine how digital tools can be used to provide formative response. Formative response actually occurs while a student is still writing and revising. It is helpful and advisory, and it places the teacher in the role of a coach. Typical modes of formative response include comments on drafts, conferences with students, peer-to-peer discussions, or tutoring (see the National Council of Teachers of English report *Formative Assessment That Truly Informs Instruction*, 2013.) In contrast, summative response evaluates a final product and assigns a grade or score. Summative response is more judgmental and final, and it places the teacher in the role of a critic. It often involves a set of evaluation criteria, or a rubric. We cover methods for summative response in digital environments in chapter 11, along with descriptions of use of e-portfolios for use in summative assessment, although e-portfolios can also be used for formative assessment during a course.

ASSESSMENT *OF* LEARNING VERSUS *FOR* LEARNING

A primary purpose for assessing students is to foster their learning of certain social practices, such as those described in chapter 2—for example, their ability to infer themes based on making connections among texts. To do so, you may provide them with assessment of their learning with a grade or rating on a rubric, what could be described as assessment *of* their learning. Or, students may take a standardized reading or writing test that provides them with a single score or scores indicating their "reading ability" or "writing ability," scores reflecting their performance just on those particular tests at a particular time.

However, assessment *of* their learning, what we are describing as summative assessment, may not provide the useful feedback that they can receive from assessment *for* learning (P. Black, Harrison, Lee, Marshall, & Wiliam, 2003). Assessment *for* learning is designed to foster students' metacognitive reflection about their use of social practices to achieve certain goals—for example, their use of hyperlinks in a blog post to their peers' posts to build social connections.

However, students, particularly early adolescent students, have difficulty engaging in metacognitive reflection. They often lack the ability to infer how their use of certain tools—for example, making hyperlinks—is related to the use of certain social practices—how using hyperlinks serves to build social connections. And they may lack knowledge of the criteria that constitute effective use of tools related to using those tools within a social context—how their use of hyperlinks to particularly relevant or useful topics in their peers' posts can serve to engage their audiences.

Recognizing How Students' Learning Preferences Shape Reflection

One argument for the flipped classroom is that it provides more time for students to interact with one another and therefore devote more time to engaging in collaborative peer conferences. However, it is useful for teachers to recognize that some students have learning preferences associated with being introverts that supports their working alone, while more extroverted students have learning preferences supporting peer interactions (Honeycutt & Warren, 2014). The former students can often adopt a reflective stance associated with thinking on their own about their writing that, in the middle of a lot of interaction, the latter students may not experience, suggesting the need for activities that foster individual student reflection. One strategy for fostering such reflection is the "Think, Write, Share" strategy that begins with individual student reflection, writing about the reflection, and then sharing that writing with peers (Honeycutt & Warren, 2014).

USE OF FORMATIVE ASSESSMENT TO PROVIDE DESCRIPTIVE FEEDBACK TO FOSTER REFLECTION

Assessment *for* learning therefore serves to foster students' use of metacognitive reflection on their uses of social practices. By providing formative assessment through descriptive feedback to students, you are helping students learn to reflect on their uses of specific social practices, leading to changes and improvement in their future uses of these social practices. For example, students are employing iMovie video-editing tools to create a digital story. You can invite them to engage in self-assessment by describing how you as their audience were engaged in, overwhelmed by, intrigued by, anticipating further developments in, puzzled by, or wanting more of certain elements, in responding to their digital story. From receiving that feedback, students then reflect on what specific aspects of their digital story generated your responses, so their reflection leads to future improvements in creating digital stories.

Student Self-Assessment of Use of Social Practices

It is also useful to include criteria in assignments to foster students' self-assessment of the degree to which they have effectively employed certain social practices. For example, given our social practice of working collaboratively and recognizing alternative perspectives, you can provide students with a set of criteria associated with their ability to do the following:

- Identify goals for determining tasks to achieve these goals.
- Identify roles and responsibilities for completing these tasks.
- Recognize the value of peers' alternative perspectives and expertise that may differ from your own perspective and expertise.
- Facilitate collaboration through providing direction and positive support of successful collaboration.
- Cope with challenges in working collaboratively through negotiation of differences.

Students could then use these criteria to reflect on changes over time during the school year to work collaboratively with others.

You can also tie completion of specific assignments to students' self-assessments of their use of practices specific to those assignments. One example of designing a series of assignments linked to criteria is the Youth Voices Challenges and Tasks Grid http://youthvoices.net/grid, developed by Paul Allison. This guide contains 20 assignments to be completed by students during the school year, organized by different "challenges" associated with use of the Youth Voices site described in chapter 9 related to the Common Core standards: "Citing Evidence in Conversations," "Independent Reading," "Text-Dependent Research," and "Formulating Arguments in Areas of Interest." These tasks are then further organized according to the following tasks, involving use of certain practices:

Reflect & Connect Tasks: Keep Track and Make Connections
Wonder & Dream Tasks: Point to What's Important and Ask Questions
Notice & Investigate Tasks: Analyze and Draw Conclusions
Construct & Express Tasks: Create and Collaborate With Multimedia

Students then use the Youth Voice site to find examples of assignments specific to different subject matter areas http://youthvoices.net/grid. Students also draw on "Guides" http://www.youthvoices.net/guide/archives from the Youth Voices site that provide templates for completing these tasks.

In their discussion of implications for assessment related to using this assignment grid, Charles Moran and Anne Herrington (2013) http://tinyurl.com/m3p3wtq note that the Youth Voices site fosters students' self-assessment of their contributions to the site that could also apply to their completion of these tasks. On the site, students can complete one of the "How Am I Doing?" templates that asks students to respond to questions such as the following:

> *How do you contribute to the Youth Voices community?*
>
> I contribute to the Youth Voices community by uploading my photos and posts featuring my ideas on my photography. By doing this, it lets other people on Youth Voices to access what I have written and comment on my ideas and what they think about it. I am also on a member of the Youth Voices group on Flickr which also helps spread ideas and share my photography with other people.

> *What is easy for you to do here?*
>
> Writing about my work and having discussions on it is easy for me because I know how I feel about my photography and what I want to do to improve. It is easy to share my ideas with everybody else and the message that I want to get across in my photography.

> *What is hard, but worth the struggle?*
>
> At times, Photoshop can be very hard and not go the way that you want it to go. But in the end, once you figure out what you're doing, it is definitely worth the struggle.

> *What do you wish you could do, but can't?*
>
> I wish that I could do more cool tricks on Photoshop (which I want to learn more about).

They quote Allison's (2009) focus on the importance of student self-assessment related to achieving goals, which motivates them.

> No longer am I working to motivate students to do work for me. Instead, I am working to help each student to accomplish his or her own goals as readers and writers in a school-based social network. No longer am I assessing them; after the shift the students assess themselves, and decide what to do next. This shift, this turning point from teacher-centered to student-centered self-assessment, has come each semester since I put blogging in a social network at the center of my curriculum. (p. 79)

However, previous research on the use of formative response shows mixed gains in fostering self-assessment and revision (Beach & Friedrich, 2006). But there is little question that digital tools such as conference-style synchronous discussions, small group student chats, online peer review, and annotated sample papers can be used to provide effective formative response fostering self-assessment. Digital technologies for such response vary widely and can affect the nature of the response as well as the consequences for students' learning. For this reason, it is important to choose a medium or technology that is best suited to the particular goals of response (e.g., to provide global, reader-based thoughts about the relationship between text and visuals versus demonstrating ways that sentences can be edited for style). In addition, although all the technologies that we describe here can be used by any respondent, some may be more appropriate to generate peer response, while others may best be used by teachers. You can employ a range of different digital tools for providing feedback, as described by Andrew Schoenborn (2013) in his presentation http://tinyurl.com/lxqqqkl at the 2013 National Council of Teachers of English conference, for use in his English class at Mount Pleasant High School, Mount Pleasant, Michigan.

Responding to the kinds of digital writing discussed in this book also requires some new perspectives and criteria that differ from those typically applied to print texts. How do we respond to features of multimodality, hypertextuality, and interactivity? For example, an effective student blog may include images and/or video, links to other blogs or sites, and strategies for engaging audiences, considerations that are not usually relevant to evaluating students' print essays.

Using a Reader-Based Perspective for Formative Response

In providing formative response, it is important to focus on a few central aspects that need the most work, as opposed to overwhelming students with too many issues. It is also helpful to give descriptive, reader-based comments (Elbow, 1973) regarding aspects of a draft that engage, confuse, please, puzzle, or require more information, as opposed to judgmental feedback (Beach & Friedrich, 2006). When a reader describes what happens to her as she tries to make sense of a text, that form of response can provide the writer with more helpful, meaning-based information than if the reader simply hunts for errors. It also helps to develop reflective capacities in student writers.

For example, teachers can frame their response in ways that encourage students to engage in processes of reflection as taxonomized by Pappas (2010; see Figure 10.1). In the higher reaches of this taxonomy, students begin to see patterns and relationships in their work:

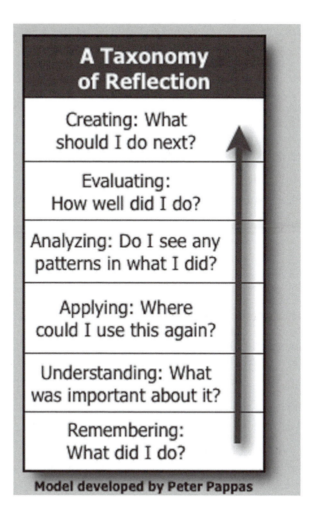

Figure 10.1.   A Taxonomy of Reflection *Source: Figure, A Taxonomy of Reflection, from Peter Pappas, A Taxonomy of Reflection: Critical Thinking for Students, Teachers, and Principals (Part 1). Copy/Paste. Used with permission of Peter Pappas.*

Were the strategies, skills and procedures I used effective for this assignment? Do I see any patterns in how I approached my work, such as following an outline, keeping to deadlines? What were the results of the approach I used—was it efficient, or could I have eliminated or reorganized steps?

Coached by response, this analysis can then generate evaluation of their drafts: "Did I do an effective job of communicating my learning to others? What have I learned about my strengths and my areas in need of improvement? How am I progressing as a learner?" Finally, the insights gained are then projected into their plans for revision: "How can I best use my strengths to improve? What steps should I take or resources should I use to meet my challenges?" (http://tinyurl.com/mm94xde).

Reader-based response also alleviates a number of problems often encountered when students read and comment on one another's drafts, such as ego conflicts or differences in ability (when a relatively skilled writer must "take advice" from a less skilled writer). When providing reader-based response, students are not telling one another what to do or playing the role of a teacher. The writer can take the raw experience of reading for what it is worth—one reader's experience, including potential confusions, disagreements, enlightenments, and pleasurable reactions. In responding to an argument about high school students' gambling problems in a blog post, for example, a reader-based response might focus on the need for more detail: "When I read your opinion about problems with high school students' gambling, I was expecting some specific examples to be sure I understood the depth of the problem." In this feedback, the teacher is describing how she is responding as a reader based on her genre expectations for responding to an argument.

Static and Dynamic Formative Response

As illustrated in Figure 10.2, response to students' writing can be described along a continuum from static to dynamic. Static response includes comments in the margins or at the end of a paper returned to the student. Such response is "one-way," from a reader to the writer, and is therefore monologic (the writer is silent). Static, fixed comments include those inserted in the text (through Insert Comments, Track Changes, markup programs—anything that is applied "on" or to the text for consumption and reflection). This kind of response becomes more dynamic when it is accompanied by deeper explanation, such as oral recorded commentary, or when students write a "memo" to the teacher about their draft, and the teacher responds in writing to acknowledge the student's intentions.

One-way oral and screen-capture response, which involves different modes and media of production and consumption, takes on more socially dynamic characteristics. At the other end of the spectrum are highly interactive conversations, which involve synchronous and asynchronous chat and other forms of live communication. A highly dynamic form of response is represented by a conference between teacher and student or between peers. The resulting conversation about the student's text is reciprocal, allowing the writer to explain his or her intentions, clarify meanings, and ask questions of the respondent, who can also offer suggestions or reader-based feedback. In such meetings, the participants actively negotiate possibilities for improvement. Although physical face-to-face conferences are viewed as the most effective way to help students to improve as writers (L. J. Black, 1998), they are also the most time-consuming and place bound, and in typical (physical) school or college settings, it is very difficult for teachers to provide them for all students.

TECHNOLOGIES FOR STATIC FORMATIVE RESPONSE

Two common forms of static electronic feedback include *intertextual commentary* and *marginal and end commentary*. In choosing which form to use with students, it is important to recognize the effect that your choice may have on their learning, revision, and interpretation of the relationship that you are establishing with them. Where do you want the responses to appear? How much do the responses "take over" or "appropriate" (Brannon & Knoblauch, 1982) the student's work? Is the technology better suited to identifying small problems, such as word choice, or larger issues that require more explanation? Do you want to use a combination of different methods of response? (Doing so can be helpful, but it can also lead to overload, with too many different kinds of comments for students to interpret effectively.)

Intertextual commentary involves line-by-line comments, suggestions, even grammatical or mechanical corrections and edits to text (Monroe, 1998). Most word-processing programs provide electronic intertextual commenting tools, such as "Track Changes." Anne, the teacher mentioned earlier, uses the "Track Changes" function (found under Tools in MS Word). When enabled, this feature allows a writer to delete, add, or change text using underlining and strikethrough visuals that preserve the original text. Figure 10.3 shows a fragment of a student paper on which we have added our own comments under the name of a fictitious teacher, Susan Pruett, using Track Changes.

In addition to these tools, reviewers can use simple techniques, such as writing text in a different color or font to distinguish teacher, tutor, or student peer comments from

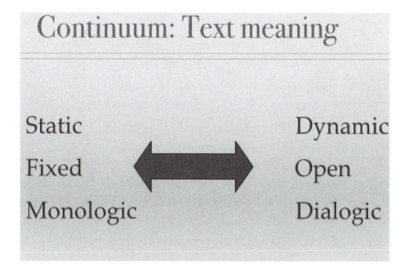

Figure 10.2. Continuum of Text Meaning

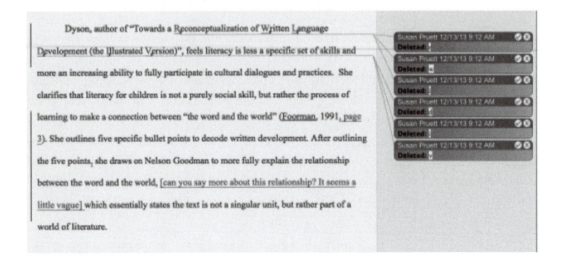

Figure 10.3.   Teacher Track Changes Comments

the author's text (Monroe, 1998), as employed in the following sample paper with comments made using simple font and boldface changes:

> My writing process is very hard to predict. It varies from paper to paper; I often don't do the same thing twice. But many times I start my paper by sitting down to watch my favorite TV program. ****How does this help you write your paper?**** It seems that I can't start writing until the very last moment, sometimes at 10 pm the night before the paper is due. When I am finally forced to start writing a paper, then the words start coming. I usually sit down for a half hour and write until I can't write anymore. ****What happens then? Are you done?****

Notice how both these methods of commenting involve inserting text into the student's work (and how Susan even corrects some errors within the text). Depending on your goals for response and your relationship with your students, you may decide to use these methods cautiously or not at all because of the way that they intrude on the student's writing. Among peers, such markup can be useful to teach editing. April Stasko, an English teacher at Mayo High School, Rochester, Minnesota, notes that her students benefit from learning to edit one another's writing:

> They like getting into their classmates' papers with a different font and making comments. Students don't know who did the purple font versus the green font so the anonymity is safe. When I have students' edit online, they have certain guided questions (restate the thesis) that they answer on paper that the author can see and I eventually get and score. Then they also comment in the paper. Most students walk away from this with a better picture of where they are. They have read several class-

mates' papers and can see if they are on the right track or completely missing the boat. When they see several papers it can give them the guidance or reassurance they need to get to work on theirs. I think they get more out of the reading of other's papers than they do the actual comments on the written paper. I do feel though most use the comments in their paper in the other color font to improve their paper. Overall I really enjoy this activity and see improvements in writing as a result of the activity.

Marginal and End Commentary

Anne also uses the "Insert Comment" feature in MS Word, which places comments into the margin of the text, as we demonstrate with our comments under the fictional name of a teacher, Mr. Castle, in Figure 10.4. This feature is now among the most popular of all static response methods because it links comments to specific words, sentences, or sections of students' text, easing comprehension. Notice how now the text is annotated with highlights but that the commentary resides next to the text rather than within it.

Some annotation programs allow teachers to create preestablished comments for cases when they write similar things repeatedly on students' drafts. Breevy http://tinyurl.com/yzsowjn and 11Trees Annotation Tool http://11trees.com/live, for example, are add-on programs that work in conjunction with Microsoft Word. You can also use tools such as EssayGrader for the Mac http://tinyurl.com/85t2t3e, Easy Assessment http://tinyurl.com/7zbmotb, GoClass http://tinyurl.com/7st4pja, and GradePad: Mobile

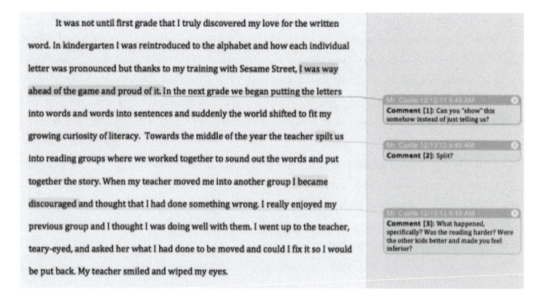

Figure 10.4. Teacher Annotation Comments

Performance Assessment http://tinyurl.com/4k5n8sk to attach comments to students' writing.

Teachers can create frequently used annotations, saving and organizing those in a file. When a comment is called for, it is easy to insert an annotation with one click into the margin of a student's paper. For example, if a teacher wants to save time explaining the need for an interesting title that captures the essence of a paper and also draws the reader in, she might create three coded comments in Breevy. The code "T1" might be associated with this text: "Great title! This immediately makes me want to read your paper." The code "T2" could be associated with the comment "Remember that titles can provide a kind of trigger that helps to prepare the reader for what you have to say and draw him or her into your paper. Can you create a more interesting, relevant, or captivating title here?" "T3" could be reserved for a formatting problem, such as "Don't forget that all the 'important' words in a title must be capitalized; see pp. 58–59 of the text to determine the difference between which words need to be capitalized and which do not." Once a student's paper is open on-screen, the teacher can use the "Insert Comment" feature in Word, choose an insert function on the Breevy toolbar (such as T1), and then hit the "Command" key. The entire comment is then inserted instantly into the margin of the student's paper.

It is important for students to know when you are using these "macro"-generating tools to save time by not having to type generalized advice over and over. If you do not explain how the macro tools work, they may begin to see repeated patterns in your responses or compare their papers with those of other students and think that you are "cheating" on providing personal responses. You can always edit the auto-inserted comments to customize them, and, of course, you always have the option of inserting unique comments specific to each paper.

Other annotation programs, such as Markin http://tinyurl.com/lvqsdz3 and Bluebeam http://www.bluebeam.com, allow for a combination of intertextual, marginal, and footnoted comments, as well as prewritten annotations. While especially robust, they can encourage teachers to become too heavy with their shaded texts, comments, and notes, overwhelming learners and making it difficult to focus on salient issues. It is important to use any such programs judiciously and be constantly mindful of the learner's experience. You can also use different programs at different stages of the process. For example, you can provide content-based comments as endnotes on students' electronically submitted papers but then later, in a subsequent revision, have students work with one another's texts using "Track Changes" to help them learn about (and improve) style and mechanics.

Readers can also provide comments using simple footnote or comments features in word-processing programs or employ Comments in Google Docs. These can appear in the conventional space at the bottom of the screen or in a parallel space using a split screen. These comments work well to provide suggestions and explanations about specific passages in the text, much like handwritten comments in the margins. Typically such comments are seen as less invasive and provide ample space for longer comments. Naturally, the footnote feature of any word-processing program can be used to create these comments. But some websites are actually designed to accommodate endnote commentary on drafts, such as FanFiction http://www.fanfiction.net, The Next Big Writer http://www.thenextbigwriter.com, or Writing.Com, where people post writing and others can write reviews or rate the writing. The benefit of endnote commentary is to provide a general sense of reader response and overall thoughts about revising a document. Usually, suggestions involve global concerns, such as organization, thesis development, or content.

Annotation and tagging tools such as Diigo or Trailfire (a Firefox extension) can also be used to highlight and write notes or annotations on students' online texts and post their notes for group members to see. For a screencast demonstration of using Diigo for highlighting and annotating students' online texts, see Diigo: A Social Bookmarking Research Tool http://www.screencast-o-matic.com/watch/cij0ev4l (for annotation tools: http://tinyurl.com/k2n3d8t, also described in chapter 5).

One final technology for providing static response bears mention. Impressive advances in voice recognition technology have yielded speech-to-text dictation tools listed on the website http://tinyurl.com/kvk4qu9, such as Dragon Dictate for Mac http://tinyurl.com/4qkh5dr and its PC counterpart, Dragon Home 12 http://tinyurl.com/26rcknk, which allow teachers to voice their comments directly into written text. These programs require about 30 minutes of "training" in which you read passages presented on-screen, using a headset and microphone that come with the product. The program adjusts itself to the features of the user's voice and articulation. After reading a student's paper, you can then activate the program and provide your orally formulated response and suggestions. The program types all your comments as you speak. The few errors that sometimes result (e.g., when the program does not recognize a specific word) can be easily edited before you convey the paper back to the student. Although speech-to-text takes some getting used to, many teachers find that they can say much more about students' papers in much less time but still provide their feedback as written text.

TOOLS FOR DYNAMIC FORMATIVE RESPONSE

Dynamic formative response involves a greater degree of interaction—give and take—between the writer and his or her readers. While inexperienced teachers may need some coaching about how to interact with students around their writing, teachers are usually skilled at providing feedback in diplomatic, helpful ways, and they have the language to render important rhetorical concepts clearly. However, most teachers find that students lack these skills and need ongoing instruction in how to provide effective peer response. This is especially true for online peer response, when students' unfamiliarity with the technology or their unhelpful prior experience with social media (e.g., flaming) can become a problem.

Past research does not suggest that peer review automatically results in better papers; students do not often offer constructive criticism, and they may not know how to comment, resorting to quickly determined and unhelpful impressions, such as "sounds good to me" (Beach & Friedrich, 2006). However, past research also suggests that when coordinated carefully, peer review supports process-based writing, encourages students to think about their audience, and provides them with practice talking about writing (Lu & Law, 2012; Strijbos & Sluijsmans, 2010).

Research is also beginning to show that online peer response can be useful in two interesting ways (Hewett, 2000; Breuch, 2004). First, some studies have reported that online peer response tends to be more focused than face-to-face comments, with concrete and specific reactions, resulting in increased revision. Second, comments can be easily stored and shared as examples for training peers to give peer feedback and for showing what revisions students made as a result of specific comments.

In preparing for online peer review, it is helpful to organize a series of steps and deadlines for students to follow. Barbara Monroe (1998) suggests using intertextual comments throughout a document, followed by an endnote that summarizes overall impressions and suggestions. The intertextual comments can be made using word-processing tools, and the endnote can be typed as an e-mail message. When used initially, this protocol creates an expectation for the online experience, which is helpful to students unfamiliar with online environments.

Students also need to be trained to give reader-based feedback. For example, David Nunez, a teacher at North Vista School, Minneapolis, Minnesota, focuses on providing constructive criticism:

> The way that I am training my students to perform online feedback is that we spent some time talking about constructive criticism. We looked at a simple poem that I wrote badly and we went around the room and came up with ways to write criticism. Next, they are required to post three times on other's blogs, but I moderate all the comments initially. I haven't had to deny publication for any of my students' comments. Then, as a class, we look at the first comments and try to figure out which ones are good and why they're good. I require that they have three good comments, and they will keep posting until they have given three interesting constructive comments to their peers. (On a feedback sheet I let them know how many they have that count and why they are good comments.)

Interactive Bulletin Boards

Teachers or peers can provide asynchronous feedback using a threaded bulletin board forum, such as those included in Moodle, Drupal, Ning, Joomla, and Nicenet.org platforms (see chapter 3). Students post their writing and receive immediate comments from peers on the bulletin board. One value of using a bulletin board rather than personal e-mail is that a teacher can control student access and comments, which then discourages students from making overly judgmental or derogatory comments. Rather than the more ephemeral chat interactions, the students' comments can also be saved for later use.

Sandy Hayes, from Becker Middle School, Becker, Minnesota, describes how she uses bulletin board technology for large class peer review at the middle school level:

> The most successful activity I've found to engage students in more thoughtful and productive responses than in typical peer conferences or read-arounds is the use of an online bulletin board. Although I do not promote it initially as a revision activity, it yields higher quality work on on-going assignments as students internalize perceptions of quality, encounter an array of possibilities they could try, gain a sense of writing for an audience, and show improved attitude and motivation toward writing. For middle school students, the activity works best for units in writing poetry or short prose pieces, where a single comment or two is adequate. With older students and longer pieces of writing, I would initially provide a list of reflective prompts to guide substantive responses and to discourage focusing on editing issues.

Oral and Screencast Response

A number of new digital tools now provide teachers and students with the option of commenting orally on students' writing without the usual time-consuming process of meeting with them face-to-face (for more on formative assessment digital tools: http://tinyurl.com/mt7ugme).

With the advent of Web 2.0 and cloud technology, however, oral response has not only become viable; large audio files resulting from voice recordings can also be uploaded to servers for retrieval by students, solving the problem of conveying such files via e-mail (for more on instructor and peer feedback tools: http://tinyurl.com/kvk4qu9).

Some programs allow for voice recording only; that is, the teacher reads the student's paper, activates the program, then talks about the paper to the student and conveys that commentary digitally. Among the programs that you can use to provide podcast-like audio comments to specific places in a student's writing are Kaizena http://www.kaizena.com for use with Google Docs, VoiceThread http://voicethread.com, Evernote https://evernote.com, and Turnitin's GradeMark http://tinyurl.com/qg2olsf.

For providing audio comments to students' Google Docs writing, as noted, you can employ the Google Kaizena https://kaizena.com audio feedback feature in Google Drive. You can activate Kaizena simply by going to the Kaizena site https://kaizena.com to authorize use of Kaizena with Google Docs and then selecting the Google Docs file to which you want to add comments; there is also a Chrome OS Kaizena app http://tinyurl.com/kkuvzvm. For a video tutorial on using Kaizena, see http://tinyurl.com/kthv4ep on providing voice comments (Roberts, 2013). And students can also use the Pirate Pad http://piratepad.net/front-page for sharing writing with peers to then engage in chat and collaborative revision.

If students save their files as PDFs, you can also employ annotation apps such as iOS iAnnotate http://tinyurl.com/b7g38ma, PDF Max http://tinyurl.com/l882q29, GoodReader http://tinyurl.com/c8h9lqg, and Readdle http://tinyurl.com/n7rwv5f to provide voice or written annotations as comments. You can then e-mail back the files or save them on DropBox for students to review.

One advantage of using these screencasting or annotation tools is that you or a peer can visually focus feedback on specific sections or parts of a text or image so that you do not need to verbally indicate what sections or aspects of student's work you are referencing. Then, when a student is replaying the screencast, she or he knows what sections or aspects are being referenced in the feedback.

Screencast tools allow teachers or peers to make a video as they scroll through a student's paper and talk about what they see, perhaps using their cursor or other highlighting methods to call attention to specific words, lines, or paragraphs. Among the most popular of these tools is Jing http://tinyurl.com/3kkw4am, which creates 5-minute (maximum) screencasts using a very user-friendly download. The files can be uploaded to a server associated with the program up to certain limit, beyond which there is a small subscription fee. Students can also provide responses to two or three peers using Jing and never come close to reaching the data use threshold. Other simple screencast programs include MyScreen Recorder http://tinyurl.com/7dewssk, CamStudio http://camstudio.org, Screencast-O-Matic http://www.screencast-o-matic.com, and Wink http://www.debugmode.com/wink. More sophisticated video production programs, such as Camtasia, allow users to edit their screencasts, but in most situations, you will not want to spend a lot of time "perfecting" your screencasts for responding to students' papers. In fact, the spontaneity and informality of quickly created screencasts is one of the strengths, offering students something more like a face-to-face interaction.

As you or your students experiment with screencast programs, it helps to keep some general suggestions in mind (these are also useful in any kind of digitally produced oral response). We have oriented these as tips for teachers, but if you use screencasts for peer response, simply convert them into lessons for your students.

First, become thoroughly familiar with the technology that you are using. Then decide how you want to respond or want your students to respond, based on your goals and context. Oral response gives you an opportunity to demonstrate your reading process by commenting as you read, explaining your predictions about what is to follow, noting confusions along the way, and so on. This is less common than an after-reading response, but if you use it, be aware that it is very spontaneous and takes unpredictable amounts of time (try turning the equipment on and off as you read).

In the after-reading response, first read the entire paper once through, making shorthand marks in the margins as reminders of specific issues. When you begin the screencast session, have the paper on-screen (make it as large as you can to fill the screen), greet the student, and explain the context—for example, "Hey, Susan. I like the direction you've taken here in this draft. Let me offer some comments about what works well for me and what else you can think about." Then work through the paper, explaining your reactions, noting both strengths and weaknesses. With your cursor, highlight parts of the text that you are discussing so that they are visible. When you are done, provide a summary statement—for example, "So overall, this paper responds effectively to the assignment, especially the use of outside sources. You should continue to work on paragraph development, and also be sure to . . ."

As you speak, keep your eye on the time bar so that you do not run over the screen capture program's limit (Jing allows 5 minutes). At the same time, try not to rush your comments. Students cannot process fast talk, especially if they are trying to see what you are referring to in a paper. It is better to focus on fewer issues more slowly than to race through a hundred concerns, even though they can replay the screen capture many times. Use an informal, friendly tone. Although oral response tends to have a more casual demeanor, it can also accentuate sarcasm and negative attitudes. Talk as if you are having a pleasant chat, and the student will pay more attention. If you need to think or review, pause the screen capture, then continue. Often, the starting and stopping is not even noticeable.

Although most teachers work linearly (from the beginning of a paper to the end), it helps to sequence your comments starting with larger issues and save the smaller surface details for last. You can also use the oral response as an opportunity to read confusing sentences aloud to show the student what happens to you when you are thrown off track or cannot make sense of garbled syntax. This is one of the most powerful advantages of oral feedback.

Conference-Style Synchronous Chats

A key aspect of providing feedback is to create conversations about a student's writing that allow teachers or peers to scaffold students' self-assessing so that they learn to identify issues and revisions on their own using synchronous chat tools such as Face-Time, Skype, and Google+ Hangouts, as well as video conference chat tools. Synchronous chats tend to be used in ways similar to face-to-face writing conferences, such as brainstorming ideas for topics and revisions, discussing progress on writing, and providing interpersonal support for writers (for more on synchronous conference chat tools: http://tinyurl.com/kamjlsk).

Why use online conferencing when you can provide feedback in what could be more intimate face-to-face conferences? One major advantage of online conferences is that students are not limited to scheduling conferences during class time; students can hold conferences at any time—for example, when they are working on their writing in the evening. Another advantage is that students then have a record of the feedback to use later as they revise. For example, by conducting chat conferences on Hangouts, students can create a video copy of their chat.

Chats can work well for a series of conferences that allow teacher and student to brainstorm ideas on the fly but also document those ideas for future reference. In an account of a student-teacher conference, Eric Crump (1998) describes online chat in terms of a "hybrid" language—somewhere between "talk" and "writing." He suggests that chats are great for brainstorming ideas, that they are engaging to students, and that they create positive energy about writing and revision. Another advantage of chat environments is that they help form social ties, as they tend to be less formal.

Similarly, you can set up "virtual office hours" in which more than one student could "stop by" and ask questions about an assignment. Many students have experience with IMing environments; opening the door of teacher-student communication in this way can be a powerful source of formative feedback on student assignments, as well as serving as a way to model peer group feedback.

Conference-style chats also occur in tutor-student online environments, such as online writing centers (for more on online writing labs: http://tinyurl.com/k83g8mv). For example, at the University of Minnesota Writing Center http://writing.umn.edu/sws/index.htm#sessions, students submit their drafts online to the tutoring site, and then, after 30 minutes (which gives time for the tutor to prepare feedback), they engage in a synchronous chat with the tutor. Both tutor and student can view the draft on the computer window, and the student can make revisions.

Eventually, sites such as this one will include a webcam shot of the tutor's and student's talking heads. For example, Wimba Pronto http://www.wimba.com combines IMing with audio or video sharing for audio or video conferencing along with the students' writing displayed on the screen. In one study, Beth Hewett (2006) describes how synchronous conferencing in an online tutoring center involved whiteboard interactions. Her analysis demonstrated that two-thirds of synchronous dialogue reflected discussion about ideas for revision, generated by either student or tutor.

Schools can also set up an online writing center staffed by trained student tutors or even volunteer adults. If these centers can be staffed during and after school, students could then obtain feedback when they are most likely to need that feedback. One model for online peer feedback sites is Scaffolded Writing and Reviewing in the Discipline (SWoRD), developed at the University of Pittsburgh http://www.lrdc.pitt.edu/schunn/SWoRD/index.html (Cho & Schunn, 2007). On this site, students submit their drafts to the site, which assigns them to peers, who then give feedback and grade the drafts. Students then revise their drafts, which are then returned to the same peers for further review. Because students rate the helpfulness of their peers' feedback, peers are then graded according to these helpfulness ratings.

Teachers can also provide peer-feedback training using face-to-face conferences with online synchronous conferencing via synchronous chat tools to model real-time discussion of students' drafts. For example, tutors at the University of Minnesota Student Writing Support Online provide feedback to students, modeling peer feedback for high school students taking courses for college credit on a site that allows students to view comments on their drafts and then discuss needed revisions, resulting in enhanced participation in revisions (Beach, Clemens, & Jamsen, 2010; Breuch & Clemens, 2009). Tenth graders' use of online peer assessment significantly improved their writing due to use of peer feedback; the peers' scores were highly correlated with expert scores, suggesting high validity for the peers' scores (Tseng & Tsai, 2007; for more on online writing centers: http://tinyurl.com/mpsgxyg).

TURNING SUMMATIVE RESPONSE DYNAMIC

So far, we have reviewed formative feedback strategies, such as conference-style chats, small group student chats, and online peer review. We end this section by reviewing one other formative feedback strategy: creating annotated sample papers.

New approaches to formative feedback argue that students can benefit from knowing the criteria or expectations for writing a paper before they start to work on it (Anson, 2006). Because students need to internalize standards for what counts as a successful performance in a genre, they can think about appropriate criteria for an assignment using annotated sample papers. This process involves taking what is usually part of the process of summative evaluation and making it formative.

The Writing Standards in Action Project http://tinyurl.com/k8su3yz, developed by the Massachusetts Department of Education, provides examples for teachers and students of exemplary student writing with annotations linked to specific Common Core writing standards to provide illustrations of how specific features of that writing demonstrate competence in learning standards at each grade level. Similarly, the iWrite program http://tinyurl.com/khtwra5 includes examples of student papers with instructor annotations within specific courses based on the criteria operating within those courses. The site also includes an interactive module (the Prompter) for assisting students in writing papers.

Creating annotated sample papers begins with a set of criteria or a rubric that can be used to evaluate the final drafts of an assignment that students are completing—criteria associated with three to five categories based on the learning goals of the assignment. A summary, for example, might include a category about the accuracy of the content, a category about how well the summary captures the gist or main points of the original, a category about the style and structure of the summary, and so on. Each of these categories then needs to be defined in writing in terms of what features are associated with good performance within the category.

Next, choose one or two existing responses to the assignment. It helps to save papers from previous classes. (Erase the students' names or create pseudonyms, and, when possible, have each class sign a form that gives permission to use their work in future classes.) It is always best to choose "interestingly problematic" papers—not excellent ones and not really bad ones but ones that have complex strengths and weaknesses of different types. Next, create a verbatim copy of the first sample paper in digital form. At the end of the paper, place a rubric with its different categories and their appropriate values (e.g., five categories each worth 20% of the grade). Show how many points the sample paper received in each category with a final score for the whole paper. This allows students to acquire a feel for the entire paper, with its problems and successes, its errors and effective turns of phrase; it also shows them the overall judgment of the paper based on the rubric.

For each category, create a hyperlink to another version of the paper, exactly like the first version. Then look for salient features in the paper that explain the judgment made for a particular category. If one category is "style," for example, choose words, phrases, and sentences that are either problematic or effective stylistically, and highlight those textual places. Use an appropriate commenting method, creating links to each high-lighted piece of text. (This can be done using a split-screen approach with comments on the right screen, adjacent to the highlighted text.) Or, use a pop-up approach—as students scroll over a highlighted word or text, a pop-up window appears that explains what is at stake in the highlighted text. You can also use a link approach—taking students to separate screens with explanations. At the end of the paper, offer an overall comment on the criterion from the rubric that is being discussed and why it received the points that it did from that perspective.

Creating these annotations for each element or criterion in the rubric provides students with a series of "lenses" or criteria for determining the quality of certain features employed in an assignment. Creating annotations can also elicit student input on creating their own set of criteria for a given assignment. Per assignment, provide students with some students' previous sample writings (with names removed) for that assignment. Have students discuss differences in the quality of these samples and reasons for their judgments: what in the *text* led them to judge differences in quality?

Then, after students complete their own writing for this assignment, have them post their writing to a class website, blog, or wiki. Students then annotate their writing and, working in small groups, consolidate their annotations and create a set of criteria. Each group then shares its criteria, leading to a final composite set of class-decided criteria. These criteria then become a guide not only for students as they write their papers but also for how they will be evaluated on those papers.

Teachers also can readily store examples of their comments for use in training peers to give peer feedback and share examples of students' revisions—for example, displaying revisions on a wiki platform created as a result of feedback. Teachers' use of video-conferencing for the purpose of giving feedback led to positive increases in students' reading test scores (Houge & Geier, 2009) and writing test scores.

TRAINING STUDENTS TO PROVIDE PEER FEEDBACK

As this chapter demonstrates, integrating feedback—whether summative or formative—is key to helping students improve writing. However, it is also important that student writers learn to provide peer feedback for other student writers. Unfortunately, this is a much harder exercise than it seems. As previously noted, some research on peer review suggests that peer review feedback is limited to local revisions, such as spelling and other mechanical edits, and that peer reviewers are not as capable in making global comments that address the rhetorical effectiveness of student writing (Beach & Friedrich, 2006). Simply stated, providing constructive peer review feedback is not an intuitive exercise, and peer review training can provide helpful and important preparation.

Peer review training can be designed to address a variety of goals, but three central goals include (1) helping students understand peer review as a conversation about writing, (2) providing a variety of commenting strategies, and (3) avoiding the "sounds good" comment. The first goal, conversation, addresses the myth that peer review is only an "editing" exercise that requires students to copyedit their peers' work for spelling, grammar, or other mechanical errors. Thinking about peer review as a conversation rather than an editing session changes the overall conceptual model that students may have about peer review. Thinking about peer review as a conversation means that students need to read and engage with their peers' texts and respond to what authors are saying. Peer reviewers can respond as interested readers with questions, comments,

uggestions. The idea of conversation helps students understand that they are valued
ticipants in the conversation of writing.

Students can also use Google Docs to provide peer feedback to one another. At the
ience Leadership Academy in Philadephia, 11th-grade students engage in writing
he 2Fer" essay every 2 weeks on any topic using Google Docs so that peers can then
dd comments to one another's drafts (Pahomov, 2014). Peers sitting next to one another provide comments on Google Docs and then revise their drafts. Their teacher,
Larissa Pahomov, notes that use of comments enhances student engagement:

> The fun of computerized comments has definitely increased participation. Teenage
> students type much more than they would ever write by hand and get deeper into the
> feedback left for them. Students take pride in their work as editors, and I give "shout-
> outs" to high-quality edits throughout the year, projecting a student's Google Doc on
> the board and reading prudent comments to the class. Students often refer to peer
> comments when listing their own strengths and weaknesses in the reflection after the
> final draft.
>
> The ease of sharing also encourages students to seek multiple editors and share
> their work with friends. As the year the assignment was instituted continued, "I read
> that 2Fer!" was not an uncommon exclamation among the grade.

After completing final drafts, students are assessed by Larissa on a rubric with five
categories—thesis/focus, content/development, organization, style, and conventions—
as well as receiving written comments. Students then reflect on how they can improve
on their next "2Fer" essay. These self-reflections are important given that students'
grades are based on the degree to which they improve over time versus comparisons
with peers' writing. Students then post their best writing for each quarter to a website
http://2ferquarterly.org and for use for their quarterly portfolio grade (for a description
of this project: http://tinyurl.com/43zvdmx).

A second goal of peer review training, commenting strategies, addresses some concrete methods that students can practice as peer reviewers. As found in WRIT VID
instructional videos, commenting strategies can include the following: (1) "asking questions as an interested reader," (2) "focusing on global before local aspects," (3) "using
the language of assignment criteria," (4) "offering constructive criticism using 'I statements,'" (5) "offering reasons for your positive comments," and (6) "writing a summary
endnote" ("Peer Review: Commenting Strategies" WRIT VID: http://www.youtube.
com/watch?v=GlSCMx9-fGA). For many instructors, these are intuitive suggestions,
but for most students, these strategies present a new way of thinking about review.

Of the commenting strategies mentioned here, the strategy "focusing on global
before local aspects," might require the most explanation. By "global," we mean aspects
relating to the overall paper as well as rhetorical concerns, such as audience, message,

purpose, and context. One way to address global aspects is to remind students to read the entire paper before commenting. Reading the entire paper before commenting is a good first step toward addressing peer review as a participant in a conversation. After reading the entire paper, peer reviewers can reflect on rhetorical aspects, such as message ("What was the main idea or thesis?"), purpose ("What is the goal of the author—to persuade? inform? entertain?"), and audience ("Who is the paper addressing?").

Another strategy that is difficult for students is "offering constructive criticism using 'I statements.'" As peer reviewers, many students feel uncomfortable offering criticism of their peers' writing, or they do not know how to express criticism in productive ways. Using "I statements" can help in that students can offer observations about writing that demonstrate how another reader understands the material (or not). So instead of saying "This part doesn't make sense," a reviewer could write the observation "I am confused about the main idea of this paragraph. I don't know where you are going." "I statements" offer peer reviewers a concrete strategy to share their observations as readers. And authors really appreciate hearing authentic feedback on parts of their work that may not be clear to readers.

A third goal of training peer reviewers is to more fully engage reviewers and remind them to avoid the "sounds good" comment. Anecdotally, the "sounds good" comment is one of the most frequent comments made by peer reviewers, and it is often connected with the reluctance of peers to offer substantive, constructive suggestions. You can address use of the "sounds good" comment by reading aloud transcripts of peer review sessions with and without "sounds good." Students are able to quickly see which sessions are productive and which sessions are not. Avoiding the "sounds good" comment means that peer reviewers need to provide detail and reasons for their observations. They simply need to be more descriptive about their observations as readers. Often, peers think that they must be professional editors, but this is not necessary for productive peer review. We need to train peer reviewers to be careful and responsive readers, engaging in a larger conversation about what is being said and demonstrated through the texts they read.

Training programs might require devoting an entire class period or two just to focus on peer review. Such class sessions might include exercises such as viewing videos on effective peer review, reading the "peer review training transcript" and discussing it, or practicing peer review commenting strategies on a sample paper for large class review (for some sample transcripts, see the appendix at the end of this chapter).

The following videos are also useful resources: WRIT VID: What Is Peer Review? http://www.youtube.com/watch?v=O3lkm8LsgoU, WRIT VID: Commenting Strategies http://www.youtube.com/watch?v=GlSCMx9-fGA, Writing Peer Review Top 10 Mistakes http://www.youtube.com/watch?v=iBuq4qgRhCc.

Peer reviewers can also receive training through digital programs specifically designed for peer review. One tool designed at Michigan State University to support peer feedback is Eli Review http://www.elireview.com for use by teachers and students to foster peer feedback. In using this site, teachers can create assignments and due dates; students then respond to these assignments and upload their writing directly to the site. Teachers can then assign certain students to review their peers' writing, as well as ask students to employ certain specific "response types" for providing feedback:

> *Trait identification*: These features ask you to identify traits, characteristics, or features in the writing. You will be given a series of checkboxes—just check each one that you find as you read.
>
> *Scaled responses*: These features ask you to respond to a question on a scale. These can take two forms: rating scales, which ask you to respond on a scale (like a star rating), or a Likert scale, which gives you a set of responses from which you pick one answer.
>
> *Contextual comments*: This feature allows you to leave multiple comments for the writer. Comments can be made simply by clicking the "Add Comment" button, but you can also attach a comment to a piece of the text by highlighting that piece and then clicking the "Add Comment" button. Note that you will not be able to highlight passages in uploaded files, only in writing composed in Eli.
>
> *Final comment*: This feature allows you to leave a single comment that the writer will see at the end of the report. Instructors often give specific instructions for this final comment.

Teachers have access to these reviews, so they can assist students in providing productive feedback. Students then engage in reviews of their peers' writing and submit their reviews to peers. Peers then develop "revision plans" defining their goals for revision and "revise and resubmit tasks" to implement those revisions. Teachers can also create survey questions to ascertain peers' perceptions of the effectiveness of peer feedback. All of this provides teachers with extensive data on students' revision process, peers' feedback strategies, and students' perceptions of feedback—data that can be used for assessing students' work and for providing additional instruction on revision processes and feedback strategies.

Another similar peer review site is the Writing Studio http://writing.colostate.edu developed at Colorado State University in which students can share documents with peers and provide feedback based on certain criteria (for more on online review sites: http://tinyurl.com/kos4ctn).

SUMMARY

In this chapter, we discuss strategies for using digital tools to provide formative response to students' writing. In the beginning of this chapter, we claim that using digital tools for feedback is an exercise of technological literacy, or the ability to not only use technology but think critically about it. We hope that this chapter demonstrates the careful thought and time that go into using digital tools for formative feedback for purposes of improving their writing.

APPENDIX: TRANSCRIPT AND TRAINING EXERCISE

Activity: Peer Review Training Transcripts

To help students practice a peer review dialogue, read aloud the following two peer review transcripts in class. Select two students to read the parts of the reviewer and the author. After reading through the transcripts, discuss the questions following each version. (R = Reviewer, A= Author)

Sample Transcript: Version 1

R: OK, I've completed the worksheet and now we should probably discuss your paper for a few minutes.

A: OK.

R: Basically, I didn't find anything huge or big that needed to be changed.

A: Really? I thought there were a few sections that were confusing.

R: Like which ones?

A: My introduction that discusses literature about my topic. I didn't know if I had included the sources correctly there or not.

R: Oh, yeah, that was where you referred to two sources.

A: Yes

R: Well, I thought that was OK. I mean, we don't need to do anything too elaborate, just so we refer to the source, I guess. I thought it was fine.

A: Well, did you understand the introduction?

R: Yeah, I thought, um, basically you were saying . . . um, let me see here. [*Reads through introduction quickly.*] Yeah, that was OK. Your sources address one aspect of your topic, but isn't your paper about the other aspect of your topic? I guess it's alright what you've done here. Yeah, I get it just fine. Sounds good.

Questions for Discussion

- In what ways was this dialogue productive? If not, why?
- What constructive feedback did the reviewer provide the author? Explain.
- What areas were addressed in this dialogue: content, context, audience, purpose, organization, support, design, or expression?

Sample Transcript: Version 2

R: OK, I've completed the worksheet and now we should probably discuss your paper for a few minutes.

A: OK. Where do you want to start?

R: Let's start with the introduction. One of the questions on the worksheet talks about documenting sources.

A: Yeah. I included two sources in my introduction.

R: Yes, but I was wondering why you chose those sources? It was hard for me to tell how they introduced your topic. They didn't address the subject of your paper. Can you tell me what you were trying to do here?

A: I was trying to introduce the opposite viewpoint, you know, to set the stage for my topic, so that I would introduce the point of view that I thought was best. I was trying to contrast the two viewpoints.

R: I was thinking that it might help to include one source that backs up your viewpoint. Then it would be easier for me to see what your main topic was.

A: OK, that's a good idea. Thanks.

R: Also, did you include your sources on a bibliography? I didn't see them on your bibliography.

A: OK, so I should add the intro sources to the bibliography?

R: Yeah, I think that is what we are supposed to do.

Questions for Discussion

- In what ways was this dialogue productive? If not, why?
- What constructive feedback did the reviewer provide the author? Explain.
- Did the reviewer's comments come across as constructive or negative?
- What dialogue strategies did the reviewer use?

11

SUMMATIVE ASSESSMENT OF DIGITAL READING AND WRITING

In this chapter, we describe summative assessment *of* learning, recognizing that this assessment draws on formative assessment *for* learning described in the last chapter. For example, in using e-portfolios (described later in this chapter), students are collecting illustrative examples of their work during your course and then reflecting on that work. Their reflection serves to support their learning as a form of assessment *for* learning. E-portfolios can also serve to support assessment *of* learning as documentation of learning over time in terms of changes in student use of certain social practices and dispositions. Junior high students employing e-portfolios demonstrated higher levels of self-evaluation and motivation than did students who were receiving traditional assessment (Chang, 2009).

All of this raises questions about the validity of summative assessments as a measure of student learning. For the purposes of assessment *of* learning, students often take standardized reading and writing tests that are assumed to be valid and reliable of "reading ability" or "writing ability." The results of these tests are then used to provide information about the presumed level of learning in a teacher's classroom, school, district, or state so that a teacher's evaluation can be based on these test results. The results, often a single score, are used to label students' ability in reading or writing (defined as those literacy practices measured by the tests). Unfortunately, it is possible that students may internalize these labels in ways that undermine their motivation to learn—for example, to assume that they are not "good readers" or "good writers."

One limitation of these tests is that they occur in a decontextualized testing environment in which there is no particular rhetorical purpose motivating students to do well other than doing well on a test within a test-taking domain. Such decontextualized assessment tasks fail to recognize that there is a wide range of domains or contexts in which students are motivated to engage in reading or writing—for example, writing paratext instructions on how to play a video game for peers.

All of this raises questions about singular generalized notions of "reading ability" or "writing ability." As James Gee (2003) notes, students

> don't read "in general," but read specific sorts of texts in specific ways; we don't learn "in general," but learn specific "semiotic domains." Indeed, any text is itself associated with one or more specific semiotic domains. By a semiotic domain I mean any set of practices that recruit one or more modalities (e.g., oral or written language, images, equations, symbols, sounds, gestures, graphs, artifacts, and so forth) to communicate distinctive types of meanings. Here are some examples of semiotic domains: cellular biology, postmodern literary criticism, first-person-shooter video games, high fashion advertisements, Roman Catholic theology, modernist painting, midwifery, rap music, wine connoisseurship. (p. 31)

Historically, assessment *of* learning has also been limited by high-stakes assessment for selection according to ranking in which the assessor controls what constitutes learning, as opposed to the student. In contrast, assessment *for* learning places more control in the hands of the student.

Notwithstanding issues about the lack of validity of summative reading and writing assessments, whether they actually measure the complexities of reading and writing is compounded by the fact that these assessments are largely designed to measure practices associated with print-based reading and writing, which, as we argue in this book, differ from practices involved in reading and writing digital texts. This suggests the need to employ valid and reliable summative assessments of social practices constituting digital reading and writing for specific rhetorical purposes within authentic classroom contexts.

In this chapter, we discuss two key forms of digital reading and writing that are ripe for summative assessment: blogs and e-portfolios. Both have the potential to include authentic samples of student writing as well as invite other digital writing social practices, such as social media in connection to student writing. In the remainder of this chapter, we outline key summative assessment issues, such as selecting authentic approaches and tools for assessment. We also discuss summative assessment specific to blogs and e-portfolios—student work that encourages thoughtful and useful evaluation of digital reading and writing.

SUMMATIVE ASSESSMENT APPROACHES

Although standardized tests provide a quantitative score regarding student reading and writing, we advocate an approach that evaluates authentic student writing. Such an approach requires discussion and planning in terms of which aspects of digital reading and writing are valued and worthy of evaluation. We discuss four approaches: use of criteria and rubrics, assessment of dispositions, organic assessment and instructor training, and automated machine-scoring evaluation of student texts (for more on summative assessment approaches: http://tinyurl.com/kdg9m2q).

Devising Criteria and Rubrics for Summative Assessments

In providing summative assessments of authentic student writing, it is important to base those assessments on clearly defined criteria specific to the use of social practices in particular projects. These criteria could include some basic aspects of effective communication based on relevance, sufficiency, validity, coherence, and significance (Grice, 1975). Ideally, for particular assignments, you and your students could collaboratively identify those criteria that you will use to assess their work so that students have a clear understanding of the criteria as well as a sense of ownership over them.

These criteria can then be employed to devise either holistic rubrics based an overall assessment of a students' work or more specific analytic or criteria-based rubrics that break down specific criteria or dimensions of a student's work—for example, the degree to which students provide supporting, relevant evidence for their claims in a blog post (for tools for creating and using rubrics: http://tinyurl.com/la2wn37).

You can then add qualifiers such as "none," "some," "a lot," and "extensive" for the amount of evidence employed and "irrelevant," "marginally relevant," "somewhat relevant," and "highly relevant" for the relevance of the supporting evidence (for a rubric devised by Clarence Fisher for use with blogs: http://tinyurl.com/lro662m). Ideally, these qualities should be relatively specific as opposed to general categories such as "good" or "excellent" (Broad, 2003). Once you have selected criteria, create columns to represent the scales, and save the document as a template. Then, for evaluation of each student's paper, copy and paste the rubric into a new document and type comments into each criterion table cell. When finished, these comments can be sent to the student. For example, students in Elizabeth Erdmann's class were applying different critical perspectives to engage in collaborative writing about the novel *Beloved* (Morrison, 2004). She provided students with the following criteria that she would draw on to give a holistic rating to the students' group draft essays:

- Make a claim (based on your interpretation of one of the characters and his/her actions and words in the novel through your critical lens) and explain the significance.
- Support the claim with evidence that is selected and presented in a manner that your audience will find persuasive.
- Anticipate and respond to any important counter-arguments to the claim.
- Incorporate relevant references to the text and to published authors.

- Present ideas in a clear, cohesive, and logical manner that supports the purpose of the paper as well as communication with the intended audience.
- Cite the text: use quotes from Toni Morrison's *Beloved*.
- Cite your research on literary theory.

Then, for the students' revision of their writing in their final drafts, she indicated that they needed to draw on the following:

- Ideas about this text from one or more classmates in other writing groups.
- Professionally published writing about the text or author.
- Professionally published writing about the literary theory as applied to similar texts.
- You MUST consult and cite Toni Morrison's *Beloved* as well as at least three outside sources: books, papers, essays, articles, etc. that add support to your argument. In other words, you should incorporate the ideas from your writing group, *Beloved,* and at least three published authors into your paper, either to illuminate or support some point you wish to make or to show a contrasting or alternative point of view. You may quote, paraphrase, or summarize; you should use MLA parenthetical citations and works cited entries to acknowledge your sources.

Providing students with these criteria served to clarify the meaning of her holistic scoring of their writing.

Using Rubrics

You can also create specific rubrics either for holistic scoring or for rating each specific criterion. You can use a number of rubric designer tools to devise rubrics: Rubistar http://rubistar.4teachers.org/index.php, iRubric http://tinyurl.com/4atrap, eRubric Assistant http://tinyurl.com/pbgaqgg for use with Word, ForAllRubrics https://www.forallrubrics.com, iOS http://tinyurl.com/kmsqyud, Android Easy Assessment http://tinyurl.com/mrww5f7, or iOS Grade Rubric http://tinyurl.com/kfynmde. While these tools can be useful for devising your own rubrics, simply borrowing predetermined, canned rubrics can undermine giving authentic assessments. An important step is determining your criteria based on the goals of your assignment.

Another option is the use of the Calibrated Peer Review http://cpr.molsci.ucla.edu, an online program designed to help students learn to apply a rubric to some sample writing by comparing their evaluations with those of the teacher. Before using the rubric, students must complete an exercise in which they apply the rubric to a sample of student writing that has already been evaluated by the instructor using the same rubric. Calibrated Peer Review will calibrate the student's evaluation with the teacher's evaluation to provide a comparison for the student. When students conduct evaluations of other students' writing, Calibrated Peer Review keeps track of comments and multiple submissions of writing to see if improvements have been made.

For creating rubrics, it is also useful to involve students in co-creating the rubrics during a project so that they have some understanding and ownership of those rubrics. For example, for assessing students' remix projects, students identified 8 to 10 categories relevant to creating remix texts, noted examples of successful remixes to specify criteria for each category, engaged in formative reflection using the rubric as they were creating their remixes, and then employed the rubric for summative assessment (Delagrange, McCorkle, & Braun, 2013).

In analyzing an example of a successful remix, students examined a *Time* magazine remix using the photograph of Marines raising the flag at Iwo Jima where the flag is replaced with a large redwood tree, along with the text "How to Win the War on Global Warming," surrounded with a green border. Students noted the importance of the rhetorical use of the tree portrayed in a precarious position to appeal to audiences with environmental concerns, suggesting the importance of criteria related to audience, purpose, and context. They also applied criteria of "image or text—color, size, pacing, scale, alignment, repetition, proximity, contrast, framing, angle, balance, focus, line, shape, pattern, proportion, clarity, emphasis, technique" related to the categories of aesthetic, visual, technical, and cultural aspects of remix design. Consistent with our social practice of collaboration, students were collaboratively constructing these rubrics with the teacher, which serves to foster application of alternative perspectives on different ways to assess digital texts.

Assessment of Dispositions

If you are interested in evaluating digital writing in conjunction with national guidelines for learning to write effectively, you may also consider assessing students' dispositions toward learning described in chapter 2—their level of interest, engagement, motivation, sense of responsibility, and persistence (Council of Writing Program Administrators, National Council of Teachers of English, and National Writing Project, 2011). To foster self-reflection of student writing, you can draw on these dispositions to ask students to reflect on changes in those dispositions over time. For example, students could reflect on changes in their ability to identify differences in their purpose, audience, and context related to the disposition of being flexible in adopting their writing to differences in rhetorical contexts.

This exercise of tracking dispositions would be particularly useful for e-portfolios, which typically include samples of students' work across a time span. You can also track changes in their use of social practices as they relate to the development of these dispositions. For example, in the beginning of a course, you may note that in their blog writing, students posit their opinions about a topic or issue with little recognition of alternative perspectives. However, as the course progresses, you note that in their blog posts, they begin to acknowledge alternative perspectives, leading to your commending them on increasing their openness to alternative perspectives.

Organic Writing Assessment

Another approach to summative assessment of writing includes an "organic" assessment that involves "dynamic criteria mapping" (Broad et al., 2009). Dynamic criteria mapping provides an alternative to set rubrics that may be used in a standard fashion to evaluate student writing. In contrast, dynamic criteria mapping advocates evaluation that is inductive and grounded in student work: "Symbiotic, smart, organic and locally grown: those are the qualities we seek in our assessments" (p. 4).

In five college and university settings where the dynamic criteria mapping approach was piloted, some settings focused on a particular course, such as first-year writing, while others looked at writing assessment for an entire program or major. The pilots required examination of student work and discussions among instructors regarding the true goals of various writing assignments as well as key criteria for writing improvement. The pilots revealed that a dynamic approach to assessment is complex; it involved constant discussion among instructors, detailed attention to student writing, and frequent updates to assessment plans. Nevertheless, Broad et al. (2009) argue that the "messiness" of this approach garnered a more authentic view of assessment of student writing.

One of the criticisms of dynamic criteria mapping is whether or not it simply produces another kind of rubric, albeit one that is thoughtfully and thoroughly created. After all, instructors must articulate the criteria that they use to evaluate student writing, whether static or dynamic. However, what makes dynamic criteria mapping unique is the insistence that criteria emerge from student work (rather than institutional goals) and that it remains flexible as goals for student writing change.

A similar dynamic approach to summative writing is found in the Writing Enriched Curriculum program at the University of Minnesota http://wec.umn.edu, where academic departments are asked to construct a "writing plan" for students that outlines key abilities and writing tasks that students are expected to complete in each major. Faculty members are invited to examine student work and discuss their goals for student writing and the strengths and weaknesses that they see in it. Each department's writing plan outlines writing abilities and tasks suited to individual disciplines (thus "dynamic"), and departments are encouraged to revisit and update these writing plans every few years. Not surprising, writing plans highlight different kinds of abilities and writing tasks depending on the discipline. Also not surprising, digital writing plays an increasingly important role in writing across disciplines, through various forms, such as blogs, wikis, websites, and writing programs and software.

Dynamic criteria mapping requires time and effort on the part of writing instructors to review student writing and discuss goals for student writing with other instructors. Although this approach is time-intensive, it is inductively grounded in student writing and yields authentic assessment.

Use of Automated Response and Evaluation Programs

A fourth approach to summative assessment is the use of automated response and evaluation programs, also known as *machine scoring*. It is important that we discuss this approach to writing assessment to raise awareness of its strengths and weaknesses, especially as we consider digital writing. With the increased use of standardized computer writing assessments (e.g., those associated with the Partnership for Assessment of Readiness for College and Careers [PARCC] and Smarter Balanced Common Core assessments), there has been and could be increased use of machine-based scoring, raising questions about the validity and reliability of such scoring relative to human scoring (for more on machine-based scoring: http://tinyurl.com/k7qbfvu).

In an ideal digital world, when students submit their writing electronically to a computer program, the program could read the writing and then give the student a human-like, helpful response, in a sympathetic and approachable "voice," offering reactions, suggestions, examples, and other information of the quality that a human reader would provide under the most ideal teaching circumstances—all in a fraction of a second. These programs could also grade students' writing, assigning points based on preestablished criteria.

A number of companies now offer schools and teachers opportunities to pay for machine scoring or automated evaluation of writing. Most of these services are not designed to do what our ideal-world scenario described; they simply evaluate the writing and provide a score. But their marketing claims make them seem very attractive, especially to overburdened schools and teachers (see the National Council of Teachers of English's position statement "Machine Scoring Fails the Test," at http://www.ncte.org/positions/statements/machine_scoring).

The underlying programs that allow computers to read and analyze student writing fall into two types of systems. One system is based on "mining" existing scored papers for certain features, creating a sophisticated matrix of those features, then consistently and reliably applying the matrix to new, unscored cases to come up with a prediction of how humans would score them. But this system needs to be "trained." For this reason, these programs do not work well for teachers who like to create new, unique assignments and who change their teaching from year to year. Typically, such programs are used for large-scale scoring of standardized test essays, when students are not given any information about their performance anyway, other than a score.

Another system examines students' texts for certain features, almost all of them at the surface of a text. For example, it is relatively easy to scan a paper for common and less common words, using a large lexicon with an index of their use frequency. Papers with less common words might be scored higher because students with a more sophisticated vocabulary could be thought to be better writers. Or a computer can look for errors of syntax and word usage. The problems with such analyses are obvious: They ignore deeper aspects of writing, and they can be unreliable at judging the surface features that they do look for. They assume that students who use less common words are better writers or that sentence fragments are problematic.

Programs can also use semantic analysis to look for the cohesion of words across a document, but they are unable to say anything about broader rhetorical concerns, such as whether a writer has successfully met the expectations of his or her audience or whether a style is appropriate to the specific occasion of an assignment, such as a scenario. And programs cannot detect the use of irony, humor, or other nuances of prose that we want our students to acquire.

Put simply, these programs are unable to read for meaning, subverting the reasons for students to write (for further critiques of specific programs, see Ericsson & Haswell, 2006). We strongly recommend, therefore, that teachers and administrators approach the use of automated or computerized response and evaluation with a high degree of skepticism. Such programs will not become effective at understanding human discourse for generations, long after this book has served its useful purposes.

Given these issues, we offer a set of questions to ask of anyone claiming to have a scoring system that will reduce or eliminate the need to evaluate students' writing:

1. Does the program rely on a corpus of existing graded papers to grade new papers? Does this then mean that teachers need to keep using the same assignments?

2. Will students know that their writing is being read and evaluated by a computer? What will knowing that they are writing for a nonhuman reader do to their sense of purpose and audience?

3. What happens when the system has been tested, particularly with random texts? What information does it provide? Is that information valid (measures important aspects of "writing quality"), reliable (measurements are consistent across similar papers), and useful for students (helps them in their writing)?

4. How does this information compare to information provided by a teacher in terms of offering a personal, helpful response?

5. If "teaching" writing is accomplished in part through feedback designed to foster self-assessment, how well does the program provide that feedback?

6. What are the ethics of paying for a service that replaces or substitutes for teacher feedback? By whom and how is this service being funded?

7. If teaching conditions are poor—if class sizes are such that there are too many students so that teachers are overwhelmed and cannot provide adequate feedback—does paying for a service to do some of that work really change the underlying problem?

This list of questions provides a helpful step in considering whether to use machine scoring as a method of summative writing assessment. At the end of the day, it is important to ask whether machine scoring can deliver authentic evaluation on student writing that helps students work toward improvement of that writing.

In this section, we reviewed four approaches to summative writing evaluation: use of rubrics and criteria, student dispositions, dynamic criteria mapping, and machine scoring. For any of these approaches, it will be useful to track multiple assessments to see how students develop and improve their writing over time. In the next section, we discuss tools for tracking student writing for purposes of summative assessment.

TOOLS FOR KEEPING TRACK OF ASSESSMENTS OF STUDENTS' WORK

Keeping track of your assessments of large numbers of different students' work over time can be a challenge. To address this challenge, you can employ a number of tools for recording, storing, and sharing your assessments of those students http://tinyurl.com/mk9lpbm.

You can use these tools for record keeping to share information about students' work with parents and administrators, as well as for tracking changes in students' performance over time. We particularly like the PowerTeacher Mobile http://tinyurl.com/kdv9tqc tool for record keeping, adding notes about students, and sharing information with students and parents. The Collaborize Classroom desktop http://www.collaborizeclassroom.com and Collaborize Classroom Pro iOS app http://tinyurl.com/ke4h2yz described in chapter 6 can be used to keep track of students' discussion participation. One advantage of platform apps such as the Engrade desktop https://www.engrade.com, iOS Engrade Class Pro http://tinyurl.com/leffwet, and Android Engrade http://tinyurl.com/mkcet92 is that because they are based on the same app, they can be used across different platforms, as well as connecting student performance to specific standards.

The desktop http://www.classdojo.com, iOS http://tinyurl.com/aog3bxt, and Android http://tinyurl.com/keujqwv ClassDojo apps can be used with younger students to record instances of students' positive and problematic practices, such as participation, helping others, creativity, having useful insights, hard work, and effective presentations, as well as problematic practices such as disruption, being late, not turning in homework, showing disrespect, and interrupting peers; students then receive feedback on their devices about their practices. At the same time, it is important that ClassDojo not be employed as a behavior reinforcement tool so that students engage in certain behaviors simply to be recorded as employing those behaviors.

The Geddit desktop http://letsgeddit.com and iOS http://tinyurl.com/l9g685r apps allow students to share their perceptions with you of their sense of success in completing certain tasks. You can then determine which students in your class are doing well versus having difficulty on a task based on a color coding of lists of names on your screen. You can then have students who are doing well on a task assist students who need more assistance.

You can also use tools such as the audio, screencasting, and annotation tools described throughout this book and in the previous chapter to provide summative assessments. You can also use the GoClass desktop http://tinyurl.com/m6rowef, iOS http://tinyurl.com/ls2albf, and Android http://tinyurl.com/jwr2bb6 apps referred to in chapter 2 to provide feedback, or you can use the Essay Grader desktop http://tinyurl.com/knxyur7 and iOS http://tinyurl.com/n558kfx apps designed for use in giving feedback to students' writing http://tinyurl.com/mts4f64. Jeffrey Bradbury (2012) describes how he uses Essay Grader for his music performance classes:

> All of the data fully syncs between the iPad and the Mac application. I found it easy to set up my categories and comments on my iMac. After doing an iTunes sync, I was ready to go into the class with the iPad and grade my students musical skills. I use the following process [to provide feedback to students' writing]:
>
> 1. Import class lists
> 2. Access student files from a simple drop-down menu in the "Student Name" field
> 3. Export the comment database for editing, sharing, and archival
> 4. Import your own personalized comment database for use in Essay Grader
> 5. Edit all tab and comment labels
> 6. Add additional comments to any column on any tab
> 7. Print feedback documents directly from the "List" screen
> 8. Print Feedback documents and save as MS Word .doc files in the following format: "student name assignment name.doc"

For Bradbury's video description of use of Essay Grader, see http://appreview.teachercast.net/essay-grader. As described in chapter 10, you can use Google Docs Forms to create forms to keep track of your summative assessment of students' work to then publish in a spreadsheet or share with students. Given these tools, we turn our attention to assessment of specific forms of digital writing, such as blogs and e-portfolios.

EVALUATING BLOGS

Blogs are a common form of digital writing that encourage sustained student writing over time, whether responding to readings, responding to other students, or sharing ideas for writing. In using blogs for assignment, instructors often ask students to contribute to blogs at regular intervals. They provide an ideal vehicle for summative assessment because the collective blog can demonstrate development of writing skills or rhetorical awareness over time.

Blogs are an excellent example of how digital writing can be assessed by rubrics or by dynamic criteria. Evaluating blogs requires a different set of criteria that are more appropriate for the kinds of practices involved in creating and commenting on posts (a kind of "dynamic" criteria). In reflecting on her experience of evaluating her students' blogs at Edina High School, Edina, Minnesota, Kathleen West noted,

> We can grade blog entries in at least three different ways at different points in any blog project. Since I felt like my 8-week blog project really only allowed my freshmen to become beginning blog writers, I "graded" their entries on completion. That's one way to let everyone know that you're serious and that the work needs to be done. It also allows the students to get a quick base of entries under their belts and gives them a new experience to feel good about.
>
> I'm thinking that another way is to grade the entry on the quality of content based on the understood audience. If it's understood (either implicitly or explicitly) that the audience is academic, that the post is a scholarly response to a scholarly topic, grade accordingly. If it's understood that the audience is wider and less sophisticated, other language would be appropriate. So part of the blog requirements would involve a certain number of posts for each audience that the teacher is concerned with addressing. That might mean that each entry now begins with a short audience statement, but that's not such a bad thing, and kids can get creative with how that statement manifests itself.
>
> The latest idea I've had about this is to grade certain entries based on the amount of conversation it generates, based on comments and other entries that address their post. So the quality of the writing isn't as important as the quality of the idea. This helps create a culture of commenting and interacting with other bloggers.

In addition to those criteria suggested by Kathleen, other criteria or rubrics can be related to the extent to which students do the following:

- Clearly formulate their positions or opinions.
- Address topics and issues dealt with in class discussions or readings.
- Provide supporting evidence for positions or opinions.
- Employ links to others' posts within and outside the classroom.
- Reformulate others' material/links in one's own words.
- Engage in comments to peers' posts and reactions to those comments.

No matter which criteria are selected, it is important that instructors share these criteria with students and provide clear feedback on how well students are doing *before* the blogs are completed. We would suggest weekly or, at the very least, monthly comments. This timing is important so that students can redirect their blog writing if and when necessary. The periodic instructor feedback might consist of paragraph-length comments regarding observations about how the students employed criteria in their blog posts. You may find it useful to share this feedback individually (rather than publicly, as through blog comments); e-mail or any of the assessment tools described earlier would work well for this purpose.

USE OF E-PORTFOLIOS FOR FORMATIVE AND SUMMATIVE ASSESSMENT

While blogs provide a clear example of student digital writing and while instructors can literally see writing development across time through blogs, electronic portfolios (e-portfolios) present another form of digital writing that is ripe for summative assessment. Over the period of a course or school career, students produce a range of these different digital writing texts in different courses and contexts. In addition to providing students with separate evaluations for each text, it is useful to evaluate their growth and development across these texts as they improve in their uses of social practices—for example, their ability to employ hyperlinks to make connections. In this chapter, we discuss how e-portfolios can be used to provide this long-term evaluation of students' growth over time. Because students are producing digital texts, these texts can be readily linked to an e-portfolio to showcase students' work.

E-portfolios are collections of digital texts or material organized and linked by students to foster their reflections on their development as writers over time (Dimarco, 2006; Maklary, 2010). They can be used for a variety of purposes:

- Presenting the sum of all the different work in a specific course
- Creating a series of documents and other materials in different modes and genres, all focusing on a specific topic, problem, or subject

- Displaying a "record" of all the work that went into responding to a specific assignment—for example, a blog as an invention activity or one or more rough drafts with comments by other class members, perhaps with some metareflection by the author, and then a final draft
- Reflecting on growth with an introduction that comments on the work and introducing the viewer to it
- Displaying one's "best work," perhaps to meet an assessment benchmark, apply for a job, or just to document progress

Although e-portfolios are commonly created as a semester-long project in a specific course, some institutions—such as Indiana University–Purdue University at Indianapolis, Alverno College, and Kalamazoo College—have large-scale electronic portfolio systems in which all undergraduates document their writing and other work during their academic careers (for examples of school and college portfolios: http://tinyurl.com/mvlbrn5).

Advantages and Challenges of E-Portfolios

Why use e-portfolios rather than print portfolios? One key advantage of e-portfolios is that they provide extensive space for storing writing based on folders or links. This makes it far easier to access and review students' work than is the case with a paper file folder (Hewett, 2006). Because students' writing, as well as resumes, transcripts, letters of recommendation, awards, and course work, is all online, students can grant selected access to advisors, professors, classmates, family, friends, potential employers, and graduate admissions officers, who can review their work online—something not possible with paper portfolios. Because digital texts can be more readily linked through digital mapping or links than with paper portfolios, students can reflect on connections in their work. For example, they may organize their e-portfolios using a digital map displaying connections among the different topics and texts that they addressed in their courses, leading to reflection on what they learned from making those connections.

Another advantage of e-portfolios over paper portfolios is that students can organize their work according to digital pages based on certain categories as well as employ hyperlinks to connect texts to define consistent patterns in their work within and across these categories—for example, "my argumentative writing," "my report writing," "my narrative writing," "my philosophy of learning," and "my reflections on development over time."

Another major advantage of e-portfolios is that students' selective work during a course can be readily displayed for other students, teachers, and parents to access that work. For example, an e-portfolio was developed at Timilty Middle School, Roxbury,

Massachusetts, http://www.savetimilty.com/nuke as part of a forum related to issues facing students in their school experience and lives. The purpose of this forum was to create a school community in which "(1) everyone writes for everyone else and not just the teacher, and (2) everyone, not just the teacher, cares about everyone's writing" (Fahey, Lawrence, & Paratore, 2007, p. 463). High school students in two Ohio high schools shared their work with Ohio State University composition instructors to receive feedback from their own high school instructor as well as college instructors in terms of how their work was consistent with expectations of college instructors (Acker & Halasek, 2008).

At the same time, one of the challenges in using e-portfolios is how to foster authentic reflection of strengths and areas that need improvement (Belgrad, Burke, & Fogarty, 2008). If students perceive e-portfolio as just one more school assignment, they may employ inauthentic reflection simply to please their teacher. This relates to the need to broaden the use of e-portfolios "as a way of being and of interacting, as well as an artifact" (p. 202) so that students reflect on changes in their identity construction over time in an authentic manner (Hughes, 2010).

Another challenge has to do with achieving valid and reliable assessment of e-portfolios given the subjective nature of assessing e-portfolio work. A study of high school students' e-portfolios indicated low interrater reliability for peer raters and low agreement between peer and teacher ratings (Chang, Tseng, Chou, & Chen, 2011).

Another issue in the use of e-portfolios is how users can readily search for material on an e-portfolio and how long students can retain e-portfolios when they are stored on a school's server or on a commercial server. One advantage of using a tool such as Blogger or Evernote for creating e-portfolios is that students can retain use of the content after graduation from their school or college.

Process- and Product-Based E-Portfolios

It is helpful to determine the purposes for using e-portfolios—whether a portfolio will be used as a product-based portfolio or a process-based portfolio (Cambridge, Cambridge, & Yancey, 2009; Maklary, 2010).

Product-based e-portfolios focus on finished drafts of papers or other artifacts (websites, design projects, etc.) that students have worked on throughout a class. Using an e-portfolio for this purpose allows students to post their best work and save or archive it for future reference. Grades reflect the finished product posted on the e-portfolio site. Contents of a product-based portfolio might include a table of contents, final papers, design projects (e.g., newsletter or brochure), blog entries, websites, digital stories, and reflections on their portfolio texts (for examples of other student portfolios http://tinyurl.com/lb6kmdf).

Process-based e-portfolios are more inclusive of drafts and other formative work leading to the finished products. In writing classes, for example, an e-portfolio might include first and second drafts of a paper with peer feedback. Process-based portfolios show work as it progresses in that students make the process visible. Grades reflect effort and their improvement throughout the process.

Tools for Creating E-Portfolios

D. Gibson and Barrett (2003) contrast two types of structures for creating e-portfolios: "generic tools" versus "customized systems." Barrett (2007) perceives a generic tools structure associated with teacher-developed tools as more consistent with a Web 2.0 orientation in that they are focused more on bottom-up student interactivity, emergent development, creativity, and constructivist learning, with open-ended feedback from peers or teachers (for a list of different e-portfolio tools: http://tinyurl.com/lgjobgn).

In contrast, customized systems structures employed by commercial e-portfolio products are more top-down, structured, standardized, and accountability driven. For example, many of the commercial digital portfolio programs employ server-based customized templates based on categories for storing texts and using rating scales or rubrics for self-assessing those texts (for resources on creating e-portfolios: http://tinyurl.com/lsy3sj8).

iOS or Android apps such as Three Rings or Easy Portfolio tend to be less structured and standardized options to many commercial customized systems structures. For a podcast discussion on creating e-portfolios using apps such as Three Rings (Bradbury, 2014), see http://tinyurl.com/kmmxgjp.

Using Blogs, Wikis, or Websites as E-Portfolios

Rather than employing a separate e-portfolio tool, students can use the blogs, wikis, or personal websites that they are already using in a course to serve as their e-portfolios, by adding reflections of their writing on their blogs, wikis, or personal websites (Dunn, Luke, & Nassar, 2013). In addition to the blog and wiki platforms previously described, students can use website creation tools such as Google Sites http://sites.google.com, Weebly http://www.weebly.com, Silk http://www.silk.co, Dropr http://dropr.com, PortfolioGen http://www.portfoliogen.com/classroom, or eduClipper https://educlipper.net to create e-portfolios (Byrne, 2013a, 2013e, 2014). For example, they can use eduClipper to access work that they have stored on different sites to then drag and drop content on their e-portfolio canvasses (Byrne, 2013a; for more on using blogs, wikis, or websites as e-portfolios: http://tinyurl.com/ko8bhfd).

Incoming students at Macaulay Honors College, City University of New York, employed a Wordpress blog platform to include "artifacts" as images, photos, quotes, essays, videos, conversations, and so on, for their e-portfolios representing their learning and identities, as well as using a BuddyPress plug-in to participate in a social network to create profiles, friend peers, participate in groups, and view one another's posts (Klein, 2013). In one course, students used their e-portfolios to create a multimedia collage project based on physical materials or found objects portraying a personal "cultural encounter," then scanned and shared them on e-portfolios along with a critical essay. Because the e-portfolios were housed within a social media platform, students actively engaged in responding to one another's collages. One student created his collage using artifacts from his youth in China that reflected his membership in the Chinese Communist Party, including red scarves that he wore to indicate his party membership. A student who grew up in Russia noted, "I could relate to this because of the red scarves that my parents also had to wear in the Soviet Union" (p. 60).

One limitation in using blog posts, wikis, or websites for possible inclusion in e-portfolios is that students may be intimidated by the idea of having their writing evaluated, particularly if they are just starting to blog or write wikis and are experimenting with adopting different voices and styles. It helps, then, to have students distinguish between including all of their work in an e-portfolio and selecting those texts that best illustrate their use of certain composing processes or digital literacies based on certain criteria. To store all their work, students could use their school's or course management system's digital archive or cloud-storage sites such as DropBox, Google Drive, iCloud, Box, or SkyDrive and then select those texts for inclusion in their e-portfolios.

It is also useful to involve parents in assisting students with the e-portfolio construction, including informing them about the nature and purpose for using e-portfolios (Clark, 2013a).

Using E-Portfolios to Foster Reflection

A primary reason for using e-portfolios is to foster student reflection about writing. It is important to provide specific directions for students' reflections—for example, having students describe "1) where the project was done (its context), 2) why the project was done (its purpose), and 3) what learning experiences were accomplished (learning demonstrated)" (Bergman, 2006). Teachers can also model portfolio construction by creating their own e-portfolios to reflect on their teaching (Kilbane & Milman, 2003).

Students can reflect on reasons for differences in their writing quality due to differences in their sense of purpose and audience, interest, engagement, knowledge of the topic, expertise in using digital writing tools, and so on. For example, they may note that because they did not have a clear sense of their audience in Assignment A, they had more difficulty with that assignment than with Assignment B, when they had a clear sense of their audience. This may lead them to attempt to clarify their sense of audience in their future writing assignments.

Students can also reflect on how their texts display their proficiencies in various digital literacies. For example, Elizabeth Erdmann asked her college writing students to use some blog posts to reflect on their uses of digital writing in the class in response to some prompts:

What did you learn to do well? How do you know this?

I learned how to express my opinion. I know this because I was always scared to share my opinion because I was scared of what other people would think, but now I learned that no matter what your opinion there is always information to back up your theory and if people don't think the same way you do then you prove your opinion and come up with things to support you. (Shannon Saleck)

What kinds of digital skills did you learn?

I think I will start blogging more now because I realized that it helped me a lot to express my feelings about things without having to talk about it because I am so scared of confrontation. I also really enjoyed making the wiki because I never heard of a PB-works and I thought it was so cool that I actually got to make one and have something that people can look at and it can help other people with research. (Shannon Saleck)

I learned how to link other pages to certain wikis and also link research to certain pages and find research links, the easy way. (Breanna Ramroop)

Copy and paste in some examples of your best work (or the work for which you are most proud) from your blog or wiki. Make a working link to that material. Explain why you think it's particularly good.

I think this is one of the better blogs I have done on the group book I had read. It makes it seem that I went more into depth with this book and tried to figure out what some of the chapters or passages might have meant. I took it on a more psychological level: As I read the last few chapters, it made me realize that most of these men are normal with a slight disability. Even though they are in a mental ward, they seem completely normal on the inside of this facility. Some of the men are just like children, because they have been cooped up like such and don't necessarily get their way when they have a group therapy session. I take it to be the Nurse Ratchet is a stern mother (sort of) and she just wants what is right for her patients. Though she does a bit more than a normal mother would, she is also killing these men little by little. (Breanna Ramroop)

On which paper do you think you did your best writing? Do you feel this way because of how peers evaluated your work, how much effort you put into it, or the grade the teacher assigned? Explain your feelings.

I think I did my best writing on the group book paper. I think I did my best on this because the paper we were writing about had a great topic and it was a strong paper that anyone could've written, but I just got a good feeling from finishing it and also writing. I got a good feel from it because the other group members had some of the same ideas as me and it just all worked together. (Breanna Ramroop)

What are some things you want to work on in the future in your writing?

The main thing that I have been deeply thinking about is using my digital skills combined with writing skills I both learned in this class also combined with my passion for film and documentary to create a homelessness-awareness blog through journal entries and a short documentary series that creates awareness and a push for involvement in youth when it comes to homelessness. (Josh Hiben)

How was peer feedback valuable to your learning?

It helped me to hear when my peers thought something was awkward, or wordy. Sometimes my own ear doesn't catch that stuff because I wrote it. It was always nice and helpful to hear their opinion, although usually there aren't really spelling errors or anything. I wrote a better paper when there was peer feedback. (Kate Mackin)

It's different when you get comments on your work by your teacher, but when you get comments on your work by other students, you get the opinions from students your age. It's a different and helpful way to get critiqued on your work. (Kyle Rusnacko)

When it came to comments on the blogs or wikis, it really helped me see what others think and what their true opinions were on the subjects at hand. It was a mind opener. (Breanna Ramroop)

How did teacher comments influence or change your writing?

One of the biggest things I appreciated from you being my teacher is your feedbacks and comments on all my papers. I was so happy when I got my first paper back full of read because I was like SHE REALLY CARES. And every comment you made always made my paper that much more dominant. When it comes to college I will most likely email you my papers. (Josh Hiben)

Explain which project you worked on that you liked the best or that you found most interesting. Explain where the project was done (its context, blog, wiki, paper, Power-Point, etc.), why the project was done (it's purpose), and what learning experiences were accomplished.

I really liked the blogging for *The Perks of Being a Wallflower*. I thought writing letters was a really good idea. It helped me get more involved in the book, because as I was reading it I became more engaged. I thought to myself, "What will I write about this? What is an appropriate response?" Instead of just reading, I felt like I was involved in the book. (Kate Mackin)

How did your digital writing change at all over the last two terms? Do you think you will use any of these tools in the future because of these changes?

It became more comfortable and confident for sure. I was into every response and made sure it counted. Because of this digital writing, I have become a much better writer. I will guarantee using almost all of these learning experiences next semester in my college career and in my career after college. (Josh Hiben)

My writing changed a lot over the two terms. I became a lot more outgoing in my writing instead of being scared to share my feelings. I became a lot more advanced in my writing skills. I also became more knowledgeable about many different kinds of writing styles. I think I will use a lot of these skills in the future. I plan on making a blog just to talk about things because that really helped me express my feelings instead of not talking about it. I hope to someday make another PB works, maybe in college, because I found it really helpful and easy to organize my thoughts and information. (Shannon Saleck)

Teachers can provide students with standards and criteria to foster self-reflection (for more on evaluating portfolios: http://tinyurl.com/kvovpub). Rather than importing generic standards and criteria often employed in customized systems e-portfolios, it is important to employ standards and criteria specific to digital writing in your class so that students have some ownership and understanding of these criteria (Broad, 2003). Students can then use these standards and criteria to identify illustrative examples to demonstrate that they have achieved certain standards. For example, if one of the standards requires the ability to integrate images and video into their writing, students would then seek out examples that illustrate this standard and include it in their e-portfolios.

Students can also use their e-portfolios to provide evidence of their ability to revise their texts, and they can reflect on how those revisions improved their writing quality. To document revisions with wikis, they can include different versions of their writing housed in wikis under "history." They can then highlight changes across different versions, noting how, for example, adding more information served to bolster the strength of their arguments.

One of the challenges of e-portfolios is that creating, responding to, and evaluating them can be time-consuming. Students often need time during class to work with one another on constructing their portfolios. In doing so, they can then provide face-to-face or online feedback to one another about their portfolios using the criteria that you have developed. When faced with 120 students' portfolios in his high school English classes,

Richard Kent (2006) employed a writing-center model in which each student was paired up with an editor, who provided written feedback to the student's writing included in the portfolio. After students wrote a cover letter introducing their work, as well as a reflection, they also received letters from peers, parents, Kent, and other readers responding to their portfolio work.

Uses of E-Portfolios for Writing Assessments

E-portfolios have been used as part of school or statewide writing assessments in lieu of standardized writing tests as a more valid measure of "writing quality" than is the case with a standardized timed exam written for unknown audiences about a topic about which students may have little knowledge. The use of print portfolios in the past in states such as Kentucky has been shown to have a positive influence on writing instruction in classrooms because teachers are then focusing more on composing processes than is the case in states with standardized writing tests (Hillocks, 2002).

However, using e-portfolios for external district or statewide assessments creates a very different purpose for selecting texts and reflection on those texts than is the case with students' own uses of e-portfolios in their own classroom, particularly if the district or state e-portfolios employ a customized systems structure. When e-portfolios are used for school or statewide assessment, they are judged according to external assessment criteria that may not be consistent with their classroom writing experiences. Helen Barrett (2007) argues that this use of e-portfolios for high-stakes assessment assumes that the meaning of e-portfolio texts is "constant across users, contexts, and purposes" (p. 436). In contrast, from a student's perspective, the meaning of their texts written within their unique classroom content according to standards operating in that classroom cannot necessarily be judged by using externally defined standards.

Yet, given the need to employ e-portfolios as a more valid alternative to standardized writing tests, Barrett (2007) proposes that students create three different kinds of collections that serve different purposes:

1. a digital archive as an ongoing collection that serves their own individual needs,
2. an e-portfolio based on selected texts from the archive that captures students' use of their own voice and stories in their selected texts and reflections unique to their classroom context, and
3. an "institution-centered database, or assessment management system" (p. 441) based on specific writing tasks and scoring rubrics that can be used for school or district assessment purposes.

For Barrett, the archive serves the need for "assessment for learning" while the database serves the purpose of "assessment of learning" (p. 440).

Furthermore, the purpose for the archive and e-portfolio is defined by the student, organized by students based on their own selections, maintained over a long period, used to foster students' self-reflection, and is not related to high-stakes decisions. The purpose for the database is defined by the institution on the basis of a predetermined selection of texts; the development occurs at the end of a course; and the writing is scored according to an external set of rubrics related to making high-stakes decisions (Barrett, 2007). All of this reflects the importance of defining the purposes for which e-portfolios are being used.

SUMMARY

In this chapter, we advocate for summative assessment based on authentic student writing rather than on standardized tests. We evaluate options for evaluating digital writing, such as the use of criteria and rubrics, dispositions, dynamic criteria mapping, and automated text evaluation. We argue that blogs and e-portfolios can both be used to foster student reflection on digital writing. E-portfolios allow students to include a range of multimodal texts illustrative of their work, to organize that work, and to create links within that work to foster reflections on patterns across their writing. While e-portfolios can be used for district and statewide assessments, this represents a different purpose for using e-portfolios than is the case with classroom e-portfolios. In addition to using commercial e-portfolio platforms, students can use blogs or wikis to create e-portfolios. From documenting and reflecting on their digital writing, students learn to reflect on strengths and weaknesses in their writing, leading to growth in their writing.

12

PROFESSIONAL DEVELOPMENT FOR TEACHERS

Our recommendations for effective use of digital tools in the classroom will only occur if you are provided with supportive, ongoing professional development resulting in redefining curriculum through the use of digital tools. In a national survey of 1,441 literacy and language arts teachers (Hutchison & Reinking, 2011), 81.6% reported that a lack of professional development on how to integrate technology is a barrier to their use of technology in the classroom. Furthermore, 73% of teachers reported that they do not have time to teach students the skills needed for complex tasks, with 45.7% of teachers reporting their own inability to use technology.

Teachers expressed their need for access to digital devices and tools, for knowledge about integration of these devices and tools into their curriculum, and for ongoing support for the use of digital tools through individual coaching and small group work (Hutchison, 2012). They also indicated the limitations of one-shot professional development that does not include follow-up support to address issues that they encounter in the use of digital devices and tools. Teachers said that given all the demands of teaching, they need additional time for exploring, practicing, and preparing to use devices and tools in a timely manner relevant to their particular classroom needs. One teacher noted, "We need a chance to apply the professional development. We are never given time to figure out how to use the things taught us" (p. 47). They also indicated the value of having examples of curriculum that represents effective technology integration as well as knowledgeable mentors or coaches who demonstrate this integration.

The Need for Professional Development

Professional development therefore needs to go beyond simply describing how to use certain tools or devices to focusing on ways to effectively integrate these tools or devices into curriculum and instruction (for a free book: *Preparing Teachers to Teach Writing Using Technology* http://tinyurl.com/writingtech). In a program in which there was no direct technology training of teachers but a major focus on teachers working together to plan curriculum around technology, teachers made major gains in using technology in their teaching (Blocher, Armfield, Sujo-Montes, Tucker, & Willis, 2011).

Effective professional development involves going beyond teachers simply acquiring the ability to employ different digital tools to fostering substantive, long-term change in their instruction and student learning. This involves understanding and applying new literacy theories of digital learning to redefine curriculum related to teachers' particular courses (Cervetti, Damico, & Pearson, 2006; Collet, 2013). Having some theoretical framework justifies the value of using digital tools to one's students, administrators, and parents, and it defines objectives to determine student learning. Teachers could use the social practices identified in chapter 2 linked to the Common Core standards to identify relevant tools for fostering the use of these practices, thereby framing the use of tools in terms of learning.

Professional development also needs to be carefully planned, differentiated through multiple options according to teachers' knowledge and needs, cohesive as opposed to fragmented, ongoing as opposed to single events, and based on expectations for follow-up support and holding teachers accountable for implementation (Summey, 2013). It should include a realistic needs assessment of teachers' actual, priority needs, using, for example, a needs assessment form developed by Dustin Summey http://tinyurl.com/ksllr9e.

One successful long-term professional development project involved 50 hours of work over a year and a half focusing on digital writing (Collet, 2013). In an initial 1-day event, teachers shared examples of the use of digital writing in the classroom and worked in small groups to share responses to articles about the use of digital writing. For the next 2 months, teachers met twice a month after school for 2-hour, just-in-time training where they experimented with use of different tools. Teachers then participated in a 2-day summer institute in which they created their own digital stories or podcasts, followed by further training the following school year.

Analysis of the effects of this training found that the teachers successfully applied their conceptions of new literacies learning to devising activities that effectively integrated digital tools in their writing instruction. Students whose teachers participated in this professional development had higher gains in their writing quality than did students of teachers in a control group who had not participated in the training, all of which points to the centrality of professional development in terms of change in instruction.

Another form of job-embedded professional development involves the use of school or district technology coaches working collaboratively with teachers in using digital tools. In the Stillwater, Minnesota, district, technology coaches employ "flipped professional development" by providing teachers with relevant how-to videos on using different tools as follow-up support after small group and workshop sessions focusing on individual projects (Flanigan, 2013).

Preservice Education

One key component of professional development is preservice education. Preservice teachers can benefit from employing the use of digital tools during their methods courses by interacting with secondary students (Rhodes, 2013). Through this experience, they recognize firsthand the value of using digital tools from witnessing students' engagement, as well as some limitations in how students may employ certain tools. Preservice teachers in a literacy methods course interacted with middle school students as "buddies" by providing comments on the students' blog posts (Colwell, 2012). Sharing their posts with the preservice teachers provided the middle school students with a sense of purpose and audience, which helped to improve their writing over time in terms of the students' need to create a positive ethos and adopt disciplinary literacies as modeled by their preservice teacher "buddies."

For preservice education, preservice teachers can also use blogging to reflect on their observations in schools as well as any of their own teaching experience, including the use of the Sanderling http://beta.sanderling.io blog tailored for such observations. In his MIT methods courses, Justin Reich (2013b) has his preservice teachers use blogs to write about their in-school experiences. He noted that the complexity of teaching itself involves a "multifaceted running inner monologue about what's happening in the classroom, and that thinking about blogging is a way to practice that multi-process thinking" (p. 2). One preservice teacher noted,

> When I tried to put my observations in sentences, the result often contained holes in my understanding that I had not noticed when my thoughts were in my head. Writing allowed me to notice those holes and think about what I needed to understand better. I returned to the following class with something to pay particular attention to. (p. 3)

In a children's literature course using the blogging feature of a Ning social networking platform, preservice teachers were most likely to read one another's literary responses when the posts included a visual image, often of the book cover, suggesting the importance of using multimodal features (Colwell, Hutchison, & Reinking, 2012). Analysis of the preservice teachers' blogging indicated the importance of modeling and encouraging the use of the comments feature to foster interactions.

University of Delaware preservice English education students in Jill Flynn's Literacy and Technology class in fall of 2013 created a resource wiki http://tinyurl.com/mnw9ovv for English language arts teachers using a PBworks wiki platform. Students provided descriptions of different digital tools as well as how these tools could be used in the classroom.

Professional Learning Networks

As previously noted, one approach to organizing professional development within a school involves creating a schoolwide professional learning network or community that supports schoolwide collaborative sharing of curriculum and resources (Beach, 2012; Easton, 2011; Kear, 2010; Ross, 2011). Having all teachers, administrators, and technology coordinators work together means that digital tools are more likely to be used across the curriculum (Masters, De Kramer, O'Dwyer, Dash, & Russell, 2010). To create a professional learning network or community, you can access the free edWeb.net http://home.edweb.net organization for resources.

Establishing an effective professional learning network or community requires a long-term planning process that begins with a small group of initial planners who then expand their group over time to include an entire school (Richardson & Mancabelli, 2011). To address the challenge of lack of time for professional development, a school or district may develop a "time-study team" to determine when and how teachers would have time for professional development through repurposing existing time or creating new, alternative times (Killion, 2013).

In addition to face-to-face meetings, given the lack of time for such meetings, teachers can employ blogs, wikis, or social networking/course management sites for sharing lesson plans, curriculum documents, resources, and students' work/e-portfolios that then function as a central repository or "learning commons" (Baker-Doyle, 2011; Beach, 2012; Koechlin, Luhtala, & Loertscher, 2011). Having this online repository can help to focus shared discussions around examples of activities, student work, or reports for collaborative curriculum assessment and planning (Beach & O'Brien, 2014).

As part of a professional learning network or community, teachers can conduct their own teacher action research projects about specific issues or questions about using digital tools related to student learning (for more on teacher action research http://tinyurl.com/ke3m6bw). Focusing on observations, interviews, and examples of students' work as data allows for systematically reflecting on students' learning in terms of benefits and limitations of the use of digital tools.

As noted in the last chapter, teachers can create teacher e-portfolios that include examples of teaching philosophy/beliefs, curriculum materials, student work, and professional development activities, along with reflection on the influence of their instruction on student work—documentation that can be useful for tenure review or administrative evaluations (for more on teaching e-portfolios: http://tinyurl.com/k2hvdm3). Sharing these e-portfolios within a professional learning network or community can serve to model veteran teachers' use of portfolio reflection for beginning teachers as well as foster exchange of teaching ideas within a network or community. Teachers can also access examples of online "course portfolios" to perceive how other teachers reflect on their courses, as illustrated by the "course portfolios" housed at the Peer Review of Teaching Project http://tinyurl.com/56pykt.

Another component of a professional learning network or community involves teachers observing one another's instruction, a central aspect of professional development in Japan using the "teaching lessons" model. Teachers could collaboratively share their observation notes or comments using tools such as Evernote or Google Forms (Stephenson, 2012) or the iOS Classroom Mosaic http://tinyurl.com/mchujeq app for recording notes on an iPad or iPhone and then e-mailing them directly to the teacher being observed. The iOS http://tinyurl.com/m8hkbhd and Android http://tinyurl.com/mlvjk8j Teacher Compass apps, which include self-reflection tools connected to videos, tutorials, and online modules; or the iOS Reflect Live http://tinyurl.com/mr8e9cg app can be used by observing teachers to dictate observation notes or for a teacher to dictate self-reflections before and after a lesson for sharing within a community.

Teachers could also organize small writing groups composed of colleagues who share their perceptions of teaching on a regular basis using social networking or cloud-based tools. For example, one group consisting of two middle school teachers, one high school teacher, and one college teacher meets every Thursday night on Google Hangouts to share their writing about the uses of digital tools through Google Docs (T. Hicks, Bush-Grabmeyer, Hyler, & Smoker, 2013).

ONLINE PROFESSIONAL DEVELOPMENT RESOURCES

In addition to participating in these formal professional development activities, there is a wide range of different online resources that you can access for your own individual professional development (Beach & O'Brien, 2014).

Professional Development Sites

Many online professional development sites are created by organizations to provide teachers with support on using digital tools (for online professional development sites: http://tinyurl.com/nyk3arx). Some particularly relevant sites related to understanding and creating digital texts include

Digital Media and Learning Central http://dmlcentral.net
The National Writing Project Digital IS http://digitalis.nwp.org
Google for Education http://tinyurl.com/mx6yrf5

Classroom 2.0 http://www.classroom20.com

School 2.0 http://school20.ning.com

English Companion Ning http://englishcompanion.ning.com

National Writing Project sites http://tinyurl.com/lr6dnyh

Education World http://www.educationworld.com/a_tech/index.shtml

4Teachers http://www.4teachers.org

University of South Florida iTeach Initiative http://tinyurl.com/bvfougv

Literacy Research Association Digital Texts and Tools https://sites.google.com/site/textsandtools

The Arizona State University NETS Teaching With Technology Video Library app http://tinyurl.com/mh4z6oh

Resources Curation Sites

There are resources curation sites that provide lesson plans and curriculum for use with professional development: Sophia http://www.sophia.org/teacher-resources, Gooru http://edtechtalk.com/node/5211, ReadWriteThink http://tinyurl.com/yb45dhu, Better Lesson http://betterlesson.com, Share My Lesson http://www.sharemylesson.com, Edu-Teacher http://www.edutecher.net/links.php, Learnzillion http://tinyurl.com/moal76z, Edusitement http://tinyurl.com/blguqoa, Teachers.net http://teachers.net/lessons/posts/posts.html, and Curriki http://tinyurl.com/locfg4.

The iTunes U site http://www.apple.com/education/ipad/itunes-u includes courses and related reading and video resources; the PBS Learning Media site http://www.pbslearningmedia.org includes videos, games, audio clips, and lesson plans linked to your local PBS station organized by grade level, subjects, collections, and Common Core standards, along with related resources. And the iOS http://tinyurl.com/n8rt3nr and Android http://tinyurl.com/kxuw6mu eduTecher Backpack apps provide access to a range of relevant resources for curriculum development.

Educators' Blogs

You can subscribe to different educators' blogs (for more examples of educators' blogs: http://tinyurl.com/kz5x2q5). The Research Blogging site http://researchblogging.org includes blog posts by research scholars.

Twitter

You can employ Twitter to receive and share links to teaching ideas and resources (for more on use of Twitter: http://tinyurl.com/c22qlad). One study analyzing Twitter feeds employed by classroom teachers found that teachers engaged in conversations with peers used Twitter 61% of the time, with the majority of their posts related to education, particularly in terms of practice, questions, and resource sharing (Alderton, Brunsell, & Bariexca, 2011). For 82% of the time, they followed experts in the field to obtain information related to building their professional learning networks.

You can also employ Twitter to follow scholars in a particular field who will cite references to scholarly research publications; that is, 1 in every 40 scholars is on Twitter, tweeting an average of five times per week (Valenza, 2014). You can also use Twitter hashtags to follow people organized according to certain topics (for suggestions http://cybraryman.xom/chats.html). And you can access Tweets focused on topics related to technology education by employing the following Twitter hashtags:

General education topics: #edchat (Tuesday, 12–1 pm/7–8 pm est), new teachers (#ntchat, Wednesday, 8–9 pm est), middle school (#mschat, Thursday 8–9 pm est), gifted and talented (#gtchat, Friday, 7–8 pm est), and rethinking education (#rechat, Saturday 9–10 am est)

Technology: technology in education (#techeducator, Sunday, 7–8 pm est), #smedu (social media), #BYODchat, #musedchat, #web20chat, #tichat, #BYOT, social media (#smchat), #vitalcpd, #slide2learn, #edapp, #elearning, #mlearning, #edtech, games-based learning (#gbl)

English: reading and literacy (#titletalk, Sunday, 8–9 pm est), English education (#engchat, Monday, 7–8 pm est), first-year composition (#FYC)

Podcasts

There are professional development podcasts on using digital tools available on the EdReach Channel http://edreach.us, including MobileReach, MacReach, Google Educast, Te@cher Tech T@lk, and LadyGeek shows; Teachers Teaching Teachers http://www.teachersteachingteachers.org; and the TeacherEducator Podcast http://tinyurl.com/l6vfl4a. These podcasts are created and produced by teachers so that they are describing their everyday classroom experiences in using digital tools (for more on educators and classroom podcasts: http://tinyurl.com/l6vfl4a).

Conferences/EdCamps

You can attend or access conferences or EdCamps http://edcamp.wikispaces.com related to technology integration as listed on the website http://tinyurl.com/k9zxrjn. Even without attending conferences face-to-face, you can often obtain online handouts and presentations from conference websites, including Google in Education Summits http://www.gafesummit.com, International Society for Technology in Education https://www.

iste.org, Digital Media and Learning Conference http://dml2013.dmlhub.net, Texas Computer Education Association http://www.tcea.org, K–12 Online Conference http://www.k12onlineconference.org, Global Education Conference http://www.globaleducationconference.com, and Technology Integration Education Service http://www.ties.k12.mn.us/Conferences.html

Webinars

You can access free webinars for professional development, including webinars provided by the American Society for Curriculum and Development http://tinyurl.com/mzmmyov, School Improvement Network http://tinyurl.com/kwv2nam, edWeb.net http://tinyurl.com/kbl5yvj, Center for Learning http://tinyurl.com/n7r7h3o, Google Apps for Education http://tinyurl.com/kwm495g, *Education Week* http://tinyurl.com/behlwp, EdTechTeacher http://tinyurl.com/mrlfw6h, Annenberg Learner http://tinyurl.com/79vqkch, or Discovery Education http://tinyurl.com/ld3peyv.

Journals/Magazines

There are a number of online journals/magazines related to uses of digital tools listed on the website http://tinyurl.com/me8lz6j.

Online Teacher Cases

You can access online cases of teachers describing and reflecting on their teaching that include video clips of students' learning, examples of student work, and teacher reflection within specific classroom contexts demonstrating how teachers adopt and employ tools within their own unique contexts (Anson, 2002; for online teacher cases: http://tinyurl.com/kpf6k8e). For example, the Goldman-Carnegie Quest Program site http://tinyurl.com/mt7rso3 includes a "teaching gallery" of K–12 online teaching cases that contains inquiry-based teacher reflections about teaching English language arts.

SUMMARY AND CONCLUDING REMARKS

In this chapter, given the essential need for professional development in use of digital tools, we described the value of creating a professional learning network or community to support teachers' integration of tools into their curriculum and instruction. We also described a range of different online resources to support professional development: professional development sites, resources curation sites, educators' blogs, Twitter, podcasts, conferences/EdCamps, webinars, journals/magazines, and online teacher cases designed to keep teachers informed about and reflecting on methods for teaching digital writing.

We hope that the information and ideas in this book will be useful for you in employing digital tools in the classroom to foster understanding and creating digital texts, particularly in terms of enhancing student engagement. We close with an invitation to the book's resource wiki http://digitalwriting.pbworks.com for sharing with other readers examples of your own activities and lesson plans. You can request editing privileges from Richard at rbeach@umn.edu or send links or resources directly to Richard, who will add them to the wiki.

REFERENCES

AbuSeileek, A. F., & Qatawneh, K. (2013). Effects of synchronous and asynchronous computer-mediated communication (CMC) oral conversations on English language learners' discourse functions. *Computers & Education, 62*, 181–190.

Acker, S. R., & Halasek, K. (2008). Preparing high school students for college-level writing: Using ePortfolio to support a successful transition. *Journal of General Education, 57*(2), 1–14.

Adams, J. (2013, March 17). The part played by instructional media in distance education. *Journal of Studies in Media & Information Literacy Education, 6*(2). Retrieved from http://tinyurl.com/5dm6ag

Adams, P. (2014, January 31). News literacy: Critical-thinking skills for the 21st century [web log post]. Retrieved from http://tinyurl.com/n9y4mop

Ady, K. (2013, March 15). 10 ways to get started using Google+ in your classroom [web log post]. Retrieved from http://tinyurl.com/bs8bbhh

Alderton, E., Brunsell, E., & Bariexca, D. (2011). The end of isolation. *MERLOT Journal of Online Learning and Teaching, 7*(3), 354–365. Retrieved from http://jolt.merlot.org/vol7no3/alderton_0911.pdf

Alexander, B. (2011). *The new digital storytelling: Creating narratives with new media*. New York: Praeger.

Allen, M. (2012). An education in Facebook. *Digital Culture & Education, 4*(3), 213–225.

Allison, P. (2009). Be a blogger: Social networking in the classroom. In A. Herrington, K. Hodgson, & C. Moran (Eds.), *Teaching the new writing: Technology, change, and assessment in the 21st-century classroom* (pp. 75–91). New York: Teacher's College Press.

Alvermann, D. E., Marshall, J. D., McLean, C. A., Huddleston, A. P., Joaquin, J., & Bishop, J. (2012). Adolescents' web-based literacies, identity construction, and skill development. *Literacy Research and Instruction, 51*(3), 179–195.

Anders, A., Duin, A. H., & Moses, J. (2013, July 29). *Personal learning networks: PLNs for educators*. Presentation at eLearning Summit 2013. Retrieved from http://tinyurl.com/jwcfu6a

Anderson, L. H. (2006). *Speak*. New York: Smith.

Anderson, S. (2013). Google+ for educators [web log post]. Retrieved from http://tinyurl.com/kjj3fpf

Annan, J. (2006). Literacy scrapbooks online: An electronic reader-response project [web log post]. Retrieved from http://tinyurl.com/lhq2ntm

Anson, C. M. (2002). *The WAC casebook: Scenes for faculty reflection and program development*. New York: Oxford University Press.

Anson, C. (2006). Assessing writing in cross-curricular programs; Determining the locus of activity. *Assessing Writing, 11*, 100–112.

Anson, C. (2008). We never wanted to be cops: Plagiarism, institutional paranoia, and shared responsibility. In R. M. Howard & A. Robillard (Eds.), *Pluralizing plagiarism: Identities, contexts, pedagogies* (pp. 231–246). Portsmouth, NH: Boynton/Cook.

Ash, K. (2009, July 13). Digital voice recorders turn students into interviewers [web log post]. Retrieved from http://www.edweek.org/dd/articles/2009/07/16/04recorders.h02.html

Aukerman, M. (2013). Rereading comprehension pedagogies: Toward a dialogic teaching ethic that honors student sensemaking. *Dialogic Pedagogy: An International Online Journal, 1*. Retrieved from http://dpj.pitt.edu/ojs/index.php/dpj1/article/view/9

Aydin, S. (2012). A review of research on Facebook as an educational tool. *Educational Technology Research and Development, 60*(6), 1093–1106.

Bach, J., &. Watson, J. A. (2014). Soft(a)ware in the English classroom: What's worth sharing? *English Journal, 103*(3), 108–111.

Baepler, P., & Reynolds, T. (in press). The digital manifesto: Engaging student writers with digital video assignments. *Computers & Composition*.

Baker-Doyle, K. J. (2011). *The networked teacher: How new teachers build social networks for professional support*. New York: Teachers College Press.

Balzhiser, D., Polk, J. D., Grover, M., Lauer, E., McNeely, S., & Zmikly, J. (2011, March 14). The Facebook papers. *KAIROS, 16*(1). Retrieved from http://kairos.technorhetoric.net/16.1/praxis/balzhiser-et-al/notes.html#spoiler

Barnes, S. B. (2012). *Socializing the classroom: Social networks and online learning*. Lanham, MD: Lexington Books.

Barondeau, R. (2014). Wiki. In H. Rheingold (Ed.), *The peeragogy handbook* (pp. 233–239). Retrieved from http://peeragogy.org/

Barrett, H. C. (2007). Researching electronic portfolios and learner engagement: The REFLECT Initiative. *Journal of Adolescent and Adult Literacy, 50*(6), 436–449.

Barron, B. (2006). Configurations of learning settings and networks: Implications of a learning ecology perspective. *Human Development, 49*, 229–231.

Barron, B., & Gomez, K. (2009). *The Digital Youth Network project*. Retrieved from http://www.digitalyouthnetwork.org/

Barseghian, T. (2011, December 27). 12 ways to be more search savvy [web log post]. Retrieved from http://tinyurl.com/kztemc5

Barton, D., & Lee, C. (2013). *Language online: Investigating digital texts and practices*. New York: Routledge.

Barton, M., & Klint, K. (2011). A student's guide to collaborative writing technologies. In *Writing spaces: Readings on writing* (Vol. 2). Anderson, SC: Parlor Press. Retrieved from http://wac.colostate.edu/books/writingspaces2/

Bazalgette, C., & Buckingham, D. (2013). Literacy, media and multimodality: A critical response. *Literacy, 47*(2), 95–102.

Bazerman, C. (1994). Systems of genres and the enactment of social intentions. In A. Freedman & P. Medway (Eds.), *Genre and the new rhetoric* (pp. 79–101). London: Taylor & Francis.

Bazerman, C. (2014). *A rhetoric of literate action*. Anderson, SC: Parlor Press.

Beach, R. (2012). Can online learning communities foster professional development? *Language Arts, 89*(4), 256–262.

Beach, R., Campano, G., Edmiston, B., & Borgmann, M. (2010). *Literacy tools in the classroom: Teaching through critical inquiry, Grades 5–12*. New York: Teachers College Press.

Beach, R., Clemens, L., & Jamsen, K. (2010). Digital tools: Assessing digital communication and providing feedback to student writers. In A. Burke & R. F. Hammett (Eds.), *Assessing new literacies: Perspectives from the classroom* (pp. 157–176). New York: Lang.

Beach, R., & Doerr-Stevens, C. (2011). Using social networks for online role-play: Play that builds rhetorical capacity. *Journal of Educational Computing Research, 44*(1), 165–181.

Beach, R., & Doerr-Stevens, C. (2009). Learning argument practices through online role-play: Toward a rhetoric of significance and trasnformation. *Journal of Adolescent & Adult Literacy, 52*(6), 460–468.

Beach, R., & Friedrich, T. (2006). Response to writing. In C. A. MacAuthur, S. Graham, & J. Fitzgerald (Eds.), *Handbook of writing research* (pp. 222–234). New York: Guilford Press.

Beach, R., Heartling-Thein, A., & Webb, A. (2012). *Teaching to exceed the English language arts Common Core State Standards: A literacy practices approach for 6–12 classrooms*. New York: Routledge.

Beach, R., & Myers, J. (2001). *Inquiry-based English instruction: Engaging students in life and literature*. New York: Teachers College Press.

Beach, R., & O'Brien, D. (2013). Fostering student writing-to-learn through app affordances. In K. E. Pytash, R. E. Ferdig, & T. V. Rasinski (Eds.), *Preparing teachers to teach writing using technology* (pp. 71–82). Pittsburgh, PA: ETC Press. Retrieved from http://tinyurl.com/writingtech

Beach, R., & O'Brien, D. (2014). *Using apps for learning across the curriculum: A literacy-based framework and guide*. New York: Routledge.

Beach, R., & O'Brien, D. (in press). Enhancing struggling students' engagement through the affordances of interactivity, connectivity, and collaboration. *Reading & Writing Quarterly*.

Beach, R., & Swiss, T. (2010). Digital literacies, aesthetics, and pedagogies involved in digital video production. In P. Albers & J. Sanders (Eds.), *Perspectives on research and practice in integrating arts, multimodality, and new literacies into English language arts classes* (pp. 300–320). Urbana, IL: National Council of Teachers of English.

Beeghly, D. G. (2005). It's about time: Using electronic literature discussion groups with adult learners. *Journal of Adolescent & Adult Literacy, 49*(1), 12–21.

Belgrad, S. F., Burke, K. B., & Fogarty, R. J. (Eds.). (2008). *The portfolio connection: Student work linked to standards*. Los Angeles: Corwin.

Bergman, H. (2006). About digital portfolios. [web log post]. Retrieved from http://www.mehs.educ.state.ak.us/portfolios/portfolio.html

Bergmann, J., & Sams, A. (2012). *Flip your classroom: Reach every student in every class every day*. Washington, DC: International Society for Technology in Education.

Bezemer, J., & Kress, G. (2008). Writing in multimodal texts: A social semiotic account of design for learning. *Written Communication, 25*(2), 166–195.

Bisson, R., & Vazquez, A. W. (2013, December 10). *iChoose: Academic choice and iPads*. Presentation at the annual TIES Conference, Minneapolis, MN.

Black, A. (2005). The use of asynchronous discussion: Creating a text of talk. *Contemporary Issues in Technology and Teacher Education, 5*(1). Retrieved from http://www.citejournal.org/vol5/iss1/languagearts/article1.cfm

Black, L. J. (1998). *Between talk and teaching: Reconsidering the writing conference*. Logan: Utah State University Press.

Black, P., Harrison, C., Lee, C., Marshall, B., & Wiliam, D. (2003). *Assessment for Learning*. Berkshire, UK: Open University Press.

Black, R. W. (2009a). English language learners, fan communities, and twenty-first century skills. *Journal of Adolescent and Adult Literacy, 52*(8), 688–697.

Black, R. W. (2009b). Online fan fiction, global identities, and imagination. *Research in the Teaching of English, 43*(4), 397–425.

Blocher, J. M., Armfield, S. W., Sujo-Montes, L., Tucker, G., & Willis, E. (2011). Contextually based professional development. *Computers in the Schools, 28*(2), 158–169.

Bloome, D., Carter, S. P., Christian, B. M., Otto, S., & Shuart-Faris, N. (2005). *Discourse analysis and the study of classroom language and literacy events: A microethnographic perspective*. Mahwah, NJ: Erlbaum.

Bodemer, B. B. (2014). They CAN and they SHOULD: Undergraduates providing peer reference and instruction. *College & Research Libraries, 75*, 162–178.

Boss, S. (2012, September 25). QuadBlogging connects student writers with global audiences [web log post]. Retrieved from http://tinyurl.com/ccagcat

Botzakis, S. (2013). Visual and digital texts. *Journal of Adolescent and Adult Literacy, 57*(2), 162–164.

Boyd, D. (2006). A blogger's blog: Exploring the definition of a medium. *Reconstruction, 6*(4). Retrieved from http://reconstruction.eserver.org/064/boyd.shtml

Boyd, D. (2010). Social network sites as networked publics: Affordances, dynamics, and implications. In Z. Papacharissi (Ed.), *A networked self: Identity, community, and culture on social networks* (pp. 39–58). New York: Routledge.

Boyd, D. (2014). *It's complicated: The social lives of networked teens*. New Haven: Yale University Press.

Boyle, J. R. (2011). Thinking strategically to record notes in content classes. *American Secondary Education, 40*(1), 51–66.

Bradbury, J. (2012, February 28). Easy grader [web log post]. Retrieved from http://appreview.teachercast.net/essay-grader/

Bradbury, J. (2014, February 18). Learn how to create digital portfolios [audio podcast]. *TechEducator Podcast*. Retrieved from http://tinyurl.com/kmmxgjp

Brahier, B. (2006). *Teachers' uses of students' digital annotations: Implications for the formative assessment of reading comprehension*. Unpublished doctoral dissertation, University of Minnesota, Minneapolis.

Brannon, L., & Knoblauch, C. H. (1982). On students' rights to their own texts: A model of teacher response. *College Composition and Communication, 33*(2), 157–166.

Breuch, L.-A. (2004). *Virtual peer review: Teaching and learning about writing in online environments*. Albany: State University of New York Press.

Breuch, L.-A. K., & Clemens, L. (2009). Tutoring ESL students in online hybrid (synchronous and asynchronous) writing centers. In S. Bruce & B. Rafoth (Eds.), *ESL writers: A guide for writing center tutors* (2nd ed., pp. 132–148). Portsmouth, NH: Boynton/Cook.

Broad, B. (2003). *What we really value: Beyond rubrics in teaching and assessing writing*. Logan: Utah State University Press.

Broad, B., Adler-Kassner, L., Alford, B., Detweiler, J., Estrem, H., Harrington, S., et al. (2009). *Organic writing assessment: Dynamic criteria mapping in action*. Logan: Utah State Press.

Brooks, J., & Brooks, M. (1993). *In search of understanding: The case for constructivist classrooms*. Alexandria, VA: Association for Supervision and Curriculum Development.

Bruce, B. C., & Bishop, A. P. (2002). Using the web to support inquiry-based literacy development. *Journal of Adolescent and Adult Literacy, 45*(8), 706–714.

Bruce, B. C., & Casey, L. (2012). The practice of inquiry: A pedagogical "sweet spot" for digital literacy? *Computers in the Schools, 29*(1–2), 191–206.

Brunk-Chavez, B. L., & Miller, S. J. (2006, May). Decentered, disconnected, and digitized: Why students successfully adapt to the online environment. Paper presented at the Computers and Writing Conference, Lubbock, Texas

Brunk-Chavez, B. L., & Miller, S. J. (2007). Decentered, disconnected, and digitized: The importance of shared space. *Kairos, 11*(2) 1–29. Retrieved from http://english.ttu.edu/Kairos/11.2/binder.html?topoi/brunk-miller/index.html

Burbules, N. C., & Callister, T. A., Jr. (2000). *Watch IT: The risks and promises of information technologies for education*. Oxford, UK: Westview Press.

Burgess, A., & Ivanič, R. (2010). Writing and being written: Issues of identity across timescales. *Written Communication, 27*(2), 228–255.

Burke, K. (1969). *Language as symbolic action*. Berkeley: University of California Press.

Burns, M. (2013, September 25). Using QR codes to differentiate instruction [web log post]. Retrieved from http://tinyurl.com/kjvbrcx

Burwell, C. (2013). The pedagogical potential of video remix: Critical conversations about culture, creativity, and copyright. *Journal of Adolescent & Adult Literacy, 57*(3), 205–213.

Byrne, R. (2013a, September 10). Create digital portfolios on eduClipper [web log post]. Retrieved from http://www.freetech4teachers.com/2013/09/create-digital-portfolios-on-educlipper.html

Byrne, R. (2013b, December 19). Five tools that help students plan stories [web log post]. Retrieved from http://www.freetech4teachers.com/2013/12/five-tools-that-help-students-plan.html

Byrne, R. (2013c, November 21). Student blogging activities that don't rely on text [web log post]. Retrieved from http://tinyurl.com/kj8e2rq

Byrne, R. (2013d, November 8). Studying through text messages [web log post]. Retrieved from http://tinyurl.com/kk78xmn

Byrne, R. (2013e, August 2). Three good options for creating digital portfolios [web log post]. Retrieved from http://www.freetech4teachers.com/2013/08/three-good-options-for-creating-digital.html

Byrne, R. (2013f, August 27). A tip about drafting posts outside of your blog post editor [web log post]. Retrieved from http://tinyurl.com/kslsszp

Byrne, R. (2014, January 2). PortfolioGen classroom: A digital portfolio tool for students and teachers [web log post]. Retrieved from http://www.freetech4teachers.com/2014/01/portfoliogen-classroom-digital.html

Cambridge, D., Cambridge, B. L., & Yancey, K. B. (2009). *Electronic portfolios 2.0: Emergent research on implementation and impact*. Sterling, VA: Stylus.

Carey, J. (2013, October 8). Don't let Google Drive leave tire marks on your lesson plans. The how of 21st century teaching, voices, web tools that deepen learning. *Powerful Learning Practice*. Retrieved from http://tinyurl.com/mxtpowk

Carmody, T. (2011, December 9). The future of context: Mobile reading from Google to Flipboard to FLUD. *Wired Magazine*. Retrieved from http://www.wired.com/epicenter/2011/12/google-to-flipboard-to-flud

Carrington, A. (2013, August 2). The Padagogy Wheel V3.0: Learning design starts with graduate attributes, capabilities and motivation [web log post]. Retrieved from http://tinyurl.com/k8zh95f

Castek, J., & Beach, R. (2013). Using apps to support disciplinary learning and science learning. *Journal of Adolescent and Adult Literacy, 56*(7), 544–554.

Castek, J., Beach, R., Cotanch, H., & Scott, J. (in press). Exploiting the affordances of multimodal tools for writing in the science classroom. In R. S. Anderson, & C. Mims (Eds.), *Digital tools for writing instruction in K–12 settings: Student perception and experience.* Hershey, PA: IGI Global.

Castek, J., Zawilinski, L., McVerry, G., O'Byrne, I., & Leu, D. J. (2010). The new literacies of online reading comprehension: New opportunities and challenges for students with learning difficulties In C. Wyatt-Smith, J. Elkins, & S. Gunn (Eds.), *Multiple perspectives on difficulties in learning literacy and numeracy* (pp. 91–110). New York: Springer.

CCCC Committee for Best Practices in Online Writing Instruction. (2011, April 12). The state-of-the-art of OWI: Initial report of the CCCC committee on best practices in online writing instruction. Urbana, IL: National Council of Teachers of English. Retrieved from http://www.ncte.org/cccc/resources/positions/owiprinciples

Center for Media & Social Impact. (2012). The code of best practices in fair use for academic and research libraries. Author. Retrieved from http://tinyurl.com/kn69jw5

Cervetti, G., Damico, J. S., & Pearson, P. D. (2006). Multiple literacies, new literacies, and teacher education. *Theory into Practice, 45*(4), 378–386.

Chang, C., Tseng, K., Chou, P., & Chen, L. (2011). Reliability and validity of web-based portfolio peer assessment: A case study for a senior high school's students taking computer course. *Computers & Education, 57*(1), 1306–1316.

Chang, C.-C. (2009). Self-evaluated effects of web-based portfolio assessment system for various student motivation levels. *Journal of Educational Computing Research, 41,* 391–405.

Chartier, D. (2014, March). Unleash Google Drive. *MacWorld,* pp. 64–65.

Chbosky, S. (1999). *The perks of being a wallflower.* New York: MTV Books.

Cho, K., & Schunn, C. D. (2007). Scaffolded writing and rewriting in the discipline: A web-based reciprocal peer review system. *Computers and Education, 48*(3), 409–426.

Cingel, D. P., & Sundar, S. (2012). Texting, techspeak, and tweens: The relationship between text messaging and English grammar skills. *New Media & Society, 14*(8), 1304–1320.

Clark, H. (2013a, December 16). The beginner's guide to creating digital portfolios [web log post]. Retrieved from http://tinyurl.com/lcrawpl

Clark, H. (2013b, October 22). Critical search skills students should know [web log post]. Retrieved from http://tinyurl.com/k2qwgem

Coad, D. T. (2013). Developing critical literacy and critical thinking through Facebook. *KAIROS, 18*(1). Retrieved from http://kairos.technorhetoric.net/praxis/index.php/Developing_Critical_Literacy_and_Critical_Thinking_through_Facebook

Cockrum, T. (2013). *Flipping your English class to reach all learners: Strategies and lesson plans.* Amazon Kindle Bookstore. Retrieved from http://tinyurl.com/kehtbpo

Coiro, J. (2003). Reading comprehension on the Internet: Exploring our understanding of reading comprehension to encompass new literacies. *The Reading Teacher, 56*(5), 458–464.

Collet, V. S. (2013). Helping teachers make the shift: professional development for renovated writing instruction. In K. E. Pytash, R. E. Ferdig, & T.V. Rasinki (Eds.)., *Preparing teachers to teach writing using technology* (pp. 111–124). Pittsburgh, PA: ETC Press.

Colwell, J. (2012). A formative experiment to promote disciplinary literacy in middle-school and pre-service teacher education through blogging (Unpublished doctoral dissertation, Clemson University). *All Dissertations* (Paper No. 958). Retrieved from http://tigerprints.clemson.edu/all_dissertations

Colwell, J., Hutchison, A., & Reinking, D. (2012). Using blogs to promote literary response. *Language Arts, 89*(4), 232–243.

Common Sense Media. (2012, June 26). Social media, social life: How teens view their digital lives [web log post]. Retrieved from http://www.commonsensemedia.org/research/social-media-social-life

Comstock, M., & Hocks, M. E. (2006). Voice in the cultural soundscape: Sonic literacy in composition studies. *Computers & Composition Online.* Retrieved from http://www.bgsu.edu/cconline/comstock_hocks/

Conrad, R., & Donaldson, J. A. (2004). *Engaging the online learner: Activities and resources for creative instruction.* San Francisco: Jossey-Bass.

Council of Chief State School Officers & the National Governors Association. (2010). *Common Core State Standards for English language arts and literacy in history/social studies, science, and technical subjects.* Washington, DC: Author.

Council of Writing Program Administrators, National Council of Teachers of English, and National Writing Project. (2011). Framework for success in postsecondary writing. Authors. Retrieved from http://tinyurl.com/k5wfutf

Council of Writing Program Administrators. (2003, January). *Defining and avoiding plagiarism: The WPA statement on best practices.* Retrieved from http://wpacouncil.org/node/9

Crump, E. (1998). As home in the mud: Writing centers learn to wallow. In C. Hayes & J. R. Holmevik (Eds.), *High wired: On the design, use, and theory of educational MOOs* (pp. 177–191). Ann Arbor: University of Michigan Press.

Curran, B., & Wetherbee, N. (2012). An ebook: I think therefore I blog: Blogging with Blogger [web log post]. Retrieved from http://tinyurl.com/ld9qzhc

Curtis, D. (2006). Building online learning communities. i.e. magazine, 23–27. Retrieved from http://education.smarttech.com/ste/en-US/Ed+Resource/Community/I.E.+Magazine/Current+issue.htm

Damasceno, C., Daouk, O., Davidson, C. N., Davidson, C. C., Davis, J. E., Morgan, P. T., et al. (2013, August 1). *Field notes for 21st century literacies: A guide to new theories, methods, and practices for open peer teaching and learning.* Retrieved from http://tinyurl.com/molzz7e

Davidson, C. (2011). *Now you see it: How the brain science of attention will transform the way we live, work, and learn.* New York: Viking Press.

Davidson, C. (2012, January 21). *Should we really abolish the term paper? A response to the* New York Times. Retrieved from http://tinyurl.com/pghszvt

Davidson, C. (2013, August 1). *How a class becomes a community: Theory, method, examples.* Retrieved from http://tinyurl.com/kwzznaj

Davis, A. (2007). Student-to-student blogging questions. [web log post]. Retrieved from http://anne.teachesme.com/2007/03/28/student-to-student-blogging-questions

De Abreu, B. (2010). Glogster: A poster-sized look at student movie stars. In M. Christel & S. Sullivan (Eds.), *Lesson plans for developing digital literacies* (pp. 45–52). Urbana, IL: National Council of Teachers of English.

Dexter, D. D., Park, Y. J., & Hughes, C. A. (2011). A meta-analytic review of graphic organizers and science instruction for adolescents with learning disabilities: Implications for the intermediate and secondary classroom. *Learning Disabilities Research and Practice, 26*(4), 204–213.

de Milliano, I., van Gelderen, A., & Sleegers, P. (2012). Patterns of cognitive self-regulation of adolescent struggling writers. *Written Communication, 29*(3), 303–325.

De Smet, M. J. R., Brand-Gruwel, S., Broekkamp, H., & Kirschner, P. A. (2012). Write between the lines: Electronic outlining and the organization of text ideas. *Computers in Human Behavior, 28*(6), 2107–2116.

Delagrange, S. H., McCorkle, B., & Braun, C. C. (2013). Stirred, not shaken: An assessment remixology. In H. A. McKee & D. N. DeVoss (Eds.), *Digital writing: Assessment and evaluation.* Logan, UT: Computers and Composition Digital Press. Retrieved from http://tinyurl.com/mve6xle

Devaney, L. (2013, November 1). Leveraging Pinterest for administrators [web log post]. Retrieved from http://www.eschoolnews.com/2013/11/01/leveraging-pinterest-administrators-145/

DigiRhet.org. (2006). Teaching Digital rhetoric: Community, critical engagement, and application. *Pedagogy: Critical Approaches to Teaching Literature, Language, Composition, and Culture, 6*(2), 231–259.

Di Lauro, F., & Shetler, A. M. (2013). Writing with Wikipedia: Building ethos through collaborative academic research. In K. E. Pytash, R. E. Ferdig, & T. V. Rasinki (Eds.), *Preparing teachers to teach writing using technology* (pp. 209–223). Pittsburgh, PA: ETC Press.

Dimarco, J. (2006). *Web portfolio design and applications.* Hershey, PA: Idea Group.

Dobie, A. (2007). One idea—Many audiences. [web log post]. Retrieved from http://tinyurl.com/q3vy9ok

Dobson, T. M. (2006, September). The love of a good narrative: Textuality and digitality. *English Teaching: Practice and Critique, 5*(2), 56–68. Retrieved from http://education.waikato.ac.nz/research/files/etpc/2006v5n2art4.pdf

Dodge, B. (1995). WebQuests: A technique for Internet-based learning. *Distance Educator, 1*(2), 10–13.

Doerr-Stevens, C., Beach, R., & Boeser, E. (2011). Using online role-play to promote collaborative argument and collective action. *English Journal, 100*(5), 33–39.

Donath, J. (1996, November 12). *MIT Media Lab, identity and deception in the virtual community.* Retrieved from http://smg.media.mit.edu/people/judith/Identity/IdentityDeception.html

Dredger, K., Woods, D., Beach, C., & Sagstetter, V. (2010). Engage me: Using new literacies to create third space classrooms that engage student writers. *Journal of Media Literacy Education, 2*(2), 85–101.

Dreyfus, H. (2001). *On the Internet.* London: Routledge.

Driscoll, T. (2012, December 20). Flipped learning & democratic education: The complete report. [web log post]. Retrieved from http://tinyurl.com/nkvzmbl

Ducate, L. C., & Lomicka, L. L. (2008). Adventures in the blogosphere: From blog readers to blog writers. *Computer Assisted Language Learning, 21*(1), 9–28.

Duggan, M., & Brenner, J. (2013, February 14). *The demographics of social media users: 2012.* Washington, DC: Pew Research Center. Retrieved from http://pewinternet.org/Reports/2013/Social-media-users.aspx

Dunn, J. S., Luke, C., & Nassar, D. (2013). Valuing the resources of infrastructure: Beyond from-scratch and off-the-shelf technology options for electronic portfolio assessment in first-year writing. *Computers & Composition, 30*(1), 61–73.

Durkin, K., Conti-Ramsden, G., & Walker, A. J. (2011). Txt lang: Texting, textism use and literacy abilities in adolescents with and without specific language impairments. *Journal of Computer Assisted Learning, 27,* 49–57.

Dymoke, S., & Hughes, J. (2009). Using a poetry wiki: How can the medium support pre-service teachers of English in their professional learning about writing poetry and teaching poetry writing in a digital age? *English Teaching: Practice and Critique, 8*(3), 91–106.

Easton, L. E. B. (2011). *Professional learning communities by design: Putting the learning back into PLCs.* Los Angeles: Corwin Press.

EdTechTeacher (2013). Citation generators. Chestnut Hill, MA: EdTechTeacher. Retrieved from http://tewt.org/index.php/research/citation-generators

Eidman-Aadahl, E., Blair, K., DeVoss, D. N., Hochman, W., Jimerson, L., & Jurich, C., et. al. (2013). Developing domains for multimodal writing assessment: The language of evaluation, the language of instruction multimodal assessment project (MAP) group. In H. A. McKee & D. N. DeVoss (Eds.), *Digital writing: Assessment and evaluation.* Logan, UT: Computer and Composition Digital Press/Utah State University Press. Retrieved from http://ccdigitalpress.org/dwae/07_nwp.html#top

Eijkman, H. (2010). Academics and Wikipedia: Reframing Web 2.0+ as a disruptor of traditional academic power-knowledge arrangements. *Campus-Wide Information Systems, 27*(3), 173–185.

Elbow, P. (1973). *Writing without teachers.* New York: Oxford University Press.

Ellison, N. B., Lampe, C., Steinfield, C., & Vitak, J. (2010). With a little help from my friends: How social network sites affect social capital processes. In Z. Papacharissi (Ed.), *A networked self: Identity, community, and culture on social networks* (pp. 124–145). New York: Routledge.

Elmborg, J. (2012). Critical information literacy: Definitions and challenges. In C. W. Wilkinson & C. Bruch (Eds.), *Transforming information literacy programs: Intersecting frontiers of self, library culture and campus community* (pp. 75–95). Chicago: Association of College & Research Libraries.

English, C. (2007). Finding a voice in a threaded discussion group: Talking about literature online. *English Journal, 97*(1), 56–91.

Engstrom, Y. (2009). From learning environments and implementation to activity systems and expansive learning. *Actio: An International Journal of Human Activity Theory, 2,* 17–33.

Estus, E. (2010). Using Facebook within a geriatric pharmacotherapy course. *American Journal of Pharmacy Education, 74*(8), 145.

Fahey, K., Lawrence, J., & Paratore, J. (2007). Using electronic portfolios to make learning public. *Journal of Adolescent and Adult Literacy, 50*(6), 460–471.

Farkas, M. (2009, October). Pathfinder in a box: Crafting your own authoritative meta search engine. *American Librarians, 45,* 27.

Felix, J. P. (2008). Edublogging: Instruction for the digital age learner. *Talking Points, 19*(2), 14–21.

Ferguson, K. (2012). *Everything is a remix* [Video]. Retrieved from http://vimeo.com/14912890

Ferlazzo, L. (2014, January 2). Response: "Flipped learning makes teachers more valuable" [web log post]. Retrieved from http://tinyurl.com/kuevxmv

Finder, A. (2007, May 9). Telling bogus from true: A class in reading news. *New York Times.* Retrieved from http://tinyurl.com/ln76b7y

Findings. (2012, April 5). How we will read: Clay Shirky [web log post]. Retrieved from http://blog.findings.com/post/20527246081/how-we-will-read-clay-shirky

Fisher, C. (2007). Studying societies at JHK [web log post]. Retrieved from http://studyingsocietiesatjhk.pbwiki.com

Fitzgerald, F. S. (1992). *The great Gatsby.* New York: Scribner.

Flanigan, R. L. (2013, June 11). "Flipped" PD initiative boosts teachers' tech skills. *Education Week*. Retrieved from http://www.edweek.org/dd/articles/2013/06/12/03whatworks.h06.html

Foter. (2012, November 14). How to attribute creative commons photos. [web log post]. Retrieved from http://tinyurl.com/k5m46d6

Freadman, A. (2002). Uptake. In R. Coe, L. Lingard, & T. Teslenko (Eds.), *The rhetoric and ideology of genre: Strategies for stability and change* (pp. 39–53). Cresskill, NJ: Hampton Press.

Freeman, S., Eddy, S. L., McDonough, M., Smith, M. K., Okoroafor, N., Jordt, H., et al. (2014). *Active learning increases student performance in science, engineering, and mathematics*. Retrieved from http://tinyurl.com/kc6dtd5

Fryer, W. (2013a). *Mapping media to the Common Core: Vol. 1. A handbook for creating digital teaching and learning* [Kindle edition]. Retrieved from http://tinyurl.com/lkttej8

Galbraith, D., Ford, S., Walker, G., & Ford, J. (2005). The contribution of different components of working memory to planning in writing. *L1–Educational Studies in Language and Literature, 15*, 113–145.

Garber, M. E. (2012, November 25). Editing with Wordle clouds [web log post]. Retrieved from http://tinyurl.com/kvol42e

Garrison, K. (2010). An empirical analysis of using text-to-speech software to revise first-year college students' essays. *Computers & Composition, 26*(4), 288–301.

Garrison, M. (2013, May 10). *Apps 25*. Presentation at the 2013 Minnesota Google Summit, Edina, MN. Retrieved from http://tinyurl.com/kd67t9x

Gee, J. P. (2003). *What video games have to teach us about learning and literacy*. New York: Palgrave MacMillan.

Gee, J. P. (2010). Digital media and learning as an emerging field, part 1: How we got here. *International Journal of Learning and Media, 1*(2), 13–23.

Gee, J. P. (2013a). *The anti-education era: Creating smarter students through digital learning*. New York: Palgrave Macmillan.

Gee, J. P. (2013b). *Good video games + good learning* (2nd ed.). New York: Peter Lang.

Gibson, D., & Barrett, H. (2003). Directors in electronic portfolio development. *Contemporary Issues in Technology and Teacher Education, 2*(4), 559–576.

Gibson, J. J. (1986). *The ecological approach to visual perception*. New York: Taylor & Francis Group.

Gil, L., Ávila, V., & Ferrer, A. (2011). Note-taking in multiple-text reading: Analysis of individual differences. *Infancia y Aprendizaje, 34*(4), 449–446.

Giles, J. (2005, December 15). Internet encyclopedias go head to head. *Nature, 438*(7070). Retrieved from http://www.nature.com/nature/journal/v438/n7070/full/438900a.html

Gillispie, M. D. (2013). *From notepad to iPad: Using apps and web tools in engage a new generation of students*. New York: Routledge.

Glader, P. (2013, November 13). These gorgeous iPad notes could lead to the paperless classroom. *THE Journal*. Retrieved from http://tinyurl.com/qg6m92j

Glikmans, S. (2013). *iPad in education for dummies*. Hoboken, NJ: Wiley.

Glogowski, K. (2006, June 29). Progressive discourse. Blog of possible development. [web log post]. Retrieved from http://www.teachandlearn.ca/blog/2006/06/29/progressive-discourse

Goel, V. (2013, October 16). Logging into Facebook: Its new privacy rules caused dismay among some child advocate groups. *New York Times*. Retrieved from http://www.nytimes.com/2013/10/17/technology/facebook-changes-privacy-policy-for-teenagers.html?nl=technology&emc=edit_ct_20131017&_r=0

Gordon, D., Proctor, C. P., & Dalton, B. (2012). Reading strategy instruction, universal design for learning, and digital texts: Examples of an integrated approach. In T. E. Hall, A. Meyer, & D. H. Rose (Eds.), *Universal design for learning in the classroom: Practical applications* (pp. 25–37). New York: Guilford.

Gover, E., & Selleck, C. (2013, December 9). Twitter as a teaching tool [web log post]. Retrieved from http://edtechdigest.wordpress.com/2013/12/09/twitter-as-a-teaching-tool

Grady, H. M., & Davis, M. T. (2005). Teaching well online in a collaborative, interactive mode. In K. C. Cook & K. Grant-Davie (Eds.), *Online education: global questions, local answers* (pp. 101–122). Amityville, NY: Baywood.

Graham, S., & Harris, K. R. (2013). Common Core state standards, writing, and students with LD: Recommendations. *Learning Disabilities Research & Practice, 28*(1), 28–37.

Grice, H. P. (1975). Logic and conversation. In A. Jaworski & N. Coupland (Eds.), *The discourse reader* (pp. 76–87). New York: Routledge.

Grisham, D. L., & Wolsey, T. D. (2006). Recentering the middle school classroom as a vibrant learning community: Students, literacy, and technology intersect. *Journal of Adolescent & Adult Literacy, 49*(8), 648–660.

Griswold, M. (2013). Rekindling reading: On the use of e-readers in the English classroom. *English Journal, 103*(2), 101–104.

Gruenbaum, E. A. (2010, May). Creating online professional learning communities: And how to translate practices to the virtual classroom. *eLearn Magazine*. Retrieved from http://tinyurl.com/n3otjqw

Gruman, G. (2012). *iBooks Author for dummies*. Indianapolis, IN: Wiley.

Gunelius, S. (2012). *Blogging all-in-one for dummies*. Hoboken, NJ: Wiley.

Gunter, G. A., & Kenny, R. F. (2012). UB the director: Utilizing digital book trailers to engage gifted and twice-exceptional students in reading. *Gifted Education International, 28*(2), 146–160.

Guthrie, J. T., Wigfield, A., & Perencevich, K. C. (Ed.). (2004). *Motivating reading comprehension: Concept-oriented reading instruction*. Mahwah, NJ: Erlbaum.

Haas, C., Takayoshi, P., Carr, B., Hudson, K., & Pollock, R. (2011). Young people's everyday literacies: The language features of instant messaging. *Research in the Teaching of English, 45*(4), 378–404.

Haber, K. (2014, January 23). Preparing for standardized testing [web log post]. Retrieved from http://tinyurl.com/mowz78t

Harris, C. (2013, June 28). "Here be fiction" launches: New site features ebook fiction available to schools on library-friendly terms [web log post]. Retrieved from http://tinyurl.com/qe4pe2r

Harris, J. (2006). *Rewriting: How to do things with texts*. Logan: Utah State University Press.

Harris, M., & Pemberton, M. (1995). Online writing labs (OWLs): A taxonomy of options and issues. *Computers and Composition, 12*(2), 145–159.

Harris, R. (2013, March 27). Storify for composition: Some successes and some epic fails [web log post]. Retrieved from http://tinyurl.com/mrmwog9

Hattie, J. (2011). *Visible learning for teachers: Maximizing impact on learning*. New York: Routledge.

Hawisher, G. E., Selfe, C. L., Moraski, B., & Pearson, M. (2004). Becoming literate in the information age: Cultural ecologies and the literacies of technology. *College Composition and Communication, 55*(4), 642–692.

Head, A. J., & Eisenberg, M. B. (2009, February 4). *Finding context: What today's college students say about conducting research in the digital age*. Retrieved from http://projectinfolit.org/pdfs/PIL_ProgressReport_2_2009.pdf

Head, A. J., & Eisenberg, M. B. (2010, November 1). *Truth be told: How college students find and use information in the digital age*. Retrieved from http://projectinfolit.org/pdfs/PIL_Fall2010_Survey_FullReport1.pdf

Head, A. J., & Eisenberg, M. B. (2011, April 4). How college students use the web to conduct everyday life research. *First Monday, 16*(4). Retrieved from http://firstmonday.org/htbin/cgiwrap/bin/ojs/index.php/fm/article/view/3484

Heinrich, P. (2012). *The iPad as a tool for education: A study of the introduction of iPads at Longfield Academy, Kent*. Nottingham, UK: Naace. Retrieved from http://www.naace.co.uk/publications/longfieldipadresearch

Hesse, K. (1999). *Out of the dust*. New York: Scholastic.

Hewett, B. L. (2000). Characteristics of interactive oral and computer-mediated peer group talk and its influence on revision. *Computers and Composition, 17*(3), 265–288.

Hewett, B. L. (2006). Electronic portfolios and education: A different way to assess academic success. In L. T. W. Hin & R. Subramaniam (Eds.), *Handbook of research on literacy in technology at the K–12 level* (pp. 437–450). Hershey, PA: Idea Group.

Hicks, K. (2013a, December 13). The benefits of blogging as a learning tool, part 1 [web log post]. Retrieved from http://tinyurl.com/katvgld

Hicks, K. (2013b, December 16). The benefits of blogging as a learning tool, part 2 [web log post]. Retrieved from http://tinyurl.com/ktbt4sj

Hicks, T. (2009). *The digital writing workshop*. Portsmouth, NH: Heinemann.

Hicks, T. (2013). *Crafting digital writing: Composing texts across media and genres*. Portsmouth, NH: Heinemann.

Hicks, T., Bush-Grabmeyer, E., Hyler, J., & Smoker, A. (2013). Writer, respond, repeat: A model for teachers' professional writing groups in a digital age. In K. E. Pytash, R. E. Ferdig, & T. V. Rasinki (Eds.), *Preparing teachers to teach writing using technology* (pp. 194–162). Pittsburgh, PA; ETC Press. Retrieved from http://tinyurl.com/writingtech

Hillocks, G. (2002). *The testing trap: How state writing assessments control learning*. New York: Teachers College Press.

Hissey, I. (2011). *How to draw digital cartoons: A step-by-step guide with 200 illustrations—From getting started to advanced techniques, with 70 practical exercises and projects.* Lanham, MD: Anness.

Hobbs, R. R. (2010). *Copyright clarity: How fair use supports digital learning.* Los Angeles: Corwin.

Hocks, M. R. (2003). Understanding visual rhetoric. *College Composition and Communication, 54*(4), 629–654.

Hodgson, K. (2014, January 5). Why we're learning about coding in our 6th grade writing class [web log post]. Retrieved from http://tinyurl.com/kc6vo3k

Hoffman, A. M. (2013). Students' perceptions of on-task behavior and classroom engagement in a 1:1 iPad school. *English Leadership Quarterly, 36*(2), 9–18.

Holland, B. (2013a, October 2). Apps for note-taking with iPads [web log post]. Retrieved from http://tinyurl.com/lhgqcws

Holland, B. (2013b, September 5). Redefining learning through screencasting [web log post]. Retrieved from http://tinyurl.com/m8oqy6y

Honeycutt, B., & Warren, S. E. (2014, February 17). The flipped classroom: Tips for integrating moments of reflection [web log post]. Retrieved from http://tinyurl.com/kvc9g2z

Horney, M. A., Anderson-Inman, L., Terrazas-Arellanes, F., Schulte, W., Mundorf, K., Wiseman, S. et al. (2009). Exploring the effects of digital note taking on student comprehension of science texts. *Journal of Special Education Technology, 24*(3), 45–61.

Hosseini, K. (2004). *The kite runner.* New York: Riverhead Trade.

Houge, T. T., & Geier, C. (2009). Delivering one-to-one tutoring in literacy via videoconferencing. *Journal of Adolescent & Adult Literacy, 53*(2), 154–163.

Housen, A. (2007). Art viewing and aesthetic development: Designing for the viewer. In P. Villeneuve (Ed.), *From periphery to center: Art museum education in the 21st century* (pp. 102–134). Reston, VA: the National Art Education Association.

Hsu, H., & Wang, S. (2011). The impact of using blogs on college students' reading comprehension and learning motivation. *Literacy Research and Instruction, 50*(1), 68–88.

Hsu, H.-Y., Wang, S.-W., & Comac, L. (2008). Using audioblogs to assist English-language learning: An investigation into student perception. *Computer Assisted Language Learning, 21*(2), 181–198.

Huang, H.-C. (2013). From web-based readers to voice bloggers: EFL learners' perspectives. *Computer Assisted Language Learning, 26*(3), 258–281.

Hudson, H. (2013, July 22). 10 ways to use Instagram in the classroom [web log post]. Retrieved from http://tinyurl.com/kj3kzlv

Hughes, J. (2010). "But it's not just developing like a learner, it's developing as a person": Reflections on e-portfolio based learning. In R. Sharpe, H. Beetham, & D. de Freitas (Eds.), *Rethinking learning for a digital age* (pp. 199–211). New York: Routledge.

Hunt, B. (2006, March 17). Sample blog acceptable use policy [web log post]. Retrieved from http://budtheteacher.com/wiki/index.php?title=Sample_Blog_Acceptable_Use_Policy

Hur, J. W., & Suh, S. (2012). Making learning active with interactive whiteboards, podcasts, and digital storytelling in ELL classrooms. *Computers in the Schools, 29*(4), 320–338.

Hutchison, A. (2012). Literacy teachers' perceptions of professional development that increases integration of technology into literacy instruction. *Pedagogy and Education, 21*(1), 37–56.

Hutchison, A. (2013, June 28). Connecting, curating and changing [web log post]. Retrieved from http://digitalis.nwp.org/resource/5227

Hutchison, A., & Reinking, D. (2011). Teachers' perceptions of integrating information and communication technologies into literacy instruction: A national survey in the U.S. *Reading Research Quarterly, 46*(4), 308–329.

Hutchison, A., & Woodward, L. (2013). A planning cycle for integrating digital technology into literacy instruction. *The Reading Teacher, 67*(6), 455–464.

Ingalls, R. (2011). Writing "eyeball to eyeball": Building a successful collaboration. In *Writing spaces: Readings on writing* (Vol. 2). Anderson, SC: Parlor Press. Retrieved from http://writingspaces.org/ingalls--writing-eyeball-to-eyeball

Ingber, H. (2013, October 23). Twitter illiterate? Mastering the @BC's. *New York Times.* Retrieved from http://tinyurl.com/kz5s2yq

Ito, M., Gutiérrez, K., Livingstone, S., Penuel, B., Rhodes, J., Salen, K., et al. (2013). *Connected learning: An agenda for research and design.* Digital Media Learning. Retrieved from http://tinyurl.com/9wmfeqt

Ivanic, R. (2004). Discourses of writing and learning to write. *Language and Education, 18*(3), 220–245.

Jackson, H. J. (2001). *Marginalia: Readers writing in books.* New Haven, CT: Yale University Press.

Jacobs, H. L. M. (2010). Posing the Wikipedia "problem": Information literacy and praxis of problem-posing in library instruction. In M. T. Accardi, E. Drabinski, & A. Kumbier (Eds.). *Critical library instruction: Theories and methods* (pp. 179–197). Sacramento, CA: Library Juice Press.

Jaschik, S. (2013, October 21). Texting in class [web log post]. Retrieved from http://www.insidehighered.com/news/2013/10/21/study-documents-how-much-students-text-during-class

Jenkins, H. (2007). What Wikipedia can teach us about the new media literacies: Confessions of an Aca fan [web log post]. Retrieved from http://henryjenkins.org/2007/06/what_wikipedia_can_teach_us_ab.html

Jenkins, H., Ford, S., & Green, J. (2013). *Spreadable media: Creating value and meaning in a networked culture.* New York: New York University Press.

Jenkins, H., & Kelley, W. (Eds.). (2013). *Reading in a participatory culture: Remixing* Moby-Dick *in the English classroom.* New York: Teachers College Press.

Johnson, D. W., & Johnson, R. T. (2009). An educational psychology success story: Social interdependence theory and cooperative learning. *Educational Researcher, 38*(5), 365–379.

Johnson, G., & Corneli, J. (2014). Building your co-learning group. In H. Rheingold (Ed.). *The peeragogy handbook* (pp. 95–101). Retrieved from http://peeragogy.org

Junco, R. (2012). The relationship between frequency of Facebook use, participation in Facebook activities, and student engagement. *Computers & Education, 58*(1), 162–171.

Junco, R. (2014). In-class multitasking and academic performance. *Computers in Human Behavior, 28*(6), 2236–2243.

Juzwiak, R. (2009). *"I'm not here to make friends"* [Video]. Retrieved from http://tinyurl.com/ly8blqs

Kasesniemi, E.-L., & Rautianinen, P. (2002). Mobile culture of children and teenagers in Finland. In J. E. Katz & M. Aakus (Eds.), *Perceptual contact: Mobile communications, private talk, public performance* (pp. 170–192). New York: Cambridge University Press.

Kear, K. (2010). *Online and social networking communities: A best practice guide for educators.* New York: Routledge.

Kelly, A. (2013). *iPads in the classroom.* Brooklyn, NY: JMC. Apple iBooks https://itun.es/us/RLkzJ.l

Kent, R. (2006). Room 109's portfolios and our high school writing center. *The Clearing House, 80*(2), 56–58.

Kessler, S. (2010, October 16). 7 free fantastic social media tools for teachers [web log post]. Retrieved from http://tinyurl.com/mouoax6

Kharbach, M. (2012). 11 steps to create a google plus community for your class [web log post]. Retrieved from http://tinyurl.com/mv5ztvc

Kies, D. (2012). Evaluating grammar checkers: A comparative ten-year study. [web log post]. Retrieved from http://tinyurl.com/3uza8c

Kiili, C., Laurinen, L., Marttunen, M., & Leu, D. J. (2012). Working on understanding during collaborative online reading. *Journal of Literacy Research, 44*(4), 448–483.

Kilbane, C. R., & Milman, N. B. (2003). *The digital teaching portfolio handbook: A how-to guide for educators.* Boston: Allyn & Bacon.

Killion, J. (2013, October 9). *Establishing time for professional learning.* Oxford, OH: Learning Forward. Retrieved from http://tinyurl.com/ley4mnn

Kinash, S., Brand, J., & Mathew, T. (2012). Challenging mobile learning discourse through research: Student perceptions of Blackboard Mobile Learn and iPads. *Australasian Journal of Educational Technology, 28,* 639–655.

King-Sears, M. E., Swanson, C., & Mainzer, L. (2011). TECHnology and literacy for adolescents with disabilities. *Journal of Adolescent & Adult Literacy, 54*(8), 569–578.

Kirschner, P. A., Sweller, J., & Clark, R. E. (2006). Why minimal guidance during instruction does not work: an analysis of the failure of constructivist, discovery, problem-based, experiential, and inquiry-based teaching. *Educational Psychologist, 41*(2), 75–86.

Klein, L. F. (2013). Eportfolio: Performance support systems—Constructing, presenting, and assessing portfolios. In K. V. Wills & R. Rice (Eds.), *The social eportfolio: Integrating social media and models of learning in academic eportfolios* (pp. 53–70). Fort Collins, CO: WAC Clearinghouse.

Kleinfeld, E. (2013). One hundred audio essays in four semesters with one iPod: innovating and making do in the underfunded classroom. *Computers and Composition Online.* Retrieved from http://www.bgsu.edu/departments/english/cconline/spring2013_special_issue/Kleinfeld/

Knobel, M. (2013, November 12). *Digital cultures, literacies and schooling.* Paper presented at the Auditorio DIE, Mexico DF. Retrieved from http://tinyurl.com/lqpn8a3

Koechlin, C. K., Luhtala, M., & Loertscher, D. V. (2011). Knowledge building in the learning commons. *Teacher Librarian, 38*(3), 20–26.

Konieczny, P. (2012, September 3). Wikis and Wikipedia as a teaching tool: Five years later. *First Monday, 17*(9). Retrieved from http://www.firstmonday.org/ojs/index.php/fm/article/view/3583/3313

Koutamanis, M., Vossen, H. G. M., Jochen P. J., & Valkenburg, P. M. (2013). Practice makes perfect: The longitudinal effect of adolescents' instant messaging on their ability to initiate offline friendships. *Computers in Human Behavior, 29*(6), 2265–2272.

Krakauer, J. (2009). *Into the wild.* New York: Anchor.

Kress, G. (2003). *Literacy in the new media age.* New York: Routledge.

Kumar, S., Liu, F., & Black, E. W. (2012). Undergraduates' collaboration and integration of new technologies in higher education: Blurring the lines between informal and educational contexts. *Digital Culture & Education, 4*(2), 248–259. Retrieved from http://www.digitalcultureandeducation.com/cms/wp-content/uploads/2012/09/dce_1060_kumar.pdf

Kurt, S. (2012). Issues to consider in designing WebQuests: A literature review. *Computers in the Schools, 29*(3), 300–314.

Kuteeva, M. (2010). Wikis and academic writing: Changing the writer–reader relationship. *English for Specific Purposes, 30*(1), 44–57.

Lambert, J. (2012). *Digital storytelling: Capturing lives, creating community* (4th ed.). New York: Routledge.

Langer, M. (2012). *iBooks Author: Publishing your first eBook.* Apple Store. Retrieved from http://tinyurl.com/9hs5pl4

Lasn, K. (1999). *Culture jam: The uncooling of America.* New York: Morrow.

Leander, K. (2009). Composing with old and new media: Toward a parallel pedagogy. In V. Carrington & M. Robinson (Eds.), *Digital literacies: Social learning and classroom practices* (pp. 147–162). Los Angeles: Sage.

Lee, H. (1988). *To kill a mockingbird.* New York: Grand Central Publishing.

Lenhart, A. (2012). *Teens, smartphones and texting.* Washington, DC: Pew Research Internet Project. Retrieved from http://www.pewinternet.org/2012/03/19/teens-smartphones-texting/

Lenhart, A., Madden, M., Smith, A., Purcell, K., Zickuhr, K., & Rainie, L. (2011, November 9). *Teens, kindness and cruelty on social network sites.* Washington, DC: Pew Research Internet Project. Retrieved from http://pewinternet.org/Reports/2011/Teens-and-social-media.aspx

Leu, D. J., Jr., Kinzer, C. K., Coiro, J., Castek, J., & Henry, L. A. (2013). New literacies: A dual-level theory of the changing nature of literacy, instruction, and assessment. In R. B. Ruddell, N. Unrau, & D. Alvermann (Eds.), *Theoretical models and processes of reading* (6th ed., pp. 1150–1181). Newark, DE: International Reading Association.

Lillis, T. (2013). *A sociolinguistics of writing.* Edinburgh, Scotland: Edinburgh University Press.

Lu, J., & Law, N. (2012). Online peer assessment: Effects of cognitive and affective feedback. *Instructional Science, 40*(2), 257–275.

Luke, A. (2012). *Publishing e-books for dummies.* Indianapolis, IN: Wiley.

MacArthur, C. A. (2006). Assistive technology for writing: Tools for struggling writers. In L. V. Waes, M. Leijten, & C. Neuwirth (Eds.), *Writing and digital media.* Amsterdam, Netherlands: Kluwer Academic Press.

MacArthur, C. A., Graham, S., Haynes, J. A., & DeLaPaz, S. (1996). Spelling checkers and students with learning disabilities: Performance comparisons and impact on spelling. *Journal of Special Education, 30,* 35–57.

Madden, M., Lenhart, A., Cortesi, S., Gasser, U., Duggan, M., Smith, A., et al. (2013, May 21). *Teens, social media, and privacy.* Washington, DC: Pew Research Center. Retrieved from http://tinyurl.com/l2tef96

Mahiri, J. (2006). Digital DJ-ing: Rhythms of learning in an urban school. *Language Arts, 84*(1), 55-62.

Maklary, J. (2010). *e-portfolios* [web post link]. Retrieved from http://site.maklary.com/e-portfolios

Malin, G. (2010). Is it still considered reading? Using digital video storytelling to engage adolescent readers. *Clearing House, 83*(4), 121–125.

Mallery, S. (2011). Using a USB microphone with an iPad [web log post]. Retrieved from http://tinyurl.com/kzj6f4a

Marshall, C. (2009). *Reading and writing the electronic book.* Santa Clara, CA: Morgan & Claypool,

Masters, J., De Kramer, R. M., O'Dwyer, L. M., Dash, S., & Russell, M. (2010). The effects of online professional development on fourth-grade English language arts teachers' knowledge and instructional practices. *Journal of Educational Computing Research, 43,* 355–375.

Mateos, M., Cuevas, I., Martin, E., Martin, A., Echeita, G., & Luna, M. (2010). Reading to write an argumentation: The role of epistemological, reading and writing beliefs. *Journal of Research in Reading, 34,* 1–17.

Mattewson, J., Donatone, F., & Fishel, C. (2013). *Audience, relevance, and search: Targeting Web audiences with relevant content.* Upper Saddle River, NJ: IBM Press.

Mayer, R. E. (2008). Applying the science of learning: Evidence-based principles for the design of multimedia instruction. *American Psychologist, 63,* 760–769.

McCallum, A. (2012). *Creativity and learning in secondary English: Teaching for a creative classroom.* New York: Routledge.

McClatchy-Tribune Information. (2012, October 15). Parents see benefit in kids' Facebook time. *Education Week.* Retrieved from http://www.edweek.org/dd/articles/2012/10/17/01bits-facebook.h06.html

McClure, R. (2011). Googlepedia: Turning information behaviors into research skills. In C. Lowe & P. Zemliansky (Eds.), *Writing spaces: Readings on writing.* Anderson, SC: Palor Press. Retrieved from http://tinyurl.com/nyvxbqg

McKenna, M. C., Conradi, K., Lawrence, C., Jang, B. G., & Meyer, J. P. (2012). Reading attitudes of middle school students: Results of a U.S. survey. *Reading Research Quarterly, 47*(3), 283–306.

McKesson, N., & Witwer, A. (2012). *Publishing with iBooks Author.* Sebastopol, CA: O'Reilly Media.

McNabb, M. L., Thurber, B. B., Dibuz, B., McDermott, P., & Lee, C. A. (2006). *Literacy learning in networked classrooms: Using the Internet with middle-level students.* Newark, DE: International Reading Association.

Menchen-Trevino, E., & Hargittai, E. (2011). Young adults' credibility assessment of Wikipedia. *Information, Communication & Society, 14*(1), 24–51.

Mendenhall, A., & Johnson, T. E. (2010). Fostering the development of critical thinking skills, and reading comprehension of undergraduates using a Web 2.0 tool coupled with a learning system. *Interactive Learning Environments, 18*(3), 263–276

Mihailidis, P., & Cohen, J. N. (2013, spring). Exploring curation as a core competency in digital and media literacy education. *Journal of Interactive Media in Education.* Retrieved from http://www-jime.open.ac.uk/article/2013-02/html

Miller, C. R. (1984). Genre as social action. *Quarterly Journal of Speech, 70,* 151–67.

Miller, W. (2012). iTeaching and learning: Collegiate instruction incorporating mobile tablets. *Library Technology Reports, 48*(8), 54–59.

Miranda, T., Williams-Rossi, D., Johnson, K. A., & McKenzie, N. (2011). Reluctant readers in middle school: Successful engagement with text using the e-reader. *International Journal of Applied Science and Technology, 1*(6), 81–91.

Monroe, B. (1998). The look and feel of the OWL conference. In E. Hobsen (Ed.), *Writing the writing center* (pp. 3–24). Logan: Utah State University Press.

Montgomery, D. J., Karlan, G., Coutinho, M. (2001). The effectiveness of word processor spell checker programs to produce target words for misspellings generated by students with learning disabilities. *Journal of Special Education Technology, 16*(2), 27–41.

Montgomery, D. J., & Marks, L. J. (2006). Using technology to build independence in writing for students with disabilities. *Preventing School Failure, 50*(3), 33–38.

Moore, N., & MacArthur, C. (2012). The effects of being a reader and of observing readers on fifth-grade students' argumentative writing and revising. *Reading & Writing, 25*(6), 1449–1478.

Moran, C., & Herrington, A. (2013). Seeking guidance for assessing digital compositions/composing. In H. A. McKee & D. N. DeVoss (Eds.), *Digital writing: Assessment and evaluation.* Logan, UT: Computers and Composition Press. Retrieved from http://ccdigitalpress.org/dwae/03_moran.html

Morris, S. M., & Stommel, J. (2013, July 22). MOOCagogy: Assessment, networked learning, and the meta-MOOC. *Hybrid Pedagogy.* Retrieved from http://www.hybridpedagogy.com/Journal/files/MOOCagogy.html#unique-entry-id-145

Morrison, T. (2004). *Beloved.* New York: Vintage.

Murthy, D. (2012). Towards a sociological understanding of social media: Theorizing Twitter. *Sociology, 46*(6) 1059–1073.

Nastu, J. (2012, October 29). How "collaborative learning" is transforming higher education [web log post]. Retrieved from http://tinyurl.com/owyg9ao

National Council of Teachers of English. (2013, October 21). *Formative assessment that truly informs instruction.* Urbana, IL: Author. Retrieved from http://www.ncte.org/library/NCTEFiles/Resources/Positions/formative-assessment_single.pdf

Navas, E. (2012). *Remix theory: The aesthetics of sampling*. New York: Springer.

November, A. C. (2008). *Web literacy for educators*. Los Angeles: Corwin Press.

November, A. C., & Mull, B. (2012, October 18). Web literacy: Where the Common Core meets common sense [web log post]. Retrieved from http://tinyurl.com/movfep9

Nussbaum, E. M., & Schraw, G. (2007). Promoting argument-counterargument integration in students' writing. *The Journal of Experimental Education, 76*(1), 59–92.

O'Brien, D., Beach, R., & Scharber, C. (2007). "Struggling" middle schoolers: Engagement and literate competence in a reading writing intervention class. *Reading Psychology, 28*, 51–73.

O'Brien, T. (2009). *The things they carried*. New York: Houghton Mifflin Harcourt.

O'Byrne, I. (2013, April 6). Signing up for and using Google+ and communities [web log post]. Retrieved from http://wiobyrne.com/signing-up-for-and-using-google-and-communities/

Ohler, J. B. (2013). *Digital storytelling in the classroom: New media pathways to literacy, learning, and creativity* (2nd ed.). Los Angeles: Corwin.

Pahomov, L. (2014). Bringing "traditional" essay writing into the digital world. In A. Garcia (Ed.), *Teaching in the connected learning classroom*. (pp. 45–48). The Digital Media + Learning Research Hub. Retrieved from http://tinyurl.com/n4uua5m

Palloff, R. M., & Pratt, K. (2001). *Lessons from the cyberspace classroom: The realities of online teaching*. San Francisco: Jossey-Bass.

Pangrazio, L. (2013, June 1). Young people and Facebook: What are the challenges to adopting a critical engagement? *Digital Culture & Education, 5*(1), 34–47. Retrieved from http://www.digitalcultureandeducation.com/cms/wp-content/uploads/2013/06/DCE_1068_Pangrazio.pdf

Pappas, P. (2010, January 4). A taxonomy of reflection: Critical thinking for students, teachers, and principals (Part 1) [web log post]. Retrieved from http://tinyurl.com/mm94xde

Parker, P., & O'Byrne, I. (2013). *Online content construction*. Massachusetts New Media Literacies Conference. Retrieved from http://mnli.org/mnli13/digging-deeper/online-content-construction

PBS/Grunwald Associates. (2010). Deeping connections: Teachers increasingly rely on media and technology. Authors. Retrieved from http://tinyurl.com/ocpwz3w

Pearce, N., & Learmonth, S. (2013, Autumn). Learning beyond the classroom: evaluating the use of Pinterest in learning and teaching in an introductory anthropology class. *Journal of Interactive Media in Education*. Retrieved from http://www-jime.open.ac.uk/article/2013–12/html

Peddycord, B., & Pitts, E. A. (2013, August 1). From open programming to open learning: The cathedral, the bazaar, and the open classroom. In C. Damasceno et al. (Eds.), *Field notes for 21st century literacies: A guide to new theories, methods, and practices for open peer teaching and learning*. Retrieved from http://www.hastac.org/blogs/barrypeddycordiiiandelizabethapitts/2013/08/01/chapter-two-open-programming-open-learning-cath

Pennycook, A. (2010). *Language as local practice*. New York: Routledge.

Petersen, C., Torkelson, L., & Torkelson, Z. (2002). *Programming the Web with Visual Basic*. New York: Apress Media.

Pierce, D. (2013, April 24). Common Core testing will require digital literacy skills [web log post]. Retrieved from http://www.eschoolnews.com/2013/04/24/common-core-testing-will-require-digital-literacy-skills

Pigg, S., Grabill, J. T., Brunk-Chavez, B., Moore, J. L., Rosinski, P., & Curran, P. G. (2013). Ubiquitous writing, technologies, and the social practice of literacies of coordination. *Written Communication, 31*(1), 91–117.

Pillars, W. (2013, September 24). Digital notetaking in the classroom [web log post]. Retrieved from http://tinyurl.com/kmuhyu4

Plester, B., Wood, B., & Bell, V. (2008). Txt msg n school literacy: Does texting and knowledge of text abbreviations adversely affect children's literacy attainment. *Literacy, 42*, 137–144.

Plester, B., Wood, C., & Joshi, P. (2009). Exploring the relationship between children's knowledge of text message abbreviations and school literacy outcomes. *British Journal of Developmental Psychology, 27*, 145–161.

Porcaro, P. (2013, February 11). 7 things you should know about infographic creation tools. *EDUCAUSE*. Retrieved from http://tinyurl.com/kn3ft3r

Provenzano, N. (2012). *The complete guide to Evernote in education*. The Nerdy Teacher LLC. Kindle Edition.

Provenzano, N. (2013, August 21). 5 quick tips for getting organized at school [web log post]. Retrieved from http://blog.evernote.com/blog/2013/08/21/5–quick-tips-on-getting-organized-at-school/

Puentedura, R. R. (2011). A matrix model for designing and assessing network-enhanced courses [web log post]. Retrieved from http://www.hippasus.com/resources/matrixmodel/index.html

Purcell, K., Buchanan, J., & Friedrich, L. (2013a, July 16). *The impact of digital tools on student writing and how writing is taught in schools*. Washington, DC: Pew Research Center's Internet & American Life Project. Retrieved from http://tinyurl.com/n4x6762

Purcell, K., Heaps, A. Buchanan, J., & Friedrich, L. (2013b, February 28). *How teachers are using technology at home and in their classrooms*. Washington, DC: Pew Research Center's Internet & American Life Project. Retrieved from http://pewinternet.org/Reports/2013/Teachers-and-technology

Purcell, K., Rainie, L., Heaps, A., Buchanan, J., Friedrich, L., Jacklin, A. et al. (2012, November 1). *How teens do research in the digital world*. Washington, DC: Pew Research Center's Internet & American Life Project. Retrieved from http://www.pewinternet.org/Reports/2012/Student-Research.aspx

Purdy, J. P. (2012, September 3). Why first-year college students select online research resources as their favorite. *First Monday, 17*(9). Retrieved from http://www.firstmonday.org/ojs/index.php/fm/article/view/4088/3289

Rainie, L., & Wellman, B. (2012). *Networked: The new social operating system*. Cambridge, MA: MIT Press.

Rajagopal, K., Joosten-ten Brinke, D., Van Bruggen, J., & Sloep, P. B. (2012, January 2). Understanding personal learning networks: Their structure, content and the networking skills needed to optimally use them. *First Monday, 17*(1), 1–12. Retrieved from http://firstmonday.org/htbin/cgiwrap/bin/ojs/index.php/fm/article/view/3559/313

Rambe, P., & Bere, A. (2013). Using mobile instant messaging to leverage learner participation and transform pedagogy at a South African University of Technology. *British Journal of Educational Technology, 44*(4), 544–561.

Ramsay, C. M., & Sperling, R. A. (2011). Exploring main idea generation via electronic note-taking. *Journal of Literacy and Technology, 12*(1), 26–55.

Redish, G. (2007). *Letting go of the words: Writing web content that works*. San Francisco: Kaufmann.

Reich, J. (2013a, May 8). The future of tablets in education: Potential vs. reality of consuming media [web log post]. Retrieved from http://blogs.kqed.org/mindshift/2013/05/the-future-of-tablets-in-education-potential-vs-reality

Reich, J. (2013b, December 23). Noticing and blogging with student-teachers. *Education Week*. Retrieved from http://tinyurl.com/kgw58v4

Reich, J., Murnane, R., & Willett, J. (2012). The state of wiki usage in U.S. K–12 Schools. *Educational Researcher, 41*(1), 7–15.

Reid, D. J., & Reid, F. J. M. (2007). Text or talk? Social anxiety, loneliness, and divergent preferences for cell phone use. *CyberPsychology & Behavior, 10*(3), 424–435.

Remarque, E. M. (1996). *All quiet on the Western front: A novel*. New York: Random House.

Rentner, D. S. (2013). *Year three of implementing the common core state standards: States prepare for Common Core assessments*. Washington, DC: George Washington University Center on Education Policy.

Rheingold, H. (2014, December 13). Forums. In H. Rheingold (Ed.), *The peergogy handbook* (pp. 292–232). Retrieved from http://peeragogy.org

Rhodes, J. A. (2013). Exploring writing with iPads: Instructional change for pre-service educators. In K. E. Pytash, R. E. Ferdig, & T. V. Rasinki (Eds.), *Preparing teachers to teach writing using technology* (pp. 57–68). Pittsburgh, PA: ETC Press. Retrieved from http://tinyurl.com/writingtech

Richardson, W., & Mancabelli, R. (2011). *Personal learning networks: Using the power of connections to transform education*. Bloomington, IN: Solution Tree.

Riedel, C. (2014, February 3). 10 major technology trends in education. *The Journal*. Retrieved from http://tinyurl.com/m7aolss

Roberts, J. (2013. September 10). *Giving students feedback with Kaizena (Voice Comments) tutorial* [Video]. YouTube. Retrieved from http://tinyurl.com/kthv4ep

Roblyer, M., McDaniel, M., Webb, M., Herman, J., & Witty, V. (2010). Findings on Facebook in higher education: A comparison of college faculty and student use and perceptions of social networking sites. *The Internet and Higher Education, 13*(3), 134–140.

Roschke, K. (2008, July 2). The text generation: Is English the next dead language? Retrieved from http://www.siu-voss.net/The_text_generation.pdf

Rosen, L. D., Carrier, L. M., & Cheever, N. A. (2013). Facebook and texting made me do it: Media-induced task-switching while studying. *Computers in Human Behavior, 29*(3), 948–958.

Ross, J. D. (2011). *Online professional development: Design, deliver, succeed!* Los Angeles: Corwin Press.

Rossing, J. P. (2012). Mobile technology and liberal education. *Liberal Education, 98*(1), 68–72. Routledge

Rowan, A. (2011, July 1). How texting helps pupils with their textbooks. *The Telegraph.* Retrieved from http://tinyurl.com/6d7mq7x

Rowen, D. (2005). The write motivation: Using the Internet to engage students in writing across the curriculum. *Learning and Leading with Technology, 32*(5). 22–23, 43.

Rowsell, J., McLean, C., & Hamilton, M. (2012). Visual literacy as a classroom approach. *Journal of Adolescent & Adult Literacy, 55*(5), 444–447.

Russell, D. R. (2009). Uses of activity theory in written communication research. In A. Sannino, H. Daniels, & K. D. Gutierrez (Eds.), *Learning and expanding with activity theory* (pp. 40–52). New York: Cambridge University Press.

Russell, D. R. (2010). Writing in multiple contexts: Vygotskian CHAT meets the phenomenology of genre. In C. Bazerman et al. (Eds.), *Traditions of writing research* (pp. 353–364). New York: Routledge.

Samson, S. (2010). Information literacy learning outcomes and student success. *Journal of Academic Librarianship, 36*(3), 202–210.

Satrapi, M. (2004). *Persepolis: The story of a childhood.* New York: Pantheon.

Schmidt, R. (2013). Sketching as response and assessment: From misunderstanding to better instruction. *Voices From the Middle, 21*(2), 52–58.

Schoenborn, A. (2013, November 21). *Fostering authentic writing through digital feedback.* Paper presented at the annual meeting of the National Council of Teachers of English, Boston. Retrieved from http://tinyurl.com/lxqqqkl

Schwartz, A. (2013, July 30). How Skype became the ultimate free teaching tool [web log post]. Retrieved from http://www.fastcoexist.com/1682605/how-skype-became-the-ultimate-free-teaching-tool

Schwartz, K. (2013, October 4). Teach kids to be their own Internet filters [web log post]. Retrieved from http://tinyurl.com/np8focd

Selfe, C. L., & Hawisher, G. E. (2002). A historical look at electronic literacy. *Journal of Business and Technical Communication, 16*(3), 231–77.

Selfe, R. (2005). *Sustainable computer environments: Cultures of support for teachers of English and language arts.* Cresskill, NJ: Hampton Press.

Shahani, A. (2013, December 4). Should schools teach social media skills? [web log post]. Retrieved from http://blogs.kqed.org/mindshift/2013/12/should-schools-teach-social-media-skills/

Shriver, R. (2012). Oral history in the digital age. *Journal of Media Education, 3*(4), 24–35.

Siemens, G. (2009). What is connectivism? *Week 1: CCK09.* Retrieved from http://tinyurl.com/76dfe9

Simmons, A. (2013, November 18). Facebook has transformed my students' writing—for the better. *The Atlantic.* Retrieved from http://www.theatlantic.com/education/archive/2013/11/facebook-has-transformed-my-students-writing-for-the-better/281563/

Sirc, G. (2004). Box-logic. In A. Wysocki, J. Johnson-Eilola, C. Selfe, & G. Sirc (Eds.), *Writing new media: Theory and applications for expanding the teaching of composition* (pp. 111–146). Logan: Utah State University Press.

Smith, A., & Brenner, J. (2012, May 31). *Twitter use 2012.* Washington, DC: Pew Research Center. Retrieved from http://pewinternet.org/Reports/2012/Twitter-Use-2012.aspx

Sormunen, E., & Lehtio, L. (2011, December). Authoring Wikipedia articles as an information literacy assignment: Copy-pasting or expressing new understanding in one's own words? *Information Research: An International Electronic Journal, 16*(4). Retrieved from http://informationr.net/ir/16-4/paper503.html

Speak Up. (2013). *From chalkboards to tablets: The emergence of the K–12 Learner.* Irvine, CA: Speak Up National Research Project

Spencer, J. (2012, July 2). Ten ideas for using Instagram in the classroom [web log post]. Retrieved from http://tinyurl.com/9ztws4t

Srivastava, J. (2013). Media multitasking performance: Role of message relevance and formatting cues in online environments. *Computers in Human Behavior, 29*(3), 888–895.

Stansbury, M. (2013, July 30). Does research support flipped learning? *eSchoolNews.* Retrieved from http://www.eSchoolNews.com

Stedman, B. (2000). Hooked on 'tronics, or creating a happy union of computers and pedagogies. In S. Harrington, R. Rickly, & M. Day (Eds.), *The online writing classroom* (pp. 187–206). Cresskill, NJ: Hampton Press.

Steinbeck, J. (1993). *Of mice and men.* New York: Penguin.

Stephenson, C. (2012, October 2). Using iPads for classroom observations [web log post]. Retrieved from http://tinyurl.com/cphr43p

Stern, S. (2008). Producing sites, exploring identities: Youth online authorship. In D. Buckingham (Ed.), *Youth, identity, and digital media* (pp. 95–118). Cambridge, MA: MIT Press.

Stewart, M. (2011, June 20). Fostering student creativity and responsibility with blogging [web log post]. Retrieved from http://tinyurl.com/69rr59e

Stewart, R. (2013). Cornell note-taking method PDF generator [web log post]. Retrieved from http://www.cornell-notes.com

Stille, S. (2011a). Framing representations: Documentary filmmaking as participatory approach to research inquiry. *Journal of Curriculum and Pedagogy, 8*, 101–108.

Strijbos, J. W., & Sluijsmans, D. M. A. (2010). Unravelling peer assessment: Methodological, functional, and conceptual developments. *Learning and Instruction, 20*(4), 265–269.

Strommel, J. (2013, September 2). The digital humanities is about breaking stuff. *Hybrid Pedagogy*. Retrieved from http://tinyurl.com/nxa8ljr

Strømsø, H. I., Ivar Braten, I., Britte, M. A., & Ferguson, L. E. (2013). Spontaneous sourcing among students reading multiple documents. *Cognition and Instruction, 31*(2), 176–203.

Summey, D. C. (2013). *Developing digital literacies: A framework for professional learning*. Los Angeles: Corwin Press.

Swartz, J. (2011). MySpace, Facebook, and multimodal literacy in the writing classroom. *KAIROS, 15*(2). Retrieved from http://tinyurl.com/njdz5r9

Thomas, A. (2006). Fictional blogs. In A. Bruns & J. Jacobs (Eds.), *Uses of blogs* (pp. 199-210). New York: Peter Lang.

Tseng, S., & Tsai, C. (2007). On-line peer assessment and the role of the peer feedback: A study of high school computer course. *Computers & Education, 49*, 1161–1174.

Turnbaugh, B. (2010). Survey says! Using Google Forms to evaluate media trends and habits. In M. Christel & S. Sullivan (Eds.), *Lesson plans for developing digital literacies* (pp. 53–60). Urbana, IL: National Council of Teachers of English.

Uzuner, S., & Mehta, R. (2010, February 26). Three ways to increase the quality of students' discussion board comments [web log post]. Retrieved from http://tinyurl.com/y97dpas

Valenza, J. (2014, January 12). Follow a scholar? [web log post]. Retrieved from http://tinyurl.com/ktght5w

Van Leeuwen, T. (2008). *Discourse and practice: New tools for critical discourse analysis*. New York: Oxford University Press.

Van Meter, P., & Firetto, C. (2008). Intertextuality and the study of new literacies: Research critique and recommendations. In J. Coiro, M. Knobel, C. Lankshear, & D. Leu (Eds.), *The handbook of research in New Literacies*. Mahwah, NJ: Erlbaum.

Van Vooren, C., & Corey, B. (2013). Teacher tweets improve achievement for eighth grade science students. *Journal of Systemics, Cybernetics & Informatics, 11*(1), 33–36.

Vincent, T. (2012, March 4). Ways to evaluate educational apps [web log post]. Retrieved from http://learninginhand.com/blog/ways-to-evaluate-educational-apps.html

Vincenzini, A. (2013, October 22). 15 top-notch content curation tools [web log post]. Retrieved from http://tinyurl.com/lhln63p

Virtue, A. D. (2013). *Digital struggles: Fostering student interaction in online writing courses*. Unpublished doctoral dissertation, University of Minnesota, Minneapolis.

Walk, K. (2000). Study underscores importance of feedback. *Harvard Writing Project Bulletin Special Issue: Responding to Student Writing*. Retrieved from http://isites.harvard.edu/fs/docs/icb.topic235511.files/HWP_Bulletin_Responding_to_Student_Writing.pdf

Walraven, A., Brand-Gruwel, S., & Boshuizen, H. P. (2009). How students evaluate information and sources when searching the World Wide Web for information. *Computers & Education 52*(1), 234–46.

Warren, J. E. (2013). Rhetorical reading as a gateway to disciplinary literacy. *Journal of Adolescent & Adult Literacy, 56*(5), 391–399.

Watson, L. (1993). *Montana 1948*. Minneapolis, MN: Milkwood Press.

Waycott, J., Deng, L., & Tavares, N. J. (2013). From Moodle to Facebook: Exploring students' motivation and experiences in online communities. *Computers & Education, 68*, 86–95.

Waycott, J., Sheard, J., Thompson, C., &. Clerehan, R. (2013). Making students' work visible on the social web: A blessing or a curse? *Computers & Education, 68*, 86–95.

Webb, A. (2009). LitArchives.com: Teaching digital texts. Retrieved from http://homepages.wmich.edu/~acareywe/archives.html

Weinstein, D. (2012). Learned it at the NCTE conference, Turned it into a mind map [web log post]. Retrieved from http://tinyurl.com/myck49x

Wender, E. (2013). Blogging in the literature survey course: Making relevance, not waiting for it. *Teaching English in the Two Year College, 41*(2), 149–163.

West, K. C. (2008). Weblogs and literary response: Socially situated identities and hybrid social languages in English class blogs. *Journal of Adolescent and Adult Literacy, 51*(7), 588–598.

Wetzels, S. A. J., Kester, L., van Merriënboer, J. J. G., & Broers, N. J. (2011). The influence of prior knowledge on the retrieval-directed function of note taking in prior knowledge activation. *British Journal of Educational Psychology, 81*(2), 274–291.

White, N. (2012, July 7). Understanding content curation [web log post]. Retrieved from http://tinyurl.com/7z7jzgc

Wiesel, E. (1982). *Night*. New York: Bantam Books.

Wilhelm, J. (2014). Moving towards collaborative cultures: Remixing classroom participation. *Voices in the Middle, 21*(4), 58–60.

Willard, N. (2007). Educator's guide to cyber-bullying and cyberthreats [web log post]. Retrieved from http://www.cyberbully.org/cyberbully/docs/cbcteducator.pdf

Wilson, M. (2014, January 26). iPad teaching is NOT about iPads [web log post]. Retrieved from http://tinyurl.com/mmxpsdu

Wissman, K. K. (2008). "This is what I see": (Re)envisioning photography as a social practice. In M. L. Hill & L. Vasudevan (Eds.), *Media, learning, and sites of possibility* (pp. 13–46). New York: Peter Lang.

Wolfe, C. R., Britt, M. A., & Butler, J. A. (2009). Argumentation schema and the myside bias in written argumentation. *Written Communication, 26*(2), 183–209.

Wood, C., Jackson, E., Hart, L., Plester, B., & Wilde, L. (2011). The effect of text messaging on 9- and 10-year-old children's reading, spelling and phonological processing skills. *Journal of Computer Assisted Learning, 27*(1), 28–36.

Wood, C., Kemp, N., & Plester, B. (2013). *Text messaging and literacy: The evidence*. New York: Routledge.

Wysocki, A. (2004a). The multiple media of texts: How onscreen and paper texts incorporate words, images, and other media. In C. Bazerman & P. Prior (Eds.), *What writing does and how it does it: An introduction to analyzing texts and textual practices* (pp. 123–163). Mahwah, NJ: Erlbaum.

Wysocki, A. (2004b). Open new media to writing. In A. Wysocki, J. Johnson-Eilola, C. Selfe, & G. Sirc (Eds.), *Writing new media: Theory and applications for expanding the teaching of composition* (pp. 1–41). Logan: Utah State University Press.

Yancey, K. B. (2009). *Writing in the 21st century*. Urbana, IL: National Council of Teachers of English. Retrieved from http://www.nwp.org/cs/public/download/nwp_file/12440/Kathleen_Blake_Yancey_Writing_21st_Century.pdf?x-r=pcfile_d

Yarbro, J., Arfstrom, K. M., McKnight, K., & McKnight, P. (2014). Extension of a review of flipped learning. Flipped Learning Network/Pearson/George Mason University. Retrieved from http://www.flippedlearning.org/research

Yena, L., & Waggoner, Z. (2003). One size fits all? Student perspectives on face-to-face and online writing pedagogies. *Computers and Writing Online*. Retrieved from http://www.bgsu.edu/cconline/yena-waggoner/index.html

Zaich, H. (2012, December 18). Teaching with content curation. *THE Journal*. Retrieved from http://tinyurl.com/ohvqw8e

ADDITIONAL READING

Achieve. (2014). Educators Evaluating the Quality of Instructional Products (EQuIP) [web log post]. Retrieved from http://www.achieve.org/EQuIP

Apperley, T., & Beavis, C. (2011). Literacy into action: Digital games as action and text in the English and literacy classroom. *Pedagogies: An International Journal, 6*, 130–143.

Aukerman, M. (2012). "Why do you say yes to Pedro, but no to me?" Toward a critical literacy of dialogic engagement. *Theory Into Practice, 51*(1), 42–48.

Barawshi, A. (2006). Sites of invention: Genre and the enactment of first-year writing. In P. Vanderberg, S. Hum, & J. Clary-Lemon (Eds.), *Relations, locations, positions: Composition theory for writing teachers* (pp. 103–137). Urbana, IL: National Council of Teachers of English.

Beach, R., Anson, C., Kastman Breuch, L.-A., & Swiss, T. (2009). *Teaching writing using blogs, wikis, and other digital tools.* Norwood, MA: Christopher-Gordon.

Black, R. W. (2005). Access and affiliation: The literacy and composition practices of English-language learners in an online fanfiction community. *Journal of Adolescent & Adult Literacy 49*(2), 118–128.

Bodemer, B. B. (2012). The importance of search as intertextual practice for undergraduate research. *College & Research Libraries, 73*(4), 336–348.

Canagarajah, A. S. (2013). Negotiating translingual literacy: An enactment. *Research in the Teaching of English, 48*(1), 40–67.

Castek, J., Coiro, J., Guzniczak, L., & Bradshaw, C. (2012). Examining peer collaboration in online inquiry. *The Educational Forum, 76*(4), 479–496.

Chase, Z., & Laufenberg, D. (2011). Embracing the squishiness of digital literacy. *Journal of Adolescent & Adult Literacy 54*(7), 535–537.

Chen, A. (2013, January 19). *Why I chose Schoology over all the rest* [web blog post]. Retrieved from http://wondertechedu.blogspot.com/2013/01/why-i-chose-schoology-over-all-rest.html

Coiro, J. (2011a). Predicting reading comprehension on the Internet: Contributions of offline reading skills, online reading skills, and prior knowledge. *Journal of Literacy Research, 43*(4), 352–392.

Coiro, J. (2011b). Talking about reading as thinking: Modeling the hidden curriculum of online reading comprehension. *Theory Into Practice, 50*(2), 107–115.

Davis, V. (2011, April 27). 15 fantastic ways to use Flipboard [web log post]. Retrieved from http://coolcatteacher.blogspot.com/2011/04/15-fantastic-ways-to-use-flipboard.html

DeNisco, A. (2014, January). *Different faces of blended learning.* Retrieved from http://tinyurl.com/mbbs92y

Doerr-Stevens, C. (2011). Building fictional ethos: Analysing the rhetorical strategies of persona design for online role play. *Learning and Digital Media, 8*(4), 327–342.

Donath, J. (2007). Signals in social supernets. *Journal of Computer-Mediated Communication, 13*, 231–251.

Duggan, M. (2013, September 19). *Cell phone activities 2013.* Washington, DC: Pew Research Internet Project. Retrieved from http://pewinternet.org/Reports/2013/Cell-Activities.aspx

Ede, L., & Lunsford, A. (1990). *Singular texts/plural authors: Perspectives on Collaborative Writing.* Carbondale: Southern Illinois University Press.

Fance, C. (2013, n.d.). Top web annotation and markup tools [web log post]. Retrieved from http://www.hongkiat.com/blog/top-web-annotation-and-markup-tools

Fields, D., & Grime, S. (2012, November). Kids online: A new research agenda for understanding social networking forums [web log post]. Retrieved from http://dmlhub.net/publications/kids-online-new-research-agenda-understanding-social-networking-forums

Flanigan, R. L. (2014, January 27). Teacher colleges seek to shift to digital age. *Education Week*. Retrieved from http://tinyurl.com/kv8c3ek

Follansbee, B. (2003). Speaking to write/word for word: An overview of speech recognition. *Perspectives, 29*(4), 10–13.

Fredericksen, E., Pickett, A., Shea, P., Pelz, W., & Swan, K. (2000). Student satisfaction and perceived learning with online courses: Principles and examples from the SUNY learning network. *Journal of Asynchronous Learning Networks, 4*(2), 1–29.

Fryer, W. (2012, January 21). Create a custom digital newspaper on your iPad with Flipboard & Google Reader [web log post]. Retrieved from http://tinyurl.com/7jxhlyj

Fryer, W. (2013b). *Hopscotch challenges: Learn to code on an iPad!* [Kindle Edition]. Retrieved from http://tinyurl.com/n2t88dp

Gewertz, C. (2014, February 6). New tools gauge fidelity of lessons to Common Core. *Education Week*. Retrieved from http://tinyurl.com/mplgnan

Goffman, I. (1986). *Frame analysis: An essay on the organization of experience*. Boston: Northeastern University Press.

Graham, S., Harris, K. R., Fink, B., & MacArthur, C. A. (2003). Primary grade teachers' instructional adaptations for struggling writers: A national survey. *Journal of Educational Psychology, 95*, 279–292.

Grassian, E. (2006, October 9). Thinking critically about Web 2.0 and beyond [web log post]. Retrieved from http://www2.library.ucla.edu/libraries/college/11605_12008.cfm

Greenhow, C., & Burton, L. (2011). Help from my "friends": Social capital in the social network sites of low-income students. *Journal of Educational Computing Research, 45*(2), 223–245.

Griswold, M. (2013). Rekindling reading: On the use of E-readers in the English classroom. *English Journal, 103*(2), 101–104.

Hall, T. E., Meyer, A., Rose, D. H. (Eds.). (2012). *Universal design for learning in the classroom: Practical applications*. New York: Guilford Press.

Hanley, L. (2011). Mashing up the institution: Teacher as bricoleur. *Radical Teacher, 90*, 9–14.

Hess, A. (2011). *iPad fully loaded*. Indianapolis, IN: Wiley.

Holland, D., Lachicotte, W., Skinner, D., & Cain, C. (1998). *Identity and agency in cultural worlds*. Cambridge, MA: Harvard University Press.

Hou, H.-T. (2012). Analyzing the learning process of an online role-playing discussion activity. *Journal of Educational Technology & Society, 15*(1), 211–222.

Ivanic, R., & Kuteeva, M. (2010). Wikis and academic writing: Changing the writer–reader relationship. *English for Specific Purposes, 30*(1), 44–57.

Jadallah, M., Anderson, R. C., Nguyen-Jahiel, K., Miller, M., Kim, I.-H., Kuo, L.-J., et al. (2011). Influence of a teacher's scaffolding moves during child-led small-group discussions. *American Educational Research Journal, 48*(1), 194–230.

Jamaludin, A., Chee, Y. S., & Ho, C. M. L. (2009). Fostering argumentative knowledge construction through enactive role play in *Second Life*. *Computers & Education, 53*(2), 317–329.

Johnson, T. E., Archibald, T. N., & Tenenbaum, G. (2010). Individual and team annotation effects on students' reading comprehension, critical thinking, and meta-cognitive skills. *Computers in Human Behavior, 26*, 1496–1507.

Jones, A., Blake, C., Davies, C., & Scanlon, E. (2004). Digital maps for learning: A review and prospects. *Computers & Education, 43*(1–2), 91–107.

Keller, D. (2013). A framework for rereading in first-year composition. *Teaching English in First-Year College, 41*(1), 44–55.

Korbey, H. (2013, September 4). Beyond the iPad: Schools' choices in tablets grow [web log post]. Retrieved from http://tinyurl.com/m2anv8o

Lai, M., & Law, N. (2013). Questioning and the quality of knowledge constructed in a CSCL context: A study on two grade-levels of students. *Instructional Science, 41*(3), 597–620.

Lee, Y.-H., & Wu, J.-Y. (2013). The indirect effects of online social entertainment and information seeking activities on reading literacy. *Computers & Education, 67,* 168–177.

Leu, D. J., McVerry, G. W., O'Byrne, I., Kiili, C., Zawilinski, L., Everett-Cacopardo, H., et al. (2011). The new literacies of online reading comprehension: Expanding the literacy and learning curriculum. *Journal of Adolescent & Adult Literacy, 55*(1), 5–14.

Lewis, C., & Dockter, J. (2011). Reading literature in secondary schools: Disciplinary discourses in global times. In S. Wolf, K. Coats, P. Enciso, & C. A. Jenkins (Eds.)., *Handbook of research on children's and young adult literature.* New York: Routledge.

Lewison, M., Flint, A. S., & Van Shuys, K. (2002). Taking on critical literacy: The journey of newcomers and novices. *Language Arts, 79*(5), 382–392.

Magiera, J. (2013, February 24). Sorry Edmodo . . . Switching to Schoology [web log post]. Retrieved from http://www.teachinglikeits2999.com/2012/12/sorry-edmodo-switching-to-schoology.html

Mateos, M., Martin, E., Villalon, R., & Luna, M. (2008). Reading and writing to learn in secondary education: Online processing activity and written products in summarizing and synthesizing tasks. *Reading and Writing, 21*(7), 675–697.

McGrath, L. B. (2013, September 4). A former skeptic's story of collaboration in the humanities [web log post]. Retrieved from http://www.gradhacker.org/2013/09/04/4828

Mills, K. A., & Chandra, V. (2011). Microblogging as a literacy practice for educational communities. *Journal of Adolescent & Adult Literacy, 55*(1), 35–45.

Mupinga, D. M., Nora, R. T., & Yaw, C. D. (2006). The learning styles, expectations, and needs of online students. *College Teaching, 54*(1), 185–189.

Nagel, D. (2013). Students use smart phones and tablets for school, want more. *THE Journal.* Retrieved from http://tinyurl.com/k4rdw2m

Nielsen, L., & Webb, W. (2011). *Teaching generation text: Using cell phones to enhance learning.* San Francisco: Jossey-Bass.

Pea, R., Nass, C., Meheula, L., Rance, M., Kumar, A., Bamford, H., et al. (2012). Media use, face-to-face communication, media multitasking, and social well-being among 8- to 12-year-old girls. *Developmental Psychology, 48*(2), 327–336.

Perry, K. H. (2012). What is literacy? A critical overview of sociocultural perspectives. *Journal of Literacy and Language Learning, 8*(1). Retrieved from http://jolle.coe.uga.edu/wp-content/uploads/2012/06/What-is-Literacy_KPerry.pdf

Potter, M. J. (2012). Developing critical thinking through web research skills [web log post]. Retrieved from http://tinyurl.com/kfu6pza

Rainie, L., & Wellman, B. (2011). *Networked.* Cambridge, MA: MIT Press.

Rheingold, H. (2012). *Net smart: How to thrive online.* Cambridge, MA: MIT Press.

Scott, K. M. (2013). Does a university teacher need to change e-learning beliefs and practices when using a social networking site? A longitudinal case study. *British Journal of Educational Technology, 44*(4), 571–580.

Seaman, J., & Tinti-Kane, H. (2013, October). *Social media for teaching and learning.* Wellesley, MA: Babson Survey Research Group, Babson College.

Seidman, G. (2014). Expressing the "true self" on Facebook. *Computers in Human Behavior, 31,* 367–372.

Shaha, S., & Ellsworth, H. (2013, December). Multi-state, quasi-experimental study of the impact of internet-based, on-demand professional learning on student performance. *International Journal of Evaluation and Research in Education, 2*(4), 175–184.

Stille, S. (2011b). Re/making the ground on which they stand: Making a school garden with culturally and linguistically diverse students [web log post]. Retrieved from http://tinyurl.com/lz9kp67

Ulman, H. L., DeWitt, S. L., & Selfe, C. L. (Eds.). (2013). *Stories that speak to us.* Retrieved from http://ccdigitalpress.org/stories

Valenza, J. K. (2005/2006). Pathfinders, streaming video: Welcome to the 21st century school library. *Educational Leadership, 63*(4), 54–59.

WITO. (2012, November 14). How to attribute different Creative Commons photo options [web log post]. Retrieved from http://tinyurl.com/k5m46d6

Wohlwend, K. E., & Lewis, C. (2011). Critical literacy, critical engagement, and digital technology. In D. Lapp & D. Fisher (Eds.), *The handbook of research on teaching the English language arts* (pp. 188–194). New York: Routledge.

Wolfe, C. R., & Britt, M. A. (2008). Locus of the myside bias in written argumentation. *Thinking and Reasoning,* *14,* 1–27.

Wolpert-Gawron, H. (2013, March 1). Creating an online student lounge [web log post]. Retrieved from http://tinyurl.com/k89kxt2

INDEX

Academic Index (search engine), 50

acceptable use policy, 39, 150–151

access: to data and sources, 44, 164–165; to devices and software, 36–38, 265; to the Internet, viii, 22, 150–151

administrator, viii, 23–24, 38, 70, 150, 212, 250, 251, 266, 268

Adobe Photoshop, 81, 166, 219

Advanced Placement, ix, 86

affordance, 2–9, 19, 23, 26, 100, 104–106, 151, 158, 182

aggregation dashboard, 69

alienation, 10

Amplify (tablet manufacturer), 19

animation, 185

annotation. *See* note-taking

AP. *See* Advanced Placement

AppSmash (combining app usage), 32

archive, 73–75

argument curation, 75

argumentative writing, viii, 5, 18, 75, 80, 98, 141, 143, 197, 199, 255

assessment, xii, 94, 133, 147, 262–263; automated, 249–251; of drafts, 220–222; organic, 248–249; organization of, 251–252; standardized, 243–244; of student-created video, 189–190; for student learning, 217; student self-assessment, 218–220

Audacity, 173–175

audience, ix–x, xii, 6, 7–9, 15, 18, 23–24, 65, 79, 90, 110, 143, 146, 168, 182, 185, 191–193, 197–198, 199, 207, 217, 236, 247, 253, 258; peer audience, 24, 147, 177; invisible, 100

audio recording, 9, 34, 35, 55, 94–95, 111, 128–129, 151, 155, 167–168, 172–173, 183–184, 229–231

avatar, viii, 17. *See also* game, online

Beyond Facebook (noncredit MOOC). *See* MOOC

bias, 16, 61, 62–63, 77, 146, 172, 178; "myself bias," 26, 44. *See also* status quo

bighugelabs.com (poster-creation website), 15

blended course, ix, 32–33. *See also* flipped course

blog, 9, 18, 27, 54, 69, 140–146, 197, 253–254, 257–258; audio/video blog, 155; class blog, x, 12, 142; components of, 141–142; as e-portfolio tool, 257–258; fictional blog, 153–154; grading of, 253–254; purposes of, 142–145; reading of, 148

Bloom's taxonomy, 30. *See also* heuristic

bookmarking, social, 66, 71, 88, 90, 96–98, 227. *See also* Diigo

Boolean search, 50

"box logic" presentation, 66–67

Box.com. *See* cloud-based computing

brainstorm, 13, 25, 56–57, 84, 87, 181, 232

brochure, viii, 256

browser, Web, 46, 66, 70–72, 96, 136, 148, 176

bulletin board, 66, 70, 107, 110, 229

calendar, online, ix, 28, 125–126, 201

Canvas (course platform). *See* course platform

cartoon. *See* comic

Case of the Digital Footprint (noncredit MOOC). *See* MOOC

caucusing, viii, 87

censorship, 46, 52

chart, 25, 78–80, 93, 151, 199

chat, online, 29, 72, 107, 111–118, 126–129, 222, 231–233

Children's Internet Protection Act, 39, 150

citation, 11, 45, 50, 211–212, 246

classroom (physical space), 140

clicker, 78, 201

clip art, 1, 180, 199

cloud-based computing, 19, 28, 69, 71–73, 89, 136, 142, 152, 174, 198, 230, 258

coding, 206–207

ABOUT THE AUTHORS

Richard Beach is Professor Emeritus of English education at the University of Minnesota, Twin Cities, former President of the Literacy Research Association (2012–2013), and coauthor of *Using Apps for Learning Across the Curriculum: A Literacy-based Framework and Guide* (2014), *Teaching to Exceed the English Language Arts Common Core State Standards* (2012), and *Teaching Literature to Adolescents* (2010).

Chris M. Anson is University Distinguished Professor, Professor of English, and Director of the Campus Writing and Speaking Program, North Carolina State University. He is the author or coauthor fifteen books and over one hundred articles and book chapters. He was chair of the Conference on College Composition and Communication in 2012–2013.

Lee-Ann Kastman Breuch is Associate Professor, Department of Writing Studies, University of Minnesota, Twin Cities; author of *Virtual Peer Review: Teaching and Learning About Writing in Online Environments* (2004); and coauthor of the book chapters "A Sociocultural Approach to Using Web 2.0 Technologies in First-Year Writing" (2013) and "Tutoring ESL Students in Online Hybrid (Synchronous and Asynchronous) Writing Centers" (2009).

Thomas Reynolds is Associate Professor, Department of Writing Studies, University of Minnesota, Twin Cities, and coauthor of the article "The Digital Manifesto: Engaging Student Writers With Digital Video Assignments" (2014) and the book chapter "Reframing Improvement: Student Writing in 'Writing Studies' Composition Classes" (2010).